The Chumash World at European Contact

The publisher gratefully acknowledges the generous contribution to this book provided by the General Endowment Fund of the University of California Press Foundation.

The Chumash World at European Contact

Power, Trade, and Feasting among Complex Hunter-Gatherers

Lynn H. Gamble

UNIVERSITY OF CALIFORNIA PRESS
Berkeley / Los Angeles / London

University of California Press, one of the most distinguished university presses in the United States, enriches lives around the world by advancing scholarship in the humanities, social sciences, and natural sciences. Its activities are supported by the UC Press Foundation and by philanthropic contributions from individuals and institutions. For more information, visit www.ucpress.edu.

University of California Press
Berkeley and Los Angeles, California

University of California Press, Ltd.
London, England

First paperback printing 2011

Library of Congress Cataloging-in-Publication Data

Gamble, Lynn H.

The Chumash world at European contact : power, trade, and feasting among complex hunter-gatherers / Lynn H. Gamble.

p. cm.

Includes bibliographical references and index.

ISBN 978-0-520-27124-1 (pbk. : alk. paper)

1. Chumash Indians—History. 2. Chumash Indians—Social life and customs. 3. Indians of North America—First contact with Europeans—California. 4. Spain—Colonies—America—Administration. 5. California—Discovery and exploration. 6. California—History—To 1846. I. Title.

E99.C815.G36 2008

979.4004'9758—dc22 2007050922

Manufactured in China

13 12 11

10 9 8 7 6 5 4 3 2 1

The paper used in this publication meets the minimum requirements of ANSI/NISO Z39.48-1992 (R 1997) (*Permanence of Paper*).

Cover image: *Meeting the Chumash* (2006) by artist David Rickman.

*For my husband, Glenn,
and daughter, Naomi, for all
their patience and support.*

Contents

Preface

My initial field experience in the archaeology of the Santa Barbara Channel region was in 1979 when I surveyed the site of Dos Pueblos, named after the two large Chumash village sites situated on either side of a creek. As part of that project, I examined the site's documentation and was intrigued with the large sweatlodge that had been discovered there in 1958. Prior to this visit, I had seen photographs of the excavations of houses and associated features at the Pitas Point site, also along the Santa Barbara Channel mainland coast. When I excavated at the site of *Helo'* in 1986, I had completed an analysis of activity areas and of household archaeology at the Pitas Point site through the examination of notes, artifacts, photographs, and other documents associated with the site. The subject of household archaeology was not of great interest to scholars of Chumash archaeology, and even today remains a topic that is seldom studied. The lack of easily identifiable architectural remains is probably one reason that so few have focused on this subject over the last fifty years. I firmly believed that the nature of power, the emergence of political complexity, and the reasons that the Chumash used shell bead money could not be understood until archaeologists knew how households functioned within settlements, and whether in fact sites were once villages, towns, or places that were only temporarily visited.

Publications on the Chumash have burgeoned over the past 20 years, due in large part to the intellectually stimulating environment created by faculty and graduate students in the Department of Anthropology at the University of California, Santa Barbara (UCSB). In the late 1970s and early 1980s, the department Anthropology Club was particularly active, headed by Mike Macko and Jon Erlandson. The club even made a tule reed boat, cutting many of the reeds with chipped stone knives, which were later inspected for evidence of use wear. The reed boat was eventually launched at Refugio Beach on a calm summer day; all aboard were tempted to make the crossing to Santa Cruz Island because of the tranquil waters in the Channel that day, and the perceived seaworthiness of the boat. Other projects, usually led by Mike Macko, included the manufacture of strands of shell beads that were bestowed on unsuspecting anthropology students as a recruiting device.

Many of my colleagues from UCSB and elsewhere have made significant contributions to the understanding of the dynamic political, ideological, and economic strategies of the Chumash. Much of their data, however, are based on knowledge of the relatively pristine sites on the Santa Barbara Channel Islands. I have taken a different tack with this project, concentrating on the large mainland populations as the primary context. My intention in this book is to create a wider perspective on the Chumash. I have chosen to focus on the early historic period in the Santa Barbara Channel in part because of the wealth of information available from this era. My hope is that this work will serve as a basis for further discussions on the Chumash and will supplement the excellent material we currently have on the island Chumash.

There are numerous people that have helped me in the completion of this book, but I first want to recognize two people in particular. I am most grateful to Glenn Russell, who not only suggested the idea for this book about five years ago, but encouraged me every step of the way. His conviction in my ability to undertake this work and to carry it to completion was unwavering. The second person who was of tremendous help in the completion of this book is Thomas Blackburn. Tom is an expert in the Chumash and California Indians, is a masterful writer and editor, and has over 40 years of experience in the region. Tom read every draft chapter of the book, sometimes twice, and provided constructive criticism as well as editing.

Other individuals also read drafts of this book, including David Earle, Kent Lightfoot, Glenn Farris, and two anonymous reviewers. I greatly appreciate all of their constructive comments. Several other colleagues were particularly generous with their time and knowledge and provided significant information and insights into the Chumash, including Jon Erlandson, Mike Glassow, John Johnson, Chester King, and Phil Walker. I thank each one of them for helping me improve this book. I also had productive discussions with Joe Ball, Doug Bamforth, Lowell Bean, Brian

Fagan, Gerrit Fenenga, Bob Gibson, Phil Greenfeld, Julia Hammett, Steve Horne, Jean Hudson, Travis Hudson, Mike Jochim, Pat Lambert, Herb Maschner, Michael Macko, Chris Pierce, Jeff Rigby, Eugene Robinson, Tom Rockwell, Kathy Schreiber, Clay Singer, and Albert Spaulding.

I am most grateful to a number of people who helped me with documentation, photographs, and artifacts in archives and museums. Copies of early maps of Mescalitan Island were obtained from the Santa Barbara Airport archives, the Goleta Sanitary District map room, and the Santa Barbara Museum of Natural History. I am appreciative to Chris Coleman, Margaret Hardin, Karen Wise, and Charles Rozaire at the Los Angeles County Museum of Natural History for their assistance in uncovering photographs and other documentation from Woodward's excavations at *Muwu*. I also recognize the efforts of Ray Corbett, John Johnson, Jan Timbrook, Tim Hazeltine, Linda Agren, and Susan Davison at the Santa Barbara Museum of Natural History; Mike Glassow, Peter Paige, Cynthia Bettison, and Karen Rasmussen at the University of California Santa Barbara Repository for Archaeological and Ethnographic Collections; Wendy Teeter, Glenn Russell, and Roger Colten at the Fowler Museum of Cultural History, University of California, Los Angeles; Leslie Freund, Joan Knudsen, Ed Luby, Rosemary Joyce, Deb Porter, Diane Grady, and Kathy Shackley at the Phoebe Hearst Museum at UC Berkeley; Mark Clark, Scott Merrick, and Roberta Kirk at the Smithsonian Institution's National Museum of the American Indian; Molly Coxson at the National Museum of Natural History at the Smithsonian Institution; Kathleen Lindahl and Michael Sampson at the California Department of Parks and Recreation; and Kathryn Klar in Celtic Studies at UC Berkeley. All of these individuals, and others too numerous to mention, provided assistance that made this book possible. In addition, I especially thank Chester King for providing notes on collections from the Phoebe Hearst Museum at UC Berkeley and the Santa Barbara Museum of Natural History, and Pat Martz for sharing her notes on the *Muwu* excavations by Woodward. I especially owe my gratitude to Donald Miller, who originally excavated and documented many of the Chumash structural remains.

A number of people helped with the photographs and illustrations used in this book, and I am particularly indebted to them for their assistance and expertise. They include Melodie Tune, Glenn Russell, Chester King, Kara Johnson, Tim Seymor, Kirsten Olson, Lori Palmer, Lisa Pompelli, and Trang Do.

I am also most appreciative of the efforts of a number of people who helped edit this book. Naomi Gamble King, my daughter, assisted me with the bibliography and had an especially keen eye for missing or misplaced commas, semicolons, and other such details. Kara Johnson and Kelleen Massie also helped me with the bibliography. Kathy Sholan and Kara Johnson proofed sections of the book and provided important editorial remarks. I thank all of these individuals for their attention to detail and assistance with these matters.

I am especially indebted to Blake Edgar, principal editor at UC Press, who was interested in what I had to say and saw me through the review and publication process. I also am grateful to Matthew Winfield and Kate Hoffman at UC Press, who oversaw the details of publishing this book.

A semester sabbatical leave was granted to me in the spring of 2004 by San Diego State University (SDSU), which allowed me a block of time to focus my energies on this book. I also received a Research, Scholarly and Creativity Activity award from SDSU in 2002, which allowed me to complete some of the research for this project. I acknowledge with sincere gratitude, the support of the Department of Anthropology, which supported me in this and other endeavors. I especially thank Kathy Peck, who manages to help us all in the slippery navigation of department obligations.

Finally, my sincere thanks go to the Chumash Indian people, both past and present. They are actively committed to the preservation of their culture and ancestral lands. They have worked closely with archaeologists in the field, in the labs at UCSB, and at hearings, serving to further the continuation and protection of their culture. Their spirit, generosity, and curiosity about the present and the past are vibrant and have greatly enriched my life.

CHAPTER I

The Chumash at a Crossroads

Theoretical Considerations

> *Ever since we first began meeting with houses laid out like towns, which was at Santa Catalina de Bononia, the villages have all been continuing to be this way, and the ones encountered are much more populous every day, with the inhabitants living in regular towns with very good sized grass houses, round like half oranges, some of which are so large within that they must be able to lodge without hindrance sixty persons and more. . . . They have their own kind of government, two, three, or four chiefs, and one of these chiefs is the headman, who gives orders to everyone.*
>
> Crespí on August 20, 1769, in Brown 2001:425

Imagine how impressed Father Juan Crespí and the soldiers that accompanied Captain Gaspar de Portolá must have been as they marched into the Santa Barbara Channel region during the first land expedition to Alta California, while in search of the harbor of Monterey. They saw large towns[1] with houses lined up in rows packed closely together. As they passed these settlements with house roofs piled high with barbecued fish (Brown 2001:391), they were entertained and fed by the Chumash. The Spanish were offered so much fish and other food that they threw some away (Brown 2001:409). This was only weeks after the expedition had left San Diego, where they had been on the verge of starvation. Eventually, the Portolá expedition, after experiencing considerable hardships, established the first permanent settlements in California.

This book is about the Chumash that Crespí encountered in 1769. At the time that Crespí journeyed through the Santa Barbara area, the

Chumash were thriving, and had reached a level of considerable sociopolitical complexity. They were the nexus of a far-reaching exchange network that used shell beads as money. They had mastered the art of building plank boats *(tomols)* that allowed them to cross the Channel to the offshore islands safely and swiftly and return laden with large stone bowls and other trade goods. Canoes enabled fishermen to venture into deep waters to catch swordfish weighing as much as 600 pounds. The Chumash lived in large houses clustered in towns, some with several chiefs. They were some of the only hunter-gatherer groups in the world that had regional chiefs who wielded power beyond the boundaries of their own settlements. The Chumash buried chiefs and other high-ranking individuals inside the plank boats, surrounded by thousands of beads to honor them in their journey to the afterlife. Their cemeteries were separated from day-to-day activities and clearly marked with painted poles and grave markers. The Chumash also had large ceremonial grounds where they danced, played music, and sang, and where special initiates performed in sacred enclosures. Chumash men and women dressed differently from one another, as did people of different status. According to some of the earliest historical accounts (e.g., Crespí in Brown 2001:367–369; Fages in Priestley 1937:320), men usually went naked but painted their bodies, wore their long hair up wrapped with cords and attached shell beads, and occasionally wore waist-length fur capes. Some had feather headdresses. The chiefs could be distinguished from others by their fur capes draping to the ankles, and the carved bone pins in their hair—some inlaid with shell beads—that were attached to long chert knives. Women (as well as two-spirits)[2] wore two deer or otter skins as skirts. Both men and women adorned themselves with shell beads and ornaments.

The lives of the Chumash who resided in the large mainland settlements are reconstructed in this book on the basis of several collaborative sources of evidence. Information from ethnohistoric documents, comparative ethnography, ecology, archaeological investigations, and biological anthropology are synthesized to create a portrayal of what life was like for the Chumash Indians in a traditional mainland town before their existence was changed forever. The era of culture contact provides a tremendous source of information because of the rich ethnohistoric and ethnographic record that is available for the region. Moreover, these independent lines of evidence can be employed—in conjunction with archaeological and biological data—to evaluate interpretations using a comparative approach (e.g., Lightfoot 1995).

At the time of European contact, the mainland population centers had the highest population densities in the Santa Barbara Channel region;

the offshore islands, the interior, and the area north of Point Conception were more sparsely populated. A greater variety and number of shell beads, which were used both as currency and as status markers, were being produced. Artifact assemblages included an abundance of prestige goods, such as finely woven baskets, steatite comals and ollas, huge shaped pestles, and carefully hewn bowl mortars. The plank canoe, the most expensive possession that a Chumash owned (Gamble 2002a; Hudson et al. 1978), was an essential component in the exchange of prestige goods. Because of the costs involved, the ownership of canoes was highly restricted. Early explorers described the *tomol* during essentially every major excursion to the Santa Barbara Channel region and were clearly impressed by the watercraft.

Significance of Research

Although considerable research has been carried out on Chumash society, no one has focused on the mainland population centers at the time of historic contact. The relative lack of publications on the mainland settlements at their peak of complexity has left scholars with only a partial understanding of economic transactions, political power, and social interactions throughout the Chumash region. This book is intended to fill that void. The emphasis will be placed on settlements that were centrally located within the Chumash region, and on how the leaders in those centers managed and retained power. Sources of power are discussed in the context of socioeconomic interactions, and the role of leaders in the centers is contrasted with that of leaders in peripheral areas. Wealth finance, status differentiation, technological innovations such as the plank canoe, warfare, feasting, and other dynamics of social organization are considered and linked to theoretical discussions on the nature of power.

The period between the first documented European interaction with the Chumash in 1542 and the Portolá overland expedition in 1769 is known as the protohistoric period (Erlandson and Bartoy 1995). The Portolá expedition of 1769 initiated Spanish settlement in the region and began the period that witnessed the most drastic changes to Chumash lifeways. The year 1769 is considered the beginning of the historic period, because prior to this date contact was only sporadic. Jon Erlandson and Kevin Bartoy (1995), as well as others (Erlandson et al. 2001; Preston 1996; Walker and Hudson 1993; Walker and Johnson 1992, 1994; Walker et al. 2005), have suggested that the Chumash may have been exposed to Old World diseases between 1542 and 1769; these diseases could have reduced their population significantly. Nevertheless, conclusive evidence for devastating diseases during this period has not yet been identified. Although it is not the focus of this research, the consequences of European colonization on Chumash society will be addressed. The primary intent of this book, however, is to use independent lines of evidence to reconstruct Chumash society at the height of its sociopolitical complexity and address the question of the political strategies that probably existed in the large mainland centers.

The greatest population density in the Chumash region involved several settlements clustered around the Goleta Slough, which contained close to 2000 inhabitants. One of these towns, situated on Mescalitan Island in the middle of the slough, was the historic settlement of *Helo'* (CA-SBA-46). I focus on *Helo'* in this volume because of its prominence at the time of contact, and because various excavations at the site have revealed important information on Chumash household activities (Gamble 1990, 1991) and mortuary customs (Olson 1930; Putnam et al. 1879). House floors, storage pits, and hearths at *Helo'* have been meticulously excavated, processed, and analyzed. Floors, rarely identified on the mainland, had previously never been excavated and analyzed using modern techniques. Ethnobotanical studies were carried out for macro and micro remains from these features. These studies and other analyses have furthered our understanding of household organization and production during the historic period.

Early archaeological investigations on the mainland primarily focused on the excavation of cemeteries, in an attempt to collect museum-quality objects. These data supplement more recent information on domestic activities. H. C. Yarrow led an 1875 Smithsonian Institution expedition that excavated a portion of the historic cemetery on Mescalitan Island, where an abundance of finely crafted burial goods was discovered (Putnam et al. 1879:35). Approximately 50 years later, a different portion of the historic cemetery was excavated by a team of archaeologists from UC Berkeley led by Ronald Olson (1930). Information from both projects is significant because the cemetery was one of the largest in the region dating to the historic period. Data on status differentiation, sociopolitical organization, and household activities at *Helo'* provide the reader a glimpse of what life was like at a major mainland center at the time of contact.

One reason that most research-oriented archaeology in recent years has been focused on the northern Santa Barbara Channel Islands instead of on the mainland is that bulldozers, gophers, and other cultural and natural sources of disturbance have seriously impacted the mainland coastal strip between Point Conception and Malibu. In comparison, the offshore islands are relatively pristine, with very little development and no burrowing rodents. Numerous features on the islands are intact, and house depressions can still be seen on the surface. Many publications on the Chumash over the last thirty years reflect this unbalanced pattern of archaeological research (Arnold 1987, 1990, 1992a, 2001a, 2001b; Colten 1995; Colten and Arnold 1998; Erlandson 1991a; Erlandson and Rick 2002a; Erlandson et al. 1996, 1999; Kennett 2005; Kennett and Kennett 2000; Rick 2007). Similarly, the most up-to-date scholarly book on the prehistory of the Chumash is focused on Santa Cruz Island (Arnold 2001a, 2001b). However, the few exceptions are worth noting. John Johnson (1988, 2000), using mission documents and ethnohistoric sources, has reconstructed population figures for both the mainland and the islands and has used this information to examine sociopolitical and economic complexity. Michael Glassow (1996) published a book on Chumash prehistory and maritime adaptations in the Vandenberg region on the mainland north of Point Conception. Other books (Erlandson 1994; King 1990a) on the Chumash have discussed mainland sites, but have not concentrated on the historic period. One of the best known volumes on the Chumash (although from a much earlier era) is David Banks Rogers's (1929) *Prehistoric Man of the Santa Barbara Coast,* a classic guide to prehistoric sites over a 10,000-year period on the mainland and islands. Although Rogers provided important information on mainland Chumash sites, he did not systematically collect data, did not synthesize his data, nor did he address the nature of sociopolitical complexity in the region. In addition, Rogers did not have the wealth of comparative data that exists today that would have allowed for a regional synthesis. Archaeologists have continued to excavate mainland Chumash sites since Rogers's era, especially since the advent of environmental regulations and contract archaeology. Nevertheless, no one has synthesized information on the mainland coast in order to address the nature of Chumash political and economic complexity at the time of historic contact.

Despite the obstacles that have affected the preservation of sites on the mainland coast, a considerable body of information on this significant region does exist. During European exploration of southern California, extensive accounts were written by priests, soldiers, and others looking for areas to settle and colonize. These invaluable ethnohistoric sources, combined with data gleaned from archaeological and ethnographic investigations over the past 100 years, provide an impressive body of literature on the Chumash during this period.

Overview of the Chumash

The Chumash occupied the region from Topanga Canyon in the south to the Monterey County line in the north, and eastward to the San Joaquin Valley. In addition to this large mainland area, the Chumash lived on the northern Santa Barbara Channel Islands of Santa Cruz, Santa Rosa, San Miguel, and Anacapa. Relatively recent cultural and linguistic research, as well as DNA evidence, suggest that the Chumash probably had an ancient presence in the Santa Barbara Channel area, and that they were not a series of separate groups that entered the region and replaced or blended with the previous inhabitants (Erlandson 1994; Johnson and Lorenz 2006; King 1990a). A number of common chronologies are used in the Santa Barbara Channel region, most of which are variations of Chester King's 1990a chronology (table 1). In 1992, Jeanne Arnold introduced the concept of a Middle-Late Transitional period based on the emergence of greater sociopolitical complexity between AD 1150 and AD 1300. Jon Erlandson and Roger Colten (1991) proposed a shift in King's chronology after calibrating the radiocarbon dates for the region. Since that time, Doug Kennett (2005) has further refined the chronology based on calibrated dates. Kennett (2005:82) points out that King's Middle period, phase 5, correlates reasonably well with Arnold's Middle-Late Transitional period when the dates are calibrated.

The coastal Chumash were hunter-gatherers who subsisted primarily on marine products (including fish, shellfish, and sea mammals) and wild plant foods such as acorns. They also utilized terrestrial mammals and birds, but to a lesser extent. As did many other California Indians, the Chumash relied heavily on stored goods, especially during the winter months when many foods were less abundant. Acorns could be stored for several years. Other important foods that were stored by the Chumash included Islay (Wild Cherry), small seeds such as Chia (Sage), dried and smoked fish, and dried meat from deer and other mammals (King 2000:39–40). Storage allowed the Chumash to have a reliable source of food throughout the year, even in years when harvests proved unreliable. Without the storage of important resources, the population densities of the Chumash would not have been as great as they were.

The population of the Chumash at historic contact has been estimated to have been between 18,000 and 20,000 people (Cook 1976:37–38; Johnson 1998:i). Population figures for this period are rough estimates because of the difficulty in measuring the impact that European diseases had on population sizes during the contact era. During the protohistoric period,

TABLE 1. Chronology for the Santa Barbara Channel Region

Period	Kennett (2005), Calibrated (BC–AD)	Arnold (1992, 2001a)	King (1990)	Lambert (1994)
Historic	AD 1782–1804	Historic 1782+	Late 3, AD 1782–1804	Late
Late 2	AD 1670–1782	Late, AD 1300–1782	Late 2b, AD 1650–1782	
			Late 2a, AD 1500–1650	
Late 1	AD 1380–1670		Late 1c, AD 1400–1500	
			Late 1b, AD 1250–1400	
			Late 1a, AD 1150–1250	
		Transitional, AD 1150–1300		
Middle 5	AD 1170–1380	Middle, 600 BC–AD 1150	Middle 5 c, AD 1050–1150 Middle 5b, AD 1000–1050 Middle 5a, AD 900–1000	Late Middle
Middle 4	AD 980–1170		Middle 4, AD 700-900	
Middle 3	AD 660–980		Middle 3, AD 400-700	
Middle 2	AD 170–660		Middle 2b, AD 200–400 Middle 2a, 200 BC–AD 200	Early Middle
Middle 1	490 BC–AD 170		Middle 1, 600–200 BC	
Early z	970–490 BC	Early, 5500–600 BC	Early z, 1000–600 BC	Late Early
Early yb	3590–970 BC		Early yb, 3000–1000 BC	
Early ya	4650–3590 BC		Early ya, 4000–3000 BC	Early Early
Early x	6120–4650 BC		Early x, 5500–4000 BC	

several European expeditions entered the Chumash region after Juan Rodríguez Cabrillo's 1542 trip, including those of Pedro de Unamuno in 1587, Sebastián Rodríguez Cermeño in 1595, and Sebastián Vizcaíno in 1602–03 (Erlandson and Bartoy 1995). During the late sixteenth century, the flourishing trade between New Spain and Asia involving spices and silk affected California, since California's west coast was a significant landmark after the long ocean crossing from Manila (Beebe and Senkiwicz 2001:38). Numerous undocumented contacts between sailors involved in the Manila galleon trade and Native Californians undoubtedly occurred between 1565 and the arrival of the Portolá expedition in 1769. Diaries from some of these explorations, records from the mission period that followed, and later ethnographic research on the Chumash have allowed researchers to partially reconstruct the political, economic, religious, and social life of the Chumash at the time of European contact. A brief overview of Chumash social organization is provided here, with a more detailed discussion of different aspects of their culture in subsequent chapters.

The political system of the Chumash was primarily organized at the village level. Each village was headed by a hereditary chief; in addition, there were many other specialists who wielded considerable influence (Blackburn 1975, 1976; L. King 1969). Some settlements had more than one chief, and Johnson (1988) has suggested that these villages were political centers. There is additional evidence that the Chumash had regional chiefs with jurisdiction over many villages (Blackburn 1975; L. King 1969).

It is important to remember that although the Chumash shared many cultural traits, "the Chumash were neither a cultural nor a linguistic entity *per se*" (Blackburn 1975:8). Recently, the Chumashan language family, which appears to be a linguistic isolate, has been broken into three branches, Northern Chumash (Obispeño), Central Chumash (Purismeño, Ineseño, Barbareño, and Ventureño), and Island Chumash (Cruzeño) (Goddard 1996:320). My focus will be on the Barbareño (figure 1), although some information from coastal sites in the Ventureño, Purismeño, and other mainland regions is presented.

The Chumash had a highly developed economic system in which shell beads were used as money (King 1976). The production of shell beads as a standardized, portable medium of exchange was a complex, specialized industry that was linked to two areas of craft specialization and was centered primarily on the offshore Channel Islands (Arnold 1987; King 1976). Seaworthy plank canoes, which were costly to build and maintain, provided a means of transport for the exchange of goods between the mainland and the islands. Shell beads were also exchanged outside the Chumash

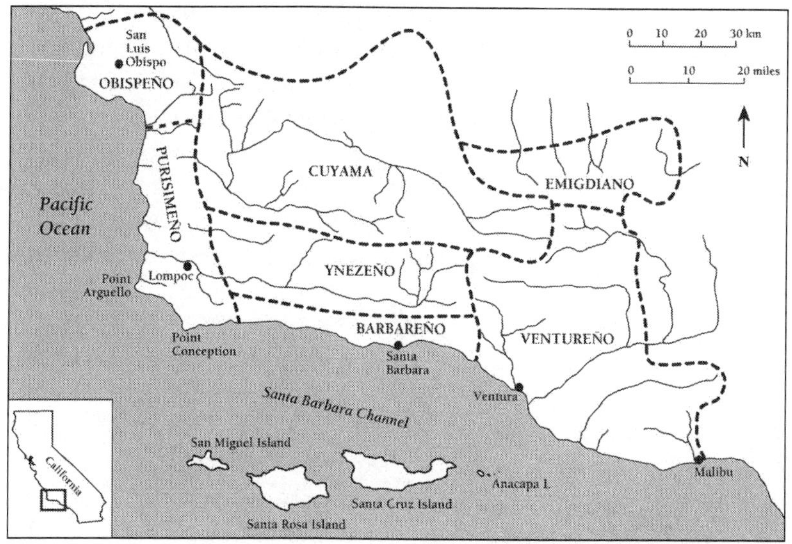

FIGURE 1 Linguistic groups of the Chumash

region; they have been found in the Southwest and the Great Basin (Bennyhoff and Hughes 1987; King 1990a).

Development of Chumash Sociopolitical Complexity

Most scholars working in the Chumash region recognize that a simple chiefdom level of organization existed at the time of historic contact (Arnold 1992a, 2001a, 2001b; Kennett and Kennett 2000; King 1990a; Martz 1984). Simple chiefdoms, in contrast to complex chiefdoms, have smaller polity sizes and a system of graduated ranking as opposed to emergent stratification (Earle 1991; Johnson and Earle 2000). There are a variety of explanations as to how the simple chiefdoms of the Chumash were organized and why they developed. Many suggest that environmental change played a critical role in the development of sociopolitical complexity in the region (Arnold 1992a; Johnson 2000; Kennett and Kennett 2000). Arnold (1992a) argues that social ranking among the Chumash developed around A.D. 1200–1300, and explains its origin as involving the manipulation of labor by rising elites within a context of political opportunism and environmental degradation. Recently, Arnold (2001a) has suggested that the control of labor by a small group of leaders, a factor that stimulated social ranking, was associated with technological innovation. Kennett and Kennett (2000) agree with Arnold that climatic change played an important role in the emergence of sociopolitical complexity, but identify a period of high marine productivity and terrestrial drought between A.D. 450–1300 as being critical. The timing and nature of their climatic reconstruction differs significantly from Arnold's. Kennett and Kennett (2000:392) propose that as a result of the earlier climatic change, the region witnessed greater sedentism, an intensification of fishing practices, more trade, and an increase in regional violence.

Others, such as King (1990a), do not recognize climatic change as significant in the emergence of sociopolitical complexity in the region. King suggests that a ranked society involving a hereditary elite first appeared in the Santa Barbara Channel area many years earlier than proposed by Arnold or the Kennetts. On the basis of detailed analyses of burial associations and their changes through time, King argues that social ranking appeared about 2,600 years ago, at the end of the Early period. However, despite differing views on the timing and reasons for sociopolitical complexity in the Chumash region, most scholars agree that by some hundreds of years before historic contact, social ranking was fully developed in the Chumash region and hereditary chiefs were in power.

Several issues relevant to the sociopolitical and economic interactions of the Chumash are addressed in this volume. One issue is the role of large population centers in the regional economic, political, and ceremonial interactions of the Chumash. I propose that important individuals in the large mainland centers played a significant role in the control of economic interactions between the mainland coast and the smaller settlements on the northern Channel Islands, in the interior of the Chumash region, on the outskirts of the Chumash territory, and outside the Chumash region. The production and ownership of canoes were undoubtedly critical factors in controlling the exchange system between the islands and the mainland. Timothy Earle (2001:30) has stated that control can more readily be applied when transportation technology is more restricted. Families with inherited political power living in the large Chumash population centers possessed considerable wealth, including the ownership of the plank canoes used to transport exchange goods between the islands and the mainland. Chiefly families intermarried with other chiefly families from surrounding Chumash settlements (Johnson 1988), thereby creating and strengthening sociopolitical ties between regions. Chiefs and wealthy individuals who owned canoes exerted considerable control in the exchange system involving the mainland and the islands.

It is likely that the demand for currency in large centers, as well as in smaller settlements both within and outside the Chumash area, served as a major impetus for the intensive bead-making activities on the islands. Moreover, beads were a form of social storage (O'Shea and Halstead 1989), the core of an institutionalized mechanism that allowed the Chumash to ensure adequate food supplies through a highly developed exchange system in which food from one region was exchanged for beads from another. The significance of durable goods (bead currency) in the development of inequalities in wealth, rank, and power is discussed in chapters 7 and 8.

Questions regarding the relationship between the islanders and the inhabitants of the mainland settlements are also addressed in this volume. Were people living on the mainland less powerful than the money-producing islanders? Or did the inhabitants of the large mainland centers strongly influence the exchange system, with the islanders performing labor-intensive specialized activities in order to acquire food and other exchange items? In order to address these and other questions, the settlement patterns and cultural landscape on the mainland coast are reconstructed through the use of ethnohistoric documents, mission register data (Johnson 1988), archaeological information, and (to a lesser extent) ethnographic sources. Multiple lines of evidence relevant to the sociopolitical and economic interactions within the Chumash network are presented in order to gain a better understanding of the production, distribution, and consumption of the goods that are found in the mainland sites.

Theoretical Considerations

Several studies have addressed the issue of complex hunter-gatherers, which Price and Brown's (1985) volume on the emergence of cultural complexity among prehistoric hunter-gatherers has brought to the forefront. Since the publication of this important volume, discussions about North American hunter-gatherer complexity on the Northwest Coast (e.g., Ames 1994, 1995; Ames and Maschner 1999; Hayden 1995; Maschner 1991), in the southeastern United States (Marquadt 2001), and in California (Arnold 1995, 2001a, 2001b; Gamble et al. 2001; Kennett 2005; Kennett and Kennett 2000) have become common. In a recent book on the Northwest Coast, Kenneth Ames and Herbert Maschner (1999) identify characteristics of complex hunter-gatherers that are relevant to this discussion. They suggest that complex hunter-gatherers were semi-sedentary or sedentary and lived in substantial houses in settlements with relatively high population densities. Large quantities of processed and stored foods were needed to feed substantial numbers of people throughout the year. Ames and Maschner propose that populations relied intensively on a few productive subsistence resources, with numerous secondary resources, and that they manipulated their environment to increase productivity. This was accomplished by means of a specialized and complex technology. Finally, complex hunter-gatherers had social hierarchies and occupational specialization (see Ames and Maschner 1999:25–29 for a full discussion). The Chumash Indians at the time of European contact exhibited all the traits described by Ames and Maschner, in addition to other traits associated with complexity. These additional traits include hereditary leadership and a monetized economic system based on shell beads.

The concept that centrally located places often become influential centers is well known and is especially relevant to this discussion. In his seminal work on social organization in Native California, Lowell Bean (1976:102) observed that a central town often served as a political, economic, and ritual center in California Indian societies. Bean described exchange mechanisms associated with these centers. "Formal or informal trade feasts were set up between groups living in different ecological areas, so that goods from the mutually advantageous but politically separate areas were exchanged for those of others" (Bean 1976:120). Similarly, in a discussion on the transition from household-based to village-level organization, Kent Lightfoot and Gary Feinman (1982:67) suggest that sociopolitical ties are strengthened through exchange and marriage networks. They propose that as part of these regional exchange systems, active participants tend to live in centrally located settlements that are much larger than other villages, because costs associated with the movement of goods and the exchange of knowledge are minimized.

When considering centrally located places, transportation is of special importance. The development of reliable ocean-going boats is an essential technological innovation if long-distance maritime exchange is to occur (Kirch 1991, 2000; Yesner 1980), allowing groups greater access to resources, including prestige goods, marriage partners, and knowledge. Patrick Kirch (1984:242–243, 2000) viewed the development of canoes for long-distance voyages among Polynesian chiefdoms as being particularly significant in the process of political consolidation and the control of exchanges of prestige goods. Similarly, prehistoric exchange in western Melanesia was dominated by specialist traders who tended to maintain a monopoly on ocean-going canoes (Kirch 1991:156). Canoes were also a significant technological innovation that provided chiefs a significant advantage in the Chumash exchange system. They were also essential in the intensification of maritime resource acquisition and the exploitation of the abundant food supply of the Chumash that was observed by the early chroniclers.

Brian Hayden (1995:21–22) has noted a strong correlation between resource abundance and the emergence of social complexity in the form of socioeconomic disparities. Hayden suggests that ample resources, paired with surpluses, were critical in creating inequalities, hierarchy, and economic complexity. Arnold (2001b:6) disagrees with Hayden on this point and instead suggests that leaders often benefit from stressful periods by manipulating resources, labor, or technology to their advantage. Certainly sustained drought conditions may have impacted Chumash subsistence practices, settlement sizes and locations, and regional interactions. Nevertheless, drought and other climactic changes generally have a greater impact on agricultural societies than on hunter-gatherer societies, particularly those that rely heavily on marine resources (Gamble 2003, 2005). It is well documented in the ethnographic and ethnohistoric record that California Indians had multiple strategies for adapting to changing environmental conditions (Blackburn and Anderson 1993). I support Hayden's (1995) argument that sociopolitical complexity developed during times of resource abundance, not scarcity. Once populations expanded and became more densely settled in the region, the Chumash became more vulnerable to risk. As a result, strategies were developed to address these greater risks. Although drought and El Niño events periodically occurred in the Santa Barbara Channel (and some were of great significance), the Chumash had developed coping mechanisms over a long period of time to reduce the risk of these recurring events (Gamble 2003). Strategies to reduce risk included exchange, storage, and the use of a system of currency. I suggest, in contrast to Arnold, that powerful individuals gained ever-increasing status and control over exchanges as the demand for prestige goods in the burgeoning mainland settlements increased.

The focus in this book is on the settlements that were centrally located within the Chumash region, their leaders, and the interactions of those leaders with each other and with individuals in more peripheral regions. An understanding of how chiefs and other powerful individuals in regional centers managed and retained power is crucial to this analysis. A useful framework for recognizing political strategies can be found in the work of both Richard Blanton et al. (1996) and others (Earle 2001; Feinman 2000; Renfrew 1974). Blanton and his colleagues, for example, have identified two types of political approaches: an exclusionary or network approach on the one hand, and a corporate approach on the other. These are not mutually exclusive and can be found within any given society, although one mode is often more pronounced than the other (Feinman 1995:264). Corporate power tends to emphasize the group, and shared collective representations with an emphasis on food production or staple finance are typical elements of corporate power strategies (Blanton et al. 1996; Earle 2001; Feinman 2000). Wealth is more evenly distributed under a corporate structure and power is shared. Examples of corporate groups include Puebloan societies (Earle 2001; Feinman et al. 2000) and the Classic Period Teotihuacan polity (Blanton et al. 1996). Material manifestations that characterize these societies frequently include monumental public architecture (with plazas and other spaces that are used for group ritual activities), a dearth of wealthy burials or royal tombs, and corporate labor systems involving irrigation canals or roads. Leaders are not easily identified in the archaeological record in societies that emphasize corporate identity.

Network power differs considerably, with an emphasis on individual power and wealth. The social relationships of individuals are tied to an extensive network system that is characterized by ceremonial displays and exchanges of marriage partners, gifts, and specialized knowledge (Blanton et al. 1996:4; Earle 2001:27). Long-distance networks that are typical of this strategy require maintenance, and can become expansive and competitive. In order to maintain and establish new trade partners and compete with other networks, there is a tendency for increased feasting, more abundant prestige goods, and heightened conflict to occur (Blanton et al. 1996; Feinman 2000). Power is revealed in ostentatious personal displays that are manifested both in life and in burial rituals. Chiefs that use network strategies attempt to control the production and/or distribution of prestige goods and valuables that represent wealth (Earle 2001).

An important component of network power is a system of wealth finance (D'Altroy and Earle 1985; Earle 1997), which involves an exchange of prestige goods, many of which have established values. These are often used to finance political officials and other individuals that maintain the system. In contrast, staple finance (which is tied to corporate political power) involves the collection of subsistence goods by a central power. One disadvantage of this strategy is the cost of transporting and storing bulky subsistence goods (D'Altroy and Earle 1985:188).

Concepts similar to network and corporate political strategies have been suggested previously but under a different rubric. Colin Renfrew (1974), for example, has recognized "group-oriented chiefdoms" and "individualizing chiefdoms" in prehistoric Europe. Renfrew suggests that group-oriented chiefdoms had limited regional ecological diversity, placed relatively little emphasis on technology, tended to use large public works for communal activities, and often lacked "princely burials." He characterizes individualizing chiefdoms as societies that emphasized warfare, personal wealth, and prestige goods, the latter of which were often found associated with burials. He suggests that in some cases these societies lacked large public works, except for structures associated with the chief such as residences and tombs (Renfrew 1974:79).

I propose that the Chumash at European contact practiced a network strategy (i.e., they had an individualizing chiefdom in Renfrew's terms), with an emphasis on wealth finance. I also believe that this strategy was not a recent development but had existed for centuries in the region (Gamble et al. 2001). The issues of social hierarchy, economic networks, sources of chiefly power, craft specialization, feasting, competition and conflict, technological intensification, and wealth finance are thoroughly investigated in this volume. The primary focus of this book is the mainland population centers and their economic, political, and ceremonial interactions with the Chumash in more peripheral areas of the region.

However, before I begin the discussion of Chumash sociopolitical and economic life, I will provide some background on the cultural ecology of the Chumash. The environment in 1769 is reconstructed on the basis of historic accounts and other documentation. Resources of significance to the Chumash are discussed, with a special emphasis on the Goleta Slough area. Next, a cultural context for the Chumash at the time of historic contact is established. I then present a brief overview of the archaeologists, anthropologists, and others who provide important information on the Chumash, with a discussion of the strengths, weaknesses, and biases inherent in their data. A more detailed description of the historic settlements in the mainland Santa Barbara coastal region follows, along with a synthesis of the available demographic data (such as the number of canoes, houses, and people in each town). Archaeological information on the size, layout, and types of settlements is also provided. The nature of houses and of the activities that occurred within them is of primary significance in understanding the patterns of production, consumption, and power at the household level. More specific information on houses, sweatlodges, other structures, and features is presented in chapter 5. This is followed by an overview of the subsistence strategies of the mainland Chumash, along with archaeological and ethnohistoric evidence that sheds light on the technological complexity of the Chumash, their storage capabilities, the importance and timing of their feasting, and their diet. The role that gender played in labor investments associated with subsistence activities and the production of feasts is also addressed, as is the impact that colonization had on the Chumash.

Ethnohistoric and ethnographic accounts have shown that chiefs and canoe owners were often the same individuals. They and other individuals with leadership roles are considered in some detail in this book, as is the overall political system of the Chumash, especially in the mainland settlements. The elaborate economic interactions of the mainland settlements, including the production, distribution, and consumption of exchange goods, are explored next. An understanding of plank canoe ownership, and of how canoe owners controlled transportation, is essential for reconstructing and understanding the Chumash economic network. The significance of bead money in the elaborate economic transactions of the Chumash, as well as the importance of the use and distribution of prestige goods, are integral to this examination. Finally, evidence of conflict within the Chumash region is documented from early historical accounts and from bioarchaeological data, although considerable evidence suggests that various mechanisms for social integration were also in operation. Data on conflict in the Chumash region are synthesized and discussed in the context of sociopolitical integration.

By the end of this book, the reader should have a coherent picture of the Chumash in the mainland centers at their height of sociopolitical complexity. The sources of Chumash political power—in the context of socioeconomic interactions—is a major subject of discussion. The role of leaders in the main population centers is contrasted with that of leaders in more peripheral areas. Wealth finance, status differentiation, technological innovations such as the plank canoe, warfare, feasting, and other dynamics of social organization are all considered and linked to theoretical discussions on the nature of power.

CHAPTER 2

The Environment and Its Management

We went the whole way over dark friable very level soil, very much clad with very fine grazing and very large clumps of very tall broad grasses, burnt off in some spots and not so in others; the unburnt [grasses] were so tall that they topped us on horseback by about a yard. All about are very large tablelands with very large tall live oaks—I have never seen larger—and a great many sycamores as well. We have come upon such vast quantities of rose bushes that in many spots the levels were full of them here. We went two leagues across this soil, which is so good it cannot be bettered. . . There is a wood close to the inlet here, of willows and cottonwoods, so that it seems as though all the lushness in the world lies there, with vast numbers of rose bushes, brambles, holythistles, and all sorts of large plants.

Crespí on August 20, 1769, in Brown 2001:419–421

Crespí was impressed with the lush environment and fine soils he saw as he approached the Goleta Slough on his journey to Monterey. In search of appropriate locations for a mission, Crespí often remarked on the suitability of a region for agricultural pursuits. Crespí and other late eighteenth century chroniclers provide detailed descriptions of the resources and environment in the Santa Barbara Channel region at the time Chumash culture was thriving. In this chapter, we look at the ecological setting of the channel region based on historical and more recent accounts in the context of the Chumash as environmental managers.

Today the Santa Barbara Channel is one of the most productive fisheries in the world due to its geographic position and the phenomenon of localized upwelling of nutrient-rich deep waters and cold California currents (Kennett 1998:90–94). Between Point Conception and Ventura, the coastline is south-facing, protected by the four northern Channel Islands, and is characterized by productive kelp beds which attract fish and sea mammals. In stark contrast is the area north of Point Conception, where the coastline primarily faces west, the surf is turbulent, strong northwesterly winds prevail, and kelp beds are scarce (Glassow and Wilcoxon 1988).

The Mediterranean climate along the Santa Barbara Channel typically is cool and wet in the winter and hot and dry in the summer, with summer fog common between May and July (Smith 1976:3–6). Greater temperature fluctuations, including occasional frosts in the winter, occur in the interior regions where the Santa Ynez Mountains dominate the landscape. Rising sharply from the coastal plain, these rugged mountains are part of the east-west-trending Transverse Ranges. The juxtaposition of the Santa Ynez Mountain range to the north and the ocean to the south protects the mainland coastal region from the more extreme summer and winter conditions found in the interior valleys (Erlandson 1994:23). The coastal plain is bisected by numerous perennial and seasonal streams and varies in breadth along the Santa Barbara Channel shore, with the widest portion in the central area between Rincon and Tecolote canyons where the canyons tend to be larger. As we will see in chapter 4, the more populous historic Chumash settlements were associated with the larger canyons on the mainland coast, where perennial streams and estuaries were situated.

At European contact, large estuary systems at Goleta, Santa Barbara, and Carpinteria provided an abundance of diverse resources (Glassow 1997). The largest of these estuaries (the Goleta Slough) was described by Crespí in the summer of 1769 in the following way: "Everyone makes lavish catches of different sorts of fish in the inlet, bonitos, needlefish, very large sardines, and other kinds" (Crespí on August 20, 1769, in Brown 2001:421–423). All three diarists on the Portolá expedition were impressed with the expansive lagoon at Goleta and noted that it was surrounded by densely populated towns (Johnson 1982:14), with the largest settlement (*Helo'*) on the "prominent" island (Mescalitan Island) in the middle of the lagoon. The soldiers on the expedition, also struck with the island, named it Mescaltitlán, after Mescaltitlán Lagoon in Nayarit, Mexico. "Mescaltitlán" is Nahuatl in origin and refers to the Aztec heartland, a place where Mother Earth resided on an island in a lagoon (Johnson 1982:14–15). The place name Mescaltitlán eventually became associated with all of the Chumash villages surrounding the Goleta Slough (Johnson 1982:15)[3]. Glassow and his colleagues have suggested that when the site on Mescalitan Island was pristine, it was "one of the two or three greatest concentrations of midden deposits anywhere within the Santa Barbara Channel" (Glassow et al. 1986:9). Radiocarbon dates and other chronological information indicate that the island was occupied for thousands of years (Gamble 1990, 1991). A brief summary of the island's occupation history is provided in Chapter 3.

The once expansive lagoon at present-day Goleta was separated from the open sea by a sandspit and was between four and eleven feet (1.2 and 3.4 m) deep at high tide; even at low tide, the island was probably accessible by canoe (Stone 1982). Immediately outside the Goleta Slough were sandy beaches and just beyond those were kelp beds (Glenn 1990). The earliest map of Mescalitan Island (figure 2) and the settlements surrounding the Goleta Slough was drawn on August 12, 1782 by Pantoja y Arriaga, who entered the estuary by boat. Based on more recent maps and aerial photographs,[4] I produced the first contour map (figure 3) of the island as it appeared before modern development (Gamble 1991). The island rose approximately 21 meters above the slough and had a circumference of less than one kilometer. In the 1930s, Van Valkenburgh and other archaeologists from the Los Angeles County Museum identified two springs on the island, one at the island's eastern edge where historic-period household deposits were identified, and another at the northwest edge of the island (Gamble 1991). These springs, along with scattered oaks, grasslands, and a vernal pool, no doubt were flourishing when the Chumash lived there.

Resources in the Santa Barbara Channel Region

The Chumash Indians lived in an environment of abundant resources, including a variety of plants that could be used for food and other purposes, fish, sea and land mammals, and birds. One of the best descriptions of food resources used by the Chumash was provided by Fages in 1769:

> There is an abundance of all seeds needed for their use, and many acorns. There are birds and land animals of the same species as above mentioned[5] besides many additional ones. The fishing is so good, and so great is the variety of fish, known in other seas, that this industry alone would suffice to provide sustenance to all the settlers which this vast stretch of country could receive. In the mountains there are seen many pines like those of Spain, *mollares*, and oaks and live oaks upon the slopes and in certain spots on level ground. On the rivers and streams there are many white and black poplars, willows, alders, elms, small poplars, some laurels, and canes (Priestley 1972:35).

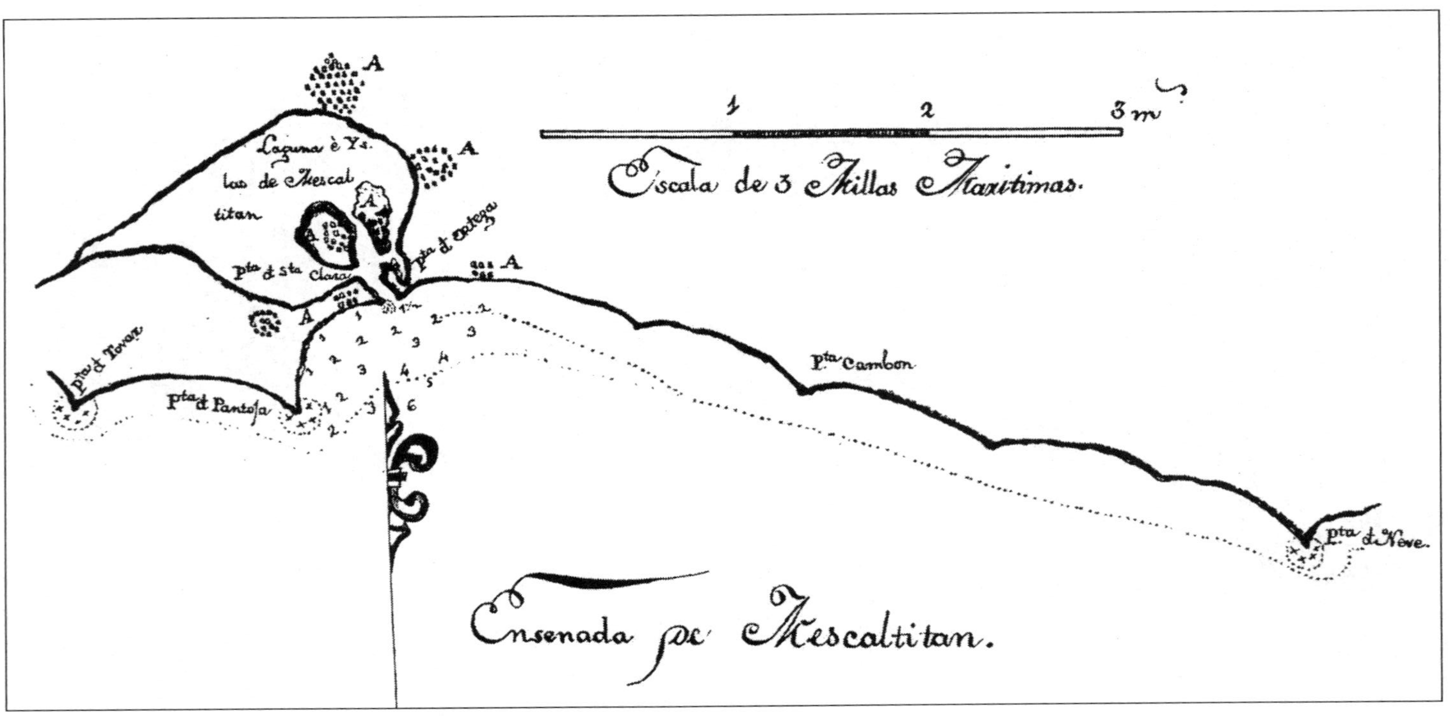

FIGURE 2 Pantoja's 1782 map of settlements around the Goleta Slough (Bolton 1930)

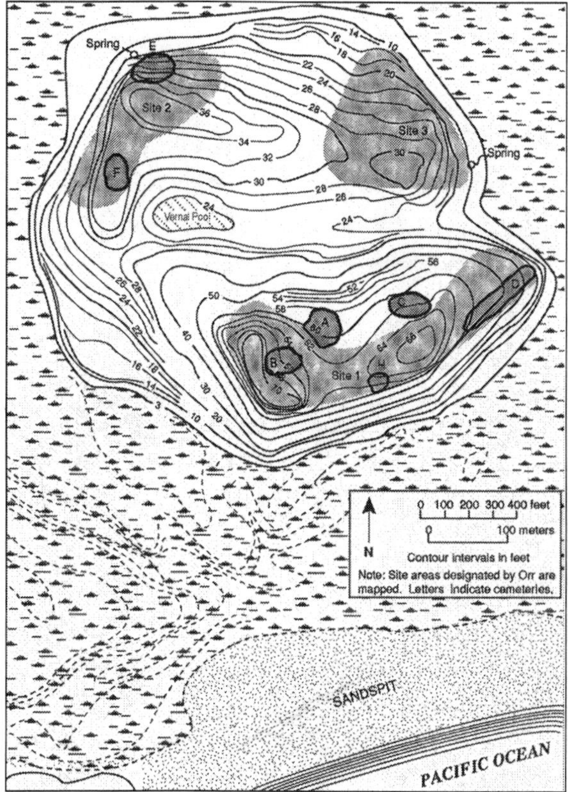

FIGURE 3 Contour map of Mescalitan Island prior to grading (compiled by Chester King)

Three general environmental regions have been identified in the Chumash area: the interior, the coastal mainland, and the northern Channel islands (King 1976). The interior consists of jagged mountains with limited areas of flat valleys that support oaks, grasses, and vegetation communities ranging from sage scrub and chaparral to riparian woodlands. In the riparian areas, live oak, sycamores, bay trees, and Wild Cherry (*Prunus* sp.) can be found. The coastal mainland, cooler than the interior region in the summers and milder in the winters, has many of the resources found in the interior and the islands; however, the proportions vary considerably. Some communities are unique to the mainland coast, such as the lagoons and salt marshes. In contrast to the mainland coast, the northern offshore islands are characterized by a cooler climate and a low diversity of plant species; there are approximately half as many plant species on the islands (King 1976:291). In addition, the seashore on the mainland tends to have greater environmental variability than the seashore environments on the Northern Channel Islands (King 1976:291). Vegetation communities on the islands include chaparral, coastal sage scrub, grasslands, pine forests, and riparian zones. One plant of significant economic importance to the Chumash that is absent from the Northern Channel Islands is *Yucca whipplei* (Smith 1976:18). The diversity of land mammals was also limited on the islands, which lacked deer, squirrels, rabbits, gophers, and rats. The largest land mammal found on the Northern Channel islands in 1769 was the island fox, a species not eaten by the Chumash. In contrast, marine resources were abundant on the islands.

The major classes of fauna and flora that were used by the Chumash Indians are summarized in tables 2 through 8. The Chumash used "at least 150 plant species for food, medicine, material culture, and religious practices" (Timbrook 1990:236), including nuts, seeds, greens, bulbs, and roots.

SEASONALITY

As in many regions of the world, the winter months were the most difficult of the Chumash annual cycle. Due to a scarcity of plant resources (with the exception of fresh greens), the Chumash gathered less at this time of year, instead relying on stored foods such as acorns, seeds, dried fish and meats, supplemented by fresh mollusks, nearshore fish, and some sea mammals (Kennett 1998; King 1990a). Cabrillo's account of the Santa Barbara Chumash on February 14, 1542, provides the earliest insight into their subsistence strategies during the lean winter months: "They did not find so many Indians as the first time nor any fishing, as it was winter; the Indians were living on acorns, another seed, and crude herbs from the field" (Wagner 1929: 91).

Over 200 years later, Crespí confirmed that few fresh fish were available during the winter months in contrast to the abundance of fish available in the summer. Additional information indicates that the Chumash rarely ventured out into the open seas during storms or inclement weather, much of which occurred during the winter months (King 1990a). Small schooling species, bottom-dwelling species, and fish associated with the kelp beds may have been a source of food during the winter months (Kennett 1998; Landberg 1965). Although land mammals were probably available in the winter, deer would have been easier to hunt during the summer months (Landberg 1965:51). Plant foods, such as yucca buds, were harvested between January and May. Other important sources of food found in the early spring were shellfish and bulbs. Sage, Red Maids, grass seeds, and other small seeds ripened in the later spring and summer. Acorns were most commonly collected in October and November. The variability of resources within microenvironments, particularly marine resources, can be very complex, and is not yet fully understood for the Chumash region.

FLORA

Many of the plants used by the Chumash required intensive processing; for example, tannins in acorns had to be repeatedly leached to make acorns edible, as did toxic substances in other plant foods. Acorns could be stored for several years and were clearly a staple for the Chumash. The procedures and technology used to harvest, process, cook, and store plant and other foods are discussed in Chapter 6; in this chapter, the resources and their habitats are the focus.

A brief review of acorn productivity is warranted here because it has been suggested that droughts may have affected the acorn harvest (Larson et al. 1994; Raab and Larson 1997; Raab et al. 1995). Oak trees are generally considered to be "mast flowerers;" they cycle irregularly through years of abundant acorn production interspersed between years of lesser production. Regardless of the weather, most oaks need at least a couple of years to recover from a year of abundant acorn production. Koenig and his colleagues (1994) recently completed a comprehensive study of acorn production in central California, where they measured the variation of acorn production in five different species of oaks (n=250) over a period of 15 years. They studied Valley Oak, Blue Oak, Canyon Live Oak, Coast Live Oak, and California Black Oak, all of which currently grow in Santa Barbara County and on Santa Cruz Island and were used by the Chumash. They found that acorn production varied considerably according to species of oak. In other words, a bad year for Coast Live Oaks is not necessarily a bad year for other species of oak. They also demonstrated that there is not a simple relationship between dry years and acorn production; even during severe drought years, one species of oak may produce ample acorns, while other species may not. It has been shown that variables other than amounts of rainfall are significant in acorn production, including the timing of rain and frosts (Bean and Saubel 1972; McCarthy 1993). For example, a heavy rainfall or freeze in the spring when the oaks are laden with pollen can be devastating.

Important plant foods other than acorns that probably were used by the Chumash in lagoon and coastal environments are presented in table 2.

TABLE 2. Important Food Plants Used by the Chumash in the Vicinity of the Goleta Slough

Plant Communities	Scientific Name	Common Name
Salt Marsh	*Atriplex californica*	California Saltbush
	Atriplex lentiformis	Quail Bush
	Atriplex watsonii	Matscale
	Distichilis spicata	Salt Grass
	Salicornia subterminalis[a]	Parish's Glasswort or Pickleweed
	Salicornia virginica[a]	Pickleweed
	Suaeda californica[a]	Seashore Blite
	Suaeda depressa[a]	Pursh Seepweed
Fresh Marsh	*Bromus carinatus*	California Brome
	Elymus condensatus	Giant Rye
	Elymus tritichoides	Alkali Rye
	Hordeum californicum	Meadow Barley
	Phalaris lemonii	Lemmon's Canarygrass
Disturbed Annual Valley Grassland Maritime	*Amsinckia intermedia*	Fiddleneck
	Amsinckia spectablis	Woolly Breeches
	Calandrinia ciliata	Red Maids
	Dichelostemma pulchella	Brodiaea, Blue Dicks
	Hemizonia australis	Spikeweed
	Hemizonia fasciculata	Clustered Tarweed
	Hemizonia paniculata	Tarweed
	Hemizonia ramosissima	Tarweed
	Hordeum californicum	Meadow Barley
South Coast Oak Woodland	*Heteromeles arbutifolia*	Toyon, Christmas Berry
	Quercus agrifolia	Coast Live Oak
	Sambucus mexicana	Elderberry
Coastal Sage Scrub	*Atriplex californica*	California Saltbush
	Malacothrix saxatilis	Cliff-Aster
	Sambucus mexicana	Elderberry
South Coast Dune Scrub	*Amsinckia spectablis*	Woolly Breeches
Coastal Strand	*Atriplex leucophylla*	Beach Saltbush
Chaparral	*Chlorogalum pomeridianum*	Soap Plant, Amole
	Heteromeles arbutifolia	Toyon, Christmas Berry
	Prunus ilicifolia	Wild Cherry or Islay
	Salvia columbariae	Chia
	Salvia leucophylla	Purple Sage
	Salvia mellifera	Black Sage
	Yucca whipplei	Our Lord's Candle

SOURCE: Compiled from Brandoff (1980).

NOTE: Some of the names of the plant communities have been slightly changed from Brandoff's terminology.

[a]Plants probably used by the Chumash, but not documented.

A few significant foods not listed in table 2 are cactus (*Opuntia* sp.), pine nuts (*Pinus* sp.), walnut (*Juglans* sp.) and onion (*Allium* sp.) (see Erlandson 1994:Table 2-1).

FAUNA

Although land mammals were more essential to the diets of interior people than to those of mainland coastal people, inhabitants of the coastal regions also hunted them. The most commonly used land mammals exploited by the Chumash are listed in table 3; their habitats have not been included because they vary considerably.

Some of the most significant staples in the diet of people living on the coast and around the lagoons were marine resources, particularly fish and sea mammals. Marine mammals such as seals, sea lions, sea otters, and dolphins were important resources for the mainland coastal and island Chumash (Colten and Arnold 1998; Landberg 1965; Porcasi and Fujita 2000). Although whalebone is found in archaeological sites, no evidence exists that the Chumash ever hunted whales. Marine mammals found in the Santa Barbara Channel and used for food by the Chumash are listed in table 4.

Fish became increasingly important in the Chumash diet over time (Glassow 1992) and were captured in several habitats, both close to shore and out in deeper waters. Near-shore kelp beds off the Santa Barbara coast

TABLE 3. Important Land Mammals Used by the Chumash

Scientific Name of Genus or Species	Common Name
Dipodomys sp.	Kangaroo Rat
Lepus californicus	Black-Tailed Jackrabbit
Lynx rufus	Bobcat
Memphitis memphitis	Striped Skunk
Neotoma sp.	Wood Rat
Odocoileus hemionus	Mule Deer
Procyon lotor	Raccoon
Scirus griseus	Western Gray Squirrel
Spermophilus beecheyi	California Ground Squirrel
Sylvilagus sp.	Rabbit
Taxidea taxus	Badger
Urocynon cineroargenteus	Gray Fox

SOURCE: Compiled from King (1988:Figure 5).

TABLE 4. Important Sea Mammals Used by the Chumash

Scientific Name	Common Name
Arctocephalus philippii	Guadalupe Fur Seal
Callorhinus ursinus	Alaska Fur Seal
Delphinus delphi	Common Dolphin
Enhydra lutris	Sea Otter
Eumatopias jubatas	Stellar Sea Lion
Lagenorynchus obliguidens	Pacific Striped Dolphin
Mirounga augustirostris	Elephant Seal
Phoca vitulina	Harbor Seal
Zalophus californianus	California Sea Lion

SOURCE: Compiled from Erlandson (1980:Table 5-2).

and around the Channel Islands are more extensive than any found elsewhere in California and are the habitat of at least 125 species of fish (Landberg 1965:68). It has been suggested that the highest density of historic-period coastal settlements coincided with the greatest extent of kelp beds on the Santa Barbara Channel (Landberg 1965:70). Pelagic fish were probably caught from plank boats. Estuarine environments, such as the Goleta Slough, are also home to many fish. Schooling species of fish, such as sardines and anchovies, were common in the Channel and attracted larger fish such as Bonito, Tuna, and Yellowtail. A list of the most common fish used by the Chumash and their general habitats is provided in table 5.

Shellfish, an important part of the Chumash diet at historic contact, were noted by Crespí (Brown 2001:649) at two settlements on January 4, 1770, a time when fish were more scarce and the expedition was hungry. At *Noqto,* north of Point Conception, the Chumash offered the expedition mussels and then just south of *Noqto*, at *Shilimaqshtush*, members of the expedition traded for "*callos* that are like limpets" (Crespí in Brown 2001: 649). Bloomer (1982:10–54) has suggested that the optimal season for gathering shellfish was in the winter and early spring in the southern Chumash area. The more common shellfish species used by the Chumash, and their habitats, are listed in table 6.

Reptiles were never a significant part of the diet, but were nevertheless eaten by the Chumash, as were birds. The most common species of reptiles and birds used by the Chumash are listed in tables 7 and 8. Most

TABLE 5. Important Fish Used by the Chumash

Scientific Name of Genus or Species	Common Name	Environment
Embiotocidae argenteus	Barred Surfperch	Surf zone
Engraulis mordax	Northern Anchovy	Open ocean, also sometimes near shore
Genyonemus lineatus	White Croaker	10–100' depth over sandy bottom
Leptocottus armatus	Pacific Sculpin	Bay/estuary
Triakas semifasciata	Leopard Shark	Bays and beaches
Myliobatus californianus	Bat Stingray	Inshore
Paralichthys californica	California Halibut	Shallow water to 200', on sand and mud bottoms
Raja spp.	Skate	Inshore
Rhinobatos productus	Shovelnose Guitarfish	Surf zone, lagoon
Squatina californica	Pacific Angel Shark	Inshore
Semicossyphus pulcher	California Sheephead	20–100' on rocky bottoms below giant kelp
Sebastes spp.	Rockfish	180–600' in some areas shallower, over rocky bottoms
Sphyraena argentea	California Barracuda	Surface to 60'
Sarda chiliensis	Pacific Bonito	Near surface in open ocean
Scorpaenichthys marmoratus	Cabezon	Bay/estuary
Scomber japonicus	Pacific Mackerel	Surface to 150' in open ocean
Sardinops sagax	Pacific Sardine	Open ocean, also sometimes near shore
Squalus acanthias	Spiny Dogfish	Open sea, often close to shore
Merluccius productus	Pacific Hake	Moderate depths in open ocean areas
Seriola dorsalis	Yellowtail	Open sea: warm waters
Euthynnus pelamus	Oceanic Skipjack	Open sea: warm waters
Trachurus symmetricus	Pacific Jackmackerel	Open ocean
Xiphius gladius	Broadbill Swordfish	Open sea
Atractoscion nobilis	White Seabass	Open sea
Isurus oxyrinchus	Mako	Open sea
Galeorhinus zypoterus	Soupfin Shark	Open sea

SOURCE: Compiled from Johnson (1980) and King (1990a: Table 2).

TABLE 6. Marine Mollusks Commonly Gathered by the Chumash

Scientific Name of Genus or Species	Common Name	Habitat
Chione spp.	California Venus	Lagoon/intertidal mudflat zone
Saxidomus nuttallii	Washington Clam	Lagoon/intertidal mudflat zone
Tagelus californianus	Jackknife Clam	Lagoon/intertidal mudflat zone
Ostrea lurida	California Oyster	Lagoon/subtidal zone
Protothaca spp.	Littleneck Clam	Lagoon/subtidal zone
Hinnites multirugosus	Giant Rock Scallop	Lagoon/subtidal zone
Macoma spp.	Macoma	Sandy beach/intertidal/subtidal
Tivela stultorum	Pismo Clam	Sandy beach/intertidal/subtidal
Mytilus spp.	Mussel	Rocky/intertidal/subtidal zone
Haliotis sp.	Abalone	Rocky/intertidal/subtidal zone

SOURCE: Compiled from Denardo (1990).

TABLE 7. Important Reptiles Used by the Chumash

Scientific Name	Common Name
Clemmys marmorata	Western Pond Turtle
Crotalus viridis	Western Rattlesnake
Lampropeltis getulus	Common Kingsnake
Lampropeltis zonata	California Mountain Kingsnake
Pituophis melanoleucus	Gopher Snake

SOURCE: Compiled from King (1988:Figure 5).

birds used as food were winter migrants associated with estuaries, but some were year-round residents.

MEDICINES AND TECHNOLOGY

The discussion so far has focused on plants and animals that were used for food by the Chumash; however, approximately 65% of the material culture goods used by the Chumash were made primarily or entirely from plant materials (Blackburn and Anderson 1993:23). Plants were gathered to make baskets, mats, net bags, fishing nets, and cordage, and for use in the construction of houses and boats. They were also gathered for medicinal purposes. Phillip Walker and Travis Hudson (1993) provide the

TABLE 8. Important Birds Used by the Chumash

Scientific Name of Family	Common Name of Family
Anatinae	Surface-Feeding Ducks
Anserinae	Geese
Aythyinae	Diving Ducks
Gaviidae	Loons
Laridae	Gulls and Terns
Oxyurinae	Stiff-Tailed Ducks
Pelicanidae	Pelicans
Phalacrocoracidae	Cormorants
Podicipedidae	Grebes
Procellariidae	Shearwaters, Fulmars, and Large Petrels

SOURCE: Compiled from King (1988:Figure 5).

most thorough discussion of medicinal plants in the Chumash region. The Chumash believed that the world was filled with pervasive, supernatural powers that brought sickness and death, but could be controlled in part by shamans. Malevolent shamans were believed to have had the ability to cause illness and subsequent death, but benevolent ones could bring good health (Blackburn 1975; Walker and Hudson 1993). A cadre of healers with specialized knowledge used herbs in the curing process. Walker and Hudson (1993) and Jan Timbrook (1990, 2007) offer thorough discussions of plants used in the healing process.

The Chumash did not use ceramic pots until after European contact, instead relying on basketry for the collection, processing, cooking, and storing of foods (Gamble 1983, 2002b). Often women not only made the baskets but also used them in food processing. Because baskets are difficult to detect in the archaeological record, the significance of women in the maintenance of high population densities and complex social organization has often been overlooked. Materials used to make baskets included *Juncus* sp., sumac shoots (*Rhus trilobata*), bullrush roots (*Scirpus* sp.), grass stems (*Epicampas regins)*, and tule rushes (*Scirpus lacustris*) (Dawson and Deetz 1965). Many of these materials were available in close proximity to the coastal estuaries.

Tule (*Scirpus* sp.) was used for a number of purposes other than basketry, including the construction of balsas (Hudson et al. 1978:28) and the thatching of houses. Wild alfalfa, fern, and carrizo were also used for house thatching. All of these plants were available to the Chumash living in the mainland coastal settlements.

The wooden frames of houses and other structures built by the Chumash were most commonly made from willow, although cottonwood and sycamore were also used (Hudson and Blackburn 1983:325-331). The Chumash used wood for many other purposes as well, with the best known application being the construction of the plank canoes or *tomols* that were so admired by the Spanish. Ethnographic evidence indicates that the Chumash utilized driftwood for the planks, with redwood considered the most prized (Hudson et al. 1978:47). Other woods that were viewed as appropriate for plank canoes were willow, cottonwood, pine, big cone spruce, juniper, piñon, and fir. The woodworking skills of the Chumash clearly impressed the early explorers. Miguel Costansó noted in 1769 that Chumash wooden bowls and plates were so well made that they appeared "as if turned in a lathe, in fact, with this machine they could not be turned out better hollowed or more perfectly formed" (Hemert-Engert and Teggart 1910:45). The exquisitely crafted wooden bowls collected by Léon de Cessac (Heizer 1951) in the latter part of the nineteenth century are further testimony to Chumash woodworking expertise. In addition to bowls, the Chumash made wooden trays, cups, dishes, ladles, spoons, bows, and arrows (Hudson and Blackburn 1983). Preferred woods for these items included oak, sycamore, willow, and California Bay Laurel. All of these trees and shrubs could be found in riparian habitats in the Santa Barbara region.

The Chumash commonly used the leaves of *Yucca whipplei* and the stems of *Apocynum cannabinum* as fiber in the making of cordage and fishnets. The fibers that surround the bulbs of soaproots (*Chlorogalum pomeridianum*), however, were preferred for brushes used to clean ground stone and for other activities that required the use of a brush (King 2000:21).

MINERAL RESOURCES

The Chumash were well acquainted with mineral resources that they fashioned into tools and jewelry, and used for other purposes. Some of these resources were readily available in the region while others had to be imported. One of the most significant mineral resources in the Barbareño area was asphaltum (also known as bitumen or tar). Asphaltum was employed for various purposes, including as a glue or fixative, to plug holes, as a sealant in basketry, for appliqué and inlay, and in the construction of plank canoes. It occurs in natural deposits, ranges in color from black to brown, and unlike modern asphalt made from petroleum, often contains minerals (Hudson et al. 1978:51). At its sources, asphaltum varies in consistency from a heavy liquid to a solid. Asphaltum was often mixed with pine pitch to decrease its viscosity. The historic Chumash recognized two types of asphaltum: *woqo*, a hard tar that was mined and used for canoes, and *malak*, a soft tar found on the beaches (Hudson et al. 1978:50–52). Several important asphaltum mines have been identified in the Chumash region (Gutman 1979:32–39; Hudson et al. 1978:51), including one at More's Cliff, just to the east of Goleta Beach. "The Chumash name for More's Cliff was *Woqwoqo*, meaning 'much tar'" (Hudson et al. 1978:51). Other important sources were at Patterson Street in Goleta, at Rincon, and at Carpinteria (Gutman 1979:37), the one at Carpinteria being the best known. When Crespí stopped at Carpinteria, he commented on the source there: "We saw, close before reaching the village here, at a small ravine about a dozen paces from the sea water, springs of pitch that had become solidified; at certain seasons, perhaps, it must boil and bubble out as is the case at the volcanoes of this sort at La Porciúncula" (Crespí on August 17, 1769, in Brown 2001:409). Crespí was so curious about the asphaltum seep that in the spring of the following year when the expedition again stopped at Carpinteria, he requested a sample be brought to him: "It was quite hot, and not intending to I got some of it stuck on my hand, so sticky that I was unable to get it off with soap and hot water; in order to do so, I had to rub myself with grasses after heating it with hot water" (Crespí on May 2, 1770, in Brown 2001:699).

The Chumash were fortunate in the abundant and high quality sources of chipped stone materials available in their region. The most common material used for flaked tools and points in the coastal settlements was Monterey chert, which occurs as thin lenses in Miocene shale deposits in western California from Mendocino County to southern Orange County (Pierce et al. 1982). Silty cherts, a less siliceous chert than the Monterery, but still valued as materials for stone tools, are often found in association. Small cobbles of Monterey chert can be found throughout the Chumash mainland region and undoubtedly would have sufficed for small points and tools, but high quality cobbles of an appropriate size for large bifaces are rare (Glassow 1996:141). The most significant outcrop of Monterey chert is in the Vandenberg region; numerous biface preforms have been recovered there that probably were traded to the large mainland settlements (Glassow 1996). A variant of Monterey chert, often identified as meta-chert or chalcedonic chert, can be found on the Northern

Channel Islands and in the Santa Monica Mountains. The most significant outcrops are on Santa Cruz Island, although other outcrops do exist on the other northern Channel Islands. It is well documented that micro-drills made from meta-chert were used in the manufacture of shell beads on the northern Channel Islands (Arnold, Preziosi, and Shattuck 2001; Kennett 1998). Nevertheless, this type of chert was not a significant source of tools for the mainland settlements. In contrast, tools made from Franciscan chert, found in sedimentary deposits of the Franciscan formation, are relatively common in the coastal region. Deposits are present in the Santa Ynez and San Rafael mountain ranges in the interior Chumash region, and Franciscan chert cobbles are widespread.

Fused shale is another chipped stone material that was highly prized by the Chumash for making points and tools. Fused shale is glassy in texture (resembling obsidian), but usually is riddled with numerous small vesicles and (unlike obsidian), is not translucent (Pierce et al. 1982:Table 7.1). It occurs in burned Miocene shale beds in the Oak Ridge area east of Ventura and ranges in color from white to red, green and black (Edberg and Singer 1981).

Long distance exchange with groups outside of the Chumash area was less significant than interregional exchange within the area; however, obsidian and steatite were significant imported mineral resources. Most obsidian on the mainland was from the Coso area and (to a lesser degree) from Casa Diablo, approximately 280 km to the east in the southeastern Sierra Nevada. In contrast to obsidian, micaceous steatite became more prevalent in mainland Chumash sites during the protohistoric and historic periods, compared with earlier eras. Steatite vessels for cooking foods were imported from Santa Catalina Island (Romani 1982; Wlodarski 1979), one of the southern Channel Islands that historically was occupied by the Gabrielino/Tongva Indians. Both obsidian and steatite are believed to have been imported as finished artifacts, rather than as raw materials. A more detailed discussion of exchange is presented in chapter 8.

The Chumash as Environmental Managers

Over the past 30 years, it has been demonstrated that the Chumash were active in managing the environment despite their lack of agriculture (Anderson 2005; Blackburn and Anderson 1993). Management through controlled burns served to reduce shrubs and increase desirable grasses, bulbs, and other plants. Crespí, who frequently mentioned the occurrence of burning while in the Chumash region (see the opening quote in this chapter), attributed the practice directly to "the heathens." Timbrook et al. (1982) have assembled the best evidence on the practice of intentional burning by the Chumash, providing numerous historical references documenting their use of fire. Timbrook and her colleagues also note that botanists and others have recorded an increase in the density and extent of chaparral since European contact, suggesting that the habitat changed when controlled burns ceased. Timbrook et al. (1982) propose that fires were set after the seeds had been harvested in the late summer, but not on an annual basis. Instead, patches were probably burned every few years. These controlled fires allowed the Chumash to discourage unwanted plants while encouraging the growth of desirable plants (see also Anderson 2005). Timbrook and her colleagues suggest that the large quantities of red maid and chia seeds that have been found with Chumash burials and reported in ethnographic accounts were obtained through controlled burns of the coastal grasslands. Burning also increased the growth of new sprouts that deer fed on, resulting in the attraction of deer to the recently burned patches. With the reduction of chaparral and the increase in grasslands, deer could also move more freely through the region, making it easier for the Chumash to be successful hunters.

In addition to controlled burns, the Chumash and other California Indians harvested resources in a manner that ensured that desirable plants continually thrived in the same locales (Anderson 1993:152). This was accomplished by leaving whole or partial plants behind to ensure adequate harvests in the future. California Indians also understood that the gathering of seeds, berries, or other plant parts often increased the yield of the plants. Through careful gathering processes, therefore, they encouraged future production of seeds and other desirable plant parts. California Indians can therefore be viewed as cultivators on the basis of practices such as pruning, tilling, weeding, coppicing, and burning; they essentially practiced horticultural techniques to encourage desirable plants and give them a competitive edge (Anderson 1993, 2005). Moreover, many taboos and social constraints typical in California Indian society served to discourage overexploitation of plants.

Environmental Changes During the Historic Period

Daniel Larson et al. (1994) provide one of the most thorough discussions of climatic changes during the historic period in the Chumash region.

They suggest that drought conditions and elevated sea surface temperatures caused several interrelated catastrophic events, which may have encouraged the Chumash Indians to move to the missions between 1786 and 1803 in order to minimize subsistence risks. According to Larson and his colleagues, the Santa Barbara area was not a "Garden of Eden," but instead a region with pronounced climatic variability. They provide a reconstruction of winter rainfall averages in Santa Barbara between 1600 and 1900, and suggest that between 1670 and 1750 little variability in rainfall occurred. This pattern changed, however, after 1750, with a severe drought occurring between 1752 and 1756, followed by moderate to severe droughts between 1780 and 1830 that fell "roughly at 10-year intervals" (Larson et al. 1994:281). Based on reconstructions made by Nicklas Pisias (1978, 1979), they suggest that a prolonged period of pronounced sea temperature increases occurred between 1787 and 1834. These higher sea surface temperatures degraded the productivity of the kelp beds and thus damaged the fish that relied on kelp as well as the sea mammals that fed on the fish.

Since Larson et al.'s significant article, Kennett and Kennett (2000) have questioned the accuracy of some of Pisias's reconstructions, although they do not directly criticize his reconstruction of the historic period. Notwithstanding, ethnohistoric evidence does indicate that the Chumash may have experienced hardship due to environmental conditions, in addition to the effects of disease and other difficulties that followed Spanish colonization. One should remember, however, that the Chumash were accustomed to periodic droughts, wet years, and warm ocean temperatures (Gamble 2005). The El Niño/Southern Oscillation (ENSO) is a natural part of the global climate system and has been active on earth for thousands of years (Allan 2000; Markgraf and Diaz 2000). ENSO events are characterized by two extremes, El Niño and La Niña. They usually reoccur every 2 to 7 years and last for 18 to 24 months, although the timing of these episodes can be irregular. El Niño and La Niña events tend to have opposite effects from each other; however, ENSO events are never the same, varying in duration, onset, cessation, magnitude, and geographic extent. During El Niño events in Southern California, sea surface temperatures (SST) tend to rise, sometimes to as high as 20 degrees C, which in turn can have a deleterious effect on kelp beds and the marine life associated with them. It is well documented that pinnipeds, birds, and other marine life can be adversely affected by an ENSO event (Colten 1993; Forrester 1997).

The effects of ENSOs on southern California resources are not straightforward. Raab and his colleagues (1995) and Raab and Larson (1997) have suggested that on Catalina Island, ENSO events were not as harmful to maritime resources as some have proposed. They demonstrate that some species, such as dolphin, yellowtail, and tuna, are attracted by warm waters, and that the inhabitants of Little Harbor on Catalina Island shifted their subsistence base to take advantage of these species. This is a clear example of diversification, or "broadening the base of the subsistence system" (Halstead and O'Shea 1989:4). Pletka (2001:238) recently analyzed fish remains from numerous sites on Santa Cruz Island and found that fishermen during the Transitional period exploited a wider variety of habitats than at other times. On the southern Channel Islands of Catalina and San Clemente and at mainland coastal sites, the remains of Giant Ocean Sunfish (*Mola mola*) have been documented (Porcasi and Andrews 2001). Some remains of *Mola mola* are found in sites that date to the Middle Holocene. These fish are rarely found north of Mexico because they prefer warmer waters. Porcasi and Andrews suggest that the presence of bones from this species may indicate that they were caught when sea surface temperatures were warmer than normal. This is another example of diversification. Today, sport fishermen rejoice during El Niño events because species such as yellowtail and tuna seek waters farther north than usual and also venture closer to the shore.

The Chumash and other southern California Indians stored both food and water, a strategy for minimizing risks associated with droughts (Gamble 2003, 2005). An early reference to the Chumash use of wells appeared in a diary kept by Father Zalvidea, who embarked on an expedition from Santa Barbara to the interior of southern California in July of 1806, visiting numerous Chumash, Yokut, and Serrano communities (Cook 1960:245). On July 23, 1806, Zalvidea noted that the countryside in the Cuyama Valley was dry and without trees (this area is in the desert portion of the Chumash region.) At two Chumash settlements in the valley (*Cuia* [*Kuyam*] and *Siguecin* [*Tsiwikon*]), Zalvidea noted that wells were being used by the inhabitants. On the same trip, he also observed wells at two Serrano villages, one of which was in the San Gabriel Mountains. It is possible that these wells were introduced by the Spanish or that there may be a problem with the translation; however, it is more likely that they were used prior to the arrival of the Spanish. We know that the Chumash were in contact with the Cahuilla and other desert groups through exchange systems, and that they had limited contact with the Spanish in the Cuyama Valley before 1806. If drought was indeed as severe on occasion as some have suggested, wells may have been used to minimize risk. It is possible that we have overlooked such features in the archaeological record, in part because they are difficult to recognize and in part because of our excavation strategies. In addition to wells, the Chumash used twined water bottles lined with asphaltum to store water, thereby again reducing risks associated with droughts (Gamble 2005).

In the eyes of the Chumash, the Spanish may have had an even more profound effect on the environment than did changing climatic events. By 1811, fields of wheat filled the areas where native grasslands once stood, and livestock such as cattle and sheep roamed where deer previously predominated (Hornbeck 1983). Agricultural pursuits continued to change the environment the Chumash had known and restricted their ability to rely on wild plant foods.

In summary, we can see that at the time of European contact the Chumash were well versed on the types of resources available to them and how to best use those resources. After living in the region for thousands of years, the Chumash had developed adaptive strategies to minimize risks associated with cyclical droughts, ENSO events, and other environmental stresses. These mechanisms included storage, exchange, the use of currencies, environmental modifications, and periodic feasts. Clearly, the Chumash did not live in a harsh environment, but in one that had an abundance of wild foods. Nevertheless, cyclical events such as those associated with El Niño challenged the Chumash, especially when their populations had reached the densities reported at European contact. In the upcoming chapters we will examine the strategies the Chumash developed to successfully cope with their environment, including these uncertainties.

CHAPTER 3

Cultural Setting

> *These heathens are all very great fishermen who, as soon as day has broken, are at sea in their canoes catching their food. They have large fish traps very well made of rushes, gigs and hooks made from shell and bone, all very well made and stowed, and very good sized nets of different hues. This is entirely a very cultivated, quick, clever folk, skilled in everything, as is bespoken by the flint knives, very gorgeous, that they carry on their heads; the gorgeous and very elegant rushen baskets and bowls worthy of the admiration of any person of good taste; and the bowls made from wood and very shiny solid stone, so splendidly carven I do not know whether anyone using tools for the purpose could do better; whereas these people have no more than bone and flint to do it with. To this, add the canoes, so well made out of planking not two fingers thick, so smooth and so even—and they not possessing any saws or planes (though I suppose they do make planes out of flint or bone).*
>
> Crespí on August 27, 1769, in Brown 2001:447

Crespí's description of the inhabitants of the region around the Santa Barbara Channel in 1769 provides an accurate overview of the Chumash, who subsisted, in part, on fish that were caught with the aid of the plank canoe. But what about thousands of years ago? Did the Chumash occupy the same general region? Some of the earliest evidence for human occupation of the Santa Barbara Channel region is from the northern Santa Barbara Islands. Human remains from Arlington Springs (SRI-173) on Santa Rosa Island have yielded approximate dates of 11,000 cal BC (Johnson et al. 2002) and the earliest deposits from Daisy Cave (SMI-261) on San Miguel Island indicate the site was occupied by about 11,500 cal BP (Erlandson 2007; Erlandson et al. 1996). Scholars have suggested that the

Chumash lived in the Santa Barbara Channel region over the past 7,000 to 9,000 years ago and were not replaced by another culture (Erlandson 1994). Recent research by Johnson and Lorenz (2006) provides mitochondrial DNA evidence for considerable antiquity of the Chumash in the region; they hypothesize that the Chumash were part of the initial peopling of the Americas.

The Chumash always utilized marine resources, but over time, these resources became more important. About 4500 years ago there is some evidence that economic and social complexity became manifest (Glassow et al. 2007). Chronological information for the Chumash can be seen in table 1. The next section of this chapter provides a brief overview of the evidence used to reconstruct Chumash society over time.

Early Documents

Despite the biases inherent in the diaries, letters, and other written texts from the early days of exploration in California, many of these sources of information provide the earliest glimpse of Chumash life before the impact of colonization drastically changed the lifeways of the Chumash and other California Indians. This section provides a brief review of the sources used in this book and their reliability.

EUROPEAN EXPLORERS' DIARIES

The earliest account of the Chumash is based on a diary written by Juan Rodríguez Cabrillo, who traveled to Baja and Alta California in 1542. Unfortunately, Cabrillo's diary did not survive. Further documentation of the journey was prepared in 1543 by Juan León, a notary in Mexico City who had seen written accounts of the expedition and had interviewed survivors upon their return (Beebe and Senkewicz 2001:31). Although Leon's report has disappeared, we have a summary that was prepared in approximately 1559 by an Augustinian friar named Andrés de Urdaneta. In his reconstruction of Cabrillo's log, de Urdaneta provided Chumash place names and their relative locations, as well as a significant description of a female Chumash chief at *Pueblos de las Sardinas* (now Santa Barbara), where the expedition stayed for several days (see chapter 4 for more details). The account also supplies significant information on the appearance of the Chumash Indians and their villages, houses, and plank canoes.

The primary goals of the Cabrillo expedition were to search for native cities with mineral wealth and to find information that might aid in trade with Asia (Beebe and Senkewicz 2001:31). Cities of gold were never found, and Cabrillo never saw Mexico again. After sailing to Monterey Bay and then returning south in late November of 1542, inclement weather forced the exploring party to land at *Posesión* (believed to be San Miguel Island by most scholars [see Erlandson and Bartoy 1995]), where the crew decided to stay for the winter (Beebe and Senkewicz 2001:31). While wintering on the island, the Chumash apparently became increasingly annoyed with the Spanish and launched a series of attacks, one of which proved fatal to Cabrillo. On or near Christmas Eve, the Chumash assaulted a group of soldiers that went ashore for water and wounded several of them. In an attempt to help, Cabrillo rowed toward shore and jumped out of the boat, catching his leg on a rocky ledge and splintering his shinbone (Kelsey 1998:158). His wound eventually became infected with gangrene and he died on January 3, 1543 on the island, where he was reportedly buried.

Despite the loss of Cabrillo's life and diary, scholars are fortunate to have accounts of his observations, although they are somewhat sketchy and confusing. Over the years, Harrington (1928), King (1975), and others (e.g., Beebe and Senkewicz 2001; Brown 1967; Kelsey 1998) have identified the locations of place names and provided other significant information related to Cabrillo's account.

For the following 225 years, between 1542 and 1769, only a limited number of accounts of relevance to the Chumash were produced. Shortly after Cabrillo's journey, the Spanish shifted their focus from the search for riches and inland waterways to the development of trade routes between Asia, New Spain, and Europe in order to meet the increasing demand for spices from South Asia and silk from China (Beebe and Senkewicz 2001:38). The Spanish conquered the Phillipine Islands in 1565, and by the early 1570s had established Manila Bay as the seat of government because of its ideal location between China and the west coast of North America. In 1566, the Spanish determined that the best route from Manila to New Spain was to Alta California, then south to Acapulco. The crossing between Manila and California was rough, and it quickly became apparent that a port was needed in California where ships could be repaired and supplied with provisions after the treacherous journey.

Only a few accounts about the Chumash from the period of the Manila galleon trade exist, including brief narratives from the 1587 voyage made by Pedro de Unamuno and from the 1595 expedition led by Sebastian Rodriguez Cermeño (Erlandson and Bartoy 1995; Lightfoot and Simmons 1998; Wagner 1929:141–151). The Unamuno account is significant because it provides the first recorded description of a Chumash sweatlodge and an early account of a Chumash village, both in the Morro Bay area (see chapter 5). The Cermeño voyage proved disastrous, as the galleon, all its cargo, and many of the crew were lost in a storm at Drake's Bay in Marin County (Beebe and Senkewicz 2001:38–45; Erlandson and Bartoy 1995). Despite this significant setback, Cermeño built a new craft, and with the remaining 70 men, sailed south. Significant stops included one in San Luis Obispo Bay in mid-December, where Chumash balsas were noted, and another a few days later on the northern Channel Islands, where—hungry and exhausted—the crew traded cloth for twelve fish and a small seal (Wagner 1929:161–162).

After the ill-fated Cermeño incident, Sebastián Vizcaíno was commissioned to chart the California coast and document as many bays and rivers as he could between Cabo San Lucas and Cape Mendocino (Beebe and Senkewicz 2001:38–45). He left Acapulco on May 5, 1602 with two ships and a frigate, approximately 200 men and three Carmelite friars, including Father António de la Ascensión (Lightfoot and Simmons 1998; Mathes 1968; Pourade 1960; Wagner 1929). The group made several stops in southern California; one was at the historic settlement of *Muwu* (see chapter 4 for a description), another at Santa Catalina Island, and a third in the Obispeño area. There are three different accounts of this expedition. The first has been identified by Bolton (1916:52-103) as Vizcaino's diary, and was based on the main ship's log. The second, entitled "Father António de la Ascensión's Account of the Voyage of Sebastián Vizcaíno," was published by Wagner in 1929. The third is a summary of Father Ascensión's diary and is entitled "A Brief Report" (Bolton 1916:104–134). Father Ascensión's diary provides the most detailed information, with descriptions of Chumash chiefs, fishing techniques, plank canoes, houses, and religious practices. In addition, Michael Mathes (1968) has written an important book about Vizcaíno and his role in the Spanish expansion in the Pacific.

After Vizcaíno's voyage, the Manila galleon trade continued over the next 150 years, but documentation on the Chumash during this period is virtually nonexistent. This changed in 1769, when the first land expedition to California, led by Gaspar de Portolá, was mounted. The Spanish were anxious to expand their horizons after the Jesuit expulsion from the missions in Baja California in 1697. The Jesuits were followed by the Franciscans, who briefly replaced them in Baja California, and then eventually by the Dominicans, who did not go beyond Baja California. Frustrated with the long standing problems of the missions, the Spanish intended to go north and establish new missions at the ports of San Diego and Monterey (Beebe and Senkewicz 2001:112–115; Brown 2001; Crosby 2003). They were also worried about the growing presence of the Russians and English on the west coast of North America and wanted to firmly establish California as their own territory. As a result of these concerns, the expedition to Alta California was arranged under the command of Portolá; it originally consisted of two land parties and three ships, but by the time the expedition reached San Diego from Mexico, one ship was lost and many men were sick, had died, or had deserted. With their numbers greatly reduced, two divisions of the land expedition, with approximately 64 individuals and 300 draft animals, left San Diego for Monterey Bay. The group consisted of 27 soldiers under the command of Fernando de Rivera y Moncada, another seven under the command of Pedro Fages, 15 Indians from Baja California, seven muleteers, two servants, the expedition's engineer, Miguel Costansó, and two priests, Frs. Juan Crespí and Francisco Gómez (Beebe and Senkewicz 2001:112-115). Three separate trips were undertaken by the Portolá expedition within Alta California. On the first, the expedition left San Diego on July 14, 1769 and arrived in San Francisco Bay on November 11, 1769. The return trip to San Diego took place between November 11, 1769, and January 24, 1770. A final trip was then initiated on April 16, 1770 to Monterey, where the group arrived on June 3, 1770. Father Crespí, who was appointed the official record keeper for the expedition, furnished detailed descriptions of the environment, the suitability of the region for settlement, and the California Indians. Most of the Crespi's notes are derived from the first leg of the trip out of San Diego. Portolá and Costansó also maintained significant logs. All of these accounts contain biases, yet all three provide a detailed picture of the Chumash and their environment.

The most significant problems with all of these early documents are the preconceptions of the authors, the most prevalent of which was a disrespect for indigenous religious and spiritual values and a belief that the native people were intellectually inferior and had limited capabilities. The Spanish, hoping to save the Indians from damnation, took a paternalistic view toward the Chumash. Most chroniclers were in California in order to settle the region, and they were preoccupied with their own problems, such as the native population's resistance to colonization and the suitability of the landscape for European settlement and agriculture. Despite these biases, the significant information derived from these accounts—such as types of foods, the appearance of chiefs, the planked canoes, and village layouts—has proven to be invaluable for anthropologists and others who wish to reconstruct traditional practices of the times before the Spanish permanently settled in the region and profoundly affected the Chumash and other groups.

MISSION DOCUMENTS

In 1769, the first mission in Alta California was established at San Diego, with others between the San Francisco Bay area and San Diego quick to follow. The Franciscan missionaries maintained five major mission registers at all of the missions in Alta California, documents that have proven to be a significant source of information on traditional marriage patterns, kinship practices, and other aspects of social organization. John Johnson (1988) has provided a detailed description of the registers, and this discussion is based on his work. The baptismal registers listed all the Indians who were baptized into the Catholic Church: the entries usually included the date and place of an individual's baptism, his or her approximate age, the village name of the person (usually including the birthplace), his or her Indian name and kin relationships. In addition, the political status of the individual in native life might be recorded. The marriage registers contained lists of the marriages that took place at the mission. In addition, information about marriages prior to affiliation with the missions was recorded when existing marriages were solemnized upon the couple's entry into the mission system. These data usually included an individual's baptismal number, place of origin, and kinship relationships. The third register, the burial register, listed the deaths of the baptized Indians and included the person's name, the date and place of burial, and whether last rites were administered. In addition, these registers occasionally listed baptismal numbers, place of death, and cause of death. The fourth type of register was the *padrón*, a type of census record that included information on baptisms, marriages, and deaths. Because the data in this register overlapped with data from the other registers, it serves as an important cross check. It may also provide new information or fill in gaps where data were missing from the other records. The final register maintained by the Franciscans, the *libro de confirmaciones*, listed the neophytes who were confirmed into the Catholic church. This record has been the least useful in reconstructing the social structure of the Chumash.

Archaeological Research on the Mainland

For over 125 years, archaeological sites in the Santa Barbara Channel region have attracted the attention of scholars, relic-hunters, museum specialists, academics, contract archaeologists, and others interested in the past. Three eras of archaeological investigations (roughly based on

Erlandson's [1994:38–41] framework) in the Santa Barbara Channel region are discussed in this section.

EARLY ARCHAEOLOGICAL INVESTIGATIONS (1860S TO 1920S)

The earliest archaeological inquiries were primarily concerned with the acquisition of "antiquities" for the recently established museums in the East, or for private collections. Investigators quickly learned that most museum-quality artifacts were found in cemeteries, and they concentrated their efforts on excavating burials for the removal of grave associations, which were hastily shipped east or sold to private interests. Several key people were associated with these early excavations.

The first documented archaeological investigations in the Chumash region have been attributed to Alexander Taylor, who conducted excavations in Goleta, in the Santa Ynez Valley, and on the northern Channel Islands. Taylor described these excavations in a series of newspaper columns, published in the 1860s, entitled "The Indianology of California." Unfortunately, these have proven to be of limited value to most researchers because of the dearth of detailed and systematic information (Benson 1997:13; Holmes and Johnson 1998:v and 45). Taylor also wrote on Chumash place names, and published other general information pertaining to southern California Indians. Compared with Taylor's contributions, the work of Paul Schumacher is of more significance to researchers, in part because he published his work and produced impressive maps with his plane table and alidade (Benson 1997:13–14; Holmes and Johnson 1998; Schumacher 1875, 1877, 1879). Schumacher excavated at numerous Chumash and Tongva sites on the Santa Barbara Channel Islands and mainland coast, initially under contract with the U.S. Coast Survey (Heizer 1978:7). He was later associated with the Smithsonian Institution and the Peabody Museum (Putnam 1879:30), and was probably the best known archaeologist working in the region prior to 1875 (Benson 1997:13). Despite the early date of his investigations, Schumacher was frustrated that collectors had already looted sites in the region (Benson 1997: 13). Schumacher went to Guaymas in Sonora, Mexico in 1880, where he worked as an engineer; he died there in 1883 at the age of 40 (Hau 1885).

The Reverend Stephen Bowers was a contemporary of Schumacher's, and the two excavated or visited many of the same sites, although there is no evidence that they worked together. Benson's excellent book on Bowers' investigations in the Santa Barbara Channel region (1997) includes the bulk of his journals. Bowers, a Methodist minister who arrived in Santa Barbara in the 1870s, immediately realized that the Chumash cemeteries had artifacts that would be of interest to museums in the East (Benson 1997:9–12). In the mid 1870s he began corresponding with the staff at the Smithsonian Institution, imploring them to initiate a collecting expedition to the Santa Barbara Channel area. Eventually the Smithsonian launched an expedition to the region, but before the project began, they relied on Bowers to supply artifacts from the Chumash area for the American Centennial Exhibition of 1876. The Smithsonian also contracted with Schumacher in the spring of 1875 to excavate Chumash sites and recover specimens for the museum. Then, in June of 1875, the Smithsonian sent a group to the region under the direction of Harry Crecy Yarrow. The day after their arrival, Bowers met with the group and showed them More's Ranch near the village of La Patera in Goleta. Subsequently, Bowers continued his work, while Schumacher investigated sites on the Santa Barbara Channel Islands. The Yarrow team eventually excavated two very significant historic-period cemeteries, one on Mescalitan Island and the other at Dos Pueblos, with some involvement by Bowers. Apparently Schumacher was also involved, as Yarrow states that Schumacher continued excavating at Dos Pueblos after they had to leave (Putnam et al. 1879:45). Because of the abundance of finely crafted burial goods from the cemetery at Mescalitan, they named the site the "Big Bonanza" (Putnam et al. 1879:35). Although the name "Big Bonanza" suggests that elaborate items were found in the historic cemetery, the term also illustrates the lack of respect for Native Americans that was typical during this period. Fortunately, Yarrow's field notes from the excavations at these sites were published; they include an account of the artifacts that were recovered from the Mescalitan Island excavations, but regrettably lack any detailed provenience information, such as grave lot identifications (Putnam et al. 1879: 35–40). Despite problematic documentation, the Yarrow collection is important because it provides information on artifacts from two historic cemeteries; many of these artifacts are illustrated in the 1879 publication.

Yarrow also remarked on the presence of León de Cessac, who had arrived on the scene from France, probably in July of 1877 (Benson 1997:15–17). Cessac spent two years in California (Moratto 1984:121), during which time he conducted excavations on the mainland, and on the Santa Barbara Channel Islands: Santa Cruz, the Anacapas, San Miguel, and San Nicolas. Eventually Cessac befriended Rafael Solares, a chief of the Ineseño Chumash community of Zanja de Cota (now the Santa Ynez Indian Reservation) (Benson 1997; Heizer 1951; Johnson 1997: Figure 90). Solares showed Cessac the location of several villages with cemeteries, including the historic sites of *Xonxon'ata*, *'Anaxuwi*, and *Soxtonocmu*. Given the amount and significance of Cessac's work, it is tragic that his field notes were lost in the late 1880s. Although his notes have never been found (Reichlen and Heizer 1964), his photographs and collections were preserved and are curated at the Musée de l'Homme in Paris. In addition, Cessac published one article on stone effigies from San Nicolas Island and a preliminary report on his investigations in California (see Heizer 1951)—unlike his colleague Alphonse Pinart, who spent less time in California and never published on the Chumash region.

The next significant excavations in the region were undertaken by Philip Mills Jones on Santa Rosa Island in 1901. Phoebe A. Hearst, a regent of the University of California, funded and commissioned a number of scholars to conduct research in various parts of the world and bring their collections back to the Department of Anthropology at Berkeley (Jones 1956). Jones was one of the archaeologists that she hired. His collections are significant in that he provided a more detailed record of his investigations than his predecessors and amassed large collections with good information on provenience.

A MORE SYSTEMATIC STUDY OF THE PAST (1920S TO 1950S)

It was not until the 1920s that archaeologists studying the region became more interested in developing regional chronological sequences than in collecting museum specimens (Erlandson 1994:39–40). Despite this new emphasis, cemeteries continued to be of considerable interest, but now stratigraphic relationships, cultural stages, and intrasite and intersite comparisons were included in the documentation and publications on the archaeology of the region. David Banks Rogers, who served as the first Head of Anthropology at the Santa Barbara Museum of Natural History in 1923, was one of the most accomplished contemporary scholars in the Chumash region (figure 4). Rogers kept detailed records that included field notes, collections, maps, and photographs. After years of fieldwork at a wide range of sites in the Santa Barbara Channel area, Rogers (1929) wrote the earliest comprehensive publication on the prehistory of the region, which included a cultural sequence that is still referred to today. Although Rogers continued to excavate cemeteries in the tradition of his predecessors, he also addressed site structure, an issue that was only cursorily touched upon by Bowers and his colleagues.

Other scholars who were active in the archaeology of the Santa Barbara Channel during this period include John P. Harrington (Smithsonian

FIGURE 4 Photograph of David Banks Rogers and John P. Harrington at Burton Mound (courtesy of the Santa Barbara Museum of Natural History)

Institution), Ronald Olson (UC Berkeley), Richard Van Valkenberg (Los Angeles County Museum of Anthropology), and Phillip Orr (Santa Barbara Museum of Natural History). John P. Harrington, best known for his work in North American linguistics and ethnography, recorded in excess of an estimated 20,000 pages of field notes on the Chumash (Johnson 1988:8). Harrington did not focus on archaeology, but he was involved in a major archaeological investigation at the Burton Mound site (figure 4) on behalf of the Smithsonian (Harrington 1928). The site had remains from several different occupational sequences, including artifacts from the historic-period village of *Syuxtun* (see chapter 4). It has been suggested that Harrington's work at the site in 1923 spurred a renewed interest in archaeological research in the region, including that of Rogers (Johnson 1998), who had been his field assistant at Burton Mound (Moratto 1984:124). Harrington also conducted archaeological investigations for a couple of weeks in the 1920s at the site of *Muwu* (VEN-11) with David Banks Rogers (see chapter 4).

During the following two decades, Ronald Olson, Arthur Woodward, and Richard Van Valkenburgh excavated at significant mainland and island sites in the Santa Barbara Channel region. The extent of Olson's collections and investigations is remarkable given the relatively short period that he worked in the area and the fact that archaeology was not his major interest (Drucker 1981). Olson was originally a logger on the Northwest Coast of North America who served in the Marines in World War I. Eventually he received his B.A. (1925) and M.A. (1926) from the University of Washington and his Ph.D. from UC Berkeley (1929), where he wrote a dissertation on clans and moieties in North America (Stewart 1980). After he left the University of Washington, and before completing his dissertation, Olson managed to find the time (between 1927 and 1929) to excavate approximately 725 burials in fourteen sites on the Santa Barbara Channel mainland and on Santa Cruz Island (Moratto 1984:124), publishing an overview of the results of his excavations in 1930. Shortly thereafter, Olson took a position at the American Museum of Natural History and used his post there to conduct excavations in Peru (Drucker 1981). In 1931, Olson was hired by the Anthropology Department at UC Berkeley, where he taught some of the most heavily attended lectures in the history of the department at that time; he never returned to his earlier archaeological investigations. Despite the brief time he spent in California, the collections and notes resulting from his excavations have provided significant information and have been a major source of data for Chester King's (1990a) work on the evolution of Chumash society.

Arthur Woodward, a curator at the Los Angeles Museum (currently the Los Angeles County Museum of Natural History), and Richard Van Valkenburgh, also associated with the Los Angeles Museum, undertook excavations at a number of significant archaeological sites in the Santa Barbara Channel region. Most of Woodward's excavations were carried out on the Channel Islands between 1939 and 1941 (Coleman and Wise 1994), after Van Valkenburgh had left for the Southwest to work with the Navajo (Young 1958). However, the two collaborated in 1929 and 1933 at the site of *Muwu*, where they excavated a sweat lodge and other structural remains (see chapter 4). Van Valkenburgh also excavated several cemeteries on Mescalitan Island between 1929 and 1930.

Meanwhile, at the Santa Barbara Museum of Natural History, Rogers retired and was succeeded by Phil Orr in 1938; Orr eventually became well known for his discovery of "Arlington Springs Man" and pygmy mammoth remains on Santa Rosa Island. In addition to his work on the northern Channel Islands, Phil Orr conducted archaeological investigations on the mainland at several major sites, including Mescalitan

Island, Carpinteria, and Rincon Point (see chapter 4). In 1968, Orr published perhaps his most significant work, a monograph on the prehistory of Santa Rosa Island that summarized 21 years of excavations.

CONTEMPORARY ARCHAEOLOGY (LATE 1950S TO THE PRESENT)

By the late 1950s, archaeologists, now equipped with new technology, became more rigorous in their methods and techniques. The most significant innovation was radiocarbon dating, and Phil Orr was one of the first in the region to use the new dating method to develop a chronological sequence of occupation for Santa Rosa Island (Erlandson 1994; Johnson 1998). It was also during this era that cultural ecology emerged as a major theoretical perspective in the Santa Barbara Channel area. An emphasis on the systemic interrelationship between the environment and culture change has continued to the present day.

William Harrison was a significant pioneer in the early development of more refined and systematic excavation and screening techniques. In 1958, at the historic site of *Mikiw* at Dos Pueblos (SBA-78), Harrison not only had the crew sieve soil deposits through screens, he used eighth-inch mesh for the first time and retained screened constituents for lab sorting, a technique that today remains rare in some parts of California but is common at most Chumash sites. In 1964, at the University of Arizona, Harrison completed his Ph.D. dissertation on the prehistory of the Santa Barbara coast, using radiocarbon dating to refine Rogers' chronology (Johnson 1998). At the time of his investigations in the Channel region, Harrison was involved in initiating a program in California archaeology in the Anthropology Department at UC Santa Barbara (UCSB), where he was a lecturer.

Both UCSB and UCLA became active in archaeological research in the Chumash region in the 1960s and 1970s. James Deetz arrived at UCSB in 1960 and pursued historic archaeology until 1967, when he left for Brown University. Deetz and his students excavated a number of significant historic-period mainland Chumash village sites, including *Sotonocmu* (SBA-167) and *Helo'* (SBA-46). At about the time that James Deetz left, Claude Warren came to UCSB where he remained until the spring of 1969. Warren excavated at a number of important sites in the region, including SBA-71 at Tecolote Canyon and at Burton Mound (SBA-28).

Albert Spaulding arrived at UCSB in 1966, after serving on the faculty at the University of Michigan, Yale University, University of Oregon, and as director of anthropology at the National Science Foundation (Voorhies

1992:198-199). Spaulding remained active in the department until 1988, during which time he excavated portions of the significant historic-period site at Prisoner's Harbor (*Xaxas*, SCRI-240) on Santa Cruz Island. Spaulding demanded methodological rigor from his students and clarity in written and verbal communication. Shortly after Spaulding's arrival and Deetz's departure, Michael Glassow, who received his Ph.D. from UCLA in 1972, was hired as the California archaeologist (in the fall of 1969) at UCSB. Glassow wrote his dissertation on the American Southwest under Jim Hill and was influenced by Lewis Binford, who taught at UCLA in the 1960s (after a brief stint at UCSB). Glassow was involved in California archaeology throughout his undergraduate and graduate career. Glassow created a vibrant program in archaeological research in the Santa Barbara Channel region that was grounded in cultural ecological theory.

When Phillip Walker arrived in 1974, the program in Santa Barbara Channel archaeology expanded to include a greater emphasis on analyses of human and faunal remains, including mortuary analysis. Glassow, Walker, Spaulding, Michael Jochim (who specialized in hunter-gatherers and cultural ecology), Brian Fagan (who stressed the importance of ethics in archaeology), and Barbara Voorhies (who specialized in the Maya region) worked together to build a program that remains active today. Many of their students (e.g., Jeanne Arnold, Brenda Bowser, Joan Brandoff, Roger Colten, Julia Costello, Steve Craig, David Earle, Jon Erlandson, Lynn Gamble, Jan Gasco, Brian Haley, Jean Hudson, Sandra Holliman, John Johnson, Doug Kennett, Pat Lambert, Dan Larson, Michael Macko, Don Miller, Madonna Moss, Jerry Moore, Ann Munns, Hector Neff, Jennifer Perry, Susan Siefkin, Larry Spanne, David Stone, Jan Timbrook, and Larry Wilcoxon) have conducted archaeological investigations and written significant publications on the Chumash in the Channel region.

During the 1960s and early 1970s, the program at UCLA was an active participant in California archaeology, particularly in the greater Los Angeles area, the Santa Monica Mountains, and the southern Channel Islands. Reports on archaeological investigations in southern California often appeared in the UCLA Archaeological Survey Annual Reports (published between 1959 and 1972). Clement Meighan was hired at UCLA in 1952 and was active in California (as well as in many other areas of the world). He led field classes in numerous locations in the Santa Monica Mountains, including at Malibu, as well as extensive excavations on the southern Santa Barbara Channel Islands. Some of the students who studied at UCLA and have made considerable contributions to the archaeology of the Santa Barbara Channel region are Tom Blackburn, Steve Craig, Jon Ericson, Robert

Gibson, Michael Glassow, Chester King, Linda King, Pat Martz, Glenn Russell, Clay Singer, Gary Stickel, Claude Warren, and David Whitley.

Although Chester King completed his degree at UC Davis in 1981, he received a Master's degree at UCLA and was an active student for many years at the UCLA Archaeological Survey. King's (1982) dissertation, *The Evolution of Chumash Society*, which was eventually published (1990a), provided a chronological sequence for the Santa Barbara Channel area—based primarily on changes in shell beads and ornaments—that most archaeologists have adopted (Johnson 1998:vii). In this book, as well as in other publications (King 1976; 1978), King proposes a model for the development of sociopolitical complexity among the Chumash (see the section entitled *Current Debates on the Origins of Sociopolitical Complexity* in this chapter). Linda King, also a dynamic force at the UCLA Survey, was one of the first researchers in the region to provide a published synthesis of some of J. P. Harrington's notes, as well as to conduct an in depth mortuary analysis at the Medea Creek cemetery in the southern Chumash region (1969, 1982).

Thomas Blackburn also worked with Harrington's notes at this time and wrote *December's Child* (1975), which today is still the best source on Chumash oral traditions. Shortly after Linda King completed her dissertation, Pat Martz (1984) wrote a dissertation that examined data from several other cemeteries at the southern end of the Santa Barbara Channel area in an attempt to examine emerging complexity. Although Claude Warren's most significant work has been in the California desert regions and San Diego County (see Moratto 1984), he briefly taught in the Anthropology Department at UCSB and excavated several significant Chumash sites. In summary, the archaeology programs at both UCSB and UCLA had a tremendous effect on the development of research directions in southern California.

Significant federal and state legislation also had a important influence on the way archaeology was conducted in the region. The National Historic Preservation Act of 1966, the National Environmental Policy Act of 1969, and the California Environmental Quality Act (CEQA), among other key legislative acts, changed the practice of archaeology throughout California (Chartkoff and Chartkoff 1984; Johnson 1998). As a result, many archaeological investigations, particularly along the mainland coast and at Vandenberg Air Force Base (see Glassow 1996), were initiated, and vast amounts of data were gathered. Although contract archaeology is not based on pure research agendas, many contract projects have provided significant information and served to further our understanding of the archaeology of the Santa Barbara region.

CURRENT DEBATES ON THE EMERGENCE OF SOCIOPOLITICAL COMPLEXITY

As a result of various programs on the archaeology of the Santa Barbara Channel region, a number of scholars have contributed significant studies focused on the Chumash. One topic that has generated considerable debate in recent years concerns the development of sociopolitical complexity among the Chumash and their neighbors. Many scholars working in the Santa Barbara Channel region argue that paleoclimatic change during the Late Holocene resulted in stressful environmental conditions that served as a trigger for punctuated change in societies in the region (Arnold 1992a, 2001a&b; Arnold et al. 2004; Glassow 1996; Johnson 2000; Kennett 1998; Kennett and Kennett 2000; Lambert 1994, 1997; Raab et al. 1995; Raab and Larson 1997). Debate continues on the timing and type of the paleoenvironmental shifts that occurred and the nature of possible responses to resource stress. (It is also worth noting that, with the exception of Raab, most of the proponents of punctuated change received their training at UCSB.)

Arnold (1987) was one of the first to propose that changing environmental conditions had a deleterious effect on Chumash resources. She suggested that these conditions, at least in part, stimulated dramatic changes in economic and political organization. Arnold expanded on her earlier arguments in 1992, relying on a paleoclimatic model developed by Pisias (1978, 1979), which in turn was based on data from a varved sediment core from the Santa Barbara Basin. Pisias suggested that there were unusually warm sea surface temperatures (a high of 21 degrees C) between about AD 1150–1300. Arnold proposed that this unfavorable warm water period adversely affected the Chumash on the northern Channel Islands, and that emerging elites took advantage of these unfortunate circumstances through the manipulation of labor. She argued that a ranked society eventually appeared in the area between AD 1200 and 1300 as a result of political opportunism in conjunction with resource stress.

Osteoarchaeological data from the Santa Barbara Channel region (Lambert 1994; Walker 1996) provides an independent source of data on resource stress. Lambert (1994) found evidence of stress in skeletal remains from Santa Cruz Island, Santa Rosa Island, and the mainland Chumash area, which she suggested might be linked to a period of aridity between AD 580 and 1350. In a separate study, Walker (1996) proposed that the northern Santa Barbara Channel Island inhabitants showed greater evidence of nutritional stress than the Chumash living on the mainland during this period. Lambert (1994) also looked for evidence of violent conflict in the remains, and found that healed cranial vault fractures were present during all time periods (between about 6000 BC and AD 1804), but were more common between approximately 1500 BC and AD 1380. Lethal projectile wounds did not increase in frequency until approximately AD 580, about the time that the bow and arrow were introduced. Lambert found that after AD 580 and until approximately AD 1350, approximately 10% of her sample exhibited evidence of projectile wounds. The majority of these individuals were from mainland sites (Lambert 2002). After AD 1350, Lambert attributed a decline in warfare to improving climatic conditions. Lambert's evidence for a warm, dry period was based on a number of studies, including one conducted by Stine (1994), who examined lake level fluctuations in the southern Sierra Nevada. Stine (1994) defined one period of drought between AD 892–1112 and another between AD 1210–1350. Larson and Michaelson (1989) also found evidence of drought in southern California, but their study relied on tree ring sequences (*Pseudotsuga macrocarpa*) from Santa Gorgonia Peak southeast of the Santa Barbara Channel region. Their data indicated that there were three drought periods, one between AD 500–800, another between AD 980–1250, and a third between AD 1650–1750.

Other scholars (Raab et al. 1995; Raab and Larson 1997) have also viewed long term dry conditions as significant, suggesting that prehistoric droughts would have caused more problems than warm sea surface temperatures (SSTs). Raab and his colleagues point out that shifting marine conditions would not have caused serious resource stress, because species that would be adversely affected by warmer SSTs would be replaced by different species, resulting in a more favorable subsistence base. They propose that the intermittent droughts that occurred between AD 800 and 1400, rather than changes in marine temperatures, had the most profound effect on southern California Indian societies (Raab and Larson 1997). They relied heavily on data derived from Stine, Larson, and Michaelson.

In 2000, Kennett and Kennett provided a new high-resolution Holocene marine record based on 20 AMS C^{14} dates and oxygen isotope analyses of two planktonic foraminifera species from a sediment core in the Santa Barbara Basin. They came up with a very different model of maritime changes than Pisias had 20 years earlier. Kennett and Kennett inferred from the new sediment record that sea surface temperatures (SSTs) were cool and marine productivity was high during the period when Pisias suggested warm waters had prevailed. They argued that these cooler waters coincided with a sustained terrestrial drought between AD 450–1300 in the Santa Barbara Channel region, and proposed that increased sedentism, trade, regional violence, and intensified fishing practices occurred at this time. Kennett and Kennett also relied on data from Stine (1994) and Larson and Michaelson (1989) for evidence of drought.

Despite Kennett and Kennett's revised record of palaeoclimatic change, Arnold (see Arnold et al. 2004; Arnold 2001c:26–31) still argued that evidence exists for a warm water event between AD 1150 and 1250 ("Middle-Late period Transition"). She cited a study of growth-sensitive variables of black abalone shells recovered from dated strata from four sites on Santa Cruz Island (Arnold and Tissot 1993) as one of the strongest indicators that there was a warm-water event off of Santa Cruz Island during the Transition period. In the same year that Kennett and Kennett presented their new paleoenvironmental reconstruction, Johnson (2000) published a significant article examining the Chumash response to climate change; he also proposed that the Chumash economic system emerged during the Middle-Late Period Transition "to buffer drought-caused food shortages" (Johnson 2000:317).

A more detailed review of the arguments for the emergence of greater sociopolitical complexity as a response to paleoclimatic change can be seen in Gamble (2005) and Johnson (2000). Although most scholars working in the region have been quick to suggest that major changes in sociopolitical complexity among the Chumash and other indigenous groups in southern California occurred as a result of climate-induced stress, there is disagreement about the nature and timing of the paleoenvironmental changes and the details of the cultural responses to these changes. Furthermore, not all researchers accept this model of punctuated cultural evolution. Chester King (1990a) views cultural change as a more gradual process, with an increasing emphasis on shell bead currency throughout time. King (1976, 1990a) was the first to seriously emphasize the fact that shell beads were used as a form of currency by the Chumash. He suggested that the initial use of *Olivella biplicata* callus beads occurred at about AD 1150 in conjunction with the development of a monetary exchange system. Prior to this period, King (1990a) believes that the political and economic systems were not clearly differentiated; however, after AD 1150, a secular economic system became distinct from the political system. As a consequence, new types of beads emerged, including the more labor intensive *Olivella biplicata* callus beads. King does not tie these changes to any particular paleoclimatic event, but instead views them as part of a gradual process of growth. King has suggested that a ranked society with a hereditary elite first appeared about 2600 years ago (at the end of the Early Period) in the Santa Barbara Channel region.

Definitive archaeological evidence for environmental change on the Santa Barbara mainland has not yet been documented. A series of radiocarbon dates from the stratified site of Corral Canyon (CA-SBA-1731) on the mainland coast indicates that the site was occupied between AD 500 and 1600, spanning Arnold's Middle/Late period (Erlandson and Rick 2002b). The faunal assemblages from the site do not provide evidence of any "serious degradation of the marine environment" (Erlandson and Rick 2002b:175–176). Erlandson and Rick do not address the possibility of an extended drought, presumably because there were no indicators for such an event. Preliminary data from another mainland coastal site that spans the Middle/Late Transition period, the Pitas Point site (VEN-27), indicate that there was a diversity of fish remains—with numerous pelagic species as well as species from other habitats—throughout the late Middle Period and Late Period (approximately AD 1000 to 1500). No hiatus in the occupation of this site was noted (Gamble 1983; Shalom 2005).

Most scholars who have accepted the hypothesis that severe environmental events triggered cultural changes suggest that sociopolitical complexity emerged rather suddenly sometime after AD 1000 (Arnold 1992, 2001a; Arnold et al. 2004; Johnson 2000; Kennett 1998; Kennett and Kennett 2000; Lambert 1994, 1997; Raab et al. 1995; Raab and Larson 1997). I have recently proposed (Gamble 2005) that the Chumash had numerous buffering mechanisms in place and were better equipped to respond to climatic changes than most agricultural societies. Furthermore, evidence for the timing and nature of paleoclimatic change is still emerging and is not currently well documented for the Santa Barbara Channel region. Data from a Middle period (~AD 950–1150) cemetery at the mainland coastal site of Malibu provide strong evidence for the existence of a ranked society with a hereditary elite prior to the Middle/Late Transition period and the ostensible drought (Gamble et al. 2001). Additional evidence for the existence of a ranked society during the late Middle period can be seen at other cemeteries in the Chumash region, including at Mescalitan Island (Gamble 2004). I argue that we lack adequate archaeological and paleoclimatic evidence to accurately define the effects and timing of an extended drought or warm-water event in the Santa Barbara region. In addition, there are compelling data to suggest that a ranked society developed in the region prior to the periods of environmental stress identified by those scholars who have been reconstructing paleoclimatic changes.

Social Sphere of the Chumash

We are fortunate in having a rich ethnohistoric and ethnographic record that can be used to reconstruct Chumash society at the peak of its development. The most detailed information on social organization can be found in the ethnographic field notes of John P. Harrington. Harrington's notes have been summarized by various authors over the years, though most notably by Blackburn (1975, 1976); Craig (1966, 1967); Hudson and Blackburn (1982, 1983, 1985, 1986, 1987); Hudson and Underhay (1978); Hudson and various colleagues (Hudson et al. 1978, 1981); Linda King (1969); and Timbrook (1990, 2007), whose syntheses are relied on in this section. In addition to ethnographic information, recent investigations of mission records and other early documents provide details on Chumash marriage patterns, descent groups, kinship systems, and other aspects of social organization that served to integrate the inhabitants of the Santa Barbara Channel region. A summary of Chumash social structure, including rank differentiation, specialization, and social roles, is presented in this section and in table 9.

SOCIAL ORGANIZATION

The analyses of mission register documents over the past 25 years have provided significant information on the kinship systems and marriage patterns of the Chumash (Johnson 1982, 1988; King 1984; King and Johnson 1999). On the basis of kinship terms found in the mission register documents and Harrington's notes, Johnson (1988:289) has argued that the Chumash had a clan type of organization based on matrilineal descent. The most common post-marital residence pattern among the Chumash was matrilocal, although patrilocal and rarely bilocal and neolocal residence have been recorded (Harrington 1942:30–31; Johnson 1988). Polygyny has been documented for Chumash chiefs, who also tended to practice patrilocal residence.

STATUS DIFFERENTIATION AND SPECIALIZATION

A person's status in Chumash society was ascribed or partially ascribed at birth, well defined, and for some, associated with substantial levels of wealth and social privileges (Blackburn 1975). Social ranks recognized by the Chumash included chiefs, elites, and commoners. High ranked people had special rights, with commoners deferring to them in public. Blackburn (1975:51) has suggested that the Chumash had an "incipient class system based on wealth." Shell beads served as social markers as well as money and were used, in part, to distinguish the wealthy from the poor.

Chiefs, their family members, and other highly ranked individuals were members of the *'antap* society (figure 5), a group of religious specialists

FIGURE 5 Photograph of Rafael Solares (*'antap* and chief) in 1878 by Cessac (courtesy of the Santa Barbara Museum of Natural History)

who performed dances and rituals at public ceremonies (Blackburn 1976:236–238). Each major Chumash settlement had an *'antap* society consisting of 12 members who were initiated into the group as children. Relatively large quantities of shell-bead money were paid by the parents of these children as a type of membership fee. Chiefs and their families were required to be members of this prestigious group. The *'antap* organization also operated at a provincial level, in that an elite council met in a capital town to oversee the religious, ceremonial, and other business that involved the settlements within the province (Hudson and Underhay 1978:29; Hudson et al. 1981). Blackburn has suggested that the *'antap* organization served to integrate chiefs and other wealthy individuals throughout Chumash territory. Because members of the *'antap* society used large deer tibia whistles during religious ceremonies (Hudson and Blackburn 1986:354), their presence can be identified in the archaeological record (Corbett 1999). The titles and duties of some of the high-ranked individuals are listed in table 9.

The Chumash recognized different types of specialists, most of which are listed in table 9. Exactly how many of these individuals were relieved from daily subsistence activities is unknown, but ethnographic data provide some insight. According to Harrington's Ventureño notes (L. King 1969:45), the Chumash had a term for "the dynasty of nobility" (*mu'alsaljewe*), who did not have to work for a living and had special privileges. One consultant even stated that "if they wanted to shit, somebody let down their pants for them" (King 1969:45). It is quite likely that boat owners were considered part of the nobility and did not have to spend much time on their own subsistence activities. One of Harrington's Barbareño consultants stated that boat owners did not have to go fishing themselves, but had fish delivered to their door, at which time they distributed the fish. This is corroborated by an account written by Font in 1776, who observed 10 or 12 fishermen carrying a canoe filled with fish to the house of the canoe captain (Bolton 1930:259). Some of the doctors recognized by the Chumash (see table 9) may have also been freed from subsistence activities, as doctors were paid when their cures worked (L. King 1969:44). A comment made by a priest from San Luis Obispo about Chumash doctors provides further evidence that they were not concerned with subsistence: "It is certain that among the Indians each one keeps secret his operation [in curing] because from it he obtains his livelihood" (Walker and Hudson 1993:46). It is likely that other individuals in Chumash society had to support themselves at a subsistence level even if they were specialists.

SOCIAL ROLES

Blackburn (1975:51) has suggested that the social roles of the Chumash appear to have been differentially ranked, with notable social distance between the members of the society. A brief summary of the more significant social roles identified by the Chumash is presented in table 9. Most members of society probably assumed more than one of these social roles

TABLE 9. Selected Social Roles Recognized by the Chumash

Chumash Name, English Name	Duties	References
	Political Roles	
wot, chief	Funded and arranged feasts, owned ceremonial paraphernalia, cared for poor and visitors, oversaw other offices, maintained stores.	Blackburn 1975:12; Harrington 1942:33; Hudson et al. 1981:100; L. King 1969: 41–42;
temi or *paqwot,* "big chief"	Had jurisdiction over several settlements. Could mobilize these villages in case of war. Other duties probably similar to those of the *wot.*	L. King 1969:41–42; Hudson et al. 1981:15
xelex (Falcon), "lesser chief"	Similar duties to the *wot.*	Blackburn 1975:53; L. King 1969 41–42.
Shan or san, assistants to the *'antap*	Group of eight. Aid the 'antap.	Hudson et al. 1981:19
ksen, messenger	Relayed messages to other settlements regarding feasts and other matters, carried money.	King 1969:43
'alseke or *'i 'enheshhesh* V, "taker of the souls," executioner	Executed people.	Hudson et al. 1981:13
ca canay y al or *jilicnash* V, judges	Determined timing of feasts and passed sentences by order of the chief if crimes were committed.	Heizer 1955:189
	Religious Roles	
paxa or *alpaxa,* ceremonial leader	Presided over ceremonies, collected offerings and fines, made announcements. Next to chief in power.	Blackburn 1975:12; Blackburn 1976:237; L. King 1969:43
'antap, member of elite religious society	Group of 12 initiates in every major village, high status individuals, performed dances and music at ceremonies.	Blackburn 1975:13; King 1969: 43
'altip'atishwi, master of herbs and keeper of poisons	Sorcerer with many herbs, poisoned wealthy individuals to insure they gave money or resources at ceremonies. Wore bags of poison. Member of *'antap.*	Blackburn 1976: 237–238; Walker and Hudson 1993:55
'alaqtsum, he who kisses	Captain of search parties at feasts to insure that no person had stolen anything.	Hudson et al. 1981:41; King 1990:57–58
'alchuklash, astronomer and astrologer, shaman/priest, smoke-doctor, pipe-doctor; included females and males	Determined phases of sun and moon, named newborns, foretold future, administered toloache, interpreted dreams, reported illnesses and social problems to the chief, cured the sick, smoked tobacco at rituals, handled charmstones, knew astrology, made rain, diverted storms, member of the *'antap.*	Blackburn 1975:13–15; Hudson and Underhay 1978: 27–38; Hudson et al. 1981:18–19, 101–102; King 1990a: 57; Walker and Hudson 1993:57–58

(*continued*)

TABLE 9. (continued)

Chumash Name, English Name	Duties	References
	Religious Roles (*continued*)	
'alalxiyepsh, regular or curing doctor, herb doctor; included females and males	Paid for curing, not a sorcerer.	Walker and Hudson 1993:55; L. King 1969:44
singer	Sung at ceremonies; used split-stick rattles.	Blackburn 1975:52, 262, 267
'alaxtut'uch, sucking doctor	Extracted disease-causing objects from victims.	Walker and Hudson 1993:58
ant doctor	Administered red ants (*shutihil*) orally to patient as a cure; usually an old woman.	Walker and Hudson 1993:58–60
kipo'omo, weather doctor/prophet	Forecast the weather; some knew how to cause wind, rain, or drought.	L. King 1969:44
	Economic Roles	
'alaleqwel 'itomol, "proprietor of a canoe"	Canoe captain or owner.	Hudson et al. 1978: 39–40; Blackburn 1975:52
rabbit drive official		King 1969:43
mortician		Blackburn 1975:52
fire tender		King 1969:43
'aqi, undertakers	Dug the graves of dead people, "two-spirits" and post-menopausal women.	King 1969:47–48, Hollimon 1997, 2001
bead maker	Produced beads.	Blackburn 1975:52
canoe maker	Made the plank canoes.	Blackburn 1975:52
fisherman		Blackburn 1975:52
hunter		Blackburn 1975:52
cordage maker		Blackburn 1975:52
tobacco maker		Blackburn 1975:52
net maker		Blackburn 1975:52
basket maker		Blackburn 1975:52
leather worker		Blackburn 1975:52
bow and arrow maker		Blackburn 1975:52
bowl maker		Blackburn 1975:52
mortar maker		Blackburn 1975:52
flint worker		Blackburn 1975:52
board maker		Blackburn 1975:52
headdress maker		Blackburn 1975:52

(e.g., see Johnson 2001:Table 3.4). As can be seen from the list, the Chumash had a remarkable degree of political, religious, and economic diversification (Blackburn 1975).

Economic Networks

The Chumash had a highly developed economic system in which shell beads were used as currency. Early historic documents and subsequent ethnographies provide important information on the Chumash exchange system. In this section, I provide a brief overview of Chumash economic networks; a more thorough discussion of the Chumash economic system is presented in chapter 8.

Chester King (1976) was the first to suggest that the elaborate exchange system practiced by the Chumash allowed them to maintain a relatively stable subsistence base. King noted that there was considerable variability in the Chumash environment, and that the three main environmental zones within the Chumash area—the inland zone, the mainland coast, and the islands—had various types of resources (see chapter 2) that were harvested at different times. Because intervillage exchanges crosscut these three zones, the Chumash were able to ensure that even those who were situated in ecological zones with relatively limited resources had adequate food supplies throughout the year.

There is abundant ethnohistoric, ethnographic, and archaeological evidence for the exchange of food and other items between Chumash settlements, and between the Chumash and other groups. Most items traded to the mainland and interior from the Channel Islands were probably manufactured goods, the most common of which were shell beads and ground stone objects. Evidence of *Olivella biplicata* shell bead making has been documented for Santa Cruz, Santa Rosa, and San Miguel islands (Arnold and Graesch 2001; Arnold and Munns 1994; Kennett and Conlee 2002; King 1976). Conlee (2000) has provided evidence for the manufacture of mortars and pestles at sites on San Miguel Island, while other scholars (Howard 2000; Romani 1982; Wlodarski 1979) have documented the manufacture of steatite ollas and comals on Santa Catalina Island. The production of shell beads, ollas, and comals was particularly pronounced during the Late and early historic periods on the islands. In contrast, the production of mortars and pestles was more significant during the Middle period, and although production continued into the Late and Historic periods, it was not as important as in the Middle period (Conlee 2000).

Ollas, comals, mortars, pestles, and shell beads were all manufactured for export to the mainland and, to a lesser extent, to other sites on the islands.

The plank canoe was critical in the transportation of these manufactured items, (especially of the heavy ground-stone items made on Santa Catalina and San Miguel Islands), and in the transportation of food and other trade goods that went from the mainland to the islands. As part of an extensive study (Gamble 2002a), artifacts associated with the plank canoe were examined to determine when this type of watercraft first appeared in the archaeological record. Evidence for its use by at least 1300 years ago was found to exist. The ownership of plank canoes was restricted to wealthy individuals and chiefs, in part because canoes were so expensive to build. The construction of plank canoes, which often took at least six months to assemble, was done by specialists who had selective, closely guarded knowledge as well as tremendous expertise (Blackburn 1975:10, Hudson et al. 1978). In 1776, Fr. Pedro Font reported that the owners of canoes were distinguished from other people by the bearskin capes they wore (Bolton 1930).

Based on ethnographic and ethnohistoric documents, Blackburn (1976:242) suggested that the exchange of resources by the Chumash, as well as by other southern California groups, involved a system of reciprocal ceremonial exchange that occurred at regular intervals during scheduled fiestas. Chester King (1976) has emphasized that the Chumash maintained a market economy, using shell beads as a medium of exchange. The ceremonial redistribution of resources discussed by Blackburn does not preclude the more open (free market) intervillage exchange described by King, or the suggestion put forth by Linda King (1982) and Arnold (1987), who proposed that the owners of the canoes controlled much of the island-mainland trade. Using data from marriage and baptismal registers, Johnson (1988; 2000) used locational analyses to test two models: (1) that trade was primarily based on redistribution; and (2) that cross-channel trade was primarily controlled by chiefs. He found that both redistribution and control over trade by chiefs were determining factors in the evolution of chiefdom organization among the Chumash.

I propose that all three forms of economic interaction (redistribution, free market trade, and commerce controlled by chiefs or wealthy individuals) were significant mechanisms for exchange among the Chumash. Redistribution of resources transpired during regularly occurring ceremonial feasts, with chiefs and their assistants instrumental in the organization of redistributive efforts. At the same time, individuals who attended ceremonial feasts came from a wide geographical range—island, mainland, and interior villages—and then traded, or bought and sold goods, among themselves. Exchange also took place outside of formal ceremonial feasts. Canoes were used to transport items between the mainland and the islands, and between coastal settlements on the mainland. Chiefs or wealthy individuals organized and paid for the materials and labor needed for the construction of a canoe. Once the canoe was built, canoe-owners probably had some control over the goods that were exchanged and—acting as middlemen in economic transactions—took a percentage of the economic transaction. In chapter 8, I investigate the nature of these transactions in more detail and document the extensive system of network power practiced by the Chumash. As part of this analysis, the role of chiefs is examined in the context of control over the production and distribution of wealth.

Chiefs and Power

Chiefs (*wots*) inherited their position and governed primarily at the village level in Chumash society (Blackburn 1975, 1976; King 1969), as in most of California. Most settlements had at least one chief. However, the smallest settlements may have had none, and larger settlements often had two or more chiefs, with one recognized as the head chief and the others identified as lesser chiefs. Johnson (1988) has suggested that settlements with more than one chief were political centers. The position of chief was usually passed down to the chief's son, generally the eldest (Harrington 1942:33). Female chiefs have been documented for all Chumash groups, and were sisters or daughters of the chief, not wives (Harrington 1942). In addition to village chiefs, the Chumash recognized paramount chiefs who had limited authority over groups of settlements that were loosely organized into federations, often around a principal town (Blackburn 1975:13; Harrington 1942; Johnson 2000). In 1785, it was noted that the son of the chief of a principal town was the chief of another town (Blackburn 1975:13; Brown 1967:48). Mission records provide evidence of widespread intermarriage between chiefly families, as well as polygamy among chiefs (Johnson 1988, 2000). Most other men apparently had only one wife. Chiefs were distinguished from others by ankle-length fur capes. They also wore bone pins attached to chert knives in their hair, although other wealthy individuals or *'antap* members may also have worn these pins.

There are limited descriptions of the duties and responsibilities of chiefs in the early historical documents, but fortunately Harrington gathered information on this subject. The chief was expected to care for the poor and for visitors, and to arrange for feasts and other ceremonies. The religious gatherings required considerable expenditures on the part of the chief, who had to furnish the property for the ceremonial grounds, pay the dancers, singers, and other personnel, and maintain extra stores of food (Blackburn 1975; Harrington 1942). The chiefs were responsible for inviting other chiefs and guests to the feasts that they organized, thereby maintaining strong relationships between chiefs and other people in surrounding settlements and providing opportunities for exchange (King 1969).

Chiefs were viewed with respect and commoners showed deference to them. One early historical account from 1769 stated that the chief traveled with a retinue of people who were not allowed to sit in front of him or his wife or sons, unless they were ordered to do so (King 1984:1–39). Among the Ventureño, according to Harrington's consultants, chiefs had larger houses than other people (King 1969:42). It is clear that chiefs had to possess considerable resources in order to insure there was enough money to pay participants in ceremonial feasts and to provide visitors and the poor with adequate food. In Crespi's diary, as in other accounts of this era, there are statements that Chumash chiefs supplied the food for the members of the expedition. (More details about a Chumash chief's power will be presented in chapter 7.) From these records, it appears that one of the most important duties of Chumash chiefs was to sponsor feasts, an activity that required significant wealth and prestige. Chiefs also had to attend the feasts sponsored by neighboring chiefs; refusing an invitation was grounds for war.

CHAPTER 4

Historic Chumash Settlements on the Mainland Coast

All of the spots here on the Channel are a joy to the sight: a great deal of good soil; good watering places; a great deal of grass for [grazing] stock; a vast number of heathen folk, all living assembled in regular towns and all of the people as kind as though they had dealt with Spaniards forever; and a great deal of wood at almost every town and each of them very freely supplied with various sorts of fish: a great many sardines, a great deal of large anchovies, a great many large, very good bonitos, large needlefish, lobsters, cuttlefish, and many other kinds of fish.

Crespí on May 3, 1770, in Brown 2001:701

The Spanish had observed other Indian villages in both Baja and Alta California, but none as spectacular as the densely populated coastal Chumash towns, with their houses neatly arranged in rows. As Crespí marched from Ventura northwest along the Santa Barbara Channel coast, he noted that the towns became ever more populous, until they arrived at the Goleta Slough, where the greatest number of people were encountered in the Chumash region (see initial quote in chapter 1). In this chapter, we take a closer look at some of the settlements that so impressed Crespí and his companions.

Population Figures for the Chumash

Reconstructing the populations of Chumash settlements during the late 18th century is a challenging endeavor, but several scholars have made solid attempts. Alan Brown (1967) provided one of the earliest thorough analyses of population figures for the mainland coastal settlements during this period, utilizing early historic accounts and mission register data for the coastal settlements between *Noqto* and *Humaliwo*. Sherburne Cook was another important demographer who provided a number of estimates of the aboriginal population in California prior to European contact (Cook 1976; Cook and Heizer 1965). Cook's (1976) most recent work on California demography was published posthumously, two years after his death. Cook reexamined Brown's population estimate for the Chumash; approximately 15,000 for the entire region. Cook carefully considered numerous sources of information, including the number of people per house and the number of houses per settlement. His original estimate with Heizer (Cook and Heizer 1965) for the entire Chumash region was 25,000 inhabitants. Cook (1976) later revised this figure to about 18,500, with a range between 15,000 and 25,000. He noted that population densities for the Chumash were of little value because of the "extreme concentration of people on the coast and the relatively sparse occupation in the interior" (Cook 1976:37–38).

More recently, John Johnson (1982, 1988) conducted research for his master's thesis and dissertation that contained even more accurate population figures for mission era populations for many mainland and northern Channel Island Chumash settlements. Chester King (King 2000; King and Johnson 1999) also worked with the mission register documents from the Santa Monica Mountains region, and added to this invaluable database. Their research has provided scholars in the region with detailed information on the population of the Chumash during the early historic period and is an essential foundation for this chapter.

The journals kept during the Portolá expedition, especially Crespí's, are considered the most accurate sources of information on Chumash settlements along the coast in the early historic period. However, several differing opinions exist regarding the reliability of the population estimates made by the members of the Portolá expedition. Cook and Heizer (1965:20) considered the accounts of the explorers relatively reliable; nevertheless, because they surmised that women, children, and fisherman were partly omitted from the population figures, they increased the numbers by a quarter when estimating populations for the period. In contrast, Landberg (1965:97–98) suggested that the population estimates from the Portolá expedition might have been inflated because of an influx of nonresidents curious to see the Spaniards; Font's calculations, made seven years later, give much lower numbers. On the contrary, Brown (1967:

49–50) believed most of Crespí's population estimates to be quite reliable, in part because Crespí counted the number of men, women, children (boys and girls), and infants. Johnson (1988:114) tends to concur with Landberg's suggestion that the diarists on the Portolá expedition might have exaggerated population figures for the Chumash communities, or that the numbers were augmented by visitors from the interior or islands who were anxious to obtain a glimpse of the Spanish. Johnson (1988:114) points out that Brown discounted both these caveats.

In table 10, I present population estimates based on three journals from the 1769 expedition: Portolá's, Crespí's, and Costansó's. I include estimates of the number of houses and canoes as these data are relevant to the population estimates provided by the explorers. Brown (1967), in his analysis of these sources, has pointed out that the explorers estimated about six persons per house; he noted that this was surprising given that they also remarked on the large size of houses. On more careful examination, Brown (1967) found that Crespí and his colleagues wrote that "some" houses were larger than others. Possibly chiefs and other leaders had larger houses. Brown (1967:1) also noted that there were close agreements between the number of houses, persons, and canoes along the mainland Channel.

Mission register data published in McLendon and Johnson (1999:Table 5.1) are presented in table 11 and mapped in figures 6 and 7. The locations of the villages are based on Johnson's most recent map of historic settlements in the Chumash region (McLendon and Johnson 1999:Figure 3.1), all of which were carefully identified based on several different sources (Johnson 1988:91–108). For the locations of the coastal villages, Johnson (1988:91–92) relied on the work of Brown (1967) and King (1975); however, locations of historic sites in the inland Chumash territory could not be identified with as much certainty (Johnson 1988:95). Mission period documents, ethnographic information on Chumash place-names from the notes of J.P. Harrington, archaeological evidence of historic-period occupation, diaries of early explorers, and information contained in the land grant diseños and expedientes from the post-mission period were used to determine locations of the inland sites (Johnson 1988:95). A question mark (?) has been placed by the villages whose positions are somewhat uncertain.

The size of settlements along the Santa Barbara Channel coast varied with some settlements being much larger than others and undoubtedly playing a different role in Chumash society. In this chapter, we examine the coastal settlements during the late 1700s and early 1800s, starting with

TABLE 10. Information from the 1769–1770 Portola Expedition about Mainland Coastal Settlements

Village	No.of People (Crespi)	No. of People (Portola)	No. of People (Costanso)	Baptisms	No. of Canoes	No. of Houses (Crespi)	No. of Houses (Portola)	No. of Houses (Costanso)	Occupation on Both Sides of Stream	Cemetery Present	Food Offered to Spanish on Trip	Population Estimate for Figure 7
Noqto	60?, 70, 100	60	60	68	0	10	n/a	n/a	n/a	yes	yes	60
Shilimaqshtush	150	200	250	106	0	n/a	n/a	n/a	yes	no	yes	150
Shisholop	n/a	150	n/a	197	6	38	50	24	yes	n/a	yes	150
Texax	n/a	n/a	n/a	41	3	20	n/a	20	n/a	yes	n/a	n/a
Kashtayit	100, 200	130	200	111	5	25	25	24	yes	n/a	n/a	200
‘Onomyo	300	300+	n/a	186	7	52	50	50	yes	n/a	yes	300
Tajiguas	400	400	800	n/a	13–15	79	80	80	yes	yes	yes	400
Qasil	n/a	n/a	n/a	116	n/a	n/a	n/a	n/a	yes	yes	yes	n/a
Dos Pueblos	600–700	1600	>1000	n/a	10	100	120	n/a	yes	yes	yes	700
Mikiw	n/a	800	n/a	325	n/a	n/a	60	n/a	n/a	n/a	n/a	n/a
Kuya’mu	n/a	800	n/a	27	n/a	n/a	60	n/a	n/a	n/a	n/a	n/a
Goleta Slough	1500, 2000	n/a	n/a	n/a	n/a	n/a	n/a	n/a	n/a	yes	yes	1500
Helo’	800	800	many	152	16	100	80+	100+	n/a	yes	yes	800
S’axpilil	n/a	n/a	n/a	324	many	n/a	n/a	n/a	n/a	yes	n/a	n/a
Alkash	n/a	n/a	n/a	78	n/a	n/a	n/a	n/a	n/a	n/a	n/a	n/a

Syuxtun	600	500	600	201	10	n/a	40	n/a	no	yes	yes	600
Q'oloq'	n/a	n/a	n/a	48	n/a	n/a	n/a	n/a	n/a	n/a	n/a	n/a
Mishopshno	500	300	n/a	135	7	38	38	32	no	yes	n/a	500
Shuku	many	300	n/a	131	7	60	30+	n/a	no	yes	n/a	300
Shisholop	n/a	300	n/a	295	3 (15)[a]	30	30	30	no	yes	n/a	300
Muwu	n/a	n/a	n/a	191	n/a	n/a	n/a	n/a	no	yes	n/a	n/a
Lisiqishi	n/a	n/a	n/a	60	n/a	n/a	n/a	n/a	n/a	n/a	n/a	n/a
Lojostogni	n/a	n/a	n/a	37	n/a	n/a	n/a	n/a	n/a	n/a	n/a	n/a
Sumo	n/a	n/a	n/a	38	n/a	n/a	n/a	n/a	n/a	n/a	n/a	n/a
Humaliwo	n/a	n/a	n/a	118	n/a	n/a	n/a	n/a	n/a	n/a	n/a	n/a

Note: n/a indicates data not available.

[a]The members of the Portola expedition saw three canoes when they were at the settlement, but were informed by the chief that there were 15 canoes from this village, but most were on the islands, informing the Chumash there about the Spanish.

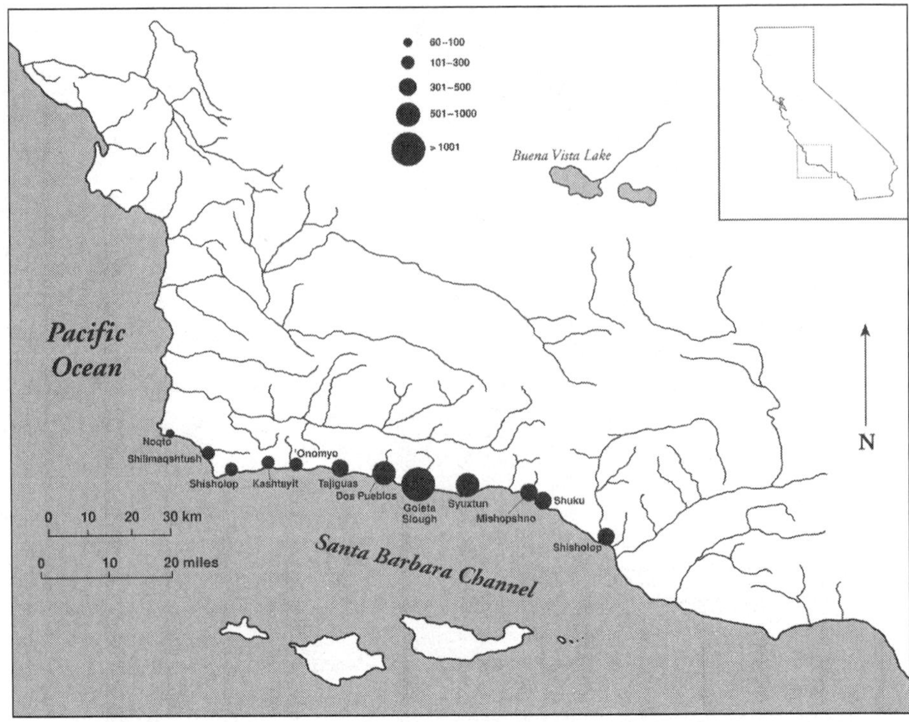

FIGURE 6 Map of population estimates based on Crespí's accounts

Noqto on the north and ending with *Humaliwu* on the south (figure 7)[6]. We will discover how many inhabitants and chiefs lived in each settlement, how many canoes were present, and what the environment was like during the different seasons. We note from Crespí's diary that the Chumash offered the members of the Portolá expedition fish, "gruel," and other foods at almost every settlement on their journey north in the summer of 1769 and on their return south in the winter of 1770; however, fish and other foods were much scarcer in some of the settlements, and the expedition often went hungry. Finally, a brief overview of the archaeological information available for each settlement is presented.

Noqto

Crespí described the setting of *Noqto* as he approached the village from the south: "From here, which is the last regular Channel town, Point La

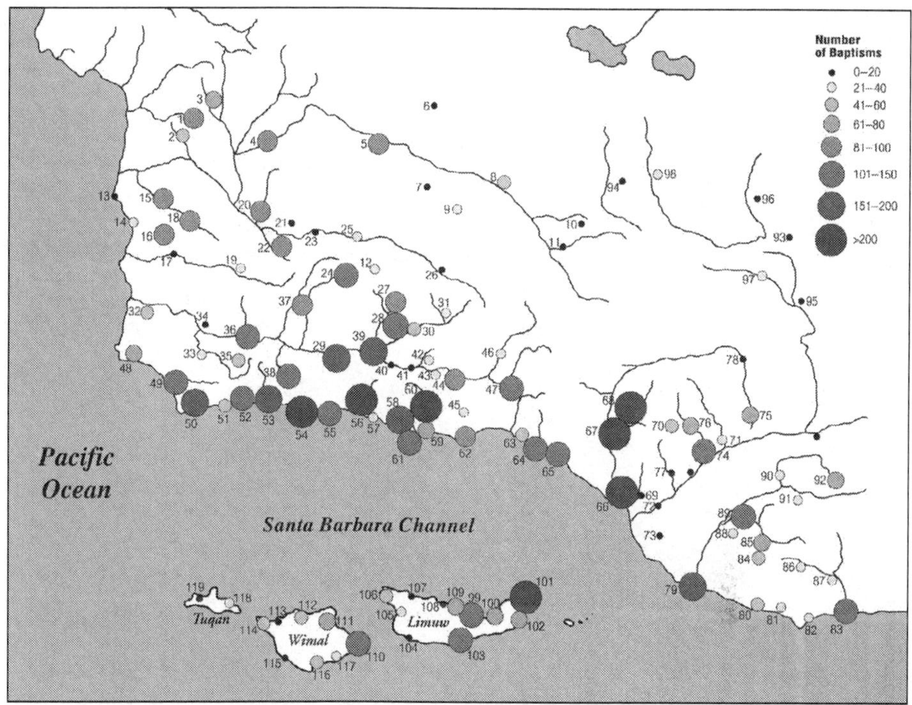

FIGURE 7 Map of population estimates based on mission register documents from Johnson (1988) and McLendon and Johnson (1999)

Concepción is in view, already well behind us, and the last island, with about half of it protruding out beyond the aforesaid point" (Crespí in Brown 2001:453). *Noqto* (translated as "eel" [Applegate 1975; Johnson 1988:93; King 1984]) marks the beginning of the Santa Barbara Channel and the larger settlements that are found there. Inhabitants of *Noqto* spoke a Purismeño dialect of the Northern Chumash language. Both Crespí and Costansó noted ten houses at *Noqto* (Brown 2001:453), indicating that it was a relatively small village compared with some of the other coastal settlements. In the field draft of his journal, Crespí estimated that about 60 or 70 people lived at *Noqto*, but changed his assessment to "sixty or more souls" in his revised notes (Brown 2001:453). This corresponds with the 60 inhabitants that both Costansó and Portolá recorded for *Noqto* (Brown 1967:17). Later, on May 7, 1770, Crespí noted 100 inhabitants and 12–14 houses at *Noqto*, increasing both population figures and house counts on this leg of the journey without explanation (table 10 and Brown 2001:711). Crespí also commented that a good source of

TABLE 11. Number of Baptisms Based on Mission Register Data and Legend for Figure 7

No. on Map	Village Name	No. of Baptisms	No. on Map	Village Name	No. of Baptisms
1	Stemeqtatimi	85	38	Naxuwi	106
2	Nipumu'	52	39	Teqepsh	180
3	Wasna	62	40	He'lxman	17
4	Wenexe'l	88	41	Wishap	56
5	Sxaliwiliumu'	81	42	Mi'asap	25
6	K'o'owshup	14	43	Shnoxsh	31
7	Lishawato'w	12	44	Shniwax	83
8	Kuyam	41	45	Xana'yan	37
9	Tsiwikon	39	46	Siwaya	35
10	Sqene'n	4	47	Shnaxalyiwi	106
11	Achililwo?	2	48	Noqto	68
12	Ahuam	36	49	Shilimaqshtush	106
13	'Ataxis	15	50	Shisholop	200
14	Lospe	30	51	Texax	41
15	'Axwapsh	88	52	Keshtayit	111
16	S'axpilil	96	53	'Onomyo	186
17	Step	19	54	Shishuch'i'	206
18	Nauca	95	55	Qasil	116
19	Saqsiyol	39	56	Mikiw	324
20	Snisewi	86	57	Kuya'mu	27
21	Siswow	5	58	Helo'	152
22	Washlayik	101	59	'Alkash	78
23	Lonsoqoq	2	60	S'axpilil	320
24	Soxtonokmu'	194	61	Heliyik	102
25	Heqep	33	62	Syuxtun	87
26	Siwil	8	63	Q'oloq'	48
27	'Aqitsu'm	98	64	Mishopshno	135
28	Stuk	111	65	Shuku	131
29	Kalwashaq'	182	66	Shisholop	295
30	Wililik'	52	67	S'omis	216
31	Saq'ka'ya	37	68	Mat'ilha	241
32	Lompo'	52	69	'Alkuy	12
33	Xalam	33	70	'Awha'y	60
34	Shipuk	14	71	'Alalhew	22
35	'Itiyaqsh	51	72	Kanaputeqnon	15
36	Sh'ahuchu	116	73	Kasunalmu	15
37	Xonxon'ata	98	74	Mupu	102

(*continued*)

TABLE 11. (continued)

No. on Map	Village Name	No. of Baptisms	No. on Map	Village Name	No. of Baptisms
75	S'eqp'e	63	98	Tashlipun	22
76	Sis'a	74	99	Xaxas	129
77	Sisxulkuy	15	100	Lu'upsh	63
78	Shumpashi	16	101	Swaxil	205
79	Muwu	191	102	Nanawani	61
80	Lisiqishi	60	103	Liyam	117
81	Loxostox'ni	37	104	Shawa	9
82	Sumo	38	105	Ch'oloshush	28
83	Humaliwo	118	106	L'akayamu	50
84	Sumuawawa	55	107	L'alale	5
85	S'apwi	62	108	Ch'ishi	2
86	Hipuk	37	109	Maschal	69
87	Ta'lopop	29	110	Qshiwqshiw	119
88	Lalimanux	28	111	Hichimin	71
89	Kayiwish	128	112	Silimihi	53
90	Kimishax	21	113	Niaqla	10
91	Shimiyi	24	114	Nimkilkil	51
92	Ta'apu	76	115	Nawani	2
93	Kashtiq	20	116	Nilal'uy	48
94	Malapwan	9	117	Helewashkuy	37
95	Mat'apxa'w	5	118	Tuqan	34
96	Mat'apxwelexwe'l	3	119	Niwoyomi	3
97	Shuxwiyuxus	21			

flint was near the site; therefore, the site was named "St. John the Baptist of the Flintstones" or Pedernales (at Pt. Pedernales) (Brown 2001:455).

When the expedition returned, hungry and tired from San Francisco on their way south in January of 1770, they stopped again at *Noqto*, where they fortunately were offered mussels, gruel, and fish (Crespí in Brown 2001:649). Approximately one league south of *Noqto*, the expedition was again provided with food, although this time it was barbecued sardines and "some things they call *callos* that are like limpets" (Crespí in Brown 2001:649). Sixty-eight individuals were baptized from the settlement of *Noqto* (table 11), a figure very close to the population estimates made by the explorers; however, by 1796 when Goycoechea completed a census there, only 12 individuals were documented. Font compared *Noqto* and *Shilimaqshtush* in 1776 and commented that these two villages had fewer people than other Channel settlements to the east and that they were "somewhat poor" (Bolton 1931:264).

The archaeological site of CA-SBA-210, where 126 glass trade beads were found during excavations in 1974, is situated on the west side of the perennial Agua Vina Creek or Wild Horse Canyon and is believed to be the site of *Noqto* (Glassow 1996:86; King 1984). Burials were excavated by Horace Smith in the late 1800s on the uppermost terrace at the site. Clarence Ruth also excavated in the cemetery, where he found disturbed burials, at least five skulls, and an undisturbed extended burial (Spanne 1970). Glassow (1996), who conducted extensive excavations here, obtained four radiocarbon dates that indicate the site was first occupied more than 4,000 years ago. He has suggested that at the time of European contact, the settlement served as a residential base in the area, and that unlike most other sites in the Vandenberg region, was more protected from the prevailing winds and cool, damp fogs. CA-SBA-552, which is on the east side of Agua Vina Creek, has also been associated with *Noqto* (Brown 1967:16; Johnson 1988:94; King 1984); however, Glassow (1996:88–89) did not find glass beads or other historic-period artifacts to indicate that this site was part of *Noqto*.

Shilimaqshtush

Crespí noted approximately 20 houses and 150 inhabitants on both sides of a "large running stream" (now known as Jalama Creek) at *Shilimaqshtush* on August 28, 1769 (Brown 2001:449). In contrast, Costansó and Portolá provided population figures that were considerably higher, with Costansó recording 250 "souls a little more or less," and Portolá estimating 200 inhabitants (table 10 and Brown 1967:17). Although Crespí explicitly noted an absence of canoes at *Shilimaqshtush*, he did observe "one or two floats of tule-rushes" (Brown 2001:451). He also stated that the inhabitants had very few fish in August. In January, however, when the expedition returned from Monterey, the Spanish were provisioned with an abundance of both fresh and barbecued sardines at *Shilimaqshtush* (Crespí in Brown 2001:649). A total of 106 baptisms were recorded for this settlement (McLendon and Johnson 1999:Table VIII.4), but according to the census taken by Goycoechea in 1796, only 12 individuals inhabited the settlement (Brown 1967:17).

Two archaeological sites that have been recorded near the mouth of the creek (CA-SBA-553 and CA-SBA-205) are believed to be the remnants of the community that Crespí observed. Lathrap and Hoover (1975) excavated at CA-SBA-205 and recovered numerous household features (see chapter 5), but did not find glass beads or other artifacts indicative of a historic-period occupation.

Shisholop North

Shisholop, the town that Crespí named Santa Teresa, was situated on both sides of a dry stream "at the very edge of the shore" (Brown 2001:445). Although the creek was dry when the expedition was there in August, springs and ponds apparently provided fresh water for its inhabitants. *Shisholop* (translated as "in the mud" [Johnson 1988:93]) was also named the "Rancheria del Cojo" (the Cripple's Village) by the soldiers on the expedition because of a crippled Chumash man observed there. This was the first settlement along the Santa Barbara coast where Crespí observed canoes. "Coming from the northward, the canoes commence here at the Santa Teresa Village; northward, between here and the inlet of San Francisco harbor, there is not a single canoe, save here and there some floats they make out of tule rushes" (Crespí on January 4, 1770, in Brown 2001:651). Crespí recorded five to six canoes and 38 "grass houses" at this settlement, but did not comment on the number of inhabitants (table 10). Portolá, however, provided an estimate of approximately 150 individuals and 50 houses. Portolá observed more houses than Costansó (who said there were 24) or Crespí (Brown 1967:20).

Members of the expedition were presented with fish on their journey north, and again on their way south, including bonito and needlefish, which they traded for with glass beads and iron implements (Crespí on January 4, 1770, in Brown 2001:651). In May 1770, when the expedition headed north for the second time, they asked for fish, but were told that none were available (Crespí in Brown 2001:707). Despite the lack of fish, the chief was given some beads and they continued their march north.

McLendon and Johnson (1999:Table VIII.4) noted that there were 197 baptisms from this settlement (table 11). In 1796, Goycoechea counted 72 inhabitants at *Shisholop*, considerably less than the number of people that were baptized from the settlement. Johnson (1988:94) has identified four archaeological sites, CA-SBA-541, CA-SBA-546, CA-SBA-1503, and CA-SBA-1522, that may be remnants of *Shisholop* (King and Craig 1978).

Texax

This was one of the smaller settlements on this stretch of the mainland coast, with only 20 houses being recorded by Crespí and Costansó (Brown 1967:20, 2001:443). None of the diarists on the expedition provided a population estimate for *Texax*, although Crespí did note three canoes (table 10). The settlement, named Santa Ana by the Spanish, was situated in the canyon that is currently known as El Bulito. Crespí reported a running stream at *Texax*, but did not state whether or not the village lay on both sides of the drainage. Forty-one baptisms were listed in the mission records for *Texax* (McLendon and Johnson 1999:Table VIII-4). In the census of 1796, Goycoechea recorded 30 individuals from *Texax*.

In 1969, Spanne noted that CA-SBA-1494 had projectile points typical of the Late period; it has been suggested that the site was *Texax* (Johnson 1988:94). Clarence Ruth (1967) noted burials eroding from the bank in 1940 and later excavated one with steatite beads. A systematic excavation of the cemetery has not been undertaken.

Kashtayit

Crespí noted 25 houses at *Kashtayit* (translated as "the willow" [Johnson 1988:93]), although in a later draft of his journal he seems to have mistakenly changed this to 50 houses (Brown 1967:21, 2001:789). The estimate of 25 houses is closer to those made by Portolá (25 houses) and Costansó (24 houses). Both Costansó and Crespí stated that about 200 people lived at the settlement, which is considerably more than the estimate of 130 provided by Portolá (Brown 1967:21). Crespí originally wrote in his journal that there were "a hundred-some souls," but altered it to "two hundred or more" and later stated that there were over 200 inhabitants (Brown 1967:21). The estimate of 200 is probably the more accurate because it corresponds more closely with the house counts. In the field draft of his journal, Crespí noted three canoes, but then later wrote in the same draft that there were four or five canoes, as he did in his revised journal (Brown 2001:441-443). Portolá only noted "some" canoes at the settlement (Brown 1967:21).

Crespí did not mention fish or other food in January 1770 on their march south, but made the following comment on their earlier journey north on August 25, 1769: "They still have the same manners as the previous heathens; here they brought us a little fish, but apparently it is no longer so plentiful as before" (Crespí in Brown 2001:441). Presumably Crespí meant that the Santa Barbara Channel towns to the south had more fish at this time of year. Crespí also noted that no trees were in sight of the settlement. The name *Kashtayit* is listed as *Estait* in the mission registers, and a total of 111 individuals were baptized from here (McLendon and Johnson 1999:Table VIII-4). The site of CA-SBA-1492 is situated on a low bench on both sides of Santa Anita Creek and is believed to be the remains of *Kashtayit* (Johnson 1988:94).

'Onomyo

Upon encountering *'Onomyo*, Crespí made the following statement: "Split between one side and the other of this inlet, and almost at the very sea's edge, there lies a well populated village where we counted 52 well-shaped large grass-roofed houses. And where we imagined there must be at least three hundred souls, young and old" (Crespí on August 24, 1769, in Brown 2001:437). Crespí also noted that the "stream has more running water than any others belonging to the last spots we have passed" and was surrounded by live oaks and willows upstream (Brown 2001: 437). *'Onomyo* was one of the larger settlements at the west end of the Santa Barbara Channel. Both Costansó ("fifty hearths") and Portolá ("fifty houses") provided estimates of houses at *'Onomyo* that were similar to Crespí's. Portolá also suggested a figure comparable to Crespí's for the population ("more than three hundred heathens") (Brown 1967:22). Crespí noted seven canoes at the settlement ("San Luis Rey de Francia"), some of which were "quite large" (Brown 2001:439). A total of 186 baptisms were recorded for this settlement (table 11; Johnson 1988: Table 4.1).

'Onomyo was the home of El Loco, a chief who accompanied the expedition from San Luis Obispo to Gaviota in the winter of 1769-1770, and who made certain that its members were entertained and well fed along the route (Crespí on January 7, 1770, in Brown 2001:653). When the expedition returned north in May 1770, Crespí wrote that El Loco greeted them and "At once on our arrival, they entertained us with dancing, with a flair and measure that I have never seen the like of" (Brown 2001:705). The expedition was also given dried fish on their first trip north in August of 1769. *'Onomyo* has been associated with CA-SBA-97 at Gaviota Creek. The site was recorded by Rogers (1929) as Canaliño or Late Period.

Tajiguas

The community of *Tajiguas* (which probably means "to leak" [Applegate 1975:43]) was bisected by a drainage and was situated next to the ocean, as were many coastal Chumash settlements. Crespí described the settlement as very large, with 42 houses on one side, 37 on the other, and a population of "at least 400 souls" (Brown 2001:433). He named the settlement "San Güido." Portolá also stated that there were 400 people in the settlement, but Costansó recorded 800 (Brown 1967:24). Brown believes that Costansó's figure may be an error of "dittography" because Costansó had just written that there were 80 houses in the settlement, the same number that Portolá noted (table 10). Crespí observed four canoes, but was informed that there were actually 15—the others had been sent to the islands (Brown 2001:435). On the return march south in January, Crespí noted "thirteen canoes, of the fifteen that they possess, out fishing" (Brown 2001:653). He also remarked on the food that they were given: "On our reaching this spot of San Güido, they brought us heaps of large sardines and some bonitos, gruel, and a little mush" (Brown 2001:653). Dried fish and gruel were also offered in August of 1769 when they headed north. Six years later, Anza passed by this settlement in February and found it completely abandoned (Brown 1967:24). It is believed that the local Chumash established new settlements at *Shishuch'i'* (Arroyo Quemado) and *Qasil* (Cañada del Refugio) at this time because of a war with their enemies (Brown 1967:24; Johnson 1988:123-124). Conflicts among the Chumash are discussed in greater detail in chapter 9.

Rogers (1929:244–247) mapped two sites (CA-SBA-89 and CA-SBA-90) near the mouth of Tajiguas Creek (figure 8) and noted that the area had been severely disturbed by railroad construction and other human activities. He remarked that the midden at CA-SBA-89 was especially deep (six feet) and noted burials, but did not believe that they were related to the late occupation at the site.

Qasil

Crespí described "an old abandoned village" at Refugio Bay when he passed by in 1769 (Brown 2001:435). The site was apparently resettled by 1776, because it is mentioned in Anza's journal (see above). It remained occupied until its inhabitants were recruited into the mission system (116 individuals were baptized from *Qasil*) (McLendon and Johnson

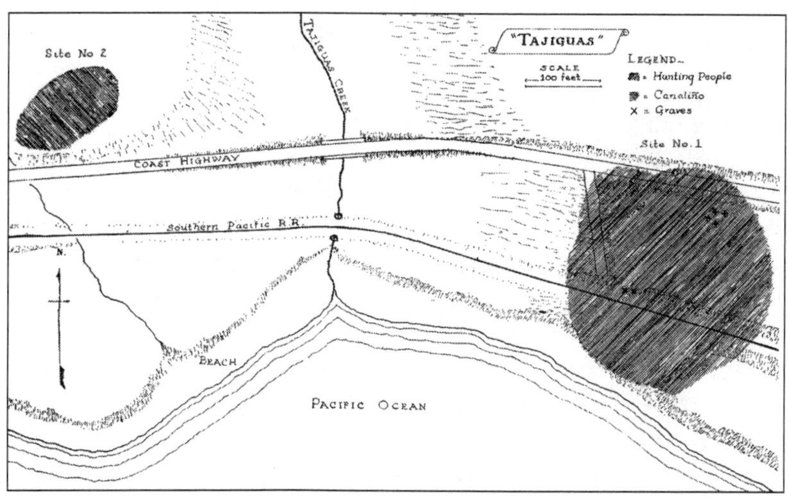

FIGURE 8 Map of *Tajiguas* made by D. B. Rogers (courtesy of the Santa Barbara Museum of Natural History)

1999:Table VIII.4). According to Goycoechea's census figures, 142 individuals lived at the settlement in 1796 (Brown 1967:24).

Harrington's consultants (King 1993:12–13) indicated that *Qasil* was an important trade center and a port for the Chumash from Santa Cruz Island. *Qasil* was strategically situated for access to the interior, with an important trail that led to the Santa Ynez Valley. In 1913, Fernando Librado told Harrington that when the Santa Cruz Island Indians came to Refugio, "there was much trade in acorns, islay, etc." (King 1993:13).

Rogers (1929:238–241) investigated three sites at Refugio Bay, one of which (CA-SBA-87) he identified as *Qasil.* Rogers noted that the site was severely disturbed by the railroad and other historic activities; however, he did observe remnants of a cemetery near the southern end of the site and a *temescal* just to the south of the cemetery. Rogers suggested that the high density of asphaltum and asphaltum caulking stones at the site indicated that boat making was an important activity there. Rogers excavated in the cemetery that King (1993:13) suggests was used during the Middle period phase 4 (ca. AD 700–900). Since Rogers' publication in 1929, construction for the Pacific Coast Highway has further impacted the site. In 1969, West (1969:26) excavated one burial at the site. Additional excavations on the east side of Cañada del Refugio Creek by Hector Neff and Terry Rudolph in 1986 found midden deposits.

Dos Pueblos: *Mikiw* and *Kuya'mu*

The two settlements on either side of Dos Pueblos Creek at the ocean's edge undoubtedly impressed Crespí: "We went to make camp about a half a league above this small hollow, close to two very large villages with vast numbers of people and a great many houses in each, where they have their towns at the very edge of the sea, at another, larger hollow with a great deal of live-oak groves, and where there is a good-sized stream of running water, very good pure water, emptying into the sea" (Crespí on August 21, 1769, in Brown 2001:429). Crespí commented that the settlements were very large; however, more definitive population estimates for the settlements vary. Crespí suggested in his field draft that there were 600–700 inhabitants, then in his revised version, 600 people, and again in his journal (January 8, 1770) on the journey south, 600–700 inhabitants (Brown 2001). Finally, in May 1770 when the expedition made its second trek to Monterey, Crespí estimated that the two settlements at Dos Pueblos (named San Luis Obispo by members of the expedition) were inhabited by "as much as a thousand souls or a bit more than that" (Brown 2001:703). Costansó recorded over 1000 individuals in both towns and Portolá suggested that each had "about 800 heathens" (Brown 1967:25). Based on these accounts, Brown (1967:25) proposed that approximately 1100 people lived in the two settlements.

Other indicators of population confirm that the two towns were in fact of considerable size. Crespí wrote that one of the settlements had approximately 10 canoes that were observed out fishing. He was uncertain how many canoes were present in the other village, but made the following statement about the number of houses at Dos Pueblos: "[I]t must have about a hundred houses, all of them round, grass-roofed, very large, and very well built" (Crespí on May 3, 1770, in Brown 2001:701). It is not clear whether he is referring to only one of the settlements at Dos Pueblos. Portolá and Costansó did not estimate the number of canoes present, but Portolá noted 60 houses in each settlement. Crespí did write that the larger settlement, *Mikiw*, was on top of "a large tableland." The other town, *Kuya'mu*, was described by Crespí as "down below within the hollow at the edge of the stream and the shore" (Crespí on May 3, 1770, in Brown 2001:701–703). Mission documents corroborate the fact that *Mikiw* was the largest settlement of the two: 325 baptisms were recorded from there compared with 27 from *Kuya'mu* (McLendon and Johnson 1999:Table VIII.4). Goycoechea noted 210 inhabitants in *Mikiw* in 1796, but did not provide an estimate for the inhabitants of *Kuya'mu*.

He did state, however, that one of the two chiefs he listed from Dos Pueblos was from *Kuya'mu* (Brown 1967:25).

Members of the expedition were treated well at Dos Pueblos as they marched northward, just as they had been in many of the settlements to the south, with the Indians offering "a great deal of fish and gruel" (Crespí on August 22, 1769, in Brown 2001:431), as well as entertainment. The expedition was provisioned again on their journey south on January 7, 1770, this time with large, fresh sardines. Although Crespí noted that the inhabitants of Dos Pueblos were fishing in May when they headed north in 1770, he made no comments about eating fish at that time.

The archaeology at Dos Pueblos has captivated the interest of museum personnel and others for over 100 years. The earliest documented excavations at the site occurred in 1875 when Yarrow, Rothrock, and Henshaw of the U. S. Geological Survey excavated a historic cemetery at the site of *Mikiw* (CA-SBA-78) for the Smithsonian Institution (figure 9) (Putnam et al. 1879:41–42). At the same time, they also investigated *Kuya'mu* (CA-SBA-77), but stated that they found only broken bones. At the historic cemetery of *Mikiw*, Yarrow (Putnam et al. 1879:42) estimated that they recovered approximately 10 to 15 tons of "specimens," including mortars, pestles, steatite ollas, steatite comals, pipes, beads, ornaments, bone awls, and iron weapons. (More detailed information on their findings are presented in subsequent chapters of this book.) As a result of their investigations, Yarrow (Putnam et al. 1879) published a brief description of the excavations with photographs and drawings of some of the objects. Paul Schumacher (1877), Stephen Bowers (Benson 1997), Alphonse Pinart, León de Cessac, Francisco Leyva, and Louis Dreyfus (Rogers 1929:202) also excavated at Dos Pueblos in the late 1800s, but their excavations were poorly documented compared with those of Yarrow. Schumacher (1877) did note that one "town" was located on the right bank of the creek on the mesa and that the other was located on the sloping bank on the other side of the creek.

Approximately 50 years later, Rogers (1929) conducted more professional archaeological investigations at Dos Pueblos (figure 10). At *Mikiw* (CA-SBA-78), Rogers (1929:207–208) excavated a couple of long trenches in two elongated refuse heaps and found shell, fish scales, faunal remains, a few human remains, and numerous fragmentary artifacts. Rogers recorded two cemeteries, including the historic cemetery that Yarrow and his colleagues excavated. Rogers placed additional trenches in this same cemetery, but found it severely disturbed from the previous excavations. Rogers recorded some of the same features as Yarrow did in the cemetery, including

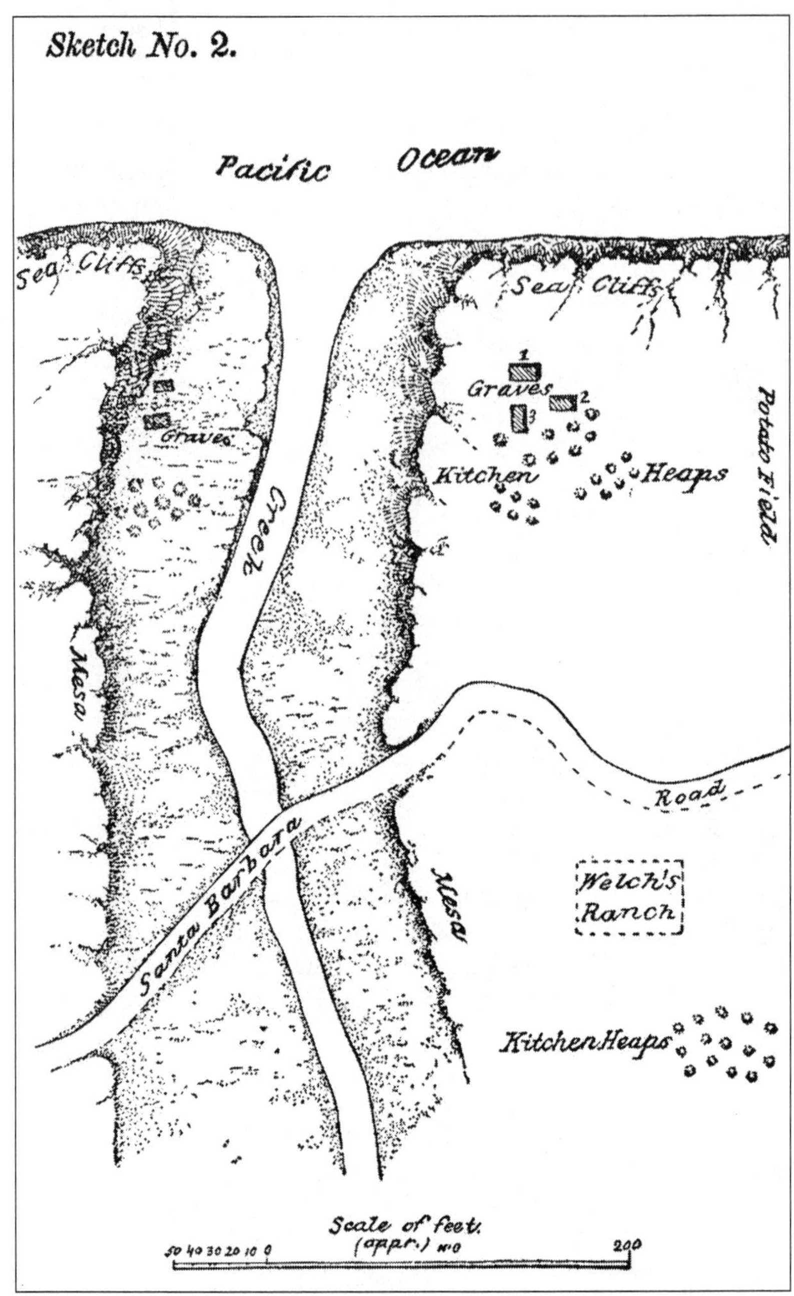

FIGURE 9 Map of Dos Pueblos made by Yarrow (Putnam et al. 1879:41)

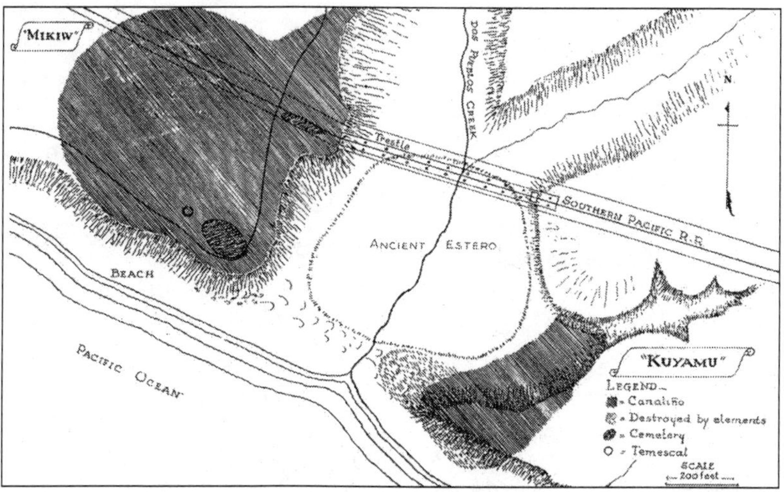

FIGURE 10 Map of Dos Pueblos made by D. B. Rogers (courtesy of the Santa Barbara Museum of Natural History)

numerous whale ribs that were no longer arched above the graves as they were when Yarrow visited the site (Rogers 1929:208–209). Rogers also noted "large slabs of whale bone, formed from the scapula or sternum" (Rogers 1929:209), which he suggested served as grave slabs along with the flat boulders in the area. He excavated a few intact burials with grave goods, such as ollas and pestles, but mostly found numerous small artifacts ("at least eight thousand"), such as beads and arrow points. These smaller remains were found strewn throughout the cemetery, presumably discarded by the earlier excavators who only collected the larger objects that they sought for museums. Rogers also excavated a sweatlodge (*temescal*) at CA-SBA-78 that consisted of layers of charred wood interspersed with ash and unburnt wood. A more detailed description of this feature can be found in chapter 5.

In addition to his excavations at *Mikiw*, Rogers (1929:211–212) also trenched at CA-SBA-77 (*Kuya'mu*), but found little that interested him, with the exception of a class of artifacts that he had never previously observed in the Chumash region. These consisted of numerous large flat boulders with clear evidence of abrading but no indication of shaping. Although Rogers explicitly distinguished these from metates, he did suggest that they were some type of milling stone. However, it is not clear if they were from the historic occupation of the site. Approximately one year after Rogers's investigations at SBA-77, two of his colleagues, Dr. William J. Mellinger and J. F. Hurlbut, followed up on Rogers's excavations (Rogers 1929:212). Rogers wrote that they found more artifacts than he had and that they were "identical in type" to those found at the village site of *Mikiw*. No human skeletal remains were found at CA-SBA-77, however, and Rogers speculated that their absence might have been a result of damage to the site from both natural and human disturbance processes.

William Harrison's excavations at the site of *Mikiw* in 1958 were in sharp contrast to those completed in the late nineteenth century, and even to those conducted by Rogers. Harrison used eighth-inch mesh screens in most of his excavations at the site, a technique that was unprecedented at the time. Moreover, he instructed the crew to remove artifacts from the screens and place the remaining constituents, such as shell, bone, and charcoal, in bags for the laboratory to sort through later. At the time Harrison conducted excavations at SBA-78, a road from the beach to the top of the mesa had already destroyed the historic cemetery (Harrison 1965). Subsequent human disturbance, including the construction of a sewage system for the ranch, further impacted the site. Nevertheless, Harrison made some unique discoveries. His most significant find was an intact sweatlodge floor dating to the historic period. (Details about the sweatlodge are reported in chapter 5. Artifacts from the historic deposits from this and other historic sites are described in later chapters.) In 1979, King and Gamble surveyed the mesa on the west side of the canyon and determined that the orchid farm road was a boundary between SBA-78 and SBA-79 (King and Gamble (1979:11–12). More recently, King (1993:18) has noted that the archaeological sites in the area appear to be the remains of different overlapping settlements that were occupied over the last 8000 years.

Goleta Slough Settlements

The most populous region along the Santa Barbara coast, the Goleta Slough area, caught the eye of several early explorers. The work of Johnson et al. (1982:12–48), who have provided a thorough synthesis of this region, serves as the basis for this discussion. Cabrillo was the first to visit and record the settlements in the area when he sailed north in October of 1542 from Baja California. Three villages named in Cabrillo's diary were apparently situated in the Goleta Slough region. *Paltuqaq* ("*Poltoltuc*")[7] was located on More Mesa and corresponds with CA-SBA-42 and the mission place name of *'Alkash* (figure 11). *Kuwa'a* ("*Gua*") was most likely the place name for Mescalitan Island and refers to the settlement on the island known in the mission registers as *Helo'* (SBA-46). Unfortunately, *Anacbuc* ("*Nacbuc*") cannot be located as precisely as the other two settlements, but it may have been at Goleta Beach where CA-SBA-1695 is located, or possibly on the UCSB campus where CA-SBA-47 or CA-SBA-48 are situated. Evidently none of the villages that Cabrillo recorded corresponded to the Mission Period settlement of *S'axpilil.*

Crespí provided much more detail on the environment and settlements in the Goleta Slough area than Cabrillo and clearly was impressed with the communities he encountered:

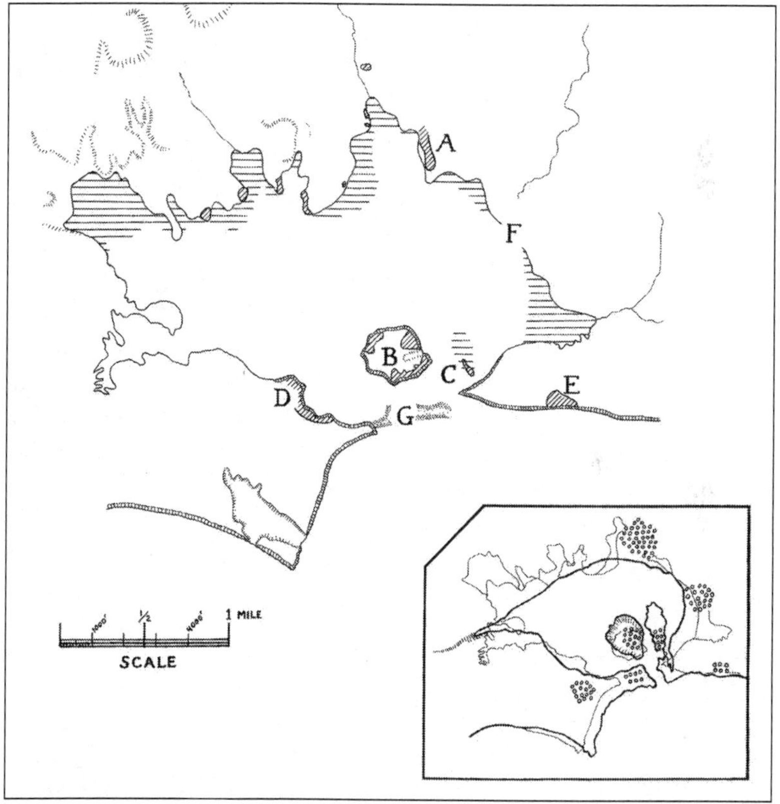

FIGURE 11 Reconstruction of Goleta Slough, with historic settlements around the Goleta Slough, by Alan Brown (1967) (courtesy of the Archaeological Research Facility at UC Berkeley and the UC Regents). Note: Inset based on map by Pantoja in 1782.

Of all the spots upon the entire Channel, this one has the greatest number of heathen folk. There are five villages, three quite large ones which we all saw, while the other two were reported of [on] by the scouts who had seen them in the surroundings of the place. One of the three lies islanded upon a knoll that must be a quarter-league in length, next to the sea, and isolated upon the inland side by a good-sized inlet that has one mouth at either end of the said knoll's length, through which the tide comes in, with the sea lying upon the other side; the inlet's width must be about half of a quarter-league. The village lying thus islanded is an extremely big one in its heathen population: so far as we could tell from the distance at which we were viewing it, there must be over a hundred very large round, very well roofed houses, and we guess that there cannot be less than eight hundred souls in this village alone (Crespí on August 20, 1769, in Brown 2001: 421).

Crespí identified *Helo'*, which was situated on the prominent island (Mescalitan Island) in the middle of the lagoon, as the largest town. This island town reminded the soldiers on the expedition so much of Mescaltitlán Lagoon in Nayarit, Mexico, that they named it *Mescaltitlán*. The name is Aztec in origin and represents the Aztec heartland, a place where "Mother Earth resided on an island in a lagoon" (Johnson et al. 1982:14–15). According to Johnson and his colleagues (1982:15), from the time of the Portolá expedition, the place name Mescaltitlán was used to refer to all of the Chumash villages in the region surrounding the Goleta Slough. Early in 1770 in correspondence from San Diego, Crespí estimated a population of 2,000 for all of the Goleta Slough towns (Brown 1967:29).

The Portolá expedition was well cared for when they stopped and camped in the region on August 20, 1769. The Chumash from the Goleta Slough towns entertained them with dancing, music, food, and gifts, including fish, seeds, skins, basketry, and feather headdresses. Crespí made the following comments about his hosts: "All of them have greatly entertained us by coming over with their flutes and pipes, many of them heavily painted and wearing their large feather headdresses for the dancing which they did for us" (Brown 2001:423). Apparently some competition developed between the settlements along the Channel Coast as to who could provide the most impressive feasts and entertainment:

They were not content with making us presents of their food, but wished also to entertains us, and it was clear that there was rivalry and emulation among the towns to come out best in the presents and feasts in order to win our approbation. . . . These dances lasted all the afternoon, and it cost us much trouble to rid ourselves of the people. They were sent away, charged with emphatic signs not to come in the night and disturb us; but it was in vain, for as soon as night fell they returned, playing on some pipes whose noise grated on our ears (Bolton 1927:168).

Crespí did not mention whether or not they were provided with food or fish on their return trip south in January 1770; however, in May 1770 on the second march north, Crespí wrote that they were again presented with "a great deal of fish" (Brown 2001:701).

Some confusion exists over the exact number of settlements in the Goleta Slough area in 1769 (figure 11). Crespí, Portolá, and Costansó provided estimates that ranged from three to seven villages. Johnson and his colleagues (1982:15) have suggested that the discrepancies in village counts may be a result of counting spatially discrete groups of households within a rancheria. Font described the villages surrounding the lagoon when he visited in 1776 as follows: "We came to Mescalititán. . . . Here there are three large villages, two somewhat apart, on the banks of the estuary, the largest one being on the road on which we were traveling" (Brown 1967:29). Six years later, on August 12, 1782, Pantoja y Arriaga entered the estuary by boat and made the following comment: "On the shores of this Lake are located five villages, and one of them, lying to the North, is very large" (Brown 1967:29). The large settlement that both Font and Pantoja y Arriaga referred to was probably *S'axpilil*. Although Pantoja y Arriaga noted five settlements in his diary, his map indicates there were actually seven clusters of houses (figure 2). The northernmost village was probably *S'axpilil*, which had the most houses (n=37) (figure 2). Mescalitan Island is represented by two lobes on this map and is shown to have 21 houses.

HELO'

Despite disparities concerning the exact number and size of the villages in the area surrounding the Goleta Slough, there is consensus that the area was densely populated. Crespí commented on the population of Mescalitan Island on three occasions. On August 20, 1769, he suggested that 800 people inhabited the island and that there were over 100 houses. He also noted 16 canoes on this date. Approximately four months later, in January 1770, Crespí estimated that "the Island Town alone must have from six hundred to eight hundred souls" (Brown 1967:33). Then in May 1770, he stated that the island "alone must hold about eight hundred souls" (Brown 1967:33). Portolá's population estimate for Mescalitan Island concurs with Crespí's higher estimate of 800 individuals (Brown 1967:33). Costansó only noted that there were numerous people living on the island.

Mission records indicate that there had been 152 baptisms from *Helo'* (translated as "the water") by 1804, when the village was virtually abandoned (table 11). Analyses of mission record documents show that three chiefs from *Helo'* were baptized at Mission Santa Barbara on the same day, May 18, 1803 (Johnson 1990:2–3), and a fourth chief was baptized on the following day. In addition, 80 inhabitants of *Helo'* were also baptized on these two days, representing most of the remaining people at *Helo'*. The chiefs from *Helo'* and other settlements are discussed in chapter 7.

Brown believed that Crespí's estimate for Mescalitan Island was too high because Crespí did not actually set foot on the island, but made his estimate from some distance (Brown 1967:33 and 77). Instead of 600 or 800 inhabitants, Brown has suggested that there were 250 or 300 people living on Mescalitan Island at the time of the Portolá expedition. Johnson agrees with Brown regarding the problems with Crespí's population estimate for Mescalitan Island. One concern for both scholars is the fact that the population was said to be 101 in 1796 when Goycoechea completed his census, much less than the figures provided by Crespí several years earlier (Johnson 1990:1–2; Brown 1967). In an attempt to reconcile the estimates, Brown (1967:77) extrapolated back in time from the census estimate of 101 (a figure that is considered reliable), using a constant rate of population decline. From this extrapolation, Brown determined that a figure of 250 to 300 people is more likely to be correct. Johnson agrees with this estimate but for different reasons.

I am less skeptical of Crespí's estimate than either Johnson or Brown, in part because Costansó, Crespí, and Portolá all suggested that *Helo'* had numerous inhabitants, and although considerably fewer people may have inhabited the settlement in 1796, other reasons for the discrepancies in the estimates should be considered. It is certainly feasible that the settlement experienced rapid population loss after 1770. The inhabitants of *Helo'* could have died at a more rapid rate than inhabitants from other historic villages because of warfare or an epidemic. This idea is particularly intriguing because *Helo'* was located on an island, where sanitary conditions may have been especially problematic. Where populations were at their densest, disease might have spread quickly, decimating the island population. It is also possible that the population at *Helo'* decreased between 1769 and 1796 for other reasons. The inhabitants may have moved to another village in the Goleta Slough or to settlements farther away. It is well documented that settlements were "either abandoned or newly occupied, or abandoned and then reoccupied" (Brown 1967:75) during the period of European contact. With the establishment of the Santa Barbara Presidio in 1782, the persistent warfare between villages in the Santa Barbara Channel area was severely suppressed. The defensive location of *Helo'* on Mescalitan Island may not have been as highly valued, and some of the inhabitants may have chosen to move to *S'axpilil*.[8] Whatever explanation is used to address the discrepancies, it is clear from the early accounts that *Helo'* was a large, impressive settlement in 1769 and a center of population.

If the population figures estimated for *Helo'* from the Portolá expedition are considered accurate, by the time Pantoja y Arriaga visited the Goleta Slough (and probably by 1776 when Font stopped in the area), the population of Mescalitan Island had apparently decreased to the point that it was no longer the largest town in the vicinity of the slough. As will be seen in chapter 5, archaeological data indicate that the village was larger in the early portion of the historic period than in the latter part.

Just as early investigators were interested in the archaeology of Dos Pueblos, they were active at *Helo'* for similar reasons. Historic cemeteries were marked with fences, poles, whale bones, and wooden boards and were readily apparent to "antiquarians" looking for museum-quality artifacts (Erlandson 1994:38–39). The earliest known archaeological investigations on Mescalitan Island were undertaken in 1875 by Dr. H. C. Yarrow and his party, including the Reverend Stephen Bowers. The group conducted their investigations in the historic (post-1782) cemetery, Cemetery D (figures 3 and 12 on Mescalitan Island (Putnam, et al. 1879:35–40; Glassow et al. 1986). Because of the abundance of finely crafted burial goods from the cemetery, they named the site the "Big Bonanza" (Putnam et al. 1879:35). The artifacts recovered from the Yarrow excavations and some of the human bones, particularly the crania, were later sent to the Smithsonian Institution, where they are currently housed. A sketch map in the Putnam report (figure 13) shows the village site to the north of the historic cemetery (Putnam et al. 1879:36). This historic village site (*Helo'*) is the same site (SBA-46, Site 3) that I investigated for my dissertation research (figures 3 and 12). In the 1920s and 1930s, several amateur collectors also worked on Mescalitan Island, including Robert Phelan and Clifford Hill (Glassow et al. 1986:13).

In the twentieth century, archaeological investigations of a more scientific nature were conducted at Mescalitan Island. Olson, who excavated three cemeteries as well as midden deposits in the 1920s, conducted some of the most extensive research at the site (Glassow et al. 1986:13; Olson 1930). The collections resulting from his excavations are housed at the Phoebe Hearst Museum at the University of California, Berkeley. One cemetery that Olson excavated was historic (Cemetery D) and was the same one that the Yarrow expedition excavated (figures 3 and 12). King (n.d.) has examined the artifacts from Olson's excavations at the cemetery (in

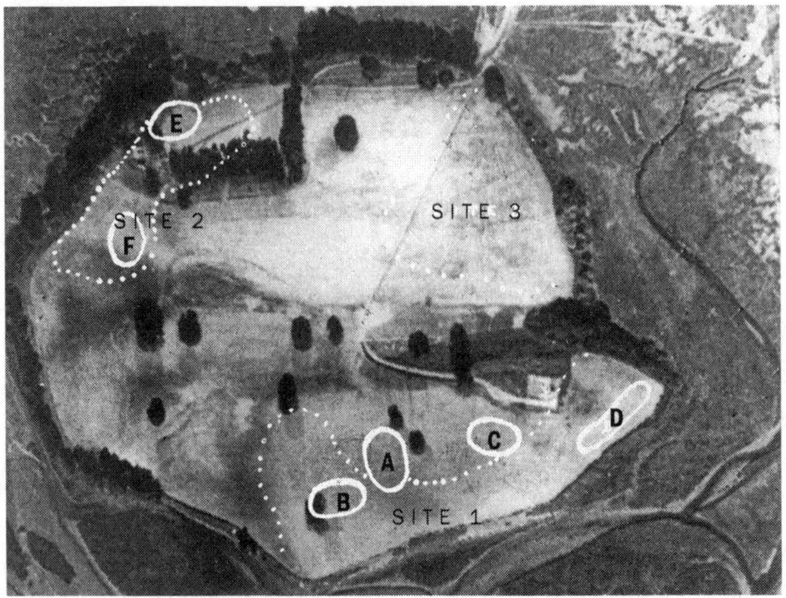

FIGURE 12 Overhead photograph of sites on Mescalitan Island

addition to the other cemeteries Olson excavated); his notes are the basis for some of this discussion. Phil Orr also conducted excavations on Mescalitan Island, working in the cemeteries in Sites 1 and 2 (Orr 1943; figure 3), but not in Cemetery D. In addition, Orr briefly excavated in Site 3, where he encountered some scattered and disarticulated human remains (Cemetery G), but a report on these excavations was never published. Other archaeologists who excavated on Mescalitan Island include Richard Van Valkenburgh (from the Los Angeles County Museum of Natural History), James Deetz, Donald S. Miller, William Allen, Roger Owen, Eugene Deuber, and Claude Warren (all from UCSB). Some of these excavations were very cursory in nature and no publications resulted from them. Many of these excavations occurred in portions of the site that predate the historic occupation.

More recent excavations took place in the 1970s and 1980s, when the Goleta Sanitation District, which has a sewage facility on the site, wanted to expand their operations in the area of Site 3, the historic village site of *Helo'*. This portion of SBA-46 is situated on an early to mid-Holocene sand-dune complex (Rockwell and Gamble 1990:3). The fact that the site is on a sand dune has significant implications for interpreting the fea-

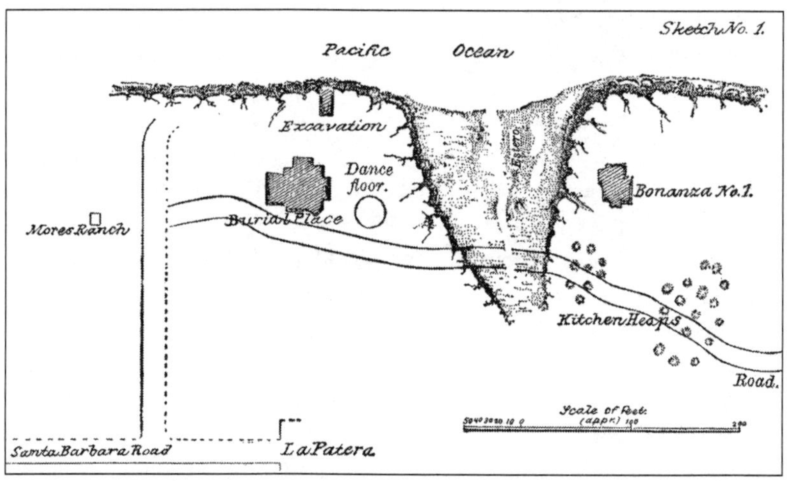

FIGURE 13 Sketch map of sites Yarrow excavated in the Goleta Slough region

tures and the artifact assemblages. Rocks that appear unused must have been deliberately brought to the location. Most rocks introduced by recent non-Indian populations are readily distinguishable from those that were used by the native inhabitants. Approximately 80% of the original site in Area 3 was undisturbed by historical earth moving before the expansion of the sanitation facility in 1987. In 1985, Scientific Resource Surveys placed 37 1 m × 1 m units in the site as part of an extensive testing program (Scientific Resource Surveys 1985:figure 4). The beads recovered from the excavations indicate that most of the excavations were in the historic component of the site (King 1985). Although not recognized as floors, several clay lenses were documented during this phase of investigations that probably were remnants of floors.

In 1986 and 1987, I undertook salvage excavations at Site 3 under the auspices of the University of California at Santa Barbara (UCSB). Stratified deposits and over 20 features were recorded during the course of these investigations. The discovery of two floors was especially significant. Although examples of excavated structural remains exist from the Chumash area (chapter 5), most remains were excavated over thirty years ago using procedures typical of that era, with relatively few excavated using refined methods such as those used in the excavations at SBA-46. Most of the features at the site were in the residential area and included the remains of hearths, roof fall, storage pits, and trash deposits. A more detailed description of these house remains, and the features and types of activities associated with them is presented in chapter 5. Since these excavations were carried out, no one has conducted archaeological investigations at SBA-46.

S'AXPILIL

This settlement was apparently the one that the Portolá expedition marched through in August 1769 (Brown 1967:32) that was located to the north of the Goleta Slough (figure 11). Crespí (Brown 2001:421) commented that in addition to the settlement on Mescalitan Island, there were two other very large villages around the slough. One of these was presumably *S'axpilil.* He also commented that these settlements had a "great many canoes", although he did not provide an exact count (nor did the others who kept records for the expedition). We also lack specific house counts for *S'axpilil.* Goyacoechea's census lists 202 inhabitants in 1796, and the mission registers list a total of 324 people for the settlement, most of whom were baptized during a 20-year period between 1787 and 1806 (Johnson 1988:135).

Archaeological investigations at the village site of *S'axpilil* (CA-SBA-60) were undertaken by UCLA archaeologists in 1960 (McKusick 1961). Three human burials and one horse burial were excavated at the site. Evidence of bead making included many micro-drills, associated platform cores, and bead blanks (Kowta 1961). Claude Warren also excavated at this site in the late 1960s when he was at UCSB.

ALKASH

This settlement was also one of the Goleta Slough towns (figure 11), although it apparently was not as large as the others around the slough. Crespí and his colleagues on the expedition did not provide detailed information on the settlement. Goycoechea gave a figure of 51 people in his 1796 census. It is believed that this site was situated on More Mesa (CA-SBA-42 and possibly CA-SBA-1696 [Johnson 1988:94]) at the southeastern side of the slough. Brown (1967:34) thought that the site was SBA-43 and was the location where Yarrow (figure 13) excavated a cemetery (labeled as "Burial Place"). Yarrow also mapped an oval-shaped feature next to the cemetery that he suggested was a dance house or "threshing floor" approximately 60 feet by 30 or 40 feet in size (Putnam et al. 1879:40).

Brown (1967:34) suggested that this site was one of two possible sites on the Pantoja map (figure 2), probably the smaller one near the cliff face. One reason that Brown believes it is the smaller site is that only 78 individuals were baptized from this settlement.

HELIYIK

Little is known about the settlement of *Heliyik* (translated as "the middle" [Johnson 1988:93]). Crespí and the other members of the Portolá expedition did not provide any specific details about the village. Goyacoechea's census lists 66 people, and a total of 102 people were baptized from *Heliyik*. Brown (1967:34) suggests that this settlement was situated to the west of the Goleta Slough and may correspond to the 16 house symbols on Pantoja's map. Johnson associates the extant village possibly with SBA-47, SBA-48, and SBA-1695.

Syuxtun

Syuxtun, situated to the west of the mouth of Mission Creek (Harrington 1928:35), was the main historic-period settlement in Santa Barbara. The earliest written record about *Syuxtun* (translated as "it forks" [Johnson 1988:93] or "where the two trails run" [Harrington 1928:31]) is from 1542, when Juan Rodríguez Cabrillo noted that the settlement (referred to as Puerto de las Sardinas) was a regional capital and had a female chief (Harrington 1928:35–36; Johnson 1986). Cabrillo spent three days at *Syuxtun*, during which time the Chumash helped supply his ship with wood and water (McLendon and Johnson 1999:30). The old female chief slept on board with some other villagers and evidently told Cabrillo that she was chief of a province between Point Conception and *Syuxtun* (Johnson 1986).

Brown has suggested that *Syuxtun* was next documented in 1603 by Geronimo Martín Palacios, who wrote the following: "It is a very large town of more than two hundred houses, and alongside it many oak-groves on the plain land and on the height many cupped pines" (Brown 1967:35). Over 150 years later, in 1769, the Portolá expedition camped within "two rifle shots" of the settlement. "We passed along one edge of the town, and so great was the press of heathen folk gathered to wait for us, that we imagined that there could not have been under seven hundred souls of all types. We greeted them, and they, all very well pleased, answered us with great noise and laughter; they were all of them weaponless" (Crespí on August 18, 1769, in Brown 2001:413–415). In Crespí's original field draft, a slightly different population estimate was given than in his final version: "and no doubt five hundred souls must have come over from the village, I should rather say six hundred: there must have been over two hundred of the men, the women also, and there were also a great many boy and girl children, grown ones and infants in arms" (Crespí on

August 18, 1769, in Brown 2001:413). On his return trip south in January of 1770, Crespí gave yet another population estimate for *Syuxtun* when he observed a funeral at the town. "There must not have been under four or five hundred souls gathered together" (Crespí on January 10, 1770, in Brown 2001:655). These somewhat conflicting population estimates are in part clarified by estimates provided by Costansó and Portolá. Costansó stated that it was "The most numerous town seen up to here: we supposed it must be over six hundred souls" (Brown 1967:36), and Portolá estimated more than 500 people lived at the settlement. Portolá also estimated approximately 40 houses at the settlement; the other diarists on the expedition did not provide any figures on house counts (Brown 1967:36). Crespí noted that there were seven canoes out fishing at *Syuxtun*, while Portolá claimed he saw 10 canoes.

Members of the Portolá expedition were treated well at *Syuxtun*. The chief of the village met the members of the expedition in Carpinteria in 1769 and guided them back to his home, where they were provided with large quantities of fresh and barbecued fish. Crespí made the following two statements upon their arrival on August 18, 1769: they brought them "So many barbecued bonito fish that seven good hundredweight-measures'[9] worth were gathered of it" (Crespí in Brown 2001:415). This would be approximately 700 pounds of fish. Crespí mentioned the fresh fish on the same day that the canoes returned from fishing. They "shortly returned in larger numbers than before, with almost every one of them bringing us two large bonitos, one in either hand, so that a great bunch of it was gotten together; I think I fall short in saying there must have been four double-hundredweights' worth of this alone" (Crespí in Brown 2001:415). Crespí was astounded with the amount of fish they were given and remarked that they must have had even more at their houses, which were virtually invisible because of all the fish laid on them. On the return trip in January of 1770, members of the expedition stopped again at "San Joaquín" in search of fish. This time it was very different; no fish were available and a large funeral was in progress. Crespí passed through *Syuxtun* a third time in May 1770.

In 1776, the Anza expedition camped near *Syuxtun*, and Pedro Font noted in his diary that the Spanish exchanged baskets for glass beads (Johnson 1986). He also saw at this time a canoe full of fish being carried to the chief, who was distinguished from others by his bearskin cape (Bolton 1930:258–259). Years later, a chief named Yanonali was mentioned when the Spanish were in the process of founding the Santa Barbara Presidio (1782) near the village of *Syuxtun*. Yanonali was described as a powerful chief whose authority reportedly extended over thirteen villages (Johnson 1986: 23–25). (Yanonali and his power as a chief are discussed in chapter 7.) Vancouver also mentioned the settlement at Santa Barbara as well as its water source when in the area in 1793. Perhaps even more significant, John Sykes, a member of the Vancouver expedition, sketched the settlement from offshore at this time (Brown 1967:35). A few years later, Goycoechea estimated that there were 125 people at *Syuxtun* for his census of 1796. Johnson (1988:84) found a total of 201 baptisms from the town.

The best documented early archaeological investigations at the site of *Syuxtun* were conducted by John P. Harrington, in conjunction with David Banks Rogers in 1923, under the auspices of Thea Hyde of the National Museum of the American Indian. Harrington, best known for his work as a linguist and ethnographer, was not considered an archaeologist, but he conducted extensive excavations at the site and published an article on the results of his investigations in 1928. Rogers (1929) wrote about these excavations independently from Harrington in a section of his 1929 book on the archaeology of the Santa Barbara Channel. Rogers returned to the site in 1924 and continued excavations for the Santa Barbara Museum of Natural History.

Harrington (1928) provided an extensive discussion of the historical accounts that mentioned *Syuxtun,* and provided a history of archaeological investigations at the site. The historic village site apparently includes both CA-SBA-27 and SBA-28 (Burton Mound), and possibly SBA-29 (Johnson 1988:94). The site has been well known in the Santa Barbara region for many years, and as a result has suffered from looting. It is believed that Cessac, who led a French archaeological expedition to southern California in the 1870s, excavated at the site in 1878. In the following decade, Bowers purportedly also excavated there (Harrington 1928:66); the mound at the northwestern end of the property was named after its owner, Lewis T. Burton, who bought the property in 1860. Rogers's (1929: Map No. 9) map of the site shows the mound surrounded by an ancient marsh. Brown (1967:35), in his analysis of the offshore sketch completed by John Sykes of the 1793 Vancouver expedition, suggests that approximately 14 to 18 houses can be seen in front of the east side of Burton Mound. Eventually, a hotel was built on the site, but it burned down on April 19, 1921 (Harrington 1928:32). It was after this event that Harrington and Rogers excavated the site.

Although Harrington's (1928) publication on Burton Mound provides a thorough discussion of the history of the site and a detailed description of the artifacts, very little data on the excavations themselves are furnished. Harrington stated that his crew placed test pits in every part of the "Ambassador" grounds and the Eaton property across the street.

Harrington (1928:71) only briefly alludes to the burials they discovered at the site. Rogers's account of the excavations at Burton Mound fills in the gaps, but still leaves scholars with a sketchy understanding of the excavations. Rogers (1929:103) stated that they shipped "no less than two tons of material and the skeletal remains of three hundred individuals" to New York, but never provides a detailed inventory of the number of burials or their grave accompaniments. In Rogers' rather general artifact descriptions, it is not clear how many artifacts were from the protohistoric and historic occupation of the site. A more detailed account of some of the artifacts is presented in chapters 6 and 7.

In 1969, Claude Warren excavated at the Burton Mound site. As part of these excavations, Warren's team found a large depression, approximately five and a half meters in diameter, which was probably the remains of a house or sweatlodge. The depth of the depression was approximately 114 cm and because of the quantity of charcoal and ash, the notes suggest that the structure may have burned. A hearth, rocks, and ash lenses were observed in the interior of the structure. A date for this structure has never been published.

Shalawa

The settlement of *Shalawa* was situated at the mouth of Sycamore Canyon, where the modern town of Montecito is located, and was probably one of the burned villages that Crespí observed between Carpinteria and Santa Barbara (Brown 1967:36). (The name was translated tentatively as "to kill" by Johnson [1988:93]; Richard Applegate [1975:23] states that *'alawah* in Barbareño means "one that spreads over"). Crespí noted two towns that had been burned approximately two to three months before their arrival (Brown 2001:413). Two chiefs who accompanied the expedition on their journey between Carpinteria and Santa Barbara, reported that "mountain heathens not long ago had destroyed two big villages, killing everyone, young and old, and afterward burning their houses as well" (Crespí on August 18, 1769, in Brown 2001:411–413). Brown (1967) determined that the larger of the two burned settlements was the one in Montecito. (More on the significance of this and other events involving conflict and warfare are presented in chaper 9). This site was recorded by Rogers (1929) as CA-SBA-17; Brown [1967] states that it is Rogers's site SBA-19. The settlement was apparently reoccupied after it was burned, as Font mentioned the site in his 1776 journal. The village also appears on Pantoja's map of 1782 (Brown 1967:36). Fourteen years later,

Goycoechea noted that there was a female chief there when he recorded 62 inhabitants in his census (Brown 1967:37). Johnson (1988:84) found 87 baptisms from *Shalawa* in the mission registers.

Rogers (1929:72–80) excavated 42 burials at the site (CA-SBA-17), but never found any historic remains. He tentatively suggested that the site was occupied between AD 900 and 1500.

Q'oloq'

This settlement, situated at the mouth of Toro Canyon, was the first and the smaller of the two burned villages noted by Crespí in August 1769 as the expedition headed to Monterey. It, too, was reoccupied by the time Font passed by in 1776; however, he listed it under the same name as the settlement of Carpinteria (Brown 1967:37). Goycoechea recorded 31 individuals at the settlement in 1796. A total of 48 people were eventually baptized from this settlement, indicating that it was one of the smaller settlements on the mainland coast.

Rogers (1929:65–68) worked at CA-SBA-13 and thought it was the site of *Q'oloq'*, but did not note historic artifacts there. He excavated numerous burials, including what he interpreted to be a single tomb with five skeletons. This consisted of a series of 12 flat slabs of stone (placed upright) that formed a ring about four feet in diameter around the burials. Within these was a bowl-shaped feature of stones covered with red baked clay. Charcoal and ash from the firing of the pit could also be seen. The five flexed burials were placed closely together on their right sides pointing northwest, lacked grave goods, and were covered with a platform of 28 flat stones. Rogers believed that they were all placed in the grave at about the same time. Another clay-lined and fired pit near this tomb was found that also had a series of stone slabs standing on end, but it was devoid of burials. Instead, there was a whale bone slab at the bottom of the pit. Rogers, who interpreted this feature as an unused tomb, noted that both features required a considerable investment of labor and were unusual. King (1993) suggested that SBA-12 or SBA-13 may be the historic site of *Q'oloq'*.

Mishopshno

Members of the Portolá expedition were impressed with this town when it was encountered on August 17, 1769, on their march from Ventura. "We saw at the very edge of the sea a large village or very regular town here at this point, appearing at a distance as though it were a shipyard, because at the moment they were building a canoe that still had its topmost plank lacking from it (and this spot was dubbed by the soldiers *La Carpintería*, the Carpenter Shop)" (Crespí in Brown 2001:407). Crespí only mentioned two canoes, in addition to the one that was under construction, at *Mishopshno* (translated tentatively as "correspondence" [Johnson 1988:93]). This differed considerably from the seven canoes that Portolá observed. Both Portolá and Crespí estimated that there were 38 houses at the settlement, in contrast to the 32 houses noted by Costansó. Crespí did not mention the number of inhabitants until May 2, 1770, when he stated that there were about 500 "souls" at the town (Crespí in Brown 2001:699). It was also on this date that Crespí noted the spring of "pitch" or asphaltum at the site (see chapter 7). Portolá's population estimate of 300 inhabitants was considerably lower than that given by Crespí. Goycoechea counted 97 individuals at *Mishopshno* and identified three chiefs there in his 1796 census (Brown 1967:38). Mission records indicate that there were 135 baptisms from *Mishopshno* (Johnson 1988:84).

The Spanish were well provisioned on their trip north in August of 1769 by the inhabitants of *Mishopshno,* who brought them fresh and barbecued bonito, bowls of gruel, and entertainment in the form of dancing and singing. On their return trip south, Crespí did not mention whether they were provided with food at specific settlements, but did make the following statement at Ventura on January 11, 1770:

> They favored us a great deal with a good many large fresh sardines at all the towns, though at these last places there was not such plenty as at the first ones; but God be thanked, everyone has been succored by a good deal of fish. Lieutenant Don Pedro Fages has gotten together about three double-hundredweights' worth of dried fish for the officers and ourselves in trade for beads and ribbons, and salt as well, which we had none of, with all of which we will be able to get along better until such times as God is pleased for us to reach the wished for harbor of San Diego once more (Crespí in Brown 2001:657).

On May 1, 1770, when the Expedition headed north for the second time, the Spanish gave the Chumash some beads in exchange for "a few large bonitos and needlefish" (Crespí in Brown 2001:697). Crespí also remarked on the sandy embayment here with numerous live oak stands, cottonwoods, and sycamores.

Unfortunately illicit looting, asphaltum mining, and development over the last 150 years has had a tremendous impact on the remains of this important settlement. Rogers (1929) identified the sites of CA-SBA-7 and CA-SBA-6 as the historic settlement, but only conducted limited excavations in the area. The sites span a long period of time, and according to Rogers, include material from his "Oak Grove," "Hunting," and "Canaliño" periods. Rogers believed the area around the asphaltum seep was associated with the Canaliño occupation. By the time Rogers first worked at SBA-7, mining of the asphaltum by the Spanish, Mexicans, and Americans had destroyed the seep. Nevertheless, Rogers was able to roughly delineate the area that he believed was used as a Late period cemetery. Although Rogers noted that SBA-7 had been heavily looted, he did find two undisturbed burials and three skulls associated with the later occupation of the site. Rogers (1929:51–52) thought he could distinguish male and female cemeteries here, but his evidence is meager at best.

Several important excavations occurred at the site before Rogers investigated it. Reverend Bowers dug a cemetery there on February 6, 1877, and recovered pestles, mortars, comals, pipes, and beads. Immediately after the Bowers investigations, Henry Chapman Ford (1887) obtained permission to continue excavating in the same area, where he uncovered an unknown number of burials two to five feet below the surface. A variety of artifacts, including mortars, steatite ollas and comals, drills, whale bone, pottery, and glass and shell beads was noted. Based on his brief description, it appears that at least some of the burials were from the historic occupation of the site. He described one burial that had slabs of redwood with asphaltum on them on each side of the individual. This person may have been buried inside a plank canoe.

Interest in the sites did not subside over the years as amateurs and archaeologists continued to excavate in cemeteries there. Lucien Higgins, who owned the land where SBA-6 was recorded, purportedly plowed up burials in a cemetery south of the marsh. In addition, his father Phineas C. Higgins (David Earle, personal communication 2006), excavated at least 40 burials behind the old asphaltum mine, including one with a bronze ornament in association (Kirkish and Smith 1997). In early December of 1929 when the Getty Oil Company made a cut towards the pier, an amateur by the name of John Rock excavated 30–40 burials to the east of the asphaltum mine (Rock 1930). He commented that the majority of burials were very shallow and listed numerous artifacts, including a porpoise effigy, charm stones, large stone beads, arrow points, red ochre, "killed" bowls (which may have been mortars), shell beads, and a pottery vase.

Bryan (1931) later reported that he excavated at the site in early 1930, after an oil company unknowingly ripped through the center of the cemetery when it built a road to the beach. This is probably the same construction episode that Rock noted. Bryan reported that numerous skeletons and artifacts were unearthed, resulting in the public descending upon the site with shovels, screens, and picks (Bryan 1931:177). Although Bryan was able to obtain a permit for excavation, he initially was only able to excavate on weekends, so the looting continued. One of the more unusual finds noted by Bryan (1931) was a skull with an arrow point embedded in the forehead. A second skeleton with an arrow point below the skull was also found. Stone grave markers, shell beads and ornaments, asphaltum lumps, mortars, and pestles are a just a few of the artifact types that he found during the excavations. He also obtained a "three-edge stone drill" that is illustrated in his article (Bryan 1931:180) and which appears to be a canoe drill (Gamble 2002a). Arthur Sanger joined Bryan in the excavations at the site and sent some of the finds to the "Los Angeles Museum" (now the Los Angeles County Museum of Natural History).

Subsequent excavations were undertaken by Ronald Olson, Phil Orr, James Bennyhoff, and Don Wood (Kirkish and Smith 1997). Olson, from UC Berkeley, excavated in four areas of the site shortly after Rogers' investigations. Not surprisingly, he found disturbed burials, but little else. In 1942, Phil Orr from the Santa Barbara Museum of Natural History excavated in a ten square foot area to the west of a small creek and estero (Kirkish and Smith 1997). He apparently found only fragmentary human remains. In 1948, Bennyhoff excavated on a knoll at Concha Loma Drive, where he found extended burials, manos, and metates (McKusick 1961). Because manos and metates are not found during the late prehistoric or historic periods in the region, it is likely that these excavations were made in the earlier components at the site.

One of the most recent significant archaeological investigations at the site was carried out in 1969 when Don Wood (1972) from the California Department of Parks and Recreation conducted excavations for a road extension south of Calle Ocho. He encountered 10 burials lacking grave associations, except for one with a highly polished whale rib. He also excavated house floors at the site, but barely reported on them. Wood mentioned that manos were found at the site, indicating that he also dug in early contexts.

Shuku

The Portolá Expedition was accompanied by 14 Chumash Indians between Pitas Point and the town of *Shuku* at Rincon Point, where they found a settlement on a small knoll "about fifty paces" from the Pacific Ocean. "Outside their houses waiting for us stood a large throng of very good, well-behaved friendly heathens.. . . On reaching here we passed in among the very houses of the village, as that was how the way lay. They were all of them unarmed, and greeted us with great noise and laughter" (Crespí in Brown 2001:403). Crespí noted that they had their house roofs packed with barbecued bonitos and needlefish, as well as with raw ones that had been cut open to dry. He counted 60 houses at the settlement, considerably more than the "thirty-some houses" observed by Portolá. In addition, Crespí (Brown 2001:403) recorded six or seven canoes that were out fishing, some of which were eight yards long. Portolá also noted seven canoes (Brown 1967:39). Later in May 1770, Crespí (Brown 2001:697) recorded three or four canoes out of the water and "as many more other ones" out fishing. Six years later when Font visited the town in February 1776, he counted nine canoes and an additional one that was "out of repair" (Brown 1967:39).

Crespí did not provide an estimate of inhabitants at Rincon, only remarking that they could not be counted because they stood so close to each other. Portolá recorded over 300 people, and Costansó noted that more people were at Rincon than at Ventura (Brown 1967:39). In May of 1770, as they passed on their way south, Crespí (in Brown 2001:697) wrote that the town was empty except for some women who were in their houses. He speculated that the men must be out gathering seeds.

An abundance of fish was offered to the expedition when they arrived at *Shuku* in August of 1769. "Once camp was set up, the whole village came over with so much fresh bonito and needlefish, and the same kinds served barbecued, that there could not have been less than three good double-hundredweights' worth of it" (Crespí in Brown 2001:405). In return for the fish, the officers gave the Chumash beads. In response, the Chumash played music and danced until they were given more beads and told to stop. In January when the expedition headed south, Crespí made the general statement about being offered fish at most of the settlements (see above), but made no comments about fish when they passed through this village in May 1770.

The mission records indicate that 131 people from *Shuku* were baptized (Johnson 1988:84), and Goycoechea counted 68 "souls" at *Shuku* in 1796 for his census (Brown 1967:39). No chiefs were identified by Goycoechea or in the mission records.

The site of *Shuku* is situated on the Ventura–Santa Barbara County line, and for many years both CA-VEN-62 and CA-SBA-1 were suggested as the historic village location (Johnson 1988:94; Rogers 1929). Brown

(1967) stated that Rogers erroneously thought that VEN-62 was the historic settlement. King (1980a) has provided evidence that Brown was wrong and that VEN-62 is the protohistoric and historic site of *Shuku*, and that SBA-1 is not associated with the historic occupation of the site.

The history of archaeological research at Rincon is complex, with numerous excavations taking place at the site during the last 125 years. Although pothunters visited the site in the late 1800s, the earliest documented excavations were those completed by Bowers in 1875, 1876, and 1878 (Benson 1997; King 1980a). Bowers, who excavated at least four cemeteries and exhumed over a hundred burials, some with steatite ollas and comals, suggested that the site covered at least 100 acres (King 1980a:4). The location of the cemeteries can be seen in a map made by Bowers published in Benson (1997:Figure 6.5). Others who conducted archaeological investigations at Rincon Point were David Banks Rogers, Ronald L. Olson, Bill Purvis, Phil Orr, J. L. Nichols, E. R. Prince, Patricia Lyon, Patrick Finnerty, Keith Johnson, Edwin Gary Stickel, Michael Glassow, John Johnson, and various UCSB archaeologists (for a complete discussion see King 1980a). Five sites, SBA-1, SBA-119, SBA-141, Area D, and VEN-62A, have been identified at Rincon Point (Erlandson 1991b; King 1980a). VEN-62A is the largest site at Rincon and apparently is the deepest, with a depth of ten to twelve feet (King 1980a). King (1980a) has suggested that the artifacts from VEN-62A indicate that this area of Rincon Point was in use from about AD 700 or 900 until the period of Spanish colonization. Olson, who also excavated at this site (though not primarily in the cemetery), found a Spanish coin dated 1790 (King 1980a:3–23).

Shisholop South

The settlement of *Shisholop* (the one near the southern end of the Channel), translated as "in the mud" (Johnson 1988:93), was situated in Ventura approximately a half mile east of the mouth of the Ventura River (Greenwood and Browne 1969). When Crespí and the other expedition members first approached this settlement, they came from Saticoy in the interior. They made particular note of the size of *Shisholop* and the houses when they encountered the first major coastal settlement in the Santa Barbara Channel region:

> We went over to the village, and they greeted us with great noise and laughter. They were all unarmed. We counted 30 very large houses, as I have said, with a great many people, and this village lies at the edge of the sea. We stopped a while,

and our Governor asked for the head chief, and out came a woman who said that she was the chief's wife but he himself was out fishing in one of three canoes that we had in sight fishing nearby (Crespí in Brown 2001:389).

After the Spanish expedition set up camp nearby, the "head chief" returned from fishing and brought the men bowls of "very well flavored gruels" and a huge quantity of fish. The Governor, Fages, Costansó, Crespí and another priest were then requested to come back to *Shisholop*, where they were invited inside the houses. Crespí wrote a detailed description of the houses and the activities that occurred inside them, leaving us with one of the best accounts on the subject (see chapter 5 for a complete description).

While at *Shisholop*, Crespí provided details on the wooden plank canoes. He was informed by the chief at *Shisholop* that there were 15 canoes associated with the town, but that most of them had gone to the islands to inform the inhabitants there about the visiting Spanish expedition (Crespí in Brown 2001:397). Portolá reported that he had seen three canoes at this settlement, similar to the count that Crespí provided. All three individuals on the expedition who kept a journal—Costansó, Portolá, and Crespí—noted 30 houses at the settlement (table 10). Portolá was the only one of the three that provided a population estimate, which was about 300 "heathens." A total of 295 individuals were baptized from *Shisholop* (McLendon and Johnson 1999:Table VIII-5). Goycoechea's census of 1796 listed a population of 86 at the village (Brown 1967:43).

The archaeological site of CA-VEN-3 is believed to be the historic settlement of *Shisholop*. The site is situated on a marine terrace that overlooks the Pacific Ocean and the four northern Channel Islands. The most extensive excavations at the site were undertaken by Greenwood and Browne (1969) in 1965 and 1967. In their report, they mistakenly identified the settlement as being equivalent to the place that Cabrillo named "Pueblo de las Canoas," but most scholars believe that that name refered to the historic settlement of *Muwu* (King 2000; Wagner 1929). Greenwood and Browne (1969:6) noted that the site was severely eroded when they worked there, with an approximate loss of land of 150 feet in one century, leaving only about one third of the original settlement. One burial, with no grave associations, and four features with fire-altered rock were recorded at the site. Thousands of beads were also found, including glass beads and *Olivella biplicata* rough disc beads typical of the historic period in the Santa Barbara Channel region (King 1990a). Aboriginal pottery, steatite vessel fragments, mortars, pestles, fish hooks, and other artifacts characteristic of the protohistoric and historic periods period were also recovered. Greenwood and Browne (1969:48) suggest that the settlement was probably a provincial capital that was occupied "not too many centuries before Cabrillo's visit and not surviving too long after the beginning of the Mission Period."

Muwu

The route of the Portolá expedition bypassed the settlement of *Muwu* (translated as "beach" [King and Johnson 1999:73]) and others to the southeast; therefore, the detailed diaries from 1769 are unavailable. Nevertheless, it is believed that Cabrillo saw *Muwu* in 1542 and named the village "Pueblo de las Canoas" (King and Johnson 1999:73; Wagner 1929:76). The next encounter of significance at *Muwu* was in 1602, when Vizcaino sailed from Catalina Island to *Muwu*. Father Antonio de la Ascensión, who was on the voyage, wrote a detailed account concerning *Muwu*:

When the fleet was in sight of the mainland, and near one of their islands, which was named "Santa Barbara," the first of the channel, a canoe came flying out from the mainland with four men propelling it. Aboard was an Indian with his son and other Indians who accompanied him, who gave us to understand that he was the king or lord of that country. This canoe came up to the Capitana, and with great assiduity and swiftness made three turns around it, all on board singing in their language in the manner and the tone in which the Indians of New Spain sing in their mitotes, or dances. They then came up to the ship and the principal Indian or petty king, grasping the end of the rope that was passed to them, came aboard without any suspicion or fear whatever, and the first thing he did upon entering the ship was to make another three turns around the waist, singing in the same tone. This ceremony being concluded, standing before the General and the rest, he commenced a long harangue in his language, of which we could not understand a word. Having finished this, he explained by intelligible signs that the people of the Isla de Santa Catalina had notified him by four posts in canoes that the ships had arrived there and that the people on board wore clothes and beards and were kind-hearted and of good demeanor, having entertained them and given them many things, and that he should come and see us. By reason of this news he had come there to offer his country and what entertainment he could supply if we wished to receive it. He begged and prayed us to come to the shore with the ship, saying he would provide us with everything necessary. As he did not see any woman on the ship, he asked by signs if we had any, pointing to his private parts and giving us clearly to understand what he wished to say. The General told him he did not have any, nor were they necessary. The Indian then importuned the General with more energy for all to go to ashore, promising to give each one ten women to serve them and entertain them. At this all of us laughed very much and the chief, thinking that we were deriding him, and that we thought he would not do as he promised, renewed his offers, and asked the General to send ashore a soldier in the canoe in which he had come to see with his own eyes if it was true that he could comply with what he promised, saying that he would remain as a hostage with his son while the soldier went and returned to inform himself about the truth of it. The General held a council about this, and it was decided as it was already night nothing should be done until the following day, but when it was dawn, some should go ashore to see if there was a safe and commodious port where the ships could remain at anchor, and if there was one, they would go there, and that the Indian should go back to his country that night to make the necessary arrangements. With this they dismissed him, the General having given him some things. He went away well paid and contented with the good behavior and kindness which he saw in those whom he expected to have as guests on the following day, and to get something ready with which to entertain them (Wagner 1929:239–240).

Ascensión appeared relieved when about an hour later a southeast wind came up and they sailed north. Wagner, who translated the Spanish journal, believed that the identification of the island in the beginning of the quote as "Santa Barbara" Island was probably incorrect and should have been Anacapa Island. In a later footnote, Wagner identified the Chumash chief as coming from the Mugu towns.

The Mugu towns consisted of several historic settlements near the Mugu lagoon, which were collectively identified in the mission registers as *Muwu* (King and Johnson 1999:74). These settlements included *Muwu*, *Simo'mo*, and *Wixatset* (CA-VEN-11, VEN-24, VEN-100, and VEN-110). Mission records indicate that more people (191 inhabitants) were baptized from *Muwu* than from any other town in the Santa Monica Mountains (McLendon and Johnson 1999:264 and Table 6.1). Mariano *Wataitset'*, the last chief from *Muwu* and the son of *Halashu* (the big chief of *Muwu*), was baptized at Mission San Buenaventura in 1802 (King 2000:54). *Muwu* was considered an important capital and ceremonial center (see chapter 7).

The archaeological site of VEN-11 is the site most often identified with the historic settlement of *Muwu* (Gamble et al. 1995; Martz et al. 1995). The site is approximately one and a quarter miles northwest of Point Mugu, and consists of a dense shell midden with dark greasy soil and an abundance of faunal remains, including whole shells, and mammal and fish bone (Gamble et al. 1995).

Like many historic village sites, VEN-11 has been investigated by numerous individuals. Some of the earliest documented excavations at *Muwu* and other sites in the region were conducted by Bowers in 1879. His notes are characteristically brief, but he does mention that they found ollas, mortars, pestles, shell beads, and ornaments at *Muwu* (VEN-11, VEN-84 or at VEN-110) (Benson 1997:140). In the mid 1920s, John P. Harrington and David B. Rogers investigated VEN-11. Harrington, who excavated for a two-week period under the auspices of the Heye Foundation (now the National Museum of the American Indian), reported that the burials were similar to those that he had found at Burton Mound. According to a 1920s newspaper article on the excavations, Harrington found "many swordfish swords," glass beads, and "broken utensils" (Martz et al. 1995:3–4).

Robert Wubben, an amateur archaeologist, also collected artifacts at VEN-11 during the 1920s, in an attempt to salvage information when the Roosevelt Highway (Route 1) cut through the site. Wubben and his father sifted through piles of soil pushed to the side by the steam shovels. One rare find was a cache of musical instruments that included three bull roarers and eight deer-bone tibia flutes (Johnson, personal communication 2002). These artifacts are now curated at the Santa Barbara Museum of Natural History.

In 1929 and 1933, Arthur Woodward and Richard Van Valkenburgh from the Anthropology Department of the Los Angeles County Museum of Natural History directed excavations at VEN-11 with funding from C. Van Bergen (Woodward 1933). They recorded ten house pits, one sweatlodge, and a cemetery. In one of the eight structures that they excavated, an infant burial was discovered. (More detailed descriptions of the structures are presented in chapter 5.) This was in addition to the twelve burials, some of which had grave goods, that they excavated in the cemetery. In 1969, Tom King filed an update letter in the site record in which he stated that Woodward's map of the site appeared highly accurate in its portrayal of site boundaries and structure locations (Gamble et al. 1995). By comparing the old site photos with the field features, King was able to identify the sweatlodge near the eastern edge of the site as Woodward's "House E," as well as backdirt piles from the 1929 excavations. He also noted a few pothunter's holes, but characterized these disturbances as light.

Fairly extensive excavations did not occur again at VEN-11 until 1976, when Holly Love and Rheta Resnick investigated the site. They excavated 50 units over a two-year period and each completed Masters theses focused on the subsistence remains recovered (Love 1980; Resnick 1980). Love and Resnick (1979:10–19) also wrote a brief article on the site and their work in progress.

In 1994, UCLA archaeologists under my direction (Gamble et al. 1995) mapped the site again and attempted to identify previous excavation units using old photographs and maps. The remains of the probable sweat lodge

(Woodward's House E) were still visible. In addition, an irregular pile of dirt in the area of Houses A, B, C, and G was observed that may represent the back-dirt pile from the 1932 excavations. Twelve looter's pits were also found in 1994, some of which were recent.

Lisiqishi

The settlement of *Lisiqishi*, which was situated 12 km to the southeast of *Muwu* near the mouth of Arroyo Sequit, was much smaller than *Muwu*. We know that 60 Chumash individuals were baptized from this village (McLendon and Johnson 1999:Table 6.1), but no early historic accounts about this or any other coastal Chumash settlement to the east of *Muwu* are known to exist.

The archaeological site of CA-LAN-52 is believed to be the remains of *Lisiqishi* (King 2000:54). O. T. Littleton conducted excavations here between 1939 and 1942 (Burnett 1944); however, many of the artifacts 're-covered' from this and other sites in the Santa Monica Mountains and published in Burnett are believed to be fakes (Gamble 2002c; Lee 1993). Gamble (2002c) studied Littleton's collection at the National Museum of the American Indian and has suggested that some items in the assemblage from CA-LAN-52 may be authentic, such as fishhooks, bone barbs, asphaltum with basketry impressions, red ochre cakes, a swordfish cup, cordage, wooden canoe planks, asphaltum canoe plugs, and other asphaltum. Most of these items are typical of the protohistoric and historic periods in the Santa Barbara Channel region. Burnett (1944:16–17) stated that the cemetery was near one end of the site and measured approximately "60 x 40 feet." He claimed that about 140 burials were excavated, 17 of which had wooden canoe planks in association. UCLA, the Archaeological Survey Association of Southern California, and the California Department of Parks and Recreation also excavated at the site (Curtis 1959, 1963; King 2000).

Sumo

It is believed that the place name *Sumo* (translated as "abundance" in the *Humaliwu* Chumash dialect [King 2000]) probably referred to all of the Point Dume area (King 2000:55). Mission records indicate that 38 individuals were baptized from *Sumo*. Numerous archaeological sites from different time periods have been recorded in the vicinity of Point Dume. One site with historic artifacts (CA-LAN-207 at Paradise Cove) was probably the settlement of *Sumo* (King 2000:55).

Lojostogni

This historic village was probably located at the mouth of Solstice Canyon (CA-LAN-210), where historic beads have been found (Dillon 1987; King 2000:55). *Lojostogni* was a relatively small settlement compared with other historic settlements; only 37 individuals from there have been identified in the baptismal records (King and Johnson 1999:71). The number of baptisms from this site may not be accurate because at Mission San Fernando, individuals were not always baptized by village, and some that were actually from *Lojostogni* evidently were baptized as coming from *Humaliwo.*

Humaliwo

The settlement of *Humaliwo* (probably translated as "the surf sounds loudly" [King 2000:55]) was located within the modern city of Malibu, which carries its name. A total of 118 individuals were baptized from *Humaliwo*, making it the second largest coastal settlement in the Santa Monica Mountains, with *Muwu* being the largest. Mission records identify one person from *Humaliwo* as the village chief, and state that he originally lived on Catalina Island (King 1994:78). Ethnographic and ethnohistoric data indicate that the Chumash Indians of the Santa Monica Mountains and their neighbors, the Western Tongva (Gabrielino), considered *Humaliwo* an important political center (King 1994:65). The role of *Humaliwo* in the Chumash political system is discussed further in chapter 7.

CA-LAN-264, situated near the Malibu Lagoon, has been identified as the historic settlement of *Humaliwo.* King suggests that CA-LAN-690, to the east of LAN-64, was also part of the historic settlement, because a number of historic period beads were found at that site. In addition to the historic component at the site, prehistoric occupation dates to approximately 2500 BP. LAN-64 was originally recorded in February of 1959 by R. S. Watson, but was not officially investigated until 1964, when a field class from UCLA under the direction of Jay Ruby excavated in some of the earlier components of the site (Gamble et al. 1996), as well as in the historic components. Subsequent excavations at the site by UCLA field classes occurred between 1972 and 1975. Collections resulting from these excavations are curated at the UCLA Fowler Museum of Cultural History Archaeological Collections Facility.

The most significant archaeological investigations of the historic component at CA-LAN-64 occurred in 1972, when the entire historic cemetery was excavated under the direction of Nelson Leonard and Christopher Donnan (Martz 1984:394). Several reports, theses, and publications resulted from these excavations (Bickford 1982; Gamble et al. 1995; Gibson 1975, 1987; Green 1999; Martz 1984; Suchey et al. 1972; Walker et al. 1996), with one of the most thorough and recent analyses completed by Gamble and her colleagues (2001). Beads indicate that use of the historic cemetery began in A.D. 1775 and ended in 1805 (Gibson 1975:117; King 1996). Gamble, Walker, and Russell (2001) examined several independent data sources from the cemetery and found strong evidence for the existence of a ranked society with a hereditary elite in the historic cemetery as well as in earlier periods. A more thorough discussion about status, rank, and leadership at *Humaliwo* can be found in chapter 7.

Considerable interaction between the Spanish and the Chumash inhabitants of *Humaliwo* apparently occurred. Grave goods from the historic cemetery show that at the time it was in use, at least some of the Chumash were working as cowboys (*vaqueros*) on the ranchos that had been established in the Los Angeles region.

Summary

Thousands of Chumash Indians inhabited the large villages and towns along the Santa Barbara Channel coast at the time of European contact. Houses were clustered in settlements at the shore's edge in places where fresh water was available in nearby streams and springs. Many settlements were near lagoons, such as those located around the Goleta Slough, where the population exceeded 2000 people in 1769. Sandy beaches, which were usually adjacent to communities, served as ideal landing spots for plank boats. Most villages south of Point Conception had at least a few plank canoes, and several larger settlements had between 10 and 16 canoes. Dome-shaped house roofs often were piled high with fresh or dried sardines, anchovies, bonito, and other fish that supplied the dense populations with an abundance of food. Fish and native seeds, nuts, and grains were so plentiful that the Chumash gave vast quantities to the Portolá expedition in 1769 and 1770. These were not trivial amounts if one considers that the expedition consisted of approximately 60 men, in addition to their mules and horses (see Beebe and Senkewicz 2001:114–115).

Dramatic demographic changes occurred in the Chumash region after European contact, only some of which have been fully documented. Erlandson and Bartoy (1995) suggest that the coastal Chumash would have been highly susceptible to Old World diseases during the protohistoric period prior to 1769. They note that contact between members of several maritime expeditions and the Chumash living along the coast in the sixteenth and seventeenth centuries was extensive and may have impacted the health of the Chumash. Preston (1996) not only concurs with Erlandson and Bartoy's suggestion that disease may have entered California prior to the establishment of the missions, but proposes that it was probable, although he too lacks definitive evidence. Clearly, the populations in the Santa Barbara Channel region were severely impacted during the mission era.

Unfortunately, population declines prior to the mission period, combined with questionable population estimates provided in early historic accounts, make it extremely difficult to accurately determine the population of the Chumash in 1769. Nevertheless, scholars in the region are fortunate to have multiple sources of information available when attempting demographic studies. Johnson (1988:108–116) has suggested that the population figures provided in the 1769–1770 accounts may have been exaggerated and has instead chosen to use the number of baptisms as an index of aboriginal population size. I believe that the population figures in the 1769–1770 accounts are on the whole reliable, and agree with Brown's (1967) strategy of using Crespí's estimates when available. I do not, however, agree with Brown's changes to the Portolá estimates, and instead have used the figures given in the diaries. I agree with Johnson that some of the estimates from the Portolá expedition are inaccurate. Nevertheless, because the coastal Chumash towns may have been impacted by disease prior to 1769 (Erlandson and Bartoy 1995; Preston 1996), the Portolá estimates may in fact be too low. Until we unearth more data on the subject, it will be difficult to derive a totally accurate population estimate for the Chumash prior to European contact; however, population sizes and densities were clearly impressive.

According to estimates provided by members of the Portolá expedition, the sizes of settlements on the mainland coast of the Santa Barbara Channel ranged between 60 and 800 or possibly 1000 people. Most communities had at least 200 inhabitants, but a number had 500 or more (figure 6). Based on mission registers and other early historic documents, Johnson (1988) has suggested that a settlement hierarchy existed, with the larger towns having some authority over smaller settlements, and that together these settlement clusters could be considered federations or "provinces" (see chapter 7 for further discussion). The data that are presented in this chapter support the idea of a settlement hierarchy at the time of historic contact. Population figures derived from multiple sources indicate that the largest settlements at the time of European contact were located in the geographic center of the Chumash region, with the smaller settlements situated at some distance from the central region (figures 6 and 7). This settlement pattern was undoubtedly influenced at least in part by the active exchange system of the Chumash involving the islands, the mainland coast, and the interior regions. In upcoming chapters, we will revisit the subject of settlement hierarchy.

In summary, the data presented in this chapter suggest that the Chumash had an abundance of food, even in the winter months, and that they were able to support relatively dense populations without agriculture. They lived in large domed houses clustered closely together in settlements. These settlements were somewhat evenly spaced at every major drainage along the coast. One question that remains to be answered is how the Chumash were able to maintain and manage such dense levels of population. This and related issues will be addressed in the following chapters. First, though, we will examine village and household organization and the role of each in the production, consumption, and exchange of goods and services at the time of historic contact.

CHAPTER 5

Village and Household Organization

This chief, after a long while, invited us to come to his village, and our Governor, Don Pedro Fages, Don Miguel Costansó, and we two Fathers, with some soldiers, went over. He showed us over his whole village, where all the house roofs were piled thick with barbecued fish, or in other cases fish of the sorts they had brought us, being dried. Some of the houses, are extremely large; for curiosity's sake, we went inside some of them, and were struck with wonder at the size, for without any doubt at all they must be able to lodge sixty persons and more without hindrance. They have hurdles about a yard and a half in height, such that we imagined that they must sleep off the floor. There were women distributed among various lodgings within these houses, some of whom were grinding for gruel, others toasting the seeds, and others making baskets and bowls, made so finely out of rushes, with such patterns and pictures, as to strike one with wonder.

Crespí on August 14, 1769, in Brown 2001:391

Crespí and other members of the expedition had the unusual opportunity to view the interior of several Chumash houses before the Europeans colonized the region. Crespí was impressed with the spacious appearance of the interior of the houses with their raised beds. He observed women busy cooking and making baskets, but did not refer to any men in the houses.

Crespí's observations serve as a starting point for this chapter, where life in a typical Chumash household along the mainland coast in the 1700s is examined. Ethnohistoric, ethnographic, and archaeological data are used to explore strategies of social organization, including settlement hierarchy, storage capabilities, feasting behavior, craft production, exchange networks, social differentiation, and gender. The roles that households and settlements played in the region's economic, political, and ceremonial interactions are also considered.

The most detailed ethnographic descriptions of Chumash villages and structures come from John P. Harrington's notes, and have been summarized in Hudson and Blackburn's (1983, 1986) volumes on Chumash material culture. Additional information comes from early diaries and other ethnohistoric accounts of the region.

Ethnohistoric and Ethnographic Descriptions of Village Organization and Structures

The Chumash lacked monumental architecture, a trait that is often associated with complex societies; however, they employed a variety of structures and outdoor spaces for a wide range of activities (figure 14). Some of the earliest descriptions of settlements indicate that the Chumash clustered their houses in rows with "streets" between them (e.g., see opening quotations in chapter 1 and in this chapter). Densely packed houses in settlements along the coast were noted in the earliest historic sources and were observed as late as 1793, when Menzies wrote the following statement about Chumash settlements along the Santa Barbara Channel coast: "These Natives live in Villages of from 20 to 40 huts each which are

FIGURE 14 Painting of the village of *Humaliwu* by Julie Van Zandt May at the Malibu Lagoon Museum.

crouded [*sic*] together & much larger than any we saw about the Settlements to the Northward" (Eastwood 1924:325). Pantoja's maps of coastal Chumash villages in 1782 (e.g., *Shisholop* at Point Conception [Brown 1967:Figure 12; King and Craig 1978:Map 1] confirm this pattern of closely-packed houses arranged in rows; however, they lack details about the types of structures and outdoor activity areas that existed in Chumash villages. Despite this lack of detail, we are able to piece that information together for traditional coastal Chumash settlements. We first look at ethnographic and ethnohistoric accounts, and then discuss archaeological data on the subject.

DANCE GROUNDS

Unlike the Patwin and other tribes in central California, the Chumash lacked large dance houses; instead, they used open-air dance grounds that were specifically dedicated for use in ceremonial gatherings. These were flat areas partially surrounded by a windbreak made of poles or mats (Hudson and Blackburn 1986:50). One of the earliest descriptions of a possible dance ground (in Chumash or Island Gabrielino territory) comes from the Cabrillo expedition of 1542:

> In their towns they have large plazas and circular enclosures around which imbedded in the ground are many stone posts which stand about three palm-lengths above it. In the middle of these enclosures there are many very thick timbers like masts sunk in the ground. These are covered with many paintings, and we thought they must worship them because when they danced they did so around the inside of the enclosure (Wagner 1929:88).

L. King (1969:53) interpreted Cabrillo's description as depicting a cemetery; however, it is unclear whether this was a cemetery or a dance area[10]. Another reference to a possible dance area is in the quote by Crespí that can be seen in the section below on cemeteries.

One of the most complete ethnographic accounts of the Chumash dance area comes from one of John P. Harrington's consultants, Fernando Librado:

> To the west of the siliyɨk [sacred enclosure] was a dancing ground with meeting areas and fireplaces for families. Every fireplace within the dancing area was a place of honor from which the families would gather to watch the ceremonies and dances. These fireplaces, which were about 25 feet from one another, were built by the local people who knew in advance how many captains and their families would be coming to the ceremonies. They made arches of tules in front of the

fireplaces of the families. Some of the fireplaces were also for the local people. Those which were for the use of a captain were marked with a banner (Hudson and Blackburn 1986:51).

SACRED ENCLOSURES

According to Harrington's consultants, sacred enclosed areas (*siliyɨks*) were found within the confines of dance grounds; they consisted of small enclosures formed by a semi-circular fence of poles and mats. These enclosures were used by religious initiates (members of the *'antap* society) for rituals and were removed upon completion of the ceremonies (Hudson and Blackburn 1986:56). Fernando Librado noted that the men who used the sacred enclosures knew the secret knowledge of the *siliyɨk* (Hudson and Blackburn 1986:58). Fernando Librado stated that when Pomposa gave her last fiesta at Saticoy, the *siliyɨk* was about 25 feet long and six feet high. In ethnohistoric accounts, sacred enclosures were often described as churches or temples (Hudson and Blackburn 1986:56–59). The most complete ethnohistoric description of a sacred enclosure is from 1602, when Vizcaino described one in a Tongva settlement on Santa Catalina Island:

> This was a large flat patio and in one part of it, where they had what we call an altar, there was a great circle all surrounded with feathers of various colors and shapes, which must come from the birds they sacrifice. Inside the circle there was a figure like a devil painted in various colors, in the way the Indians of New Spain are accustomed to paint them. At the sides of this were the sun and moon (Wagner 1929:237).

Unfortunately, detailed early historical descriptions of Chumash sacred enclosures are nonexistent. It is assumed that the enclosures described by Harrington's Chumash consultants were similar to the Tongva enclosures.

CEMETERIES

Formal cemeteries were used by the Chumash for centuries and are characteristic of most Late period Chumash settlements (Gamble et al. 2001). The best early description of a cemetery and sacred space was penned by Crespí in 1769:

> They bury their dead, and have their graveyards, one for men and the other for women[11], all being enclosures of very tall sharp-pointed poles much painted in hues, and some upright boards painted the same way, surrounding or enclosing

the graveyard, where they have placed very large whale-bones. One or two of a sort of round stone fonts are to be found at all of the graveyards, very delicately carven, so that they might serve very well for holy water fonts and even for baptismal fonts. They have another room, very clean, with many upright stones around it and with a large feather ornament set up in the center, which we suppose must be their places of prayer. They also have another very smooth clean spot, with quite a large sized whale-bone driven in the midst of it, and as soon as they die the body is brought to this last spot to hold a wake over it. They lay it out and place the head resting on the whalebone stake. From here they take it, if it is a man, for burial in the men's graveyard, and the hair of the dead person's head is left hanging upon one of the many upright poles there [that] are there. If it is a woman, they do the same as in the case of the men and take the deceased person from here to her own graveyard, and a bowl or basket of the dead woman is left hanging upon one of its poles. And so at both graveyards there are a great many objects hanging up, as a result (Crespí on August 20, 1769, in Brown 2001: 427–429).

Apparently, several areas near the cemetery were used in a ceremonial context; however, it is unclear if these areas were entirely separate from the cemetery, or if Crespí was describing a dance area or sacred enclosure.

Several early references exist on the location of Chumash cemeteries within settlements. Costansó's journal from the 1769 Portolá Expedition indicates that cemeteries were situated within the boundaries of settlements: "They bury the dead, and their burying-grounds are within the town itself" (Hemert-Engert and Teggart 1910:47). Seven years later, Font made this observation on cemeteries:

Near the villages they have a place which we called the cemetery, where they bury their dead. It is made of several poles and planks painted with various colors, white, black, and red, and set up in the ground. And on some very tall, straight and slim poles, which we called the towers, because we saw them from some distance, they place baskets which belong to the deceased, and other things which were perhaps esteemed by them, such as little skirts, shells, and likewise in places some arrows. Over the deceased they place the ribs or other large bones of the whales which are customarily stranded on these coasts (Bolton 1931:254).

PLAYING FIELDS

Gaming areas or playing fields were flat, open areas, similar in appearance to dance areas, that were used for communal sports near or within settlements (Hudson and Blackburn 1986:48). The playing fields were surrounded by low fences made of poles and mats or interwoven branches.

One of the best and earliest accounts of a gaming area is from Font's 1776 journal:

> All of the settlements or rancherias of the Channel have a community place for playing, consisting of a very smooth and level ground, like a bowling green, with low walls around it, in which they play, rolling a little half-round stick (Bolton 1931:253).

MENSTRUAL HUTS

According to Harrington's consultants, adolescent Chumash girls were secluded in isolated structures known as menstrual huts during female puberty observances (Hudson and Blackburn 1986:45). Most California Indian groups used menstrual huts, but we have very few details about those built by the Chumash. Magdalena Olivos, a Kitanemuk consultant of Harrington's, stated that a hut about eight feet in diameter was made for her puberty ceremony (Hudson and Blackburn 1986:45–46).

CHILDBIRTH HUTS

The Ventureño Chumash used a special hut in which a woman was isolated during childbirth (Hudson and Blackburn 1986:47). The same structure that was used as a menstual hut may have also been used as a childbirth hut. We have very limited information on these structures.

MALE PUBERTY HUTS

The male puberty hut was a structure located in an isolated part of the village that was used by adolescent boys to sleep in during a portion of the male puberty observances[12] (Hudson and Blackburn 1986:44).

STORAGE STRUCTURES

Although houses were one of the most important structures used for storage by the Chumash, a number of other structures and pits served as facilities for storing food and other possessions. Drying granaries were employed to dry and store acorns as well other foods outside of houses. These were large, loosely woven containers that were elevated on poles (Hudson and Blackburn 1983:55). They also used large, coiled basketry containers elevated on poles for storing foods such as acorns (Hudson and Blackburn 1983:58). In 1792, Longinós Martinez wrote about Chumash storage granaries when he traveled along the coast between Ventura and the San Luis Obispo area:

> Next to their dwelling house, they have another smaller one, in which to keep seeds, dried fish, sardines, and other foods for winter, when the cold, rain, and roughness of the sea prevent them from seeking food (Simpson 1939:41).

Storage also occurred in pits, particularly in the interior of structures, and in caves.

SMOKEHOUSES

In addition to storage granaries, smokehouses were used by the Chumash to cure dried fish or meat (Hudson and Blackburn 1983:215). According to Harrington's Ventureño consultant, Fernando Librado, the smokehouse was a specially made little house similar to a small sweatlodge, with wattle-and-daub construction. There was an opening in the top for the release of smoke from the direct fire underneath. To my knowledge, there is no information on the placement of these structures within a village.

WINDBREAKS

Windbreaks were fence-like structures consisting of vertical poles covered by mats that were associated with Chumash houses (Hudson and Blackburn 1983:351).

SWEATLODGES

Most Chumash settlements contained at least one sweatlodge (Gamble 1995). In contrast to the Plains Indian type of sweatlodge, which was heated with hot rocks, the Chumash heated theirs by direct fire. Sweatlodges were usually situated near fresh water in Chumash settlements so that participants could plunge into the water after sweating.

Sweatlodges were the most substantial structures that the Chumash built. Two types of sweatlodges were described by Harrington's consultants: a small one or *'uqstilulu* and a large one or *'apayɨk* (Harrington 1942:9–10; Hudson and Blackburn 1986:33–35, 37–41). The smaller sweatlodge was semicircular, semi-subterranean, and earth-covered, was sometimes built into an earthen bank, and was high enough that a man could stand in the center of it (Hudson and Blackburn 1986:33–34). A smoke hole was not used in these smaller sweatlodges; instead, the fire was built near the door.

Harrington noted that larger sweatlodges were usually used for ceremonial purposes and were semi-subterranean and hemispherical in shape (Hudson and Blackburn 1986:37). They were made with four forked posts, approximately 10 inches (25 cm) in diameter[13], that were placed in the interior of the structure with four cross beams placed on them. Long, straight poles made from willow were arranged closely together on the cross beams (Hudson and Blackburn 1986:38). A small opening in the roof, about 1.8 m long and 60 cm wide and directly above the central fireplace was used as a smoke hole and as a doorway. A pole made of willow with notches on the side served as the ladder (Hudson and Blackburn 1986:43). Fernando Librado told Harrington that sweatlodges were always located near water and that very few women used them (Hudson and Blackburn 1986:37–39). According to one of Harrington's consultants, Feliz Carillo, not every common person could use the sweatlodge, and only *'antap* used the large sweatlodges (Hudson and Blackburn 1986:41). In an interview with Gould in 1887, Juan de Jesús Tumamait described the large *temescal* as a structure that could hold up to 30 people and had a door in the roof and a fire in the middle (Gould n.d.).

A number of early historic accounts contain descriptions of sweatlodges. The earliest is Unamuno's 1587 report of a sweatlodge at an abandoned village on Chorro Creek:

> A little apart from the river in the other direction a hut was found among some trees, big enough for about two persons, built of sticks and covered with earth, and having only one small opening. Inside were dried grass and leaves. We supposed this was for their chief (Wagner 1929:146).

Unamuno's description is the only historic report of a small sweatlodge known for the Chumash; most accounts refer to the larger type. Crespí described sweatlodges at a Chumash village near present-day Fillmore in 1769:

> The village lay close to where we had found them encamped, with a great many very large round houses well roofed with grass. We saw some underground ones as well, with their vaulted dirt roofs, so that only the vault is visible rising out of the ground like an oven. These houses have chimney-holes on top, making a sort of doorways through which they go in and out by means of ladders. Inside these are quite large, forming a sort of porticoes[14] in which it appears they build their fires. They must go inside them during very cold seasons (Crespí on August 11, 1769, in Brown 2001:375-377).

In 1769, Fages described the use of sweatlodges used for purposes other than sweating in the San Luis Obispo area:

The men do not often sleep in their houses at night; but, carrying with them their arms, bow and quiver, they are accustomed to congregate in numbers in great subterranean caves, where they pass the nights in sheer terror; (if they stayed at home) they might be surprised in their beds by the enemy whilst defenseless on account of the presence of their wives and children (Priestley 1972:48).

Font wrote a general description of sweatlodges and their uses in the Santa Barbara Channel area in 1776:

They also have a common temescal. This is a hot, closed room for sweating, made somewhat subterranean and very firm with poles and earth, and having at the top, in the middle, an opening like a scuttle, to afford air and serve as a door, through which they go down inside by a ladder consisting of straight poles set in the ground and joined together, one being shorter than the other. I peeped into a temescal and perceived a strong heat coming up from it. In the middle of them they make a fire. The Indians enter to perspire, seated all around, and as soon as they perspire freely and wet the ground with their sweat, they run out and jump into the sea, which is close by, to bathe themselves (Bolton 1931:254).

In 1793, Menzies also described large sweatlodges he saw in the Santa Barbara Channel area:

At each village we observed a sweating place made by digging a deep pit or cavity of from 10 to 15 feet square in a bank near the water side and covering it all over with spars and earth so as to be scarcely distinguishable from the other parts of the bank, excepting for a small hole left open at the top for an entrance through which only one person could descend at a time by means of a post notched with steps; We were at first puzzled to know the use of these places, till one evening at the Village near the landing place we observed them make a large fire with dried faggots in the middle of this subterraneous oven & when it was sufficiently heated & the smoke subsided a number of the Natives went down in order to be sweated, by the time they were in a state of profuse perspiration they came up again one by one & instantly plunged themselves into the sea (Eastwood 1924:325).

The early historic chroniclers' reports of sweatlodges concur with later ethnographic descriptions on several key issues: sweatlodges were semi-subterranean, were earth-covered, had entrances in the roof through a smokehole, had center posts, and had central fireplaces for heat. In contrast, houses were constructed in a significantly different manner from sweatlodges.

HOUSES

Hudson and Blackburn (1983:323–337) provide a thorough summary of ethnohistoric and ethnographic descriptions of Chumash houses, some of which are briefly reviewed here. Chumash houses varied in size, with the smaller ones approximately 12 to 18 feet (3.7 to 5.5 m) in diameter and seven to ten feet (2.1 to 3.0 m) in height. Some houses might be considerably larger[15] but all were circular in floor plan and usually dome shaped. One of Harrington's consultants (Juan de Jesús Justo), commented that the old rancherias had taller houses which were 20 feet (6.1 m) or more in diameter. Another consultant (Fernando Librado) commented that houses were 15 feet (4.6 m) or more in diameter. Posts for houses were set in holes about one and a half feet (30 cm) apart and were usually made from willow, although cottonwood and sycamore were also mentioned. Horizontal poles were lashed to the posts, then thatching (of tule, wild alfalfa, fern, or carrizo) was attached to these poles in four or five tiers. In some houses, two or three small holes were left in the wall for windows. Fernando Librado commented that a diligent person would line the inside of the walls with mats before attaching the thatching. One remark (made by Mr. Santana Avila) in Harrington's notes states that the San Luis Obispo Indians had houses of willow, dirt, and tule. Another consultant (Luisa Ygnacio) stated that they put earth all around the house so water would not enter when it rained. The door was low and closed with a woven mat and was placed on the side of the house away from the wind. Sometimes a pit was excavated in the ground under the top of the doorway to insure that water dripping from it did not enter the house. The fireplace was near the middle of the house[16] under the smokehole; during rainy weather, a deerskin was used to cover the smokehole. The fire was kept going day and night and was used for cooking and heating, and the ashes were thrown out of the house periodically. The only mention of a floor comes from Fernando Librado, who stated that the floors were made hard by wetting them and then pounding them with rocks. Houses were arranged close to one another according to Harrington's consultants. Some of them said the houses were not arranged in rows, while others claimed they were always arranged in rows. According to Fernando Librado, each family lived in a separate house (Hudson and Blackburn 1983:325–331).

Most of the early chroniclers remarked on the types of houses that the Chumash inhabited. The earliest reference to Chumash structures comes from Cabrillo, on June 10, 1542, at what was probably the historic Chumash village of *Muwu*: "We saw on land an Indian town close to the sea with large houses like those of New Spain" (Wagner 1929:86). Later in 1542, additional references to Chumash houses were made in the ship's log, this time from elsewhere in the Santa Barbara Channel area: "They have round houses, well covered down to the ground" (Wagner 1929:88). Another reference to houses comes from 1543, while Cabrillo was on San Miguel Island:[17]

> The Indians of these Islands are very poor, being fishermen, and eat nothing except fish. They do not sleep on the ground.[18] All their business and occupation is to fish. In each house they say there are fifty souls (Wagner 1929:90).

Two descriptions of abandoned Chumash villages in the area near Morro Bay were recorded by Unamuno on October 18 and 19, 1587. The first of these refers to an abandoned village located upstream from Morro Bay, probably on Chorro Creek:

> We came upon an old Indian camp northeast of the river, in which there were seventeen large and small dugouts,[19] like Biscay charcoal pits, that is, a large round hole in the ground very well covered over with branches of trees. Judging from the size of the dug-outs, each could hold more than a dozen persons. They seemed to have been made about a month and a half before (Wagner 1929:147).

The second account by Unamuno was written the next day and probably refers to an abandoned village adjacent to another stream in the area:

> We came upon a camp on both sides of the river, where there were more than thirty dug-outs like those found the day before. Nothing was found in these but some little cord bags made like nets, in which there were some rope ends, very well made out of the bark of trees, some old baskets in which they carry their plunder, and a trough made out of a tree trunk (Wagner 1929:147).

The villages in Unamuno's accounts may have been temporary sites, which were more common among the Chumash living in the San Luis Obispo area who were not as sedentary as the Chumash in the Santa Barbara Channel region. Fifteen years after Unamuno's visit, members of the Vizcaino expedition remarked on a village that probably was situated on San Miguel Island:[20]

> They had gone into the interior of the said island and that there was a pueblo there with more than two hundred large houses, in each one of which lived more than forty Indians; and that in the midst of it two poles were nailed together, with one above, like a gallows[21] (Bolton 1916:90).

This was an unusually large village. Other descriptions of the Channel Island settlements suggest that those on the islands were smaller than this, indicating that this figure may not be accurate. Following these earlier reports, no descriptions of Chumash houses were recorded until the Portolá expedition of 1769.

Fages, a soldier on that expedition, described Chumash houses at a village near Santa Paula:

> Here a small village was seen; its peculiarity was that the inhabitants dwell in huts covered with grass, spherical in construction like a half-orange, at the apex of which an airhole was left for the escape of smoke and the entrance of light (Priestley 1972:24–25).

His comment on the peculiarity of the houses may refer to the fact that he saw villages upstream where no structural remains were apparent. In a description of the Obispeño Chumash, Fages gave the following information on structures:

> Their houses, shaped like half-globes, are neatly built; each one is capable of sheltering four or five families which, being kin, are accustomed to live together. The houses have one door on the east, and one on the west, with a skylight in the roof, halfway between. Their beds are built up high on bedsteads, which are called tapextles, of heavy sticks; a reed mat serves as a mattress, and four others as curtains, forming a bedroom. Beneath the bedsteads are the beds of the little Indians, commodiously arranged (Priestley 1972:48).

Costansó, the engineer on the 1769 Portolá expedition, also described beds in the interior of houses and reported on the sizes of houses in the Santa Barbara area:

> In their houses the married people have their beds set apart on platforms raised above the ground. Their mattresses are some plain petates, or mats of rushes, and their pillows are the same kinds of mats rolled up at the head of the bed. All the beds are hung with similar mats, which serve as decency, and as a protection from the cold (Hemert-Engert and Teggart 1910:137).
>
> They live in towns, the houses of which are spherical in form, like the half of an orange, are covered with reeds, and are as much as 20 yards[22] in diameter. Each house contains three or four families. The fireplace is in the middle, and in the upper part of the house they leave an air passage or chimney for the escape of smoke (Hemert-Engert and Teggart 1910:133–135).

Seven years later, Font also described the houses of the Chumash in the Santa Barbara Channel region, which apparently had changed little during the period of early historic settlement:

> Once I went near a hut which I saw open, to examine its structure, for among all the huts which I saw in all the journey these are the best. They are round in form,

like a half orange, very spacious, large and high. In the middle of the top, they have an aperture to afford light and to serve as a chimney, through which emerges the smoke of the fire which they make in the middle of the hut. Some of them also have two or three holes like little windows. The frames of all of them consist of arched and very strong poles, and the walls are of very thick grass interwoven. At the doors there is a mat which swings toward the inside like a screen, and another one toward the outside which they ordinarily bar with a whalebone or a stick (Bolton 1931:251–252).

In 1792, Longinós Martinez traveled in southern California and wrote about the coastal Chumash between missions San Buenaventura and San Luis Obispo. Again it appears that little had changed in house construction over the years:

These Indians live in society and have a fixed domicile. Their houses are arranged together, very well built, round like an oven; light enters through the center of the roof; they are spacious and fairly comfortable. Their beds are made on the floor (en tapeste) with skins, and covers in which to wrap themselves, and with divisions, like the cabins of a ship. Even if many sleep in one house they do not see one another. In the center of the room they make a fire for cooking seeds, fish, and other foods, for they eat everything cooked or roasted (Simpson 1939:41).

The account written by Martinez is one of the few passages that describe outside storage facilities and state that the Chumash slept on the floor. The following year, Menzies also described Chumash villages and houses along the Santa Barbara Channel coast:

These Natives live in Villages of from 20 to 40 huts each which are crouded [sic] together & much larger than any we saw about the Settlements to the Northward; They are of a hemispherical form, thatched all over with bulrushes, & each seem to contain several families; The fire is generally made in the middle of the hut & a hole is left open in the top of it as a Chimney vent for the smoke; They usually sleep on platforms which are raised 4 or 5 feet from the floor, coverd [sic] with a mat of bulrushes and decently railed round (Eastwood 1924:325).

In this account, the Chumash were described as sleeping on platforms, as was the case in the 1769 descriptions. The quotation from Martinez indicates that there may have been some variety regarding sleeping arrangements, although both accounts describe interior partitions for the sleeping areas.

These early historic accounts indicate that the houses along the Santa Barbara Channel coast were often clustered together and were large, up to 55 feet (16.8 m) in diameter. Crespí indicated that as many as 70 people could sleep in one. Evidently several families shared a house. Sleeping areas were set apart with mats, providing limited privacy, and elevated beds were used for sleeping. The houses were usually described as hemispherical, made with poles, and covered with grass or reeds. Fireplaces used for cooking were observed in the center of houses, with smoke holes directly above. Mats were used for covering doors, which faced away from the prevailing winds.

Archaeological Evidence for Village Organization and Structures

Many of the ethnographic descriptions of village organization and structures are similar to those in the early historic accounts, but what about the archaeological record? In this section, archaeological evidence on Late period Chumash settlements and structures situated along the mainland Santa Barbara Channel coast is examined.

EARLY ARCHAEOLOGICAL DOCUMENTATION

Some of the best archaeological descriptions of village organization and structures come from the notes of early archaeological investigators, in part because they were able to view historic village sites before some of the features were obscured by modern developments and natural processes. The three most significant accounts of structures and village organization were provided by the Reverend Stephen Bowers, Paul Schumacher, and David Banks Rogers. Because the data on village organization and structures on the Santa Barbara Channel coast are so meager, information on settlements throughout the Chumash mainland region is included in this section. Most of the sites date to the historic period, but some are from earlier contexts.

Reverend Stephen Bowers. Bowers provided some of the earliest information on Chumash structures and settlement layout. Most sites that Bowers visited were historic; some were so intact that mounds, dance floors, and house depressions were still discernible. Illustrations and measurements, although somewhat crude, accompany many of his notes (Benson 1997). The following discussion of Bowers' archaeological investigations is based on Benson's (1997) presentation of Bowers' notes.

Between 1875 and 1889, Bowers recorded the remains of structures in numerous abandoned villages, most of which were in the interior Chumash region. Houses[23] were probably the most common type of structure that he came across. Some were apparent because of the circles of stones that apparently had been used as foundations. One, in the Santa Ynez Valley, measured about 10 meters in diameter (Benson 1997:40), but most were smaller, ranging in size between 3.7 and 7.6 meters in diameter. Bowers also noted a variety of house depressions without stone foundations, as well as low mounds that he believed were house sites. One of the most unusual features that Bowers encountered was what he described as an "enclosure." At the historic village of *Teqepsh* (SBA-477) in the Santa Ynez Valley, Bowers described a stone enclosure that encompassed one to two acres and had two outlets (Benson 1997:40). He recorded another enclosure[24] at Prietos Rancheria (possibly the historic village of *Snihuaj*, SBA-823) that was defined by low walls of earth and was approximately 71.6 by 36.6 meters in size. West of the large enclosure was a row of rocks enclosing three sides of a rectangular area that was about 100 feet (30.5 m) long and 73 feet (22.2 m) wide (Benson 1997:110–111 and Figure 6.1).

Bowers also identified a number of structural remains as sweathouses, but the criteria that he used to distinguish these from open-air dance floors or large residential houses were not clearly defined (Benson 1997:175). Remnant sweathouses were often near cemeteries, indicating that location may be one of the criteria that Bowers used. At the historic village site of *Wenexe'l* (SLO-94/95) in the Cuyama River Valley, Bowers mapped a sweathouse that was 60 feet (18.3 m) in diameter (Benson 1997:68). Jerry Williams, who excavated features at the site in 1968 under the direction of Roger Desautels, stated that there was a large depression about 60 feet in diameter at the top of a knoll that was probably a dance floor, not a sweat lodge, as it lacked evidence of a superstructure (Benson 1997:173). However, a structure that was identified as a sweatlodge was excavated at the site by Desautels and subsequently reported on by Gamble (1995).

The remains of the structures that Bowers identified as dance features tended to be larger than those he interpreted as sweathouses. At a site in the Santa Ynez Valley (probably the historic village of *Wishap*[25] (SBA-865?), Bowers described a "perfect" circular area 100 feet (30.5 m) in diameter, carefully paved with small boulders set on edge[26] (Benson 1997), as a remnant dance area. At another historic village site in the Santa Ynez Valley, *Kalwashaq'* (SBA-516), he also interpreted a large circular depression 90 feet (27.4 m) in diameter as the remains of a dance house (Benson 1997:64). A passageway between this depression and an adjacent one that was about 40 or 50 feet (12.2 or 15.4 m) in diameter was also noted.

In 1900, Philip Jones (1956), using Bowers' journal, relocated the historic village site of "*Kallawasaw*" (*Kalwashaq'*) on the Santa Ynez River and mapped ten house depressions, with nine of them in three rows of three. The house depressions in the center row appear to be slightly larger than those to the north or the south.

Paul Schumacher. Schumacher visited and excavated several Chumash village sites on both the Channel Islands and the mainland during the late nineteenth century, including the historic village site of *Wenexe'l* (SLO- 94/95), the same site that Bowers and Desautels investigated. Schumacher (1875:Figure 5) mapped three rows of circular depressions, most of which were approximately 14 feet (4.3 m) in diameter. Two, however, were about 23 feet (7 m) in diameter, and one, on the highest point of land, was much larger, about 40 or 50 feet (12.2 or 15.2 m) in diameter; Schumacher thought it was a chief's house (Schumacher 1875:345 and Figure 5). This was probably the depression that Bowers thought was a sweathouse and that Williams interpreted as a dance floor. At a distance of about 210 feet (64 m) from the large possible house depression, a smaller, solitary circular depression, about 14 feet (4.3 m) in diameter, was also mapped by Schumacher (1875:Figure 5).

David Banks Rogers. Rogers (1929) also described the internal organization of structures and ceremonial areas at Chumash sites, many of which were along the mainland coast. Rogers' commentary, however, should also be viewed with caution. For example, Rogers described structures and artifacts in his book that were never mentioned in his field notes. Either Rogers' field notes were inconsistently kept or he embellished the archaeological record when he wrote his book, *Prehistoric Man of the Santa Barbara Coast.* Observations made by Rogers indicate that many Chumash village sites included houses, sweatlodges, cemeteries, and dance areas. When sweatlodges and dance floors were observed at the same site, they were often next to each other. At Tecolote No. 2 (SBA-73) on the mainland, Rogers (1929:197) described an elliptical dance floor approximately 100 feet (30.5 m) by 50 feet (15.24 m) in size that was situated to the south of two cemeteries (Rogers 1929:197). Stones had been piled around the borders of this elliptical dance area, presumably to clear the dance floor area (Rogers 1929:197). Rogers identified a sweatlodge near the "dance area" and the creek. This site was probably occupied between Phase 4 of the Middle period and Phase 2 of the Late period (King 1980b:60–63). Across the creek at Tecolote No. 1 (SBA-72), a similar pattern was observed (Rogers 1929:195). A large ceremonial dance floor (cleared of stones) between two cemeteries and about 100 feet (30.5 m) long was recorded next to a semi-subterranean sweatlodge, approximately 20 feet (6.1 m) in diameter (Rogers 1929:195). The lower part of the sweatlodge's walls was constructed of boulders and its interior was filled with an abundance of charred material and ashes. This site was probably late Middle or early Late period in age (King 1990a:46 and 51). At a site nearby (Winchester No. 3, SBA-71)[27] Rogers observed another elliptical dance floor approximately 100 feet (30.5 m) long, entirely cleared of stones and gravel (Rogers 1929:182). A thin layer of stones and gravel surrounded the dance floor, which appeared compacted. This site was probably occupied during Phase 2b of the Middle period (King 1990a:30). Rogers (1929:338) also observed sweatlodges at many other sites on the mainland and on the islands and found them to be more common than dance areas, more of which were reported for the mainland.

Arthur Woodward. The most extensive and best-documented investigation of village organization and structural remains during this early period of inquiry occurred at the coastal village site of *Muwu* (VEN-11) (Woodward 1938:141). Members of the Van Bergen-Los Angeles Museum Expedition, led by Richard Van Valkenburgh and photographer Milton Snow, excavated the historic-period settlement between 1929 and 1932. Arthur Woodward from the Los Angeles County Museum of Natural History oversaw the excavations, and Van Bergen funded them. As a result of their explorations, nine house depressions, the remains of a sweatlodge, and a cemetery were recorded at the site. As can be seen in figure 15, the sweatlodge and cemetery were at opposite ends of the residential area. The circular floor of the remnant sweatlodge was made from hard-packed clay about 10 centimeters in thickness, and was covered by a thin layer of eel grass. The floor was approximately 21 feet (6.4 m) in diameter and was sunken 18 to 24 inches (46 to 61 cm) below the surface. The central fire pit (91 cm in diameter) was filled with clean white ash and was unusual because of the presence of a stone slab, about two feet high, that was at one edge. Immediately behind the slab, a burned center post was recorded (Woodward 1938:141–142). No artifacts were found on the surface of the floor or in the firepit.[28]

In addition to the sweatlodge, Woodward excavated four house depressions out of the nine he mapped. Three of these were excavated in their entirety and yielded significant information.[29] The first, House A, was located in the southern part of the village and was approximately 6.6

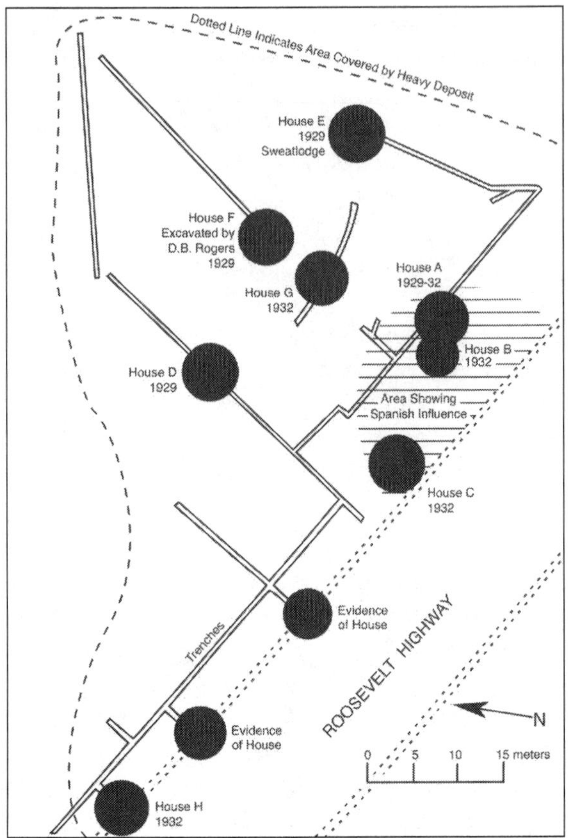

FIGURE 15 Map of *Muwu* (CA-VEN-11)

meters in diameter (figure 15). Woodward (1932) believed that a thin layer of sand mixed with ash was used as a floor cover. He noted that small fragments of bone, shell, and charcoal were embedded in the hardened ash and sand floor. No postholes were associated with this floor, but there were a few interior pits that were not described by Woodward. The remains of a hearth were recorded near the center of the floor, with numerous fire-altered rocks nearby. House B, which was approximately 5.2 meters in diameter, overlay portions of House A (figure 15). This floor, which was almost entirely covered with a layer of ash and burned shell, had two fire pits near its perimeter. However, no post holes were encountered. A variety of cultural material was recovered from the floor, including eight bone awls, bird bone tubes, three leaf-shaped arrow points, a worked copper point, two circular fish hooks, two composite fish hooks, hammerstones, pitted stones, mortar fragments, a pestle fragment, steatite fragments, and assorted bone and shell (Woodward 1932).

The largest (approximately 7 m in diameter) and most elaborate depression (House C) was delineated by 174 post holes, some of which indicated an interior house partition may have been present. Two distinctive floors overlain with masses of eel grass (*Zostera marina*) were identified in this structure. Woodward (1932) interpreted the eel grass as part of the fallen roof of the structure. In addition, House C had a number of interesting interior storage pits that were absent from the other house depressions. One of the interior pits was about 23 centimeters in diameter and (curiously) was filled with approximately 70–80 opened mussel shells (Gamble 1991:Figure 3.22A). Another two pits were linked, with the shallower one (13 cm deep) filled with ten shells and two stones. The deeper one (23 cm deep) had a bone whistle placed near the center of the pit and was surrounded by sand (Gamble 1991:Figure 3.22B). A fourth pit, 15 centimeters in diameter and 20 centimeters deep, was filled with beach sand covered with a plaster plug that was level with the floor. A final pit (61 cm in diameter and 64 cm deep), located near the two central hearths in the house, contained a burial of a child estimated to have been one year old at death. Near the top of this pit and overlying the burial was a flat, irregular flagstone in a horizontal position (Gamble 1991:Figure 3.23). Olivella beads, tubular clam beads, and glass beads were found in the fill above the burial, apparently in association with the child. Asphaltum impressions from a basket rested on the floor of the pit along with the remains of what appeared to be food (Gamble 1991:114). Artifacts and other objects associated with the floor of House C included a group of flagstones, a whale bone and worked whale rib, a mat of eel grass, asphaltum basketry impressions, tarring pebbles, fish hooks, and stone points. In addition, potsherds, metal, and glass beads were associated with the upper floor.

These excavations represent some of the most thorough investigations of Chumash structural remains and village organization for the time period. Because three houses from the Historic period were excavated in their entirety, differences between households at the site can be addressed. House C was larger than the other two houses, and had a greater subterranean interior storage capacity, suggesting that the residents were wealthier than the inhabitants of the other houses. Some of the artifacts and features in the house, especially the worked whalebone and whistle stored in the subterranean pit, may also reflect the presence of higher status inhabitants.

RECENT ARCHAEOLOGICAL DOCUMENTATION OF STRUCTURAL REMAINS

Pitas Point, CA-VEN-27. Some of the best archaeological evidence of structural remains for the mainland Chumash region was found at the Pitas Point site. The site, which is located approximately eight miles northwest of Ventura along the Santa Barbara Channel coast, was excavated in 1969 and 1970 under the direction of Chester King (Gamble 1983:103–129). King (1978:Figure 6) mapped five house depressions (each approximately 9 m in diameter) that were aligned with the beach (figure 16). In addition to structural remains, numerous rock ovens, hearths, storage pits, and other features were documented at the site. One of the more interesting features was a whale bone shrine that was found behind one of the house pits (King 1978:Figure 6). A second whale bone feature, also probably ceremonial in nature, was found at the base of the deposit in the house depression in Area 3. It consisted of a large flat whale bone with red dots painted on it in a pattern, possibly of stars (King, personal communication, 2007). Shell beads, shell ornaments, and radiocarbon dates for the site indicate that it was occupied from Middle period Phase 5c (A.D. 1050) through Phase 1 of the Late period (A.D. 1500). Excavations occurred in portions of the remains of two domestic structures, in an area that

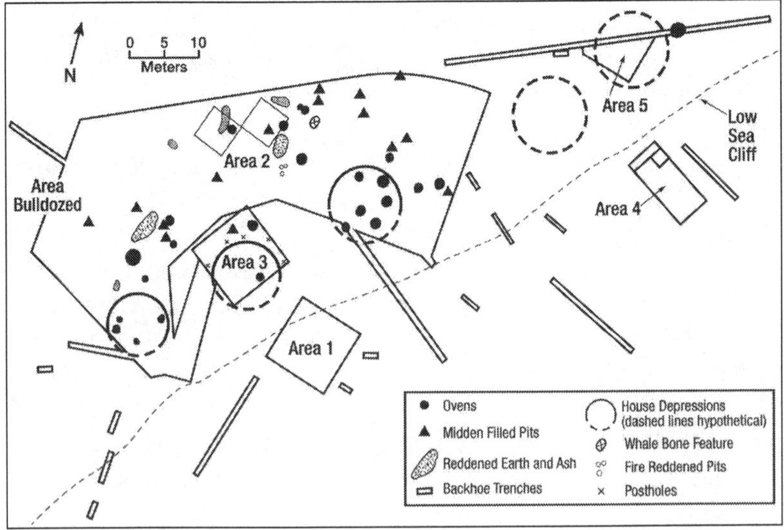

FIGURE 16 Map of the Pitas Point site (CA-VEN-27)

was used for depositing refuse, and in an outdoor activity area adjacent to the houses.

Only one of the two domestic structures at the site was excavated completely; beads in this area suggest that it was in use during the entire occupation at the site. Six hearths were found in this structure, some overlaying one another. In addition to the hearths, a large rock oven feature (approximately 150 cm in diameter and 40 cm deep) was identified at the base of the midden in the house deposits. One of the most unique features in this house was the remains of a basketmaking area (Gamble 1983, 2002b). Near one of the hearths, a sizeable pit lined with large, flat rocks, many of which had asphaltum on them, was found. A cache of 15 tarring pebbles was discovered nearby in the same level. Another cache of 20 tarring pebbles was recovered from a different level in the same part of the house, and several other tarring pebbles were mapped in the vicinity of this feature. The Chumash used tarring pebbles to coat the interior of twined basketry water bottles with asphaltum to make them watertight. Approximately six pebbles would be heated in a hearth, then placed in the interior of baskets with hardened, pulverized asphaltum and rolled around until the asphaltum was evenly distributed (Craig 1967:98). Asphaltum was abundant near the Pitas Point site, as well as at other sites along the mainland Santa Barbara Channel coast. Ethnographic and ethnohistoric data indicate that it was women who made baskets in Chumash society (Gamble 1983). This area of the house appears to have been used by women to make baskets and other items (Gamble 1983, 2002b), and it is one of the only archaeological examples of a basket-making area in California.

The distribution of artifacts and features at the site indicates that a number of activities occurred within the houses at Pitas Point, including basket making, food preparation, cooking, the production of pestles, and food storage (Gamble 1983). Activities that occurred outside the houses included butchering, the manufacture of stone tools, and the production and maintenance of fishing equipment. Some of the items that were produced at the site may have been exported to the islands and other Chumash sites.

Mikiw, CA-SBA-78. The best documented and most spectacular archaeological discovery of a sweatlodge comes from Harrison's excavations at the historic village site of *Mikiw* at Dos Pueblos in 1958 (Harrison 1965:91–178; see chapter 4 for additional information on *Mikiw*). Harrison employed excavation techniques that were advanced for the time.

He processed all remains from the sweatlodge depression though eighth-inch mesh screens, and the residues were then taken to UCSB and sorted under controlled conditions in the laboratory. Harrison excavated in six-inch (15 cm) levels when he was in the vicinity of the floor. He also left one-foot (30 cm) wide balks in place temporarily across the center of the structure and mapped large artifacts *in situ*.

The semi-subterranean structure that Harrison recorded was oval in shape and measured 19 by 21 feet (5.8 by 6.4 m) in size (figure 17) The mud-plastered floor was basin-shaped, with the top of the rim 18 inches below the ground surface. Near the center of the structure, the concave shape of the floor was interrupted by a slightly elevated rectangular platform, surrounded by an even higher raised ridge (figure 17). The center platform was about 7 by 8.5 feet (2.1 by 2.6 m) in size and was also somewhat basin-shaped. Four large postholes were found at each corner of the central platform with two more slightly smaller ones on the northern and southern sides of the ridge (figure 17). The burned remains of a post were found in the deeper levels of the post molds, with a layer of mud

FIGURE 17 Photograph of sweatlodge floor at *Mikiw* (CA-SBA-78)

and rock fill surrounding the mold in the upper layers (Harrison 1965:151). The floor was irregular and consistently broken to the northeast of the posts, suggesting that the final collapse of the posts may have occurred in this direction. The entire surface of the floor was covered with several layers of sand and mud plaster, which were considerably thicker in the central platform area. Although the floor was never excavated, cross sections of it could be observed in areas disturbed by gophers. In several instances, four separate layers of plaster between one-fourth inch and one-eighth inch in thickness were observed. The plastered floor was peppered with fine grains of sand and small splinters of charcoal, shell, and stone. Except at the southern end, the rim was apparent around the entire periphery of the floor. Harrison thought that the entrance of the structure may have been at the southern edge of the floor (Harrison 1965:151–153).

A large (110 × 76 cm) oval fire pit was found near the southern edge of the sweatlodge. The fire pit was basin-shaped and separated from a circular flue by a deflector composed of a large, flat sandstone rock set upright in mud plaster and smaller rocks (figure 17). The fire pit, which was 46 centimeters deep, was fire-reddened and filled with a large deposit of ash, charcoal, and burned rock.

Burned beams, varying in diameter from seven inches to eight inches, were found lying on the floor. Many smaller carbonized pieces of wood, ranging from twigs to poles an inch in diameter, and a large section of a carbonized, interwoven, fibrous material, were found on the surface of the floor; the latter was interpreted as thatching. A reconstruction of the roof of the structure was based on several lines of evidence (Harrison 1965:153). Harrison suggested that large support posts were set upright around the raised ridge of the central platform, with smaller logs laid across these to form a network of roof beams. Others may have sloped to the ground from this network, but they were not imbedded in the ground. The walls were made from smaller poles, twigs, and thatching material, with sterile soil packed over the entire structure. Based on stratigraphic data, Harrison (1965:153–154) suggested that after the structure burned, it was abandoned and the roof collapsed. Later the depression was used for general garbage disposal. Four radiocarbon dates, obtained from carbonized logs and shell resting on the floor level and just above it, indicate the structure was probably built in the early 1700s (A.D. 1710 ± 55) and abandoned by the last quarter of the eighteenth century (A.D. 1780 ± 55) (Harrison 1965:154–155).

Harrison suspected that the structure was deliberately destroyed by fire because the floor had been cleared of artifacts. Judging from the direction that the support posts collapsed and the location of most of the carbonized remains, the fire probably was started on the northern side of the structure. Harrison suggested that the structure might have been burned by either the Spanish or the Chumash (Harrison 1965:155–157). I have classified the remains as a sweatlodge because of its plastered floor with a raised interior rim, large hearth, large interior postholes, and a floor that was relatively devoid of domestic debris (Gamble 1995). In addition, the floor closely resembled other floors that have been identified as those of sweatlodges in the Chumash region, including two at the interior historic settlement of *He'lxman* (CA-SBA-485) in the Santa Ynez Valley, which were very similar in appearance to the one at *Mikiw* (Gamble 1995:62–63; Macko 1983).

Shilimaqshtush, CA-SBA-205. Very little archaeological evidence exists for storage facilities in the Chumash region. This makes the discovery of numerous storage facilities at the historic village site of *Shilimaqshtush* (between Point Conception and Point Arguello) all the more significant (see chapter 4 for a discussion of *Shilimaqshtush*). In 1950, Lathrap and Hoover (1975) found sealed subterranean storage pits, as well as fragments of house floors and other features, during excavations there (Lathrap and Hoover 1975).[30] Most of the features in the upper levels were probably from the Late period occupation of the site and date to about AD 1000 (Gamble 1991; Glassow 1980). I have provided a brief synopsis here of the storage and house features from the site; for a more thorough discussion, the reader should look at the original monograph (Lathrap and Hoover 1975), as well as subsequent descriptions (Gamble 1991, 1995; Glassow 1980).

At least two floors, about 9 meters or larger in diameter, were documented at the site of *Shilimaqshtush.* An abundance of rocks and artifacts, along with a series of subterranean globular pits, were recorded in the area near and around the floors. Seven of the subterranean pits had fired clay walls with asphaltum bases that overlapped the clay on the walls (Lathrap and Hoover 1975:21–23). Three additional pits varied slightly; one consisted of just an asphaltum base, another had walls and a base of baked clay, and a third had baked clay walls but no base of asphaltum or baked clay. The depth of the pits ranged from about 10 to 38 centimeters. Six of the ten pits were found within one and a half meters of each other, and one had been completely sealed by the overlying floor. One had two bifaces in it, but the contents of the others is unknown. Lathrap and Hoover (1975:21–23; 112) suggested that these pits were used for the storage of economic surpluses such as food. The pits were carefully and intentionally constructed so that they could presumably be sealed, possibly to store perishables such as food. Their location underneath floors in the interior of a structure also suggests that they were concealed in a safe location and that valuable materials were probably stored in these pits. In a review of Lathrap and Hoover's work, Glassow (1980:316) noted that the amount of storage space represented by the pits was probably about 50 cubic feet.

Helo', CA-SBA-46. If we piece together the archaeological evidence on structural remains for Late period mainland sites, we have solid clues about the form of sweatlodges, the layout of houses, and the use of storage facilities. Despite this scattered but significant body of data, we still lack a detailed study of Chumash domestic structures. However, archaeological evidence from the historic settlement of *Helo'* provides a more comprehensive picture of a Chumash household.

Portions of two house floors (figures 18 and 19) were excavated at the site in 1986 and 1987 by a team of archaeologists from the University of California at Santa Barbara (Gamble 1990, 1991, 1995). When the floors were discovered, a meticulous data recovery procedure was followed to recover pollen, carbonized seeds and plant remains, and the kind of minute artifacts and faunal remains that had never been recorded in previous excavations of structural remains in the Chumash region.

FIGURE 18 Photograph of house floor at *Helo'* (CA-SBA-46)

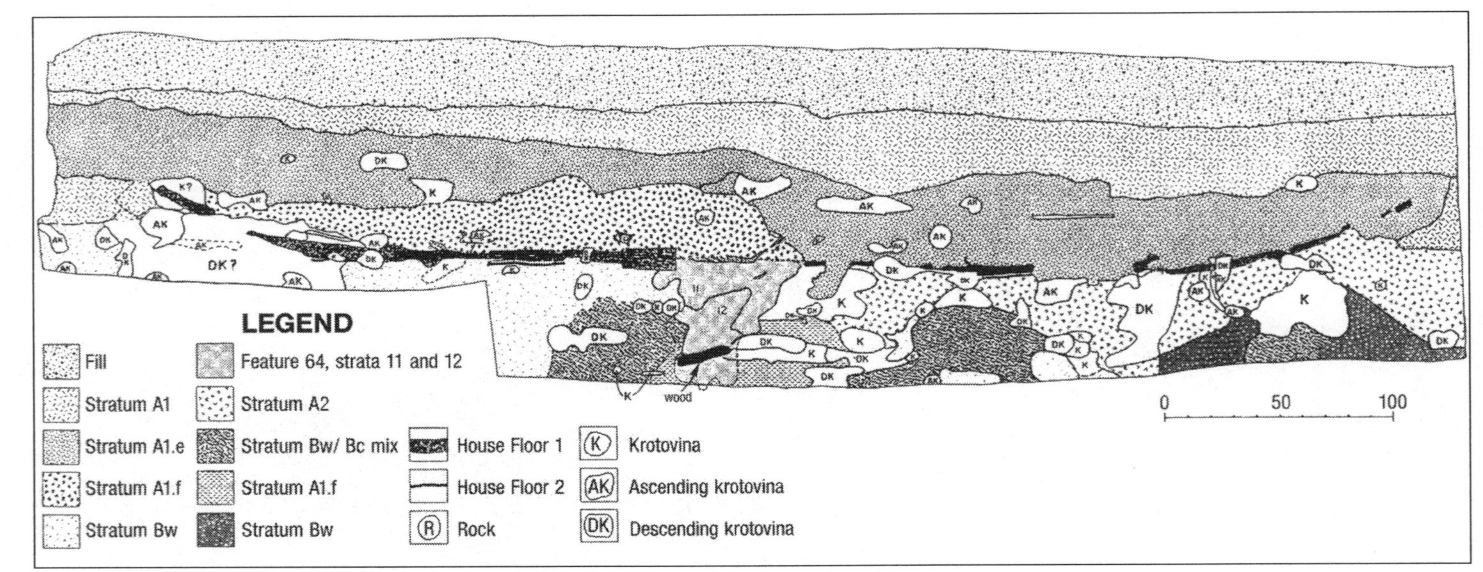

FIGURE 19 Cross section of house floors at *Helo'* (CA-SBA-46)

Floor 1 overlay or intruded into portions of Floor 2 (figure 19), and it appeared to have been purposely constructed from clay that was noticeably different from the surrounding sandy matrix.[31] A concentration of *Olivella biplicata* rough disc beads with large diameters in the vicinity of Floor 1 indicate that this floor was probably in use during the later historic occupation of the site, between 1782 and 1803 (King 1990b). Floor 2 and the dense shell deposit recorded above it (in the area where Floor 1 did not overlay it) contained *Olivella biplicata* rough disc beads that were more typical of the earlier historic occupation of the site between 1770 and 1782 (Gamble 1991:361–362). The stratigraphic relationship between floors 1 and 2 also indicates that Floor 2 was used at an earlier time than Floor 1.

Approximately one third to one half of Floor 1 was excavated[32] (figures 18 and 19). The floor was concave in cross section, about five and a half meters in diameter, and two centimeters thick in most places. Pieces of the floor remained intact when held in one's hand. In certain locations the floor had been replastered or patched with up to four layers (figure 19 and Gamble 1991). The remains of a hearth were found near the southern perimeter of the floor and a subterranean pit with a piece of wood at its base was identified near the center of the floor (figure 19). Very few artifacts were found in or directly associated with Floor 1. In an attempt to recognize spatial patterning, Floor 1 was removed separately from the deposits immediately above and below, using a 25-centimeter grid (figure 20). The floor samples that were analyzed, therefore, were relatively pure because disturbed soils were not included. Fifty-seven of the samples were floated and wet-screened through a 1/40-inch mesh screen, then sorted at the UCSB laboratory facilities (see figure 20). The remaining 20 samples were sent to PaleoResearch Laboratories for pollen analysis (Gamble 1991: Appendix 1).

An analysis of the remains found in Floor 1 was based on the descriptive and visual approach used by Spencer and Flannery (1986:331–367) at Guilá Naquitz, where grid data were collected to assess the degree to which cultural remains were clustered or distributed randomly.[33] A series of descriptive measures for faunal remains and charcoal in Floor 1 was generated to determine if the patterning across the floor was random or not (table 12).[34] All of the remains had a standard deviation that was greater than the mean, indicating an uneven distribution. The standard deviation for shell was notably high, suggesting an extremely uneven distribution for this class of remains. The coefficient of variation expresses the dispersion of a category relative to its mean value (Thomas 1976:84; Spencer and Flannery 1986:332). If the coefficient of variation is

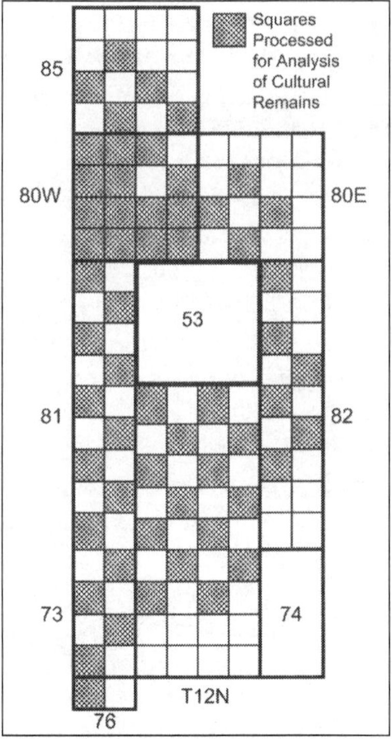

FIGURE 20 Grid map of Floor 1 at *Helo'* (CA-SBA-46)

greater than 0.1, it is likely that the distribution is multimodal, or that some squares had few or no remains while others had a high density of remains. All of the values in table 12 are considerably greater than 0.1, indicating an uneven distribution of all four classes of cultural remains. A variance-mean ratio[35] that is close to 1.0 or equal to the mean suggests a random distribution of remains. A clustered distribution of remains would produce a variance-mean ratio greater than 1.0, and an even distribution or aligned arrangement would produce a variance-mean ratio smaller than 1.0 (Carr 1984:140; Spencer and Flannery 1986:332).[36] The value for the variance-mean ratio of shell in table 12 is particularly high, indicating that the distribution of shell is clustered. Charcoal also exhibited a greater value than 1.0. Fish bone, on the other hand, has a variance-mean ratio of 1.0, indicating a random distribution (table 12). The variance-mean ratio for non-fish bone is 0.41, indicating an even distribution of non-fish bone (table 12).

TABLE 12. Descriptive Measures for Weighed Items Found in Floor 1[a]

Variable	*n*	Weight, Grams			Standard Deviation	Coefficient of Variation	Variance-Mean Ratio
		Minimum	Maximum	Mean			
Charcoal	54	0.06	10.40	1.51	1.96	1.30	2.54
Shell	54	0.12	132.30	17.56	25.91	1.48	38.24
Fish Bone	54	0.01	4.50	0.89	0.95	1.07	1.01
Non-fish Bone	54	0.00	1.44	0.31	0.36	1.14	0.41

TABLE 13. Descriptive Measures for Counted Items Found in Floor 1[a]

Variable	*n*	No. of Items			Standard Deviation	Coefficient of Variation	Variance-Mean Ratio
		Minimum	Maximum	Mean			
Flakes	54	0	14	1.50	2.47	1.65	4.07
Beads	54	0	3	0.54	0.88	1.65	1.46
Otoliths	54	0	1	0.17	0.38	2.25	0.85

SOURCE FOR TABLES 12 AND 13: Based on Spencer and Flannery 1986: Table 26.1.

[a]Explanation of column headings is as follows: *n*, number of squares; Minimum, lowest number of remains in each category per square; Maximum, greatest number of remains in each category per square; Mean, average number of remains in each category per square; Standard Deviation, measure of dispersion calculated in usual manner; Coefficient of Variation, standard deviation divided by the mean to provide a relative measure of dispersion; Variance-Mean ratio, the variance divided by the mean to yield a relative measure of clustering.

Descriptive measurements for artifacts that were counted instead of weighed are presented in table 13.[37] The values in the minimum column of table 13 indicate that some grid samples did not contain examples of the artifact types. The maximum value of otoliths in any given grid square was only one. Because of the small sample, it is questionable whether the descriptive measures for otoliths in table 13 are meaningful. The standard deviation in each category is greater than the mean, indicating that artifacts and otoliths tended to be distributed unevenly. The coefficients of variation are all above 1.0, also suggesting that the artifacts were unevenly distributed. The variance-mean ratio for the beads and flakes indicates that both of these classes of artifacts were distributed non-randomly across Floor 1. The variance-mean ratio for otoliths, however, indicates that otoliths were more randomly scattered than the beads or flakes. This pattern is similar to that of the fish bone, which makes sense. Nevertheless, given the ambiguous nature of some of these results, a visual inspection of the distribution of these remains seems warranted.

Three-dimensional grid maps of the counts and weights of cultural remains and artifacts recovered in Floor 1 were produced to aid in the identification of patterns (figures 21–23).[38] Shell was most abundant in the northern and eastern portions of the floor (figure 21); its distribution was similar to that of charcoal (see Gamble 1991:Figure 7.1). The distribution of beads and flakes, however, was notably different than the distribution of the shell (figures 22 and 23). Beads tended to cluster in the

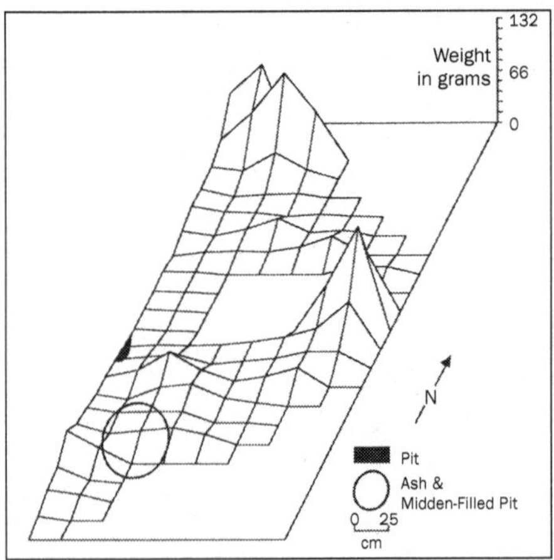

FIGURE 21 Distribution of shell on house floor at *Helo'* (CA-SBA-46)

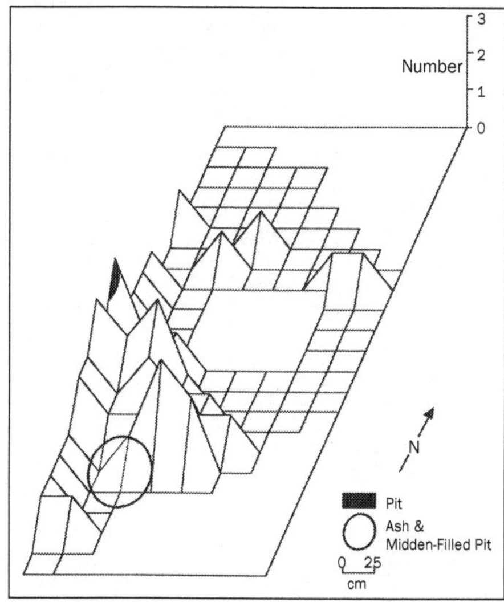

FIGURE 22 Distribution of beads on house floor at *Helo'* (CA-SBA-46)

central part of the floor, with very few or none near the northern and eastern edges. The total absence of beads at the northern end of the floor was most noticeable. The distribution of flakes was similar to that of beads, with the majority of flakes clustered in the vicinity of the hearth (figure 23).

The few additional artifact types that were associated with Floor 1 are mapped in figure 24; they appear to be distributed in a pattern that is similar to that of the beads. Except for an asphaltum plug near the eastern perimeter of the floor and an asphaltum lump in the northern part of the floor, all of these artifacts were clustered in the southern and central part of the floor (figure 24).

An analysis of the distribution of pollen provides information on the processing of plants inside the house represented by Floor 1. Several pollen types from plants of economic significance were recovered in the floor, including Cheno-Ams, Liguliflorae, Cruciferae, Poaceae, Leguminosae, Liliaceae, Malvaceae, *Rhus trilobata*, and a Rosaceae species (Gamble 1991:Appendix 1). Cheno-Ams, which were used for seeds and greens, include plants in the goosefoot (Chenopodiaceae) and pigweed (Amaranthus) families (Cummings 1991:2). Plants in the Poaceae family were most often used for their seeds. There was no evidence for the use of domesticated plants in the pollen record or in the carbonized plant remains

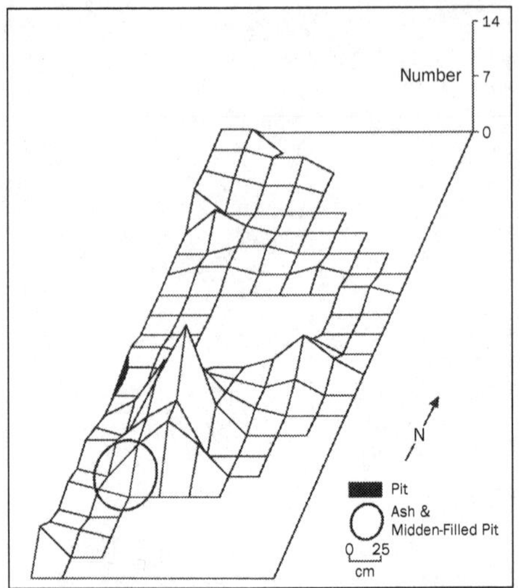

FIGURE 23 Distribution of flakes on house floor at *Helo'* (CA-SBA-46)

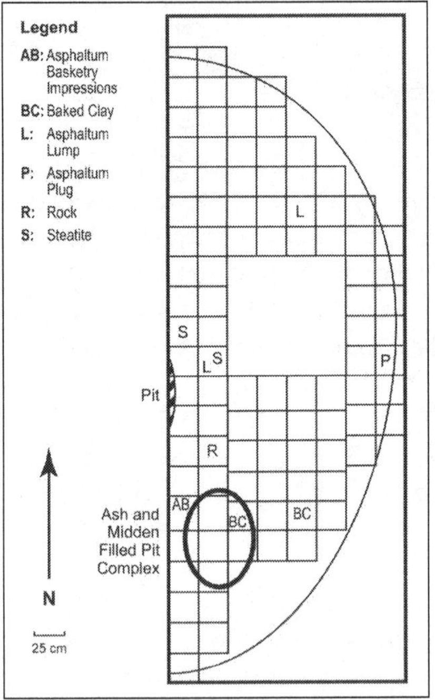

FIGURE 24 Distribution of selected artifacts on house floor at *Helo'* (CA-SBA-46)

at the site. The distribution of two pollen types of particular interest can be seen in figures 25 and 26. The aggregates[39] and elevated Cheno-Am pollen samples are clustered in the southern portion of the floor, particularly in the vicinity of the hearth near the southern end of the floor (figure 25). The distribution of Poaceae pollen is similar to that of the Cheno-Am samples (figure 26).

If these patterns are examined as a whole, we see that the artifacts, cultural remains, and at least some of the pollen were distributed in a nonrandom pattern in Floor 1. Charcoal, shell, and bone (particularly fish bone) were found in greater quantities near the perimeter of the floor (see Gamble 1991:366–395). Some of these remains may have become incorporated in the floor during its construction, either accidentally from the underlying cultural material or from an intentional addition of cultural material as a tempering agent. The cultural remains in the central portion of the floor show a very different pattern than the remains from the

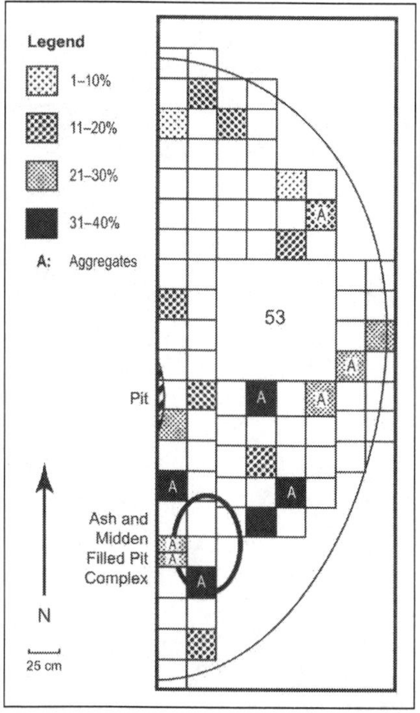

FIGURE 25 Distribution of Cheno-Am pollen on house floor at *Helo'* (CA-SBA-46)

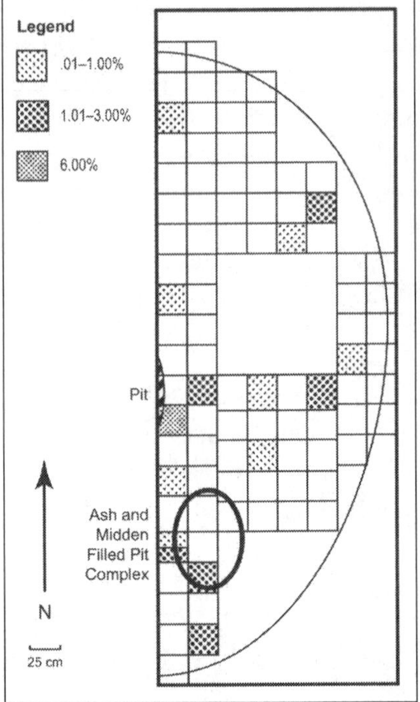

FIGURE 26 Distribution of Poaceae pollen on house floor at *Helo'* (CA-SBA-46)

floor's perimeter. Beads, flakes, steatite, the remains of baskets, and Poaceae and Cheno-am pollens occur in greater densities in the south-central portion of the floor. It is likely that these remains became incorporated in the floor as a result of activities such as food preparation.

The presence of small flakes near the hearth indicates that activities other than food preparation may have also occurred in the house. Of the 83 flakes found in Floor 1, 86 percent were recovered in the 8-mesh per inch and 16-mesh per inch screens; therefore, they were quite small and may have been a result of flakes fracturing off during tool use, a result of retouching tools for sharpening purposes, or a result of tool manufacture. Most of the flakes recovered in Floor 1 were made of cryptocrystalline materials such as chert (Bamforth 1990). Because limited evidence for tool or point manufacture occurred at SBA-46 (see chapter 8),[40] it is unlikely that any of the flakes found in Floor 1 are related to the production of a tool or point. It is more likely that these are a result of tool use or retouch. Most of the flakes in Floor 1 were found in the central portion of the floor near the hearth. Assuming that most of these flakes were a result of primary deposition, it is likely that the occupants of this structure were using and repairing chipped stone tools in this area of the house. The presence of basketry remains and the subterranean pit near the center of the floor indicate that the storage of food or water also occurred in this structure.

Floor 2 was larger than Floor 1, with a diameter of eight meters, and it differed from Floor 1 in consisting primarily of compacted sand (Gamble 1991). The floor was relatively devoid of large rocks and artifacts; however, there are a few artifacts and features worth noting. A fairly large piece of asphaltum with impressions of a coiled basket was found resting on Floor 2. Ethnographic evidence suggests that coiled baskets with asphaltum bases were used as storage baskets among the Chumash (Craig 1966, 1967). It is possible that the basket was left on the floor of the structure when the dwelling was abandoned. A stone anvil was also recovered in this area of the floor: it was fine-grained and had an undulating surface that was pecked and polished. It may have been used as a whetstone as well as an anvil. Anvils were used ethnographically for cracking acorn shells (Hudson and Blackburn 1983:89–91); therefore it is not surprising that the anvil was recovered near the remnants of an acorn storage basket. The shank portion of a bone fishhook fragment also rested on Floor 2. It was probably made of cow bone (chapter 8).[41]

In addition, several fire-altered rocks, two possible hearth features, and a concentration of ash were found in association with Floor 2. A variety of carbonized seeds and plant remains were also recovered in the southern portion of Floor 2 and were identified by Hammett (1991:Table 6.3 and 6.4). The larger plant remains recovered in the floor included Manzanita berries (*Arctostaphylos glandulosa*) and Islay (*Prunus* sp.) (Hammett 1991:Table 6.3). The small seeds from this area included *Calandrinia* sp., *Chenopodium* sp., *Amaranthus* sp., and a variety of grass seeds (Hammett 1991:Table 6.4). All of these plant remains are from important plant foods used by the Chumash. Most of the features and cultural remains in Floor 2 were associated with food preparation and cooking, indicating that these were important activities when the structure was occupied.

There is no indication that Structure 2 (the dwelling associated with Floor 2) burned. Instead, this area of the site continued to be occupied after the abandonment of Structure 2. The beads recovered in the Floor

1 matrix indicate that Structure 1 (the dwelling associated with Floor 1) may have been built soon after Structure 2 was abandoned. None of the items found on Floor 2 appeared to be objects of great value. The storage basket was probably broken and no longer of use. The anvil that remained on the floor may have had the greatest value among the items on the floor. The inhabitants of Structure 2 apparently had time to remove their esteemed possessions when they abandoned their house. Then, sometime after the abandonment of Structure 2,[42] Structure 1 was constructed in the same area of the site. Structure 2 was most likely dismantled because it was in the way of construction, and poles that were still of value may have been used in the construction of Structure 1. It is certainly possible that the inhabitants of Structure 2 were also the inhabitants of Structure 1. Although the ownership of house sites in the Chumash region has not been discussed in the ethnographic record, the inhabitants of choice dwelling locations may have been unwilling to relinquish possession, particularly to non-family members.

Although the data are limited, there are a few observations that can be made based on the excavation of structures at SBA-46; however, these should be considered preliminary until more data are collected. Changes in the size of these two domestic structures, as well as in the size of the settlement of *Helo'* (see Gamble 1991) during the Historic period, suggest that there was a shift in social organization during this period. Households apparently decreased in size,[43] possibly changing from extended family units to nuclear family units. Other evidence for a decrease in the number of inhabitants in Structure 1 include the decline in the number of large rocks and artifacts associated with Floor 1. This is an indication that not as many activities took place in Structure 1 as in Structure 2, and that probably fewer people were living in Structure 1 than in Structure 2. Moreover, on the basis of ethnohistoric evidence, we know that many Chumash villages became depopulated at this time, in part due to the increasing death rate among the Chumash during this era. Despite the fact that villages and probably structures became smaller, the effort invested in constructing the floor in Structure 1 was greater than the effort expended in constructing the floor in Structure 2. Floor 1 was made of clay that was probably brought in from the Goleta Slough; it was then later replastered or patched, in some places repeatedly. At the time that the house was occupied, both the Presidio and the Mission in Santa Barbara were established. Nevertheless, the inhabitants of Structure 1, and probably of other structures at *Helo'*, were living in, maintaining, and improving houses of the type traditionally used by the Chumash.

Evidence for Production and Consumption at the Household and Village Level

An analysis of archaeological evidence, ethnohistoric documents, and ethnographic information provides a baseline for the investigation of the role of the household in the production and consumption of foods and goods. Significant questions can be addressed with these data. How did a typical household in a mainland settlement contribute to the active exchange system of the Chumash? Was storage an integral part of village life? Is there evidence of political power or ritual behavior at the village or household level? What types of activities occurred in the mainland settlements during the Late period? Did these activities change after Spanish colonization? What role did gender play in household and village consumption and production? These questions have been briefly addressed in this chapter, and more data relevant to these issues will be presented in forthcoming chapters.

Extensive evidence for the specialized production of material goods, such as that found on the northern Channel Islands involving the manufacture of shell beads (Arnold and Munns 1994; Kennett 2005), has not been documented for the mainland sites, although limited evidence for the specialized manufacturing of Monterey chert bifaces or preforms does exist in the Vandenberg region (Glassow 1996). Glassow proposes that at least some of these preforms were probably exported out of the region, possibly to the Northern Channel Islands in exchange for shell beads. These issues will be examined in more detail in chapter 8.

The presence of caches of tarring pebbles in the house depression at the Pitas Point site, in addition to the numerous tarring pebbles recovered elsewhere at the site (Gamble 1983), suggest that water bottles were produced in large quantities, some of which were probably intended for export. Based on the ethnographic record, it was probably women that made these baskets.

Other sites with evidence of structures that are discussed in this chapter have little, if any evidence of specialized manufacture. For example, the structures and associated trash deposits at the historic site of *Helo'* lack refuse or artifacts that suggest specialized production took place there. Although there may have been specialized production that could not be seen in the archaeological record at the site, this is in stark contrast to the specialized manufacture of shell beads on the northern Channel Islands.

Storage, however, has been documented by ethnographers, ethnohistorians, and archaeologists. Storage inside of houses and other structures was used for special items, such as the bone whistle found inside the house at *Muwu*. The storage of foodstuffs inside of houses was probably also common; the clay-lined pits at *Shilimaqshtush* most likely were used to store food items. We know from early historic accounts that acorn granaries were built outside of houses and that dried fish were piled on top of houses. It is possible that more desirable foods were stored inside structures because they could be guarded more readily. Economic activities documented in the historic accounts include the processing and cooking of foods, storage of foods, basket making, fishing, and other basic subsistence pursuits.

In contrast to the meager record for specialized production at mainland settlements, there is substantial evidence for ceremonial activities. Structures and areas associated with religious rituals in Chumash sites include dance grounds, sacred enclosures, cemeteries, menstrual huts, male puberty huts, and sweatlodges. Most of these features were noted in the early historic accounts, early archaeological reports and ethnographic accounts, or appear in Chumash oral traditions (Blackburn 1975). In more recent excavations, archaeologists have had a more difficult time identifying ceremonial features, except when they are associated with burials. The most identifiable features involving Chumash ritual behavior in the archaeological record are sweatlodges and cemeteries, especially Late period or historic period lodges, in part because they became standardized in Late period Chumash sites (Gamble 1991, 1995). Bowers and Rogers describe large flat dance grounds in a number of sites, both on the coast and on the mainland. Cemeteries have been found at most major Chumash settlements on the mainland (see chapter 3 for descriptions). Whale bone features have also been found at archaeological sites, some of which were likely associated with ritual or purification, such as those found at the Pitas Point site. Ceremonial activities at Chumash sites appear to have been an important aspect of Chumash life, despite the lack of monumental architecture.

We have no evidence of Spanish ceremonial features in archaeological sites after historic contact. It appears, then (at least judging from structures and other features described in accounts or seen in the archaeological record) that the Chumash living in native settlements maintained their traditional way of life and adopted few if any architectural features associated with the Spanish. In the next chapter we look at this issue in greater depth, as we investigate the subsistence practices of the Chumash both before and after the Spanish settled in the region.

CHAPTER 6

Subsistence and Feasting

Soon we caught sight of the whole village, awaiting us while we encamped in the shade of some trees. (The scouts had come here yesterday, when the heathens of this village presented them with a great deal of seeds, gruel, and very well flavored small raisins.) One of the chiefs, at our own arrival, was making a long speech. We found about a hundred souls seated there, men, women, and children, having some 23 quite large baskets set out in front of them for us, prepared with gruel and sage, others with a kind of very small raisins, and others with water—they made signs to us to take some of this, that they were giving it to us.

Crespí in Brown 2001:363

The Chumash repeatedly held lavish feasts for the Portolá expedition as the expedition passed through their territory (see chapter 4 for descriptions). Feasts such as these required the coordination of large numbers of people to gather, process, and serve the foods. Based on early historic accounts (see Brown 2001), foods served at feasts in the mainland coastal towns included fish, seeds, berries, mush (probably acorn), gruel, sage, and a "sort of honeydew . . . commonly yielded from reed grass patches . . . " (Crespi in Brown 2001:365). The latter food was probably *panoche*, a type of sugar that is deposited by aphids on the stalks of reed grass (*Phragmites australis*) that the coastal Chumash traded for with the Chumash, Yokuts, and other Indian groups in the interior of California (King 2000:33).

In this chapter the nature of feasting and its context in Chumash society is explored, including the ceremonial setting of feasts, the types of serving vessels and foods used, the role of gender in feasting, and the significance of storage for provisions and redistribution of food. Understanding subsistence and the use of food among the Chumash is also integral to the topic of feasting.

Subsistence strategies that developed over thousands of years enabled the inhabitants of Chumash mainland settlements to produce the great feasts described by Crespí and others. An overview of diet and subsistence resources is initially presented in this chapter, followed by a comparison of floral and faunal remains from two historic-period settlements, *Helo'* and *Talepop*, both before and after European colonization. Storage and gender are then investigated. Finally, a thorough examination of the feasting behavior of the Chumash is presented.

The subsistence and political economies are also considered throughout this and subsequent chapters. The subsistence economy, also referred to as the domestic mode of production, is organized at the household level to accommodate the basic needs of the family, such as food, clothing, procurement technology, and housing (Johnson and Earle 2000:23). The political economy, although within the sphere of the subsistence economy, encompasses the exchange of services and goods between interconnected families (Johnson and Earle 2000:26). Most of this chapter focuses on the subsistence economy; however, the political economy is addressed in the context of feasting: later, in chapters 7 and 8, sociopolitical control and exchange are investigated.

Dietary Overview

The Chumash exploited a wide variety of resources in their subsistence activities. A summary of the important plant and animal resources that were used by the Chumash was presented in chapter 2, along with a brief mention of seasonality. Unfortunately, published ethnographic and archaeological information on the seasonal use of plants and animals by the mainland Chumash is incomplete at best. Seasonality data from surrounding California Indian groups must often be used to supplement the meager data for the Chumash (e.g., King 2000). Some of the best syntheses of seasonal uses of plants and animals in the Chumash area can be found in Erlandson (1994), Kennett (2005), King (1967, 1990, 2000), and Landberg (1965). The discussion of diet and seasonality in this chapter is based in part on these sources of information.

MARINE RESOURCES

Inhabitants of the large coastal settlements along the Santa Barbara Channel mainland coast relied heavily on marine resources. King (1990a:Table 2) identified 23 species of important fish that the mainland Chumash ate, all of which were caught in the summer, and many of which were also available throughout the year. Crespí and his companions on the Portolá expedition were offered large quantities of fresh and barbecued fish when they passed through the Chumash region on their journey to the San Francisco Bay area in August of 1769 (see chapter 4). On August 18, 1769, at *Syuxtun* (where the city of Santa Barbara is now located), the expedition was given "so many barbecued bonito fish that seven good hundredweight-measures' worth were gathered . . ." (Brown 2001:415). On the same day, the Chumash again brought the expedition "four double-hundredweights' worth" of fish (Brown 2001:415). There is no doubt that the Chumash on this part of the mainland coast had excessive amounts of fish in August—enough to provide numerous feasts for the many men (approximately 64) who visited the Chumash town.

Other fauna available in the summer on the mainland were sea mammals, shellfish, deer, and medium and small-sized mammals such as rabbits and squirrels. Landberg (1965:59–67) noted 24 species of sea mammals in the Santa Barbara Channel area prior to commercialization (the more significant ones are listed in table 4). Of the four species of seal and two species of sea lions in the Santa Barbara Channel, five are year-round residents in these waters; only the Northern Fur Seal is just a winter visitor. Landberg (1965:62) and King (1990a) have suggested that the most commonly hunted species of sea mammal was the Guadalupe Fur Seal, followed by the California Sea Lion. King (1990a:52) commented that sea otters were next in significance but were probably captured primarily for their pelts. Sea otters once were abundant in the kelp beds of the Santa Barbara Channel (Landberg 1965:59), but are now locally extinct.

Colten (2002) and Kennett (2005:198) have suggested that marine mammals were less important than shellfish or fish in the diet of the Chumash of the northern Channel Islands during the Late period. Certainly one would expect even less emphasis on marine mammals on the mainland, where rookeries were less common. However, some recent findings indicate marine mammal presence and exploitation on the mainland. For example, in a dietary reconstruction of faunal remains (using meat weight estimates) from the Late period site of SBA-72N in Tecolote Canyon, Erlandson and his colleagues (2005:92) found that "sea mammals contributed most of the meat consumed (41%), followed by land mammals (30%), fish (26%), shellfish (3%), and birds (<1%)." At SBA-73N, situated across the creek from SBA-72, Erlandson et al(2005:102) found a similar pattern, with sea mammals again dominating the assemblage, followed by fish. At SBA-73S, the pattern was slightly different, with fish contributing most of the edible meat represented, followed by sea mammals. Both areas of SBA-73 were occupied during the Late period. All of these dietary reconstructions are similar in that they show an emphasis on marine faunal resources when compared with terrestrial ones. More dietary reconstructions from the Late period are needed before final conclusions can be reached; nevertheless, it appears that sea mammals were a significant component of the diet during the Late period at Santa Barbara mainland coast settlements.

Procurement Technology. Landberg (1965) has provided the most detailed discussion of methods of sea mammal procurement; he noted that there are no rookeries on the mainland today, but points out that ethnographic evidence (although not specific to the Chumash) indicates that clubbing sea mammals at rookeries was probably the easiest method of capture. The Chumash may have also harpooned marine mammals from watercraft, although Landberg (1965) and others believe that this is less likely. It is possible that most sea mammals, or select portions of them, were traded from the Channel Islands to the mainland. Walker (1997) proposed that the sea mammal remains from the Pitas Point site (VEN-27), which consisted primarily of forelimb bones of Guadalupe Fur Seal, were probably traded from the Channel Islands to the mainland.

Undoubtedly the most significant maritime technology for the capture of fish and sea mammals involved the ocean-going plank canoe (figure 27), an innovation essential for the intensification of marine resource exploitation (Gamble 2002; Kirch 1991; Yesner 1980). Solid archaeological evidence indicates that this important watercraft was fully developed by at least 1300 years ago, and probably much earlier (Gamble 2002). We know from early historic records that the Chumash used at least two types of watercraft, the tule reed balsa and the sewn wooden plank canoe, and possibly a third, the dugout canoe (Hudson et al. 1978). The balsa was made from bundles of tule reeds and could be constructed in a relatively short time (about three days). It was primarily used for fishing along the coast and occasionally to access the Channel Islands in calm conditions (Hudson et al. 1978:27–28; Hudson and Blackburn 1982:331). Some of the constraints on tule balsas included their limited ability to carry large

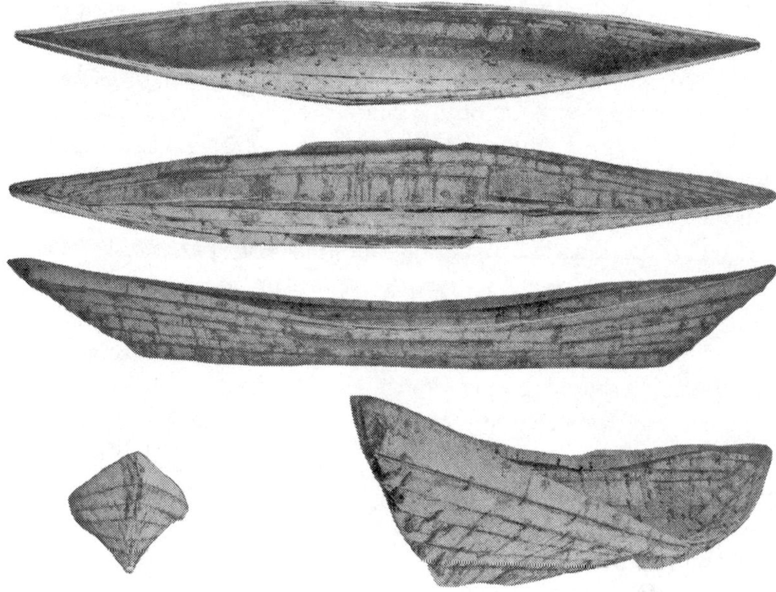

FIGURE 27 Chumash plank canoe replica made for the 1915 Panama-California Exposition by Fernando Librado (photo courtesy of the San Diego Museum of Man)

amounts or substantial weights, their likelihood of becoming waterlogged if submerged for long periods of time (e.g., Fagan 2004), and their vulnerability in rough seas (Hudson et al. 1978).

There is some doubt among scholars as to whether the dugout was used by the Chumash prior to European contact (Heizer 1940). Heizer and Massey (1953) noted that dugout boats were not mentioned in any of the historic accounts of the Santa Barbara Channel region between the sixteenth and eighteenth centuries; the authors believed that dugout canoes were a more recent introduction to the Chumash. The only early reference to the use of the dugout by the Chumash came from Hill in the 1850s (Woodward 1934:120), who described how these watercraft were constructed out of a solid tree trunk. Hill stated that the canoes were about 30 feet long and three or four feet deep and wide.

Ethnographic information from Harrington (Hudson et al. 1978:31–36) provides more details about the dugout, only some of which are summarized here. The dugout was made from a single log, often of willow, cottonwood, or poplar, that was hollowed out. Harrington does not provide information on size, but his consultants did note that the dugout was of little use in the ocean. Usually this type of watercraft was used in estuaries or in coves where the sea was calm (Hudson et al. 1978:33). Despite the lack of documentation on the dugout in the early historic period in the Chumash region, Hudson and his colleagues (1978:22) have suggested that the earliest plank canoes were probably dugouts with a few boards added to the hull to make them more seaworthy. Certainly some form of watercraft, possibly the balsa or dugout, must have been used when the offshore Channel Islands were settled approximately 10,000 years ago.

In contrast to the balsa and dugout, the *tomol* or plank canoe was considered much more seaworthy (figure 27). In early historic accounts, the plank canoe is frequently mentioned in association with fishing among the Chumash (for examples, see chapter 4). The plank canoe facilitated the capture of large, deep water fish, such as the swordfish, and was an essential element in the elaboration of the exchange network in the Santa Barbara Channel region (see chapter 8 for a discussion on the significance of the plank canoe in trade).

Seaworthy plank canoes such as those made by the Chumash involved esoteric and sophisticated technological skills. Most early historic chroniclers estimated that the watercraft could hold eight to twelve people, although usually only three to five people were observed in them (Heizer 1938; Robinson 1942, 1943). Estimates of the length of plank canoes varied between 12 and 30 feet. On the basis of early historic accounts, Robinson (1943:15) argued that the majority of canoes were small, between 12 and 18 feet long and 4 feet wide, whereas the larger ones were about 19 to 22 feet in length. One of the earliest and best descriptions of the physical appearance of a plank canoe was written by Fr. Pedro Font, a priest who accompanied the Anza expedition in 1776 (Bolton 1931). Font stated that the canoes were shaped like a little boat without ribs and that the ends of the canoe were elevated and arched with an opening at each end leaving a "V." This description is in accordance with other ethnohistoric accounts as well as with the ethnographic literature. The gap at the prow and stern of the boat (referred to as its "ears") helped in the capture of large fish. By throwing the line off the prow or the stern, rather than the side of the boat, the boat would be less likely to capsize if a large animal was captured (Hudson et al. 1978:93). The plank canoe was propelled with a wooden paddle (figure 28) with a blade at each end (Hudson and Blackburn 1982:353).

Because detailed information on canoe construction is meager in historic accounts, ethnographic data provide some of the best information

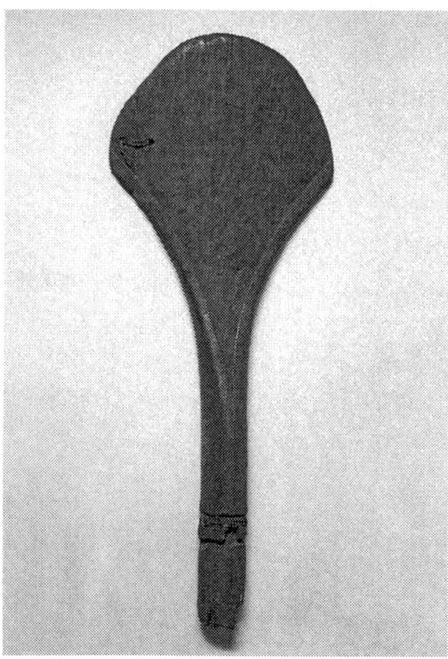

FIGURE 28 Canoe paddle blade collected by Vancouver in 1793 (copyright the Trustees of the British Museum)

on the subject. The most explicit information on the canoe comes from a replica of a Chumash plank canoe (figure 27) that Harrington had Fernando Librado make for the 1915 Panama-California Exposition in San Diego (Richie and Hager 1973; Robinson 1942, 1943). Fernando Librado was one of Harrington's most knowledgeable Chumash consultants. In Fernando's replica, the bottom board is the largest, measuring fourteen feet in length, eight and a half inches in width, and one and a half inches in thickness, and tapering to a point at each end. The sides of the replica consist of about twenty planks, each about three-quarters of an inch in thickness and between three and nine feet in length (Robinson 1943:13).

Ethnographic information and some historic accounts indicate that the wood, whether driftwood or not, was seasoned. Once seasoned, the wood was shaped into planks, using stone tools, and after that bent using steam and boiling water. The planks were first submerged in hot water (that had been heated with rocks) in a large pit that had been sealed with baked clay, and then bent immediately after removal. Afterward, the planks were shaped, sanded with sharkskin, and carefully fitted together. At least two of the planks may have been beveled: the bottom board and the adjacent plank (Hudson et al. 1978:59, 77). Gamble (2002) noted that numerous planks found in archaeological contexts had evidence of beveling.

Stone tools (figure 29) were employed to drill holes in the planks, which were later sewn together with milkweed string. High-grade hardened asphaltum from mainland tar seeps, mixed with pine pitch, provided the material used to fill the holes (figure 30) and caulk the seams where the planks were joined (Hudson et al. 1978). Obviously, because of the nature of a plank boat, the material used to plug the holes and caulk the seams was a critical component in its seaworthiness. Landberg (1965:38) believed that asphaltum was so essential to the plank canoe that without it the watercraft would not have been seaworthy. Heizer (1940:83) noted that the

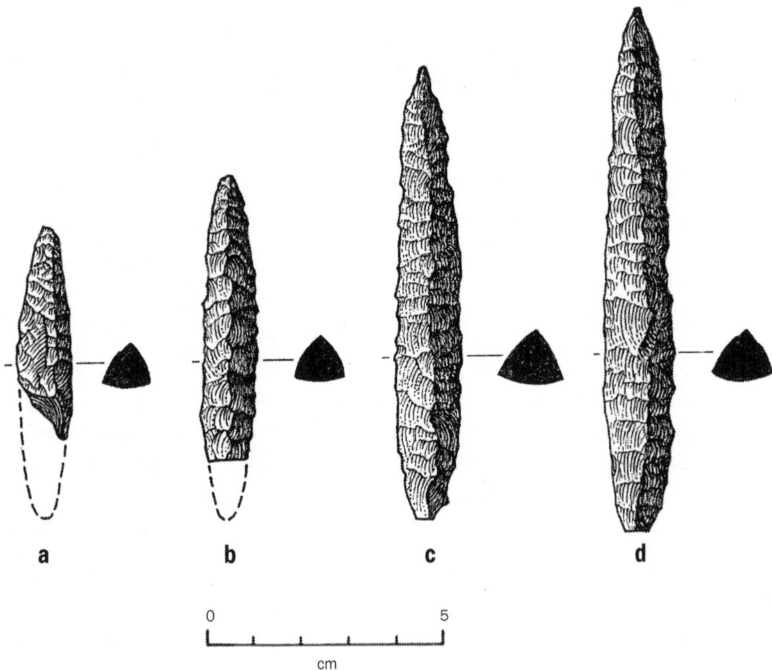

FIGURE 29 Monterey chert canoe drills: (a) UCLA catalog no. 565-929, Monterey chert drill from the Pitas Point site (CA-VEN-27); (b) UCLA catalog no. 565-2523, Monterey chert drill from the Pitas Point site (CA-VEN-27); (c) LACMNH catalog no. L-1433-32-831, Monterey chert drill from *Simoʿmo* (CA-VEN-26); (d) LACMNH catalog no. L-1433-32-832, Monterey chert drill from *Simo'mo* (CA-VEN-26). (courtesy of American Antiquity, Vol. 67, No. 2, 2002)

FIGURE 30 Photograph of canoe plank with asphaltum plugs, site #3, Christies (Berkeley SCRI-156a), catalog no. NA-CA-156a-3E (photo by Lynn Gamble, courtesy of the Santa Barbara Museum of Natural History)

plank canoe was basically frameless (like that of early Egyptian plank boats), and that construction of the boat would have been impossible without the liberal use of asphaltum. Apparently some plank canoes did have a cross beam that served as a brace for the boat (Hudson et al. 1978:90–91).

Once the plank canoes were built, the chiefs and wealthy individuals who owned them exerted considerable control over their use. In 1776, at the town of *Syuxtun* (Santa Barbara), Font observed a plank canoe filled with fish being carried by ten or twelve fishermen to the house of a chief, who stood on shore dressed in a bearskin cape (Bolton 1931; Johnson 2001; Robinson 1942:204). Harrington noted that once the canoe was brought to the owner's house, the day's catch was then redistributed among the individuals who constructed the canoe, as well as to the relatives of the canoe owner (Hudson et al. 1978:130).

No other technological innovation used in the taking of marine resources was as significant as the plank canoe. However, other items, including fishhooks, harpoons, nets and other innovations associated with fishing, were also integral to this industry. A variety of fishhooks and other technological items were used during the Late period in the Santa Barbara Channel region that were highly effective for capturing fish (figure 31). At the time of European contact, the Chumash used single-piece curved fishhooks, composite fish hooks, fish gorges, harpoons, and nets

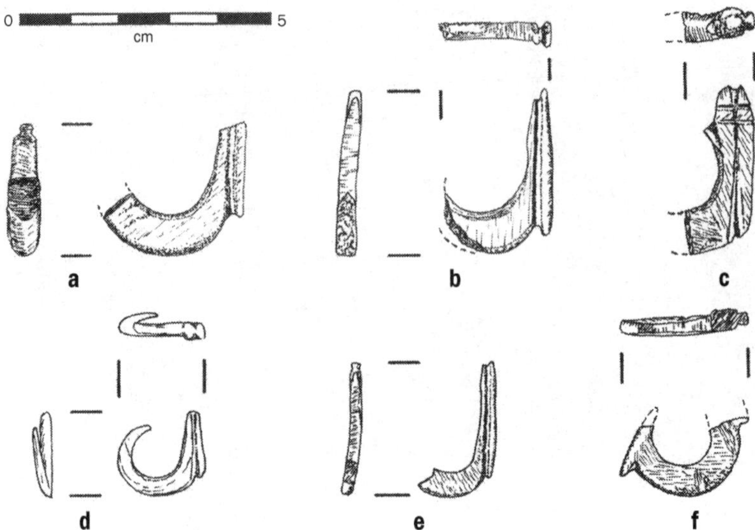

FIGURE 31 Bone and shell fishhooks from *Helo'* (CA-SBA-46): (a) bone fishhook #12443; (b) bone fishhook #12467; (c) bone fishhook #12447, (d) shell fishhook, Haliotis sp. #12451; (e) shell fishhook, *Mytilus californianus* #12456; (f) shell fishhook, *Mytilus californianus* #12454.

(Bennyhoff 1950; King 1990a; Rick et al. 2002; Strudwick 1986). Pedro Font noted that the Chumash used shell fish hooks, as well as small and large nets, when capturing fish (Bolton 1931: 259). In 1775, Fages provided even more details about fishing practices:

> The tridents they use are of bone. The barb is well shaped and well adapted to its use. The fishhooks are made of pieces of shell fashioned with great skill and art. For catching sardines they use large baskets, into which they throw the bait which these fish like, which is the ground up leaves of cactus, so that they come in great numbers; the Indians make their cast and catch great numbers of the sardines (Priestley 1972: 51).

King (1990a:48) has suggested that the tridents that Fages described might have been harpoons, and noted that Fr. Antonio de la Ascensión (Wagner 1926:236) also described the use of harpoons from canoes when he observed the Indians off the coast of Catalina Island in 1602 catching fish and sea mammals.

On the basis of the types of fish in the archaeological assemblage from the Late period site of *Shisholop* (VEN-3), Fitch (1969) proposed that the

Chumash used hook and line, gill nets, cast nets, beach seines, traps, and harpoons to capture fish. His suggestions are supported by early historic accounts of fishing practices in the Santa Barbara Channel. Of the 946 otoliths from the site, 906 were identified by Richard Huddleston (1988) to the species level, and twenty five others to the family level. A total of 40 species assignable to eleven families were identified (Huddleston 1988:Table 8.9). This represents the largest and most varied collection of otoliths from any site in the Chumash area. The types of fish represented in the sample from the historic settlement of *Helo'* are similar to those found at *Shisholop* (South) and were probably also caught using the same techniques.

The most common type of fishing gear found in Chumash archaeological sites is the single-piece curved fishhook made from bone or shell (figure 31). Rick and his colleagues (2002) have demonstrated that these fishhooks were in use for approximately 2500 years, although King (1990a) has suggested that compound fishhooks were in use for at least 6000 years. Single-piece bone fishhooks were made from deer bone; they are rarer in the archaeological record than those made from shell. After European settlement in the Chumash region, cow bone was probably used (Gamble 1991:280). Strudwick (1986) has suggested that the single-piece circular fishhook was most effective along rocky shores at a moderate depth. Several archaeological assemblages from Late period mainland coastal sites, including those from Muwu (VEN-11), Malibu (LAN-264), Helo' (SBA-46) and Pitas Point (VEN-27) include fishhook blanks, drills, and other evidence of fishhook manufacture (figure 32) (Gamble 1983; Hudson and Blackburn 1982; King n.d.).

The best archaeological evidence for the use of nets are grooved and notched stones (figure 33) that have been found in a number of Late period sites, including Pitas Point (VEN-27) and the historic settlement of *Helo'* (SBA-46). Ethnographic sources indicate that these apparent sinkers may have also been attached to a fishline (Hudson and Blackburn 1982: 159–161). King (1990a:83) has shown that these weights may have been in use for thousands of years. At the historic site of *Shisholop* (South), Fitch (1969:68) identified 7,655 White Croaker otoliths that all appeared to be about the same size. He proposed that the uniformity of the otoliths indicates that the croakers were captured with gill nets. Other fish represented at the site that were in the same size range and that were probably also caught with gill nets included Queenfish, Yellowfin Croaker, Jacksmelt, and embiotocid perch. Fitch also suggested that beach seines were used to capture surf-dwelling species such as Shovelnose Guitarfish, surf perches, and atherinids, and that cast nets were probably used for anchovies.

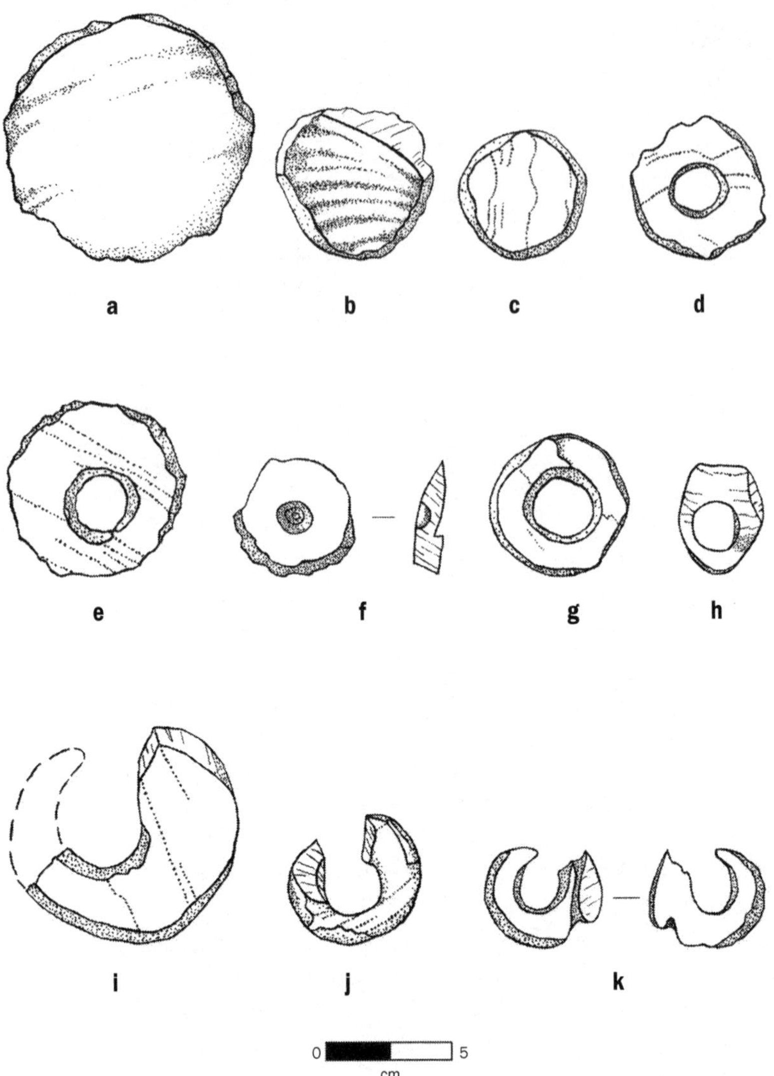

FIGURE 32 Fishhooks in different stages of manufacture from the Pitas Point Site (CA-VEN-27): (a) fishhook blank, *Haliotis* sp. #4334; (b) fishhook blank, *Mytilus californianus* #1844; (c) possible fishhook blank, *Mytilus californianus* #1203; (d) fishhook blank, *Mytilus californianus* #372; (e) fishhook blank, *Mytilus californianus* #1695; (f) fishhook blank, *Mytilus californianus* #2029; (g) fishhook blank, *Mytilus californianus* #2300; (h) possible fishhook blank, *Mytilus californianus* #4699; (i) fishhook blank, *Mytilus californianus* #1835; (j) fishhook blank, *Mytilus californianus* #2773; (k) fishhook blank, *Mytilus californianus* #1382.

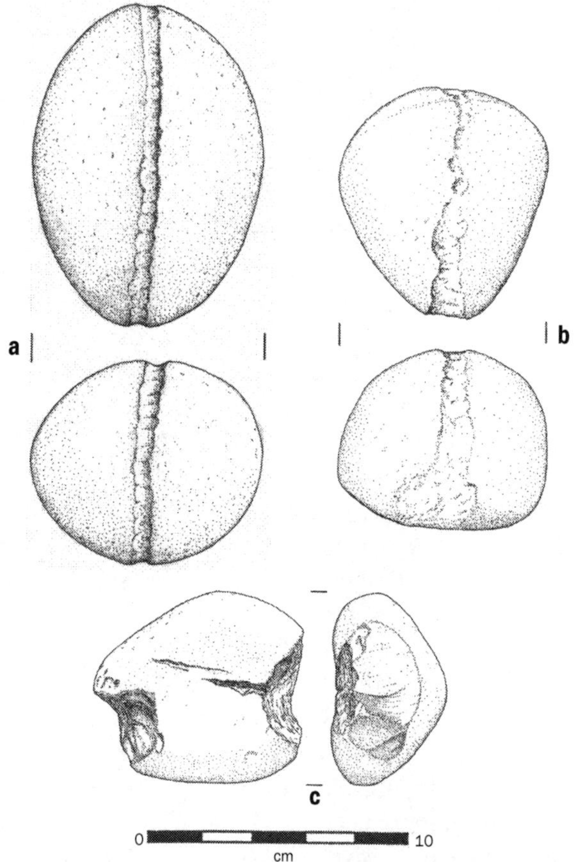

FIGURE 33 Net weights from CA-SBA-46: (a) grooved net weight, sandstone, #602; (b) grooved net weight, sandstone, #603; (c) notched net weight, siltstone, #12403.

By the Late period, it is clear that the Chumash had mastered a wide range of effective techniques for the capture of both fish and sea mammals. Evidence of intensification over time is clearly documented in the archaeological record, as can be seen in the example of the plank canoe. Innovations such as this were undoubtedly a result of intensification, as human populations in prime locations burgeoned.

TERRESTRIAL RESOURCES

Although land mammals, birds, and reptiles were exploited less frequently than marine resources in Late Period Chumash coastal sites, they were essential sources of food and provided materials for tools. Deer were the most significant large terrestrial animals that the Chumash captured. Landberg (1965) and Glassow and Wilcoxon (1988:88) have suggested that the easiest time to capture deer was probably in the late summer, because of the tendency of deer to concentrate in the lower elevations at this time of year. Several early historic accounts, including those of Costansó in 1769 and José Longinos Martinéz in 1792 (Hudson and Blackburn 1982:74–77; King 2000:34), describe the use of deer decoys by the Chumash; they wore the skin of the head and part of the neck of a deer and then, pretending to graze until they were close, the hunters shot the deer with a bow and arrow. This weapon was used to hunt deer and other mammals and was also used in warfare. Arrow points typical of the Late and Historic periods were small, with concave or convex bases (figure 34) (Gamble et al. 1982; King 2005). Although deer were a more significant part of the diet of the Chumash living in the interior, data from Tecolote Canyon (Erlandson et al. 2005, see above) indicate that the Chumash living on the mainland coast during the Late Period also relied on deer to some extent.

The data from Mescalitan Island differ from those collected by Erlandson and his colleagues in that land mammals appear to be less significant in the diet at this site than at the Tecolote sites (Anakouchine 1990; Denardo 1990; Glenn 1990; Glenn et al. 1988). The total weight and protein yield of the major non-fish faunal categories at SBA-46 are presented in table 14, with a chronological overview of non-fish faunal remains listed in table 15. Analysis of the late historic deposits indicates that there was a slight increase in terrestrial mammal bone over preceding periods in comparison with sea mammal bone. One explanation for this increase is that historic terrestrial mammal bones (such as cow and sheep bone) were present at the site during its later historic occupation. Despite this slight increase in terrestrial remains, the inhabitants of *Helo'* continued to use marine resources, particularly fish and shellfish, in greater quantities than terrestrial resources (exclusive of floral remains) (Anakouchine 1990:8; Glenn et al. 1988). Rabbits were also significant at the site of *Noqto* (McClure 2004), but were not as important as they had been in the earlier periods. We also have evidence of the use of birds for food and for feathers at the Goleta Slough; most of them came from an estuarine or bay environment (Guthrie 1985).

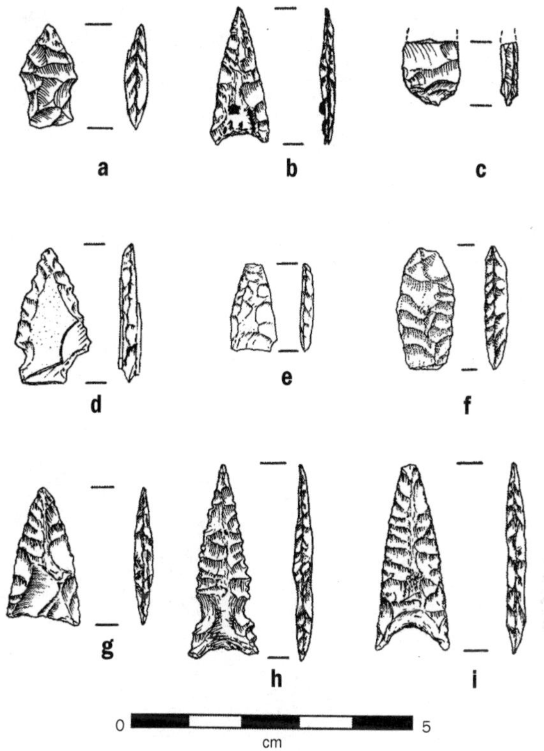

FIGURE 34 Projectile points from CA-SBA-46: (a) Franciscan chert, #2492; (b) Monterey chert, #2513; (c) Monterey chert, #2497; (d) Franciscan chert, #2489; (e) Monterey chert, #2500; (f) chert, #2516; (g) Franciscan chert, #2491; (h) Monterey chert #2515; (i) Monterey chert, #2490.

The bones of deer and other large ungulates were never very common at SBA-46 (Anakouchine 1990; Langenwalter 1985:4) and were apparently valued for technological purposes, rather than as a source of food. Langenwalter (1985:4) noted that tooth and lower limb fragments comprised the sample of deer bone from the SRS excavations at CA-SBA-46, and suggested that deer bone was brought to the site exclusively in the form of tools or tool-making materials (Langenwalter 1985:4). Tools made from deer and other large mammal bones included fishing equipment, awls, and needles (figure 35). Bone was also used as ornamentation and in rituals; bone hairpins and scepters are discussed in subsequent chapters. Walker (1990:1), in his analysis of the tool marks on the bones from

TABLE 14. Total Weight of Each Major Faunal (Non-Fish) Category and Corresponding Amounts of Edible Meat Protein, SBA-46

Category	Weight (grams)	Protein Yield (grams)[a]
Arctocephalus sp. (Southern Fur Seal)	9.55	3216.54
Callorhinus sp. (Northern Fur Seal)	6.60	
Zalophus sp. (Sea Lion)	34.75	
Undiff. Fur Seal	38.95	
Cetacea (Dolphin, Whale)	97.35	
Odocoileus sp. (Mule Deer)	54.65	233.60
Undiff. Med-Large Land Mammal	679.65	1359.30
Bos/Ovis spp.(Cow/Sheep)	48.25	
Canis sp. (Dog)	3.20	
Sylvilagus/Lepus spp. (Rabbit)	1.84	36.80
Thomomys sp.(Pocket Gopher)	34.00	
Microtus sp.(Meadow Mouse)	0.55	
Spermophilus sp.(Ground Squirrel)	1.15	
Reptile/amphibian	3.75	

[a]Converted by ratio 1:10 for sea mammals (Osborn 1977:147) and 1:21 for land mammal species (Watt and Merrill, 1963:51).

TABLE 15. Total Weight of Fauna in Grams by Chronological Period, SBA-46

Time Period	Miscellaneous	Rabbit	Rodent Mammal	Sea Mammal	Terrestrial
Early Middle Period	0.35	1.80	2.65	118.25	124.65
Early Historic	1.15	1.40	5.10	119.85	60.70
Late Historic	1.40	2.55	4.55	79.94	50.90
Mixed Transition	12.25	3.60	3.45	407.00	156.55
Unknown	32.75	9.05	25.20	674.10	523.15

SBA-46, found that about 60% of the worked bones were from land mammals. Most of the land mammal bones from the UCSB excavations appeared to be from deer, though only one specimen exhibited sufficient anatomical detail for certain identification (Walker 1990:1).

Helo': Plant Use at Contact

The remains of plants used by the Chumash are more difficult to identify in the archaeological record than are the remains of animals; therefore de-

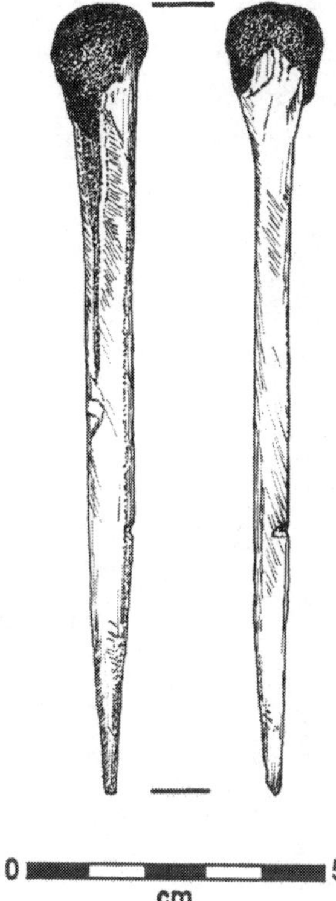

FIGURE 35 Bone awl from *Helo'* (CA-SBA-46), # 542, 12431.

termining their significance is a considerable challenge. Adding to these difficulties is the fact that many archaeologists do not collect ethnobotanical remains or have only done so recently; issues of preservation further complicate the identification of plant remains. Surpluses used in feasting required storage, yet we know very little about storage because only limited excavations have been conducted in houses, few storage pits have been carefully analyzed, and external granaries would leave little trace in the archaeological record. Although limited in scope, some of the best data on household storage come from the historic town of *Helo'* (SBA-46), where paleobotanical remains and house features were examined in detail.

Macrobotanical remains associated with two hearths and a house floor at *Helo'* were analyzed by Julia Hammett (1991). In addition, twenty-one pollen samples collected from 25-cm-square samples from Floor 1 were examined by Linda Scott Cummings (Appendix 1 in Gamble 1991). The results of these analyses are provided in table 16. The taxonomic nomenclature is based on that used by Clifton Smith (1976); some common names are provided. A few floral remains are not listed in tables 16 and 17; for example, desiccated berries of *Sambucus mexicana* (Elderberry) were observed by Hammett (1991), but are not included in this table because they were not carbonized. Many of the plant families observed in

TABLE 16. Pollen and Charcoal at SBA-46

Family	Pollen: Genus or Species	Charcoal: Genus or Species	Common Name
Agavaceae (Liliaceae)		*Yucca whipplei*	Chaparral Yucca
Amaranthaceae (Cheno-Am)	Undifferentiated[a]	*Amaranthus californicus*	Amaranth
Anacardiaceae	Undifferentiated		Sumac
Anacardiaceae	*Rhus* sp.	*Rhus* sp.	Sumac
Anacardiaceae	*Toxicodendron diverslobum*		Poison Oak
Asteraceae (Compositae)	Undifferentiated	Other	Sunflower
Asteraceae (Compositae)	*Artemisia* sp.		
Asteraceae (Tubuliflorae)	Undifferentiated	*Hemizonia* sp.	
Asteraceae (Low-Spine)	Undifferentiated		
Asteraceae (High-Spine)	Undifferentiated		
Asteraceae (Liguliflorae)	Undifferentiated		
Betulaceae	*Alnus* sp.		Alder
Boraginaceae		*Amsinckia menziessi*	Fiddleneck
Cactaceae	*Cylindropuntia* sp.		
Chenopodiaceae (Cheno-Am)	Undifferentiated	*Chenopodium* sp.	Salt Bush
Chenopodiaceae (Cheno-Am)		*Atriplex* sp.	Goosefoot
Cruciferae	Undifferentiated	Other	Mustard
Cruciferae	Undifferentiated	*Lepidium* sp.	Peppergrass
Cucurbitaceae		*Marah* sp	Wild Cucumber (Chilicothe)

(*continued*)

TABLE 16. (continued)

Family	Pollen: Genus or Species	Charcoal: Genus or Species	Common Name
Cupressaceae	*Juniperus* sp.		Juniper, Guata
Cyperaceae	Undifferentiated	*Scirpus* sp	Tule
Ericaceae		*Arctostaphylos* sp.	Manzanita
Ericaceae		*Arctostaphylos glanulosa*	
Ericaceae		*Arctostaphylos glauca*	
Euphorbiaceae	*Euphorbia* sp.		
Fabaceae (Leguminosae)	*Prosopis* sp.	Undifferentiated	Pea Family—Mesquite
Fagaceae	*Quercus* sp.	*Quercus* sp.	Oak
Geraniaceae	*Erodium* sp.		Geranium
Lamiaceae (Labiatae)		*Salvia* sp.	Sage
Liliaceae	Undifferentiated		Lily
Malvaceae	Undifferentiated		
Malvaceae	*Sphaeralcea* sp.		Mallow
Myrtaceae	*Eucalyptus* sp. (Contaminant)		Eucalyptus
Onagraceae	Undifferentiated		Evening Primrose
Pinaceae	*Pinus* sp		Pine
Plantaginaceae		*Plantago* sp.	Plantain
Poaceae (Gramineae)	Undifferentiated	Other	Grass
Poaceae (Gramineae)	Undifferentiated	*Hordeum* sp	Barley
Poaceae (Gramineae)	Undifferentiated	*Phalaris* sp.	
Polygonaceae	*Eriogonum* sp.	*Rumex* sp.	Buckwheat Family
Portulaceae		*Calandrinia* sp.	Red Maids
Portulaceae		*Montia* sp.	Miners Lettuce
Rhamnaceae	Undifferentiated		Buckthorn
Rhamnaceae	*Ceonothus* sp.		Buckbrush, Wild Lilac
Rosaceae	Undifferentiated	*Prunus* sp.	Rose Family, Islay
Saxifragaceae	Undifferentiated		Saxifrage Family
Scrophulariaceae	Undifferentiated		Figwort Family
Solanaceae		*Solanum* sp.	Nightshade
Umbelliferae	Undifferentiated		Parsley/Carrot Family
Urticaceae	*Urtica* sp.		Nettle

SOURCES: Data from this table is from Hammett 1991, Cummings 1991, and Gamble 1991.

[a]Undifferentiated indicates that the genus or species was not identified.

TABLE 17. Common Plant Resources Observed in the Pollen Record at SBA-46 and Their Uses

Group and/or Family	Plant Genus in Santa Barbara County	Common Name	Habitat	Uses by California Indians
Cheno-Am Amaranthaceae	*Amaranthus* sp.	Amaranth	Mud flats	Chumash: possibly used seeds and leaves. Talepop and Helo': seeds. Cahuilla: used seeds and leaves
Cheno-Am Chenopodiaceae	*Atriplex* sp.	Saltbush	Wetlands; many found in salt marshes	Chumash: *A. lentiformis*, whole plant burned, ashes used for lye in soap, Mission times. Talepop and Helo': seeds. Cahuilla: used seeds for food, leaves and roots for soap, flowers, stems, and leaves medicinally. Owens Valley Paiute: seeds
	Chenopodium sp.	Pigweed	Varied; some in wetlands	Chumash: *C. berlandieri*, seeds and greens; *C. californicum*, roots for soap and medicinally. *Chenopodium* sp.: seeds at Talepop and Helo'. Also used by Atsugewi, Cahuilla, Bear R., Luiseño, Miwok, Salinan, Tipai, Paiute.
	Salicornia sp.	Pickleweed	Salt marsh	Cahuilla: seeds (tips can also be eaten).
	Suaeda sp.	Blite	Salt marsh	Cahuilla: seeds and greens, used as dye for hair and in baskets.
Liguliflorae Asteraceae	*Agoseris* sp.	Mountain Dandelion, *A. heterophylla*	Grassland, woodland, chaparral	Chumash: possibly used seeds and leaves. Karok: *A. aurantiaca* (not in S.B.Cty.). Root sucked and chewed like gum.
	Aniscoma aucalis		Sandy flats in woodland, sandy slopes to deserts	Shoshone and S. Paiute: cooked greens
	Crepis occidentalis		Coniferous forest	N. Paiute: leaves eaten raw. Karok: *Crepis acuminata* (not in S.B.Cty.). Stems peeled and eaten as greens.

	Malacothrix sp.	Snake's Head	Varied. *M. californica* in sandy places	Luiseño: *M. californica*, seeds. Wintun: roots
	Microseris sp.		Varied	Roots eaten
Poaceae	*Bromus* sp.	Brome	Varied. *B. carinatus*, fresh marsh	Chumash: seeds, *B. carinatus*, Talepop: seeds. Nisenan, Miwok, Gosiute: *B. carinatus*, seeds.
	Distichlis spicata	Salt Grass	Salt marsh	Chumash: plants beaten to remove surface encrustations for possible use as salt.
	Elymus condensatus	Giant Rye	Near creeks, washes, potreros, and canyons	Chumash: stems used for arrows, tobacco tubes, gambling sticks; used for house thatching; tea of new shoots for venereal disease. Talepop: seeds. Indians from Great Basin: seeds eaten.
	Hordeum spp.	Barley	Varied	Chumash: seeds eaten as pinole. Talepop and Helo': seeds
	Muhlenbergia sp.		Varied	Chumash: stalks
	Phalaris sp.	Canary Grass	Vernal flats and wet, sandy places	Chumash: Talepop and Helo': seeds. N. Paiute: seeds
	Phragmites australis	Carrizo Grass	Near springs in canyons of inland mountains	Chumash: aphid honeydew collected from stems and eaten like sugar; stems used for arrows.

SOURCES: Chumash references primarily from Timbrook 1990:236-253 and Timbrook, Johnson, and Earle 1982:163-186. Archaeological references: Hammett 1991; Hammett and Wohlgemuth 1982. Other references: Bean and Saubel 1972; Brandoff 1980; King 1988, 2000; Kirk 1970; Mead 1972; Munz 1970; Smith 1976.

the microbotanical record were also identified at the macrobotanical level (table 16). The pollen was frequently identifiable only to the family level, whereas the charcoal was identifiable to the genus or species level.

Most of the floral remains identified in table 16 are from plants that were frequently used by the Chumash for food or other purposes. These include *Salvia* sp. (Sage), *Calandrinia* sp. (Red Maids), Poaceae (grass seeds), *Yucca whipplei,* and many species in the Cheno-am group (Timbrook 1984, 1990; Timbrook et al. 1982).

Many of the plant remains identified at SBA-46 were those of plants common in the fresh and saltwater marshes that surrounded Mescalitan Island and many other Chumash mainland coastal sites. Stone (1982) reconstructed the slough as it appeared in AD 1770 using ethnohistorical accounts, historical maps and records, and modern aerial photographs, and suggested that an extensive salt marsh existed then, with vast quantities of *Salicornia* sp. (Pickleweed) growing in the saltwater marshes (Stone 1982:7). Brandoff (1980), in her reconstruction of the historical botanical changes in the Goleta Slough, also suggested that the dominant vegetation of the slough in about 1750 was *Salicornia* sp. Characteristic salt marsh plants that were of economic significance to the Chumash in the Cheno-am pollen classification were *Atriplex californica* (Saltbush), *Suaeda californica* (Seashore Blite), and *Salicornia* sp. (Pickleweed) (see table 2). *Distichilis spicata* (Salt Grass), also a plant used by the Chumash, is a typical salt marsh plant in the Poaceae (grass) family. Common freshwater marsh species that were readily available to the inhabitants of Mescalitan Island included *Hordeum californicum* (Native Barley), *Phalaris lemonii*, and various species in the Poaceae (grass) family (see chapter 2 and Brandoff 1980). Although not all these species were identified at the site, their genus or family was determined to be present in the pollen record (tables 16 and 17).

Elevated frequencies of several pollen groups, including Cheno-Ams, Liguliflorae, and Poaceae[44] were clustered on Floor 1 (figures 25 and 26). Because of this patterning, Cummings (1991) proposed that these resources were probably processed on Floor 1. Table 17 includes information on genera associated with these three pollen groupings, including data on their habitats and use by California Indians. The list in table 17 is not exhaustive, but does encompass the most common plants used by California Indians in these pollen categories. All of these genera can be found in Santa Barbara County (Smith 1976), and many have been identified in wetland environments such as that surrounding Mescalitan Island.

A synthesis of the information gleaned from the macro- and microbotanical analysis of this significant site is important for an understanding of plant use by the inhabitants of the populous settlements near the salt marshes along the Santa Barbara Mainland coast. The Chumash living in these environments relied on plants from the *Amaranthus*, *Atriplex*, and *Chenopodium* genera, the *Poaceae* family, and the Liguliflorae subfamily for their seeds. The clustering of pollen in Floor 1 and the carbonized remains suggest that these plants were brought into the house for preparation, storage, and use as foods, as well as for medicinal and technological purposes.

With the establishment of the presidio at Santa Barbara in 1782 and the Santa Barbara Mission in 1786, Spanish foods such as corn, beans, wheat, and meat from cows and sheep must have been available to the Chumash living at *Helo'*, just as iron tools and glass beads were. No clear evidence for the use of domesticated plants was represented in the macro- or microbotanical remains examined from *Helo'*, even though numerous samples from the later house floor area were examined (1782–1803 occupation). Domesticated animal remains were present at *Helo'*, but not in great quantities; cow bones at the site were primarily used for tools such as fishhooks. In contrast, many native foods local to the area and traditionally used by the Chumash were identified at the site. The scarcity of non-native plant and animal remains indicates that domesticates were not an important food source for the inhabitants.

Only one land grant, Nuestra Senora del Refugio (established in 1795), existed in the Santa Barbara Channel region prior to 1822. It was situated some distance from the Goleta Slough and probably exerted little direct influence on the settlements in the region. Another land grant, the Reyes Rancho, was situated outside of the Santa Barbara Channel region, in northern Santa Barbara County, between 1802 and 1808 (Farris 1999). There is documentation for farming in the Goleta Valley in 1805; this was after the abandonment of *Helo'*. Perhaps historically-introduced plants and animals were relatively insignificant at *Helo'* because the rich marine resources and abundance of plant foods made a reliance on domesticated food sources unnecessary. It is also possible that the Chumash at *Helo'* may have been purposely avoiding relying on domesticated foods, just as they resisted baptism into the mission system (Bamforth 1993:58).

Evidence of domesticated plants and animals is more frequent at the historic site of *Talepop* (CA-LAN-229) than at *Helo'* (Hammett 1991). *Talepop* is in the Santa Monica Mountains, approximately 6 km from the coast, and was occupied between AD 1000 and the 1820s (King 1982).

Domesticated plant remains, including beans, corn, and wheat (or common barley) (Hammett 1991; King et al. 1982:9–78), were identified at the site, in addition to bones from cows and sheep. Several features at *Talepop* contained clusters of cow bones, some of which were whole. Many of the ranchos in the Los Angeles region were established by 1785, the year that Los Angeles was founded. The Rancho Simi land grant, for example, was awarded in 1794. In 1801 or 1802, Miguel Ortega received a provisional land grant for the Rancho Las Virgenes, which was in the Santa Monica Mountains in the immediate vicinity of *Talepop*. The Topanga-Malibu-Sequit land grant was being used by 1800, and included the area near Malibu. In the next few years, several other land grants were awarded in the Santa Monica Mountains. It is possible that some of the grants were operating prior to the dates they were licensed, thus affecting the local Indians at even earlier dates. In conclusion, inhabitants of settlements near ranchos and other European settlements were more likely to adopt European foods; nevertheless, these foods never fully supplanted the traditional diet of the Chumash that lived in their native villages.

Products from plants were important resources for food, technology, and medicines for the Chumash living on the Santa Barbara Channel mainland coast during the late prehistoric and early historic periods. Very little information on the use of plant remains can be found in the archaeological record. Ethnobotanical data from the historic settlement of *Helo'*, which has one of the best records of plant use available for the region, indicate that the Chumash primarily used local native plant resources and did not utilize Spanish cultigens. It appears that there was an overall pattern of intensive resource utilization, but that the exact resources that were used varied with the local environmental context. Hopefully, more ethnobotanical information will be collected and analyzed in the future to augment the paucity of knowledge available on the subject.

The Significance of Storage

The best evidence for storage in the Chumash region comes from early ethnohistoric descriptions, with Crespí's diary from 1769–1770 being of particular interest. He noted that the roofs of Chumash houses along the mainland Santa Barbara Channel coast were covered with accumulations of both fresh and dried fish, and repeatedly commented on the massive quantities of food that the Chumash served the expedition members on their way north. Also noted were outdoor granaries, where foods such as acorns, seeds, and fish were dried and then stored. Anderson (2005) emphasizes that Indians throughout California were successful at ensuring that outdoor storage granaries were kept free of moisture, bacteria, and fungi by such ingenious methods as waterproofing the granaries through shingling (Anderson 2005:54). California Indians were also experts at keeping small animals and birds at bay by weaving the granaries very tightly and placing them in special locations. The interiors of granaries were also insect proofed by the use of insect repellants such as Mugwort (*Artimesia* spp.).

Although archaeological documentation for storage is much rarer than that found in the historical record, both indirect and direct evidence of storage in the form of subterranean pits and storage baskets (figure 36) (see chapter 4 for details) in the interior of houses at the historic coastal settlements of *Muwu*, *Shilimaqshtush*, *Helo'*, and the earlier settlement at Pitas Point provide insight into the nature of interior storage strategies.

At the site of *Shilimaqshtush*, nine subterranean storage pits at the site had fired clay walls that served to protect the contents that were stored. Most of these also had asphaltum or baked clay bases, further insuring the contents' safekeeping. With the exception of one of the pits that had two bifaces in it, the contents of these storage pits are unknown. The excavators

FIGURE 36 Chumash storage basket (courtesy of the Santa Barbara Museum of Natural History)

never conducted flotation; however, it is highly likely that the pits contained stored food products. At several sites, fragments of storage baskets including water bottles (figure 37) are additional evidence for storage.

The only storage pit in a Chumash mainland site on which flotation has been performed was at the site of *Helo'* (see Gamble 1991 and Hammett 1991). An interior storage pit (figure 38) underneath Floor 1 at the site (Feature 59) contained plant remains from Manzanita (*Arctostaphylos glandulosa*), oaks (*Quercus* sp.), Wild Cherry or Islay (*Prunus* sp.), and the Cucurbitaceae family, in addition to unidentified nutshell fragments (Hammett 1991:Table 6.2). Smaller remains, such as small seeds and other plant remains, were recovered at the site, although it was not reported which of these were in the feature. All of the plant remains found

FIGURE 37 Twined Chumash water bottle (courtesy of the Santa Barbara Museum of Natural History)

FIGURE 38 Storage pit at *Helo'* (CA-SBA-46) (photo by Lynn Gamble)

associated with this feature were important food resources to the Chumash living on the mainland coast. It is likely that the interior storage pit at *Helo'* was used to store staples such as acorns, other nuts, seeds, and plant foods, in a safe and dry place. Undoubtedly, more foods were stored in outside storage facilities, as well as in other interior storage containers such as baskets.

The capabilities of the Chumash and other California Indian groups to maintain large stores of food allowed them to live in relatively densely populated settlements. There are few hunter-gatherer societies anywhere in the world that had densely clustered settlements with up to (and perhaps exceeding) 1000 inhabitants (see chapter 4 for population estimates for the Channel region). Blackburn and Anderson (1993), Anderson (2005), and others (Anderson 1993, Timbrook et al. 1982) have documented the extensive management of the environment by California Indians, who used controlled burns, the sowing of seeds, the transplantation of small trees and shrubs, irrigation, pruning, and weeding to improve the accessibility, yield, and quality of plant products. These techniques all served to increase the yield of foodstuffs and other important products (e.g., basketry materials, medicines, etc.), some of which could be stored to ensure adequate supplies during times of stress or to meet the needs of the apparently burgeoning populations. The intensification of fishing strategies, such as the use of plank canoes, harpoons, fishhooks, and fishnets, improved harvests of marine products which could then be dried and stored. Facilities to store acorns, other nuts, seeds, dried berries, fish, and other foods were critical once the technology was developed to obtain an abundance of significant foods.

Subsistence storage is also relevant to issues of inequality and the emergence of rank and competition. Hayden (1995:24) has argued that one characteristic of complex hunter-gatherers is the presence of subsistence surpluses that are available on a regular basis, resulting in the emergence of economically-based competition. He proposes that small groups or individuals can develop exclusive control over some resources, eventually resulting in a storage of surpluses that are used in competitive ways to institute power inequities. Associated with these processes are regional exchange systems of prestige goods. As we will see in subsequent chapters, these exchange systems were an integral component of Chumash sociopolitical and economic practices. Women played a significant role in the development and maintenance of subsistence surpluses—a role that is usually overlooked.

Gender Roles

Women, and men who adopted women's gender roles, played an important role in feasting and subsistence activities. They collected, processed, cooked, and stored the resources that enabled the Chumash to undertake lavish feasts and to live in densely populated mainland towns. Several early historic observations provide the best documentation of the roles that women played in subsistence activities. Crespí described the activities of women when the expedition stopped near present-day Ventura (see opening quotation in chapter 5) and noted that they made the baskets and cooked the food. Lt. Pedro Fages, who was also a member of the Portolá expedition, noted that women made baskets in addition to other activities:

> The women go about their seed-sowing, bringing the wood for the use of the house, the water, and other provisions. They skillfully weave trays, baskets, and pitchers for various purposes; these are well made with threads of grass roots of various colors (Priestley 1972:34–35).

Longinós Martínez, twenty-three years after Fages and Crespí visited the Chumash, documented similar women's activities when he traveled along the coast between Ventura and San Luis Obispo:

> They gather their harvests of seeds with more skill than the other nations. In this operation the women go alone about the country, many leagues if necessary, carrying a large basket on their back and another in one hand. Then with a kind of long-handled fan which has a net at one end they knock the seeds from the plants into their baskets, which are thus filled with little effort (Longinós Martínez in 1792, as translated by Simpson 1961:53).

It is clear from this account that women continued to pursue their basic subsistence activities even years after colonization. Together, these accounts document that women were proficient in the production of baskets, in the gathering of plants, and in the collection of wood. A wide variety of baskets was used for the collecting, cooking, and storing of resources. The production of these baskets and the processing of subsistence resources required specialized knowledge and considerable time (Anderson 2005), and served to supply the large populations living in the mainland coastal settlements. In part because basketry and plant remains are not preserved well in the archaeological record, and in part because archaeologists have emphasized hunting, fishing, and other aspects of subsistence that are primarily associated with the male gender, the role that women played in the maintenance of social systems has been underplayed. Without the efforts of women, the population densities and level of sociopolitical complexity that existed would not have been possible. The persistence of baskets and the continued use of traditional plant resources after the introduction of Spanish technology and foods reflect the significance of women's roles among the Chumash Indians both before and after Spanish contact.

Feasting

The Spanish, impressed with the feasts that the Chumash provided, often commented on the abundance of foods served and the accompanying entertainment in the form of music and dance. As noted in chapter 4, numerous Spanish accounts written during the earliest period of exploration and colonization emphasize the abundance of foods that the Chumash stockpiled beyond their daily needs. Clear evidence of feasting emerges from these accounts. The Chumash were perhaps attempting to gain prestige goods and forge alliances with the Europeans, but despite their motives they were participating in feasts that were undoubtedly typical of those that were enacted prior to the Spanish invasion.

Feasting is a topic that has gained greater attention in recent years among archaeologists (e.g., Dietler and Hayden 2001), yet is one that has not been extensively addressed by scholars studying the Chumash. Arnold (2001a:294) has said that the only possible evidence for feasting on Santa Cruz Island occurred during the later Historic period (1790s–1810s) at Prisoner's Harbor, where the bones of at least one swordfish and a quantity of black abalone were found. In her dissertation, Noah (2005) examined the faunal remains, in conjunction with contextual information from this same feature at Prisoner's Harbor, and compared them to other samples from the site and elsewhere on Santa Cruz Island to determine if feasting was present. She interpreted the "abalone stratum" as evidence of a public feasting event or series of events that probably occurred between 1814 and 1816, after the house structure where the remains were found was abandoned. Noah (2005:280) noted that in addition to feasting on abalone and swordfish, the participants consumed at least five pinnipeds, other fish, a minimum of one dolphin, two sea otters, a sea turtle, and many crabs, mussels, wavy top turbans, and large limpets. Besides the food remains, unusually high densities of abalone ornaments, glass beads, and Tivela tube bead-blanks were recovered in the abalone stratum (see also Arnold and Graesch 2001).

Although Noah (2005:83) rejects the hypothesis that the stratum stems from the filling of an abandoned house with trash, this still remains a possibility. The use of abandoned house depressions for depositing trash was common on the northern Channel Islands (Gamble 1991; Rogers 1929). The abalone stratum was not continuous (see Noah 2005:Figure 3.2), and detailed stratigraphic cross sections of these and the surrounding deposits have not been presented in Arnold's (2001a,b,c) edited volume nor in Noah's (2005) dissertation. The horizontal extent of these stratigraphic features is also unclear, because there are no plan views documenting this. Although Noah carried out an impressive faunal analysis and argued for a feasting event having produced the "abalone stratum," until more empirical evidence is provided on the stratigraphic relationships of these features and their size within strata, the hypothesis that these deposits represent feasting event(s) is tantalizing but unproven.

Ethnographic sources are rife with accounts of feasting. The Chumash maintained a seasonal round of ceremonial events that involved frequent feasting; in addition, normal rites of passage were often taking place. Blackburn (1976:233) identified the following types of ceremonial occasions that the Chumash observed: "Birth, the naming of children, adolescence, the drinking of *toloache*, marriage, illness and the recovery of illness, wakes, a chief's birthday, the appearance of rattlesnakes in the Spring, the completion of the harvest in the Fall, and the summer and winter solstices."

The two most significant annual ceremonies that the Chumash recognized were the *Hutash* or the fall harvest ceremony and the *Kakunupmawa* or winter solstice (Blackburn 1976; Hudson et al. 1981; Hudson and Underhay 1978). The *Hutash* ceremony occurred after the piñon harvest, during the latter part of September (or possibly in August, see Hudson et al. 1981:104 for a description of its timing), to honor the earth (*Hutash*) and its bountiful harvests. The *Kakunupmawa* ceremony was held near the winter solstice and was intended to ensure that the sun would return for the next year (Hudson et al. 1981). This was a time when debts incurred during the previous year were settled.

Chumash specialists in astronomy and astrology, named *alcuqlas*, maintained a fairly precise 12-month lunar calendar by tracking the movement of the stars, planets, and sun. They adjusted the calendar semi-annually by tying it to the solstice events (Blackburn 1976; Hudson and Underhay 1978). People who attended these two important public ceremonies, which often lasted from five to six days, traveled long distances from Chumash settlements on the mainland and the islands; California Indians from other areas, such as the Tulareños (Yokuts), attended as well (Blackburn 1976; Hudson et al. 1981). At the Hutash ceremony, attendees brought offerings such as seeds, acorns, and shell beads that were routed through their chiefs, who in turn handed them to the chief of the host settlement. These offerings, which were gifts symbolizing the renewal of social and political bonds, were intended to help the chief defray some of the expenses that were incurred in hosting such a ceremony. At the winter solstice, the *paha* received the offerings, and presumably then shared them with the chief. The chief played an important role in orchestrating ceremonies; his duties, along with those of the *paha*, included paying the singers, dancers, and other essential participants; scheduling the ceremony and ensuring that chiefs from the numerous participating settlements were notified; maintaining the ceremonial accoutrements that were used in the ceremonies; and finally, ensuring that everyone was fed and cared for during the ceremony (Blackburn 1975). Both these ceremonies, in addition to the mourning ceremony, involved large public feasting; most of the less public ceremonies that the Chumash observed also had a feasting component, but on a smaller scale than the public ceremonies.

Hayden (2001:29–33), who suggests that feasts are one of the most significant venues for displaying success among humans, asserts that such events can generate cooperative alliances, mobilize labor, create political power because of reciprocal debts, and compensate for transgressions, among other practical benefits. He groups the immediate benefits of hosting feasts into two broad categories. The first involves feasts that create alliances between groups, political support, or social distinctions. The second involves feasts that create economic benefits. Hayden (2001:36–38) suggests that competitive feasts often fall into the latter category, and that these types of feasts are different in that the foods and technology used in the feasting process diverge from the standard daily types of foods and technology used in their processing and serving. He also contends that competitive feasts have the same material characteristics as alliance or promotional feasts, but involve more costly prestige vessels or other objects and may entail the destruction of wealth items (e.g., through burial). The Chumash may have staged alliance or competitive feasts. They destroyed large quantities of shell beads, ollas, and other valuable items during mortuary events (see Gamble et al. 2002 and chapters 7 and 8). In addition, the mainland settlements along the Channel coast appeared to have competed in feeding and entertaining the Portolá expedition as it passed through the region (see chapter 4). Although it can be argued that this situation was a result of the presence of the Spanish themselves, it is unlikely that the Chumash could have successfully orchestrated such feasts unless they were accustomed to staging them. Furthermore, this was the first land expedition in the Santa Barbara Channel region, making it even less likely that the Chumash, with little notice, could have successfully produced and served such a surplus of food unless it was a customary practice.

Hayden (2001:39–42) proposes a number of archaeological signatures for feasting that are useful for detecting its presence among the Chumash. The first of these is centered on food: evidence indicative of feasting would include the presence of rare or labor-intensive plant or animal species, indications of the wasting of food, or the presence of exceptionally large quantities of food. In the Chumash case, the presence of fish that have been identified as "prestigious," such as swordfish, albacore, and shortfin mako, at numerous Late period and historic period archaeological sites in the Santa Barbara Channel (Davenport et al. 1993; Bernard 2004; Noah 2005) is an indicator of the capture of labor-intensive, rare species. All of these fish probably required the use of a *tomol* for their capture, are large, and are relatively rare, in part because of the difficulty in capturing them (especially a species such as swordfish). In addition, swordfish had great power among the Chumash, who viewed these fish as "people" of the marine world with supernatural powers.

The Chumash reverence for the swordfish is reflected in the existence of a swordfish dance (Hudson et al. 1981:75–79); a remarkable archaeological find further documents its significance. In 1926, David Banks Rogers excavated the skull of a swordfish with a 16-inch bill that was associated with a burial in a cemetery in Winchester Canyon (CA-SBA-71). Next to the swordfish skull, and apparently once attached to it, was a cape of abalone shell ornaments. The skull of the swordfish, whose eye orbit had been inlaid with iridescent shell, was placed on top of the human skull, indicating that the find was that of a swordfish dancer buried with his regalia. The abalone shell in the cape has a 13-C adjusted age of 2040±90 BP (Davenport et al. 1993). This date was calibrated recently by Johnson (2005) to calendar years (Cal AD 395–773, 2 sigma range), with the "center point" at AD 608. This extraordinary discovery provides further evidence that the reverence for the swordfish had considerable time depth, and that the eating of this fish was undoubtedly reserved for special occasions.

Hayden also suggests that the preparation and serving vessels used for feasts differ from everyday vessels in their quantity or in their size, type, or material. Several different types of special vessels were used by the Chumash and are strong indicators of feasting. Large stone ollas and comals (figure 39) made from micaceous Catalina Island talc schist were used for cooking and occasionally for storage (Hudson and Blackburn 1983:201–206). The Chumash did not make or use pottery prehistorically, but instead relied primarily on baskets for the storage and cooking of foods; stones were heated in fireplaces and then placed in baskets to cook foods. The adoption of steatite for the cooking of food represented a considerable innovation over the heating of foods in baskets, and its use may have been reserved for special occasions or for wealthier and higher status individuals. Stone ollas were finely made, with smooth interiors and exteriors, and were large—some were over 40 cm in diameter and 38 cm in height (Abbott 1879:93–96). They occasionally had incising as well as bead inlay along the rims, and many have evidence of burning on the interior and exterior surfaces.[45] Many of the bigger ollas are considerably larger than would be needed for a family, even an extended family. Fernando Librado, one of Harrington's most respected consultants, described a feast at Ventura where steatite ollas were used: "At Ventura during a fiesta there were between 30 and 40 fireplaces, each

FIGURE 39 Large steatite olla from Medea Creek (CA-LAN-243), #524-1112 (photo by Glenn Russell, courtesy of the Fowler Museum at UCLA)

with 3 or 4 ollas" (Hudson and Blackburn 1983:203). These data provide unequivocal evidence that steatite ollas were used by the Chumash for feasting.

The Catalina Island steatite vessels were most common in the Chumash area during Middle Period phase 4 (AD 700 to 900) and then again during the Late Period phase 2b and during the historic period (King 2005). King (2005) has suggested that the average size of Catalina Island talc schist cooking bowls and their frequency in mortuary contexts increased during the period of Spanish colonization (see also L. King 1982:435). Forty-three ollas were found by Yarrow in the excavations at La Patera.[46] Olson, who excavated the historic period cemetery at *Helo'*, recorded 13 ollas made from Catalina Island steatite. The use of iron tools certainly would have facilitated the manufacture of these items. The presence of fragments of steatite ollas and comals in Late period midden soils (Gamble 1991:296–297) and the presence of large steatite cooking vessels with many burials during the Late period (L. King 1982:430–436) are evidence that feasting probably occurred at many sites along the Santa Barbara Channel at this time.

Special preparation vessels that were probably used for feasting events are also present in the Chumash region during and prior to the Late period. Large, shaped mortars and pestles, some with decorations, are the most common of these. Abbott (1879:72) was one of the first archaeologists to remark that these decorated mortars were probably reserved for special occasions: "It may be possible that these large ornamented mortars were used for ceremonial more than for useful purposes, as utensils so ornamented, if in every-day use, would, probably, not long retain the laminae of so fragile a shell as the *Haliotis*." Abbott is referring to some of the large mortars from La Patera that were grooved on the rim and then decorated with asphaltum and abalone and cowry shells. A number of these larger, decorated mortars were over 50 cm in diameter (see Abbott 1879:70–86 for descriptions of these). Costansó, a member of the Portolá expedition in 1769, made this comment about the large mortars: "Some of these mortars are of extraordinary size, and as well formed as if the best tools had been used in making them. The patience, exactness and energy which they exercise in making these articles are well worthy of admiration" (Hemert-Engert and Teggart 1910:47).

An ethnographic account from Harrington's consultant María Solares confirms the use of these large mortars (figure 40) in the preparation of food for feasts: "When I asked MS [Maria Solares] what they used the very large mortars for, she says it was to grind up acorns on fiesta days" (Hudson and Blackburn 1983:109). In discussing the distribution of these large mortars, Hudson and Blackburn (1983:110) noted that they were probably used by most groups but were rare on the Channel Islands. Previously, Hudson suggested that they may have been thrown in the sea by the islanders because a number of the mortars have been recovered in underwater contexts off the Channel Islands. Hudson and Blackburn (1983:110), in the caption for a photograph of one large mortar, commented that these were probably used for ceremonies. Long, finely-

FIGURE 40 Large sandstone mortar from Medea Creek (CA-LAN-243), #524-1070 (photo by Glenn Russell, courtesy of the Fowler Museum at UCLA)

shaped pestles, which are often uniform in shape and are polished, are usually associated with these large mortars. Some of these had flanges near their tips and were over 60 cm in length (Abbott 1879:Figure 22).

I propose that most large mortars (especially the decorated ones) and long, highly finished pestles were used in preparing food for feasts. The antiquity of these large mortars and pestles is a significant issue. Although the focus of this book is on the Late period (especially the period just prior to historic contact), there is evidence that long, shaped pestles and very large decorated mortars have considerable time depth. One large, highly decorated mortar was found with Burial 1 in Cemetery #4 (also known as Cemetery E) at Mescalitan Island. Based on its context and the bead inlay, the mortar probably dates to Middle Period phase 2 (200 B.C to AD 400). The mortar is over 60 cm across at its maximum diameter, and it is inlaid with double rows of shell disc beads in asphaltum along the rim (Gamble 2004). The outside of the mortar was also inlaid with an estimated 315 beads in asphaltum. This example, along with others in the Chumash area, indicates that the use of mortars as feasting vessels has a long history in the region. The long pestles also have a considerable time depth, although according to King (2005), the flanged pestles became more elaborate after the introduction of iron tools.

Although we know very little from the archaeological record about serving vessels, the ethnographic and ethnohistoric record indicates that baskets and wooden bowls were used to serve foods. In Crespí's account, as well as in those of other early chroniclers, baskets are frequently mentioned as vessels for serving foods (Hudson and Blackburn 1983:221). Women, or men who adopted female roles, produced these often highly decorated and finely made woven containers.

In addition to baskets, wooden bowls (figure 41), plates, trays, and jars were also used to serve foods, probably during feasts. These were highly prized by the Spanish; in 1811, Fr. José Señan wrote that he sent several wooden bowls to Mexico as presents. Crespí made the following comment about the wooden bowls and steatite ollas: "They manufacture a great many bowls both of wood and of stone, so smooth and glossy that especially those made of stone are like so many mirrors, having various inlay work very well set into place. Many of the soldiers have provided themselves with one or the other sort of bowls by bartering for them" (Brown 2001:395). Costansó, in his comments, indicated that it was the men who made the wooden bowls: "The men make beautiful bowls of wood with solid inlays of coral [= shell] or of bone, and some of the vessels of great capacity. Contracted at the mouth, which appear as if turned

FIGURE 41 Inlaid wooden bowl collected by Cessac (courtesy of the Santa Barbara Museum of Natural History)

on a lathe, in fact, with this machine they could not be turned out better hollowed or more perfectly formed" (Hudson and Blackburn 1983:77).

Wooden and basketry serving vessels are only a few of the types of objects that were used in feasting that are not well preserved in the archaeological record, yet they provide researchers important evidence on the significance and antiquity of feasting. It is clear from ethnohistoric, ethnographic, and archaeological data that the Chumash had a long tradition of feasting. At the time of the Portolá expedition, feasting was a common activity that involved the use of ostentatious food preparation, cooking, and serving vessels as well as large stores of food. In the next chapter we will examine the role of chiefs in these and other activities that were a part of the Chumash religious and social sphere.

Colonial Influence and the Persistence of Native Traditions

The effects of colonization on the Chumash and other California Indian societies have been well documented (e.g., Lightfoot 2005, Milliken 1995). What is interesting about the Chumash is the persistence of traditional practices, including subsistence activities and the holding of religious feasts during the early historic period, despite missionization and the presence of the Santa Barbara Presidio. Inevitably, many traditional native practices among the Chumash changed drastically as populations declined because of introduced diseases and other consequences of colonization. Yet the production and exchange of shell beads and steatite cooking vessels, mortars, and pestles continued, as did the use of traditional foods. Feasting persisted despite the attempt of missionaries to rid the Chumash of their "pagan" activities. In fact, some of the "the padres actively encouraged the Indians to conduct some ceremonies . . . and then tied them into Christian holidays or the construction of mission buildings" (Hudson et al. 1981:104). Luisa Ignacio, one of Harrington's consultants, reported that "Fr. Antonio Ripoll ordered the Indians to manufacture shell bead money to help pay for these fiestas. According to the informant, Fr. Ripoll wanted the Indians to celebrate every year, but the Indians did not want to for it cost too much" (Hudson et al. 1981:104).

The continuation and elaboration of feasting after Spanish colonization undoubtedly shifted power among the Chumash as chiefs, religious specialists, and commoners were baptized and moved to the missions, a process that took about 50 years (Walker and Johnson 1994). Some settlements were abandoned fairly quickly once the chief was baptized into the mission system. For example, at the historic settlement of *Helo'*, four chiefs and most of the remaining inhabitants were baptized on May 18 and 19, 1803. With entire villages quickly becoming virtually depopulated, exchange networks and centers of power were altered, yet trade and feasting endured, with different chiefs and villages taking on new roles or even becoming alcaldes and other Chumash officials in the missions (Lightfoot 2005).

Prior to Spanish colonization, settlements in the less populated and more peripheral areas of the Chumash realm, such as those in the interior and on the islands, probably had less elaborate ceremonies involving fewer people than the feasts in the large central settlements on the mainland coast. Inhabitants in the inland and island settlements were recruited into the missions later than people living in the mainland settlements (Johnson 1988). This shift of power is not the focus of this book, but is a topic that warrants further investigation.

Traditional foods, along with the artifacts used in their preparation and presentation during feasting events, also prevailed after Spanish colonization. The Chumash were active agents (Lightfoot 2005; Silliman 2004) in choosing to use European technology when it served their purposes, such as in the production of large flanged pestles and steatite ollas. But they also continued to use traditional foods and tools in many contexts (see Bamforth 1993 for a discussion of post-contact stone tools at *Helo'*). Evidence that the Chumash pursued traditional subsistence practices is documented above as well as in a letter written in 1803 by Fray Gregorio Fernandez, a missionary priest at Mission La Purísima Concepción, who was protesting against a petition by Juan Francisco Reyes for a rancho in the vicinity of the mission. In this letter, Fr. Fernandez noted that the local neophytes were forced into the hills to gather grass seeds, because these 'wild' grasses had been severely impacted by grazing cattle near Rancho del Refugio (Farris 1999:177–180, 1996). He wrote to express his concern that if the Reyes Rancho was authorized, that a similar deleterious effect would occur. In addition, the production and use of baskets has persisted into the present (Gamble 2002) despite the introduction of ceramics and metal containers. Although some of this was a result of the demand for baskets by non-native people, it is significant that the Chumash were active agents in their commitment to the continuance of baskets, steatite cooking vessels, large mortars, and other objects that were central to their traditional practices.

Summary

The Chumash scheduled feasting events that were held at regular calendrical intervals, as well as during rites of passage such as funerals and mourning ceremonies. During rites of passage and other events, the Chumash destroyed (through both burial and burning) shell beads, fancy serving vessels, and other types of objects, many of which were rare, associated with the elite, and part of the political economy. The Chumash stored large quantities of subsistence items, such as fish, acorns, seeds, and other foodstuffs, which were then redistributed during feasts, along with beads and other non-edible goods. Successful feasts involved an abundance of food as well as prestigious food preparation implements and serving vessels. The Chumash relied heavily on stored fish and plant foods. Chumash women played a significant role in the intensive processing of foods such as acorns and other plants. Women produced the baskets used for the collection, processing, cooking, and serving of foods. Baskets were labor-intensive and expensive to make, especially when symbolic elements were incorporated into them, a practice common among the Chumash and other California Indians. Feasts consisted of common subsistence items augmented, most likely, by rare foods such as swordfish, *panoche*, and other Chumash delicacies. In the next chapter we examine the role of chiefs and their assistants in feasts, and discuss their power in other realms.

CHAPTER 7

Rank, Ritual, and Power

> *In the afternoon, the head chief, who at our arrival had not been at the village, came over with them all, bringing us large servings of a great many big bowls full of good gruels, a great many others full of very good mush, fresh deer meat, a few fresh fish, and a bowl of a sort of white pies that they said were very good and looked as though made from rice. This head heathen chief or petty king of this country is a tall heathen man of very majestic and grand appearance, with very good features and easily distinguished by a very large tumor that hangs from one side of his neck, large as a well swollen ox gall, because of which everyone calls him The Goitre,* El Buchón, *and by this name he has become known to everyone. Like the other heathens, this man The Goitre wears a very fine cape that they make from the otter skin, covering him from neck to ankles. He always goes around closely accompanied by many heavily armed heathens, and, as we understood it, because many villages give him tribute, whatever seeds they harvest or gather from the fields, [or] whether they slaughter any meat or catch fish, they take it all—or so we understood—to his village, where he receives it and then they take back whatever he tells them to. In their own fashion, he employs considerable pomp, and they bring a hide and lay it on the ground for him to sit down on. He has two brothers and two or three sons who are almost always with him, and no one sits down in front of him or his family unless ordered to. Great is the fear and awe in which he is held in all the surrounding parts.*
>
> Crespí in Brown 2001:477–479

Crespí describes an imposing chief whose authority was recognized throughout the region. He dressed in a full-length otter skin cape and was accompanied by men armed with bows and arrows, and villagers provided him "tribute" in the form of food. Few such detailed descriptions of chiefs exist from the early historic period, but the accounts that are available indicate that a chief's power extended beyond the confines of his or her own settlement. The exact nature and full extent of that power is not well understood and is a subject of some debate (Arnold 2001a,b; Gamble et al. 2001, 2002; Kennett 2005; Johnson 2000). According to Crespí, chiefs were protected by armed men, were able to provide enough food to feed the 64-member Portolá expedition throughout much of its journey, and were respected by the Chumash in a region that encompassed multiple settlements. In this chapter, ethnohistoric, ethnographic, and archaeological sources of information are examined in order to address the nature of political power among the Chumash Indians of the mainland coast.

Ethnohistoric and Ethnographic Perspectives on Chiefs, Elites, and Commoners

Early ethnohistoric documents provide some information on the power of chiefs, as well as on their appearance; much of this type of information was not available when Harrington started collecting ethnographic data on the Chumash, making these early comments by the explorers all the more valuable. Fages (who was commander of the Portolá expedition) noted that it was *only* the chiefs who wore full-length cloaks and that this was what distinguished a chief from other individuals (Priestley 1937:32). Crespí described other details about a Chumash chief's appearance when the expedition stopped in what is now Santa Barbara on August 18, 1769:

> These chiefs here all wear the usual device, a very long flint knife attached to a very smooth well-fashioned stick with many different-colored inlays of shell that make them very appealing, in the same way as those I spoke of before (Brown 2001:415-417).

Crespí also remarked on the appearance of dancers and other individuals who were probably part of the chief's elite retinue:

> In order to dance, they all come out wearing very large feather headdresses, with all the rest of their bodies so painted in all hues that it appears like a thick garment. All the heathen men go naked but make a great show of adorning their heads. Not only do they wear their own hair twisted up, but some of them wear a great deal more false hair than their own, so that with the feathers and other adornments they deck themselves with, their heads look like so many large turbans (Brown 2001:425–427).

The power of chiefs and their elite retinues was a topic of considerable concern to the Spanish, who were interested in their own safety and in plans for colonization and settlement in Alta California. The accounts above demonstrate that there was a group of people who were visually distinguishable from the general populace by their headdresses, clothes, or other ornamentation. But what kind of power did the chiefs and the other high-ranked leaders actually possess? How did they differ from commoners? Again, Crespí provided insight into these questions when he made the following observations in the area around present-day Ventura on August 14, 1769:

> They have their own style of government in these villages: as we have understood from the good chief here, all of these villages have three or four chiefs, one of whom is head, and gives orders to everyone and to the other chiefs, and these all have two wives while the rest of men only have a single wife apiece (Brown 2001:427).

Crespí mentions polygyny among chiefs again when he is in Gaviota, and states that all chiefs have two wives. Fages corroborates Crespí's observations on this subject:

> Although in this district the captains commonly enjoy the privilege of taking two or three wives, and putting them away at will, the ordinary men have only one, and may abandon her only in case of adultery (Priestley 1937:33).

Mission register research indicates that some Chumash men (probably chiefs) often practiced polygyny (Johnson 1988; King 1984), although Johnson noted that it can be difficult to determine if a man was married to more than one woman at the same time or if these marriages were sequential. Certainly polygyny was a custom that was not condoned by the Catholic church; as a result, the practice of polygyny was suppressed or eliminated after Spanish colonization.

Several early chroniclers remarked that chiefs were skilled orators who commanded their subjects to follow instructions (see opening quotations in chapters 1 and 6 and Father Ascensión's description of a chief's "harangue" at *Muwu* in chapter 4). The explorers also noted that chiefs distributed food, beads, and other items to their people, as well as to the Spanish, who were often hungry when they passed through the region. Crespí wrote that two chiefs, *El Loco* and *El Buchón*, were able to acquire extensive provisions from a series of villages in the Obispeño region, indicating that they had jurisdiction over more than their own settlements (see chapter 8 for details). In fact, *El Loco* obtained food for the Portolá expedition at every village between Gaviota and San Luis Obispo (Brown 2001; King 1984:1–38). A less detailed account by Cabrillo provides the earliest historic reference to the regional power of Chumash chiefs; in 1542, he described a woman chief at *Syuxtun* as being the chief of all the villages between Point Conception and Santa Barbara (Johnson 1988:117).

The power of chiefs was also alluded to in the "Interrogatorios" or list of questions that the Spanish Government sent to religious authorities in California in 1812 in order to learn more about the pagan activities of the native people. The reply to the "Interrogatorio" by the padres at Mission San Luis Obispo de Tolosa indicated that a failure to participate in fiestas and contribute to host chiefs could result in armed conflict:

> Among the Indians are all kinds of classes, poor and rich. Among the rich, however, there is one in each village whom all recognize and whose voice is respected by all who live with him. To him, I do not know by what standards, all pay tribute of fruits, goods, and beads. These headmen summon to the pagan feasts all that assemble who happen to be his friends. If perchance anyone of them should refuse the invitation, he distributes arms and after notifying his people, he sets out to avenge the injury done to him by the refusal of the invitation. He takes the life not only of the chief one but of as many as are together with him (Geiger and Meighan 1976:122; L. King 1982:172).

Ethnographic descriptions of chiefs and of their political power supplement those of the early explorers, but because they were based on the memories of individuals who had not experienced traditional Chumash life prior to European colonization (see Lightfoot 2005), they need to be examined critically and in conjunction with multiple lines of evidence. Once again, the best descriptions of chiefs and their power come from interviews between Harrington and his consultants. With the exception of smaller settlements, most communities had at least one chief and some had four or five, many of whom held office contemporaneously (table 18 and Johnson 1988; L. King 1969). Harrington's consultants described three types of chiefs: "the 'big chief' (*paqwot*) of the 'tribe' or group of villages, the 'chief' (*wot*) or captain of a village, and the 'lesser chief'" (L. King 1969:41). During the early Mission period, Yanonali, the chief of *Syuxtun*, was said to have effective influence over thirteen villages from Goleta to Rincon (Brown 1967:36, 47; Johnson 1988:117). Later, Harrington's consultant Fernando Librado noted that the chief of *Syuxtun* was chief of all the villages between Carpinteria and Dos Pueblos (Johnson 1986:25). The prominence of *Syuxtun* as a center of political power—from 1542, when Cabrillo remarked on the extent of power of the female

TABLE 18. Number of Chiefs at Chumash Political Centers on the Mainland[a]
Based on Mission Register Documents

Village Name	No. of Chiefs
Qasil	2
Dos Pueblos	5
S'axpilil	5[a,b]
Helo'	5[c]
'Alkash	2[d]
Syuxtun	2
Stuk	3
Shisholop	2[e]

SOURCE: Based on Table 4.12 in Johnson (1988).

[a]Another chief from *S'axpilil* was listed in Goycoechea's 1796 census as a capitan from *Heliyik* (Johnson et al. 1982:45).

[b]This total includes a father and son pair who were both listed as chiefs (Johnson 1988: Table 4.12).

[c]One of these chiefs was a gentile, and may not have been contemporaneous with the other four (Johnson 1988:Table 6.6).

[d]It is not clear if these two chiefs were contemporaneous (Johnson 1982:Figure 4).

[e]These two chiefs may not have been contemporaneous (Johnson, personal communication).

chief there, through the mission period, and then into the twentieth century—is significant, in that *Syuxtun* maintained its identity as an influential and predominant place of authority for centuries. The concept of a regional chief for a group of villages is found elsewhere in the notes of John P. Harrington, when Fernando Librado noted that there was one big chief for the whole of Santa Cruz Island (Hudson et al. 1981:15).

Chumash settlements were hierarchically organized, with individuals from smaller villages apparently looking to chiefs from larger towns for direction in ceremonial and political affairs (Johnson 2001:54). Henshaw noted that certain villages served as "Capitals . . . where festivals, feasts and perhaps councils were held" (Johnson 1988:118). In his analysis of mission baptismal records, Johnson (1988:Table 4:12) identified several settlements that had more than one chief in residence and probably were political centers (table 18). With the exception of *Stuk*, all of these towns were situated on or immediately adjacent to the coast. Three of them were located around the Goleta Slough, implying that this region was a significant seat of political power. Population figures presented in chapter 4 confirm the importance of this area as a center. Moreover, the central location of these towns, between the islands and the interior and in the middle of the mainland Santa Barbara Channel coast (figure 7), meant that they were strategically located for trade and for hosting political or ritual congregations for inhabitants of other Chumash settlements. Although our understanding of the relationship between large towns and smaller settlements is unclear, there is some evidence that regional territories were recognized. Based on a synthesis of ethnohistoric and ethnographic sources, Hudson and Underhay (1978:27) have referred to these regional territories as 'provinces' and to the town where the 'big chief' lived as the 'capital' of the entire province. These capitals may have served as centers of political, economic, ritual, and legal activities for the Chumash towns, villages, and hamlets within the province.

Chiefs were integrally involved in the ceremonial life of the Chumash in that they provided the property used in rituals and ensured that visitors were fed (Harrington 1942:33). Chiefs and their family members were required to belong to the *'antap* society, a formal and institutionalized group of elites and religious specialists whose members were 'baptized' into the association as children. The families of the initiates had to pay a substantial amount of money for the privilege of membership in this elite society (Blackburn 1974:104–105, 1976:236). The principal duty of its members was to perform rituals and dances at large ceremonial gatherings. According to Hudson and Underhay (1978:29): "The *'antap* owned and used all ritual paraphernalia, cured illness, maintained the essential cosmic balance, and provided the needed astrological advice to the *wots* on when and where to hold important legal, economic, political, or ritual events." Blackburn (1976) has suggested that the *'antap* society served as a social integrative mechanism that connected elite individuals throughout the Chumash region. Each major settlement was reported to have had at least 12 *'antap*; in addition, the society was organized at a provincial level, with representatives from the major settlements assembling approximately every five years to discuss important ceremonial and political issues (Hudson and Underhay 1978). Although Chumash religious beliefs and concepts of cosmology varied on a regional level, apparently all of the Chumash (and some adjacent groups such as the Kitanemuk; see Hudson and Underhay 1978:30) distinguished the elite member of the *'antap* from commoners (Gamble et al. 2001).

According to Harrington's sources, political and religious influences were profoundly interwoven in the *'antap* organization, whose associates, in addition to the chief and his family members, included the ceremonial leader (*paha*) and other religious specialists, such as shamans, singers, and dancers (L. King 1969:43). The *paha* (also known as the *al-*

paxa) was an individual who managed private functions, such as weddings, and large public ceremonies. The *paha* was second in authority to the chief; if a chief died, the *paha* was in charge until the chief's successor was determined (Blackburn 1976; L. King 1969). Blackburn provides the best summary of the relationship between the chief and the *paha* in this passage:

> The *wot* or chief among the Chumash was a prominent figure behind the scenes on every important occasion. Dancers and singers, for example, were kept on a steady salary by the chief, who received through the *alpaxa* a sizeable portion of the considerable offerings collected from spectators at their performances. Again, charmstones and other power objects were apparently considered the property of the chief, and anyone wishing to use such items for a time had to pay for the privilege. The financial transactions occurring in connection with the Winter Solstice are particularly illuminating; during the course of the ceremony a public meeting was held for the purpose of settling any and all outstanding debts contracted during the year by anyone present, before the beginning of the new year. The *alpaxa* presided at this meeting and received a portion of any money and goods offered on this occasion in honor of *xutash*, the earth; again, presumably, a part of this went to enrich the chief, the *alpaxa*, and the other '*antap* (Blackburn 1976:237).

The chief and the *paha* were closely aligned in the economic transactions associated with ceremonies. The use of shell-bead money by the Chumash was the basis of these transactions (see chapter 8), with redistribution one means of dispensing goods and services. The chief did not rely solely on his or her ability to exact beads and goods in the context of ceremonial feasts, but instead worked together with the *paha* to collect funds from the attendees and redistribute them to the performers and other active participants, while at the same time benefiting from the transactions. We have seen from the early historic accounts that the Chumash were readily prepared to host feasts for the Spanish intruders, feasts involving abundant food and accompanied by dancers and singers. These types of costly events occurred prior to European colonization; shell beads were an integral component of these occasions. As Chumash populations increased over time, and more and more attendees assembled in Chumash centers for ceremonies (coming from as far away as the central San Joaquin Valley and the Channel Islands; see chapter 6), the demand for shell beads must have increased. Beads also served as currency in individual transactions, which undoubtedly increased in frequency as populations grew and exchange flourished. Prestige goods that were employed to validate the power of chiefs and ceremonial leaders became more significant over time as the ceremonial and political roles of the elites became more defined, thus further stimulating the political economy. The chief, *paha*, and other individuals who worked together in regulating appropriate behavior among their followers took their share of these transactions, thereby amassing greater wealth and stores of food, some of which would later be redistributed. Feasts also served as events where host chiefs, chiefly families, and their community displayed their generosity to guest groups and thereby gained prestige and political influence. Probably the most important function of Chumash feasts was that they enriched chiefs politically and secured their positions.

Chiefs not only relied on the *paha* as a trusted collaborator, they also worked closely with the *'altipatishwi* or "poisoner" in what has been described for the Yokuts and the Chumash as an "unholy alliance" (Gayton 1930). Blackburn has described the relationship between the *'antap*, poisoner, and the chief in this way:

> According to popular belief, a secret meeting of the important chiefs and shamans was held some months prior to a mourning anniversary in order to select the date and location of the ceremony. At this meeting one of the *'antap* present was selected as an *'altipatishwi* or "poisoner." The identity of this individual was apparently a closely-guarded secret, although he was an obvious figure at important ceremonies because of his actions. The *'altipatishwi* wore bags of herbs on his legs or at his waist, and would get up beside the dancers while they were dancing and imitate their movements. It was generally believed that the *'altipatishwi* selected a wealthy man from a rich and populous village and began to poison him some months before the fiesta was to be held; during the course of time the *'altipatishwi* would extract large sums of money from his victim before either curing him or allowing him to die. In the latter case, the offerings presented at the fiesta would be even greater, and the *'altipatishwi* would get a percentage from the local chief. How frequently shamans actually did poison people at the instigation of the chief is, of course, debatable; however, it is abundantly clear that the widely-held belief that such practices did exist (a belief strongly reinforced by the foreboding presence of the *'altipatishwi* at Chumash ceremonies) provided a chief with indirect coercive abilities that undoubtedly augmented his political power significantly (Blackburn 1976:238).

The chief collaborated with a number of people to insure that individuals, especially wealthy members of the community, contributed appropriate sums of money. Social institutions similar to these have been documented for the Yokuts and probably for the Gabrielino and Luiseño, neighbors of the Chumash who reportedly attended some of the larger ceremonies held by the Chumash (Blackburn 1976). The chiefs' political and economic power was reinforced through their relationships with ceremonial assistants and other *'antap* members; at the same time, the chief frequently did not directly collect tribute, but instead relied on others to exert pressure on attendees to pay their fair share. As a result, the chiefs no doubt maintained their role as generous leaders who distributed wealth, food, and other items in the context of elaborate ceremonies where guests were well fed and entertained. The advantage of this relationship for the *paha*, *'altipatishwi*, and other *'antap* members was that they gained a share of wealth and prestige during these ceremonial feasts. One key aspect of the ritual mode of production is that it induces the chief's followers to work harder to amass surpluses of resources beyond the needs of the domestic sphere. Blackburn (1976), King (1976), and others (see Gamble 2005 and Kennett 2005) note that these events also served as institutionalized means for transferring and redistributing resources in a region with considerable variability in environmental settings (i.e., islands, mainland, and interior) and in an area that was (and is still) subject to irregular environmental fluctuations such as El Niño events.

Chumash chiefs also had an extensive network of marriage partners and other kin in settlements that were often situated in different environmental zones and in large important coastal centers. The best information we have on marriage ties stems from research John Johnson (1982, 1988) and Chester King (1984, 1994, 2000) have carried out using the mission registers (see chapter 3). Johnson (1988:248) examined marriage ties between Chumash settlements in order to assess political, social, and economic interactions between villages. He found that the Chumash predominantly practiced matrilocal residence (except for the chiefs, who followed a more patrilocal residence pattern). He also noted that members of chiefly families intermarried with other high ranking or chiefly families.

Using Johnson's (1988:Tables 9.1 and 9.3) mission register data, I examined the marriage ties between two historic settlements situated on the Goleta Slough (*Helo'* and *S'axpilil*) and other villages and towns on the mainland (table 19). Table 19 provides a list of marriage connections between *Helo'* and other settlements, as well as a list of endogamous marriages. Most of the marriages listed in the mission records for *Helo'* were endogamous, an indication that the settlement was large enough for people to find suitable marriage partners within the community. Four of the settlements (Dos Pueblos, *S'axpilil*, *Syuxtun*, and *Stuk*) that had marriages bonds with *Helo'* were identified by Johnson as important political centers on the basis of the number of chiefs baptized from these towns. A fifth village (*Heliyɨk*) was identified by Pio Pico as a capital. Although

TABLE 19. Marriage Ties between Partners from *Helo'* and Other Settlements, with Number of Chiefs
Based on Mission Register Documents

Village Name	No. of Marriage Ties	No. of Chiefs
Dos Pueblos	6	5
Heliyɨk	5	0[a]
S'axpilil	8	5[a,b]
Helo'	17	5[c]
'Alkash	6	2[d]
Syuxtun	5	2
Stuk	1	3
Shnoxsh	1	0
Shniwax	2	0
Shisolop[e]	1	2[f]

SOURCE: Based on Johnson's (1988:Tables 9.1 and 9.3) mission register information and personal communication.

[a]Another chief from S'axpilil was listed in Goycoechea's 1796 census as a capitan from Heliyɨk (Johnson et al. 1982:45).

[b]This total includes a father and son pair who were both listed as chiefs (Johnson 1988: Table 4.12).

[c]One of these chiefs was a gentile, and may not have been contemporaneous with the other four (Johnson 1988:Table 6.6).

[d]It is not clear if these two chiefs were contemporaneous (Johnson 1982:Figure 4).

[e]This is the *Shisholop* in Ventura.

[f]These two chiefs may not have been contemporaneous (Johnson, personal communication).

'Alkash was not designated by Johnson as a political center, it may have had two chiefs living there contemporaneously (table 19). Eight of the ten villages (including *Helo'*) listed in table 19 either possessed multiple chiefs or were identified by Pico as political centers. Ninety-four percent of the marriage ties between *Helo'* and other villages were to political centers or to settlements that possessed more than one chief. Individuals from *Helo'* had more marriage connections to inhabitants of Dos Pueblos than to any other Goleta settlement (Johnson 1990:4). This is of particular interest since Johnson (1988:248–271) has proposed that there was a strong political boundary between the Dos Pueblos region and the Goleta/Santa Barbara area. Johnson suggested that the settlements of Dos Pueblos, Refugio, and of the central Santa Ynez Valley were aligned with one another, and that the settlements near Goleta, Santa Barbara, and on the upper Santa Ynez watershed were also aligned. The marriage ties between these two regions, as well as those between *Helo'* and other centers, represent a network of political coalitions that the elite from *Helo'* and other

centers perpetuated in order to maintain their status, create alliances, and reinforce the power of the chiefs at the political centers.

Another possible explanation for the endogamous pattern of marriages at *Helo'* was that individuals were marrying people in geographic proximity. Certainly this must be considered as a partial explanation. Johnson found that geographic proximity clearly affected spousal selection, and that no mainland marriages occurred between settlements that were more that 59 km. apart (Johnson 1988:255–258). When the marriage patterns at *Helo'* are examined in detail, however, it is clear that people from *Helo'* did not marry people from some of the smaller settlements that were closer to them, but instead chose marriage partners from large centers as far away as *Suyxtun* and *Shisholop* (figures 6 and 7).

In addition to being inextricably involved with various religious specialists, chiefs were intimately involved in the complex economic system of the Chumash (see chapter 8 for more details). Their leadership helped to ensure that risks due to climatic fluctuations were minimized. The Chumash practiced a multitude of risk management strategies to insure that populations were well fed during difficult times, as well as during periods of population growth. These strategies included diversification, intensification, physical storage, redistribution, exchange, alliance formation, and the use of currency as a form of social storage (Gamble 2005). As a result of the chief's active participation in risk management, the development of a political economy occurred (Feinman and Nichols 2004; Johnson and Earle 2000), in part regulated by the chief and other Chumash elite. By the time the Portolá expedition passed through the Santa Barbara Channel region, the political economy was fully developed. Both myself and colleagues (Gamble et al. 2001; Gamble 2002; Gamble and Russell 2002; Gamble 2005; Glassow et al. 2007; King 1990) have suggested elsewhere that the emergence of sociopolitical complexity, including a political economy, probably occurred thousands of years ago.

The extensive, albeit slightly flawed, ethnohistoric and ethnographic record for the Chumash provides detailed information on chiefs, religious leaders, economic specialists, and other elites. We turn now to the archaeological record in an attempt to further understand the relationship of the chiefs, religious leaders, and other elite individuals with the commoners.

Mortuary Symbolism, Rank, and Religious Power

One of the best indicators of differentiation of rank in the archaeological record can be seen in Chumash mortuary practices. Intact burials from a variety of sites and time periods have been the focus of archaeological investigations since the 1860s (see chapter 3 and King 1990a). The notes and collections that resulted from these investigations have been the subject of several important analyses that have centered on mortuary behavior and how it is related to social structure and the emergence and development of rank (Gamble 2004; Gamble and Russell 2002; Gamble et al. 2001; Green 1999; Hollimon 1990; King 1980b, 1990a; L. King 1982; Martz 1984).

HUMALIWO CEMETERIES

Two significant historic period cemeteries on the mainland coast of the Santa Barbara Channel provide insights into mortuary practices at the time of European colonization and immediately after. The first of these is the cemetery at the historic village site of *Humaliwo*, where the modern town of Malibu is currently situated (see chapter 4 for a more complete discussion of this settlement). *Humaliwo* was not as large a settlement as *Helo'*, *Syuxtun*, or other towns situated closer to Santa Barbara and Goleta, yet it is important for this discussion because a thorough analysis of independent data sources including genetic relatedness, health status, types of grave goods, and the distribution of grave goods was conducted (Gamble et al. 2001). In addition, this cemetery was excavated in its entirety.[47]

Archaeological data from the historic period cemetery at *Humaliwo* are consistent with ethnohistoric and ethnographic accounts of Chumash social organization and of the disparity of wealth between the elite and commoners. The types of shell and glass beads (figures 42 and 43) that were apparently used as symbols of wealth and money had an uneven distribution in the Malibu cemetery. Forty-five percent (n= 65) of the individuals in this cemetery had fewer than 20 beads associated with them, and approximately half of these (n=30) had no beads at all (Gamble et al. 2001:196). In contrast to the burials with few or no associated beads, nine percent (n=12) of the burials were associated with 1000 or more beads, and they often had other lavish burial offerings. Except for one person, all of the individuals with more than 1000 beads were concentrated in the southern portion of the cemetery. They were people of all ages and both sexes, as would be expected if they were members of high ranking, wealthy families, instead of people who had attained wealth through personal achievement. Furthermore, the age distribution of burials with few or no grave goods did not differ significantly from that of

FIGURE 42 Small shell disc beads, *Mytilus sp.*, from Medea Creek (CA-LAN-264), #524-2344 (photo by Lynn Gamble, courtesy of the Fowler Museum at UCLA)

FIGURE 43 Glass beads from *Humaliwu* (CA-LAN-264) (photo by Nelson Leonard III, courtesy of the Fowler Museum at UCLA)

burials with sumptuous grave goods, suggesting that the juvenile burials with lavish grave goods did not represent an expression of intense mental anguish on the part of parents or other relatives (see Green 1999), but instead reflected inherited social status in a ranked society. There was also a significant positive correlation between the number of artifacts buried with a person and the depth of the grave (Gamble et al. 2001). The specialist class of undertakers among the Chumash, known as *'aqi* (Hollimon 2001), were paid more when graves were deeper (L. King 1969:47), indicating that deeper graves were more costly than shallower ones.

In addition to glass and shell beads, numerous other types of items were placed as offerings with Chumash burials; these included plank canoes, which (because of their expense and association with highly ranked individuals) were owned only by wealthy individuals such as chiefs (Gamble 2002, Gamble et al. 2001). Plank canoes were made from wooden planks (often redwood) that were drilled with specialized stone drills and then sewn. Finally, the holes where the planks were sewn together were sealed with a mixture of asphaltum, as were the seams between the planks. Frequently, all the evidence of canoes that remains in archaeological contexts is the asphaltum caulking and plugs, along with an occasional plank fragment. At the historic-period cemetery at *Humaliwo*, 11 burials were found buried with wood or asphaltum. Of these, three were clearly associated with plank canoes, including redwood planks with caulking and plugs. The three individuals were a 19-year-old male, a 26-year-old of unknown sex, and another person of unknown sex and age. Although all three of these burials were associated with shell and glass beads in addition to canoe parts (Gamble et al. 2001:Table 1), the 19-year-old had many more beads (n= 2395) than the others, suggesting that he was from an elite canoe-owning family, possibly a chief's family (Gamble et al. 2001).

The types of historic artifacts in the cemetery reflect the nature of the interactions occurring between the European colonizers and the Chumash people living at *Humaliwo*. Approximately 15,000 glass beads and numerous metal objects were interred with individuals. A number of the metal objects of Spanish origin that were deposited as burial offerings were typical of items associated with *vaqueros*, or cowboys, who worked on the ranchos in the region during the late eighteenth and early nineteenth centuries. These items included five small bronze and brass ornaments (*higos*) that were suspended from the *anquera* or leather saddle skirt used by the Mexicans and Spanish during the 18th and 19th centuries; an iron headstall plate which functioned as an ornamental part of the Spanish bridle; part of an iron spur that consisted of a star rowel and heel plate; (figure 44) and an iron concho, frequently worn either on the side of the pants, on bridles, or on hats by both Spanish and Indian *vaqueros* (Bickford 1982). Other artifacts of Spanish origin from the cemetery included metal adzes, four iron knives, six iron spikes, two buckles, seven metal buttons, a copper bead, a copper cup, an iron cup, pieces of firearms, a sword (Bickford 1982), and a St. Francis de Sales medal (Green 1999). It is intriguing, but not surprising, that many of the metal artifacts that were identifiable in the historic cemetery at *Humaliwo* were associated with *vaqueros*.

Several ranchos in the Los Angeles region had been granted to individuals by 1785 (when Los Angeles was founded), and native Californians were an important source of labor for these enterprises (Lightfoot 2005; Silliman 2004). The first legal claim by the Spanish to *Humaliwo* and the surrounding region occurred in 1801, when José Bartolome Tapia was given grazing rights to approximately 13,330 acres by the King of Spain. This concession became known as Rancho Topanga Malibu Sequit. Tapia settled in Malibu Canyon and grazed his cattle in the area,

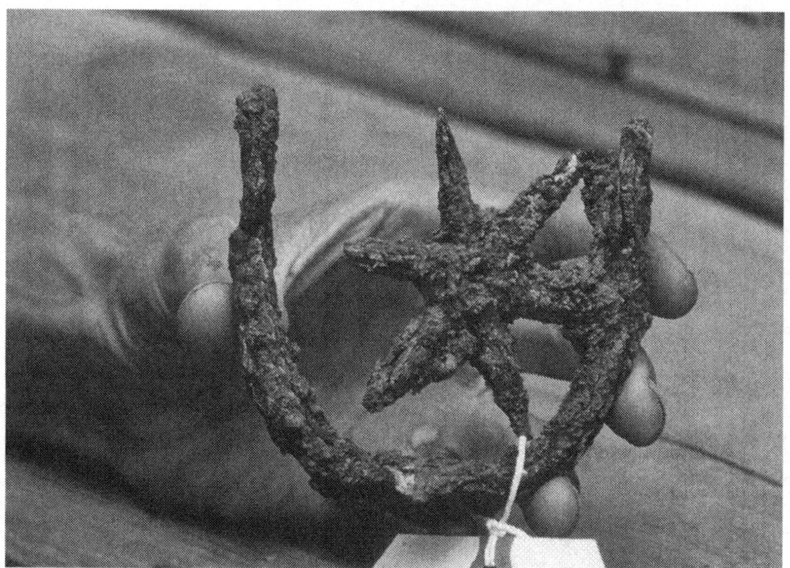

FIGURE 44 Iron spur with star rowel and heel plate from *Humaliwu* (CA-LAN-264) (photo by Nelson Leonard III, courtesy of the Fowler Museum at UCLA)

and undoubtedly hired Chumash Indians to help work the ranch. It is likely that the Chumash at *Humaliwo* were more involved with the ranchos than the missions (contra Green 1999), as most of the inhabitants of *Humaliwo* (94%) were not baptized into the mission system until 1803 (McLendon and Johnson 1999:Appendix XIII). Furthermore, the two missions where most inhabitants of *Humaliwo* (98%) were baptized, Missions San Buenaventura and San Fernando Rey (see King and Johnson 1999:Table 6. 1), were located over 25 km. away. In addition, once Indians were baptized at these missions, they lived there until they died or until mission secularization, which occurred between 1832 and 1835.

Instead of active involvement at the missions, many of the Indians from *Humaliwo* and other Chumash settlements in the region probably worked at Rancho Topanga Malibu Sequit and were paid, at least in part, with glass trade beads (Bickford 1982; Engelhardt 1927:9). A 1795 account by Padre Vicente de Santa María, who saw Indians working as "cowherds, cattlemen, irrigators, bird catchers, horsemen, etc." (Engelhardt 1927:9) between Ventura and Los Angeles, further corroborates this notion. The padre noted that the Chumash working on the ranchos wore European clothing and were not associated with the missions: "Here we see nothing but pagans passing, clad in shoes with sombreros and blankets, and serving as muleteers to the settlers and rancheros, so that if it were not for the gentiles there would be neither pueblo nor rancho . . . these pagan Indians care neither for the Mission nor for the missionaries" (Engelhardt 1927:9). The drastic changes in the lives of the Chumash living at *Humaliwo* stemming from European colonization are reflected in the burials in the historic cemetery, where European trade goods are relatively abundant. European economic influences undoubtedly affected the Chumash at this time, and opened up a new path to the accumulation of wealth. Nevertheless, the Chumash continued to be buried in a traditional cemetery, with non-European goods alongside those that were of European origin (Gamble et al. 2001).

HELO' CEMETERY

The historic cemetery at *Helo'* serves as a useful comparison to the cemetery at *Humaliwo*. This cemetery was first noted in Yarrow's field notes in 1875:

> Dr. Rothrock, who had strolled off some distance after botanical specimens, communicated to us that he had discovered, on the opposite side of a small *estero* to the northward, a locality he believed to be a burial-place, founding his belief on

the fact that he had seen a number of whales' ribs, placed so as to form arches over certain spots. As we well knew that the Santa Cruz Island burial-grounds were similarly marked, we anticipated a "good find," and, indeed, so richly were our anticipations rewarded that we named it the "*Big Bonanza*" (Putnam et al. 1879:35).

This historic cemetery is identified as Cemetery D (Site 1) in figure 12. The only other area on Mescalitan Island where historic artifacts associated with human bone were observed was in Cemetery G, Site 3. Phil Orr excavated in this area in 1944 and found scattered human bone; historic artifacts such as glass beads and a metal cross were also found in this area, though not directly associated with the human bone. It is not clear whether these historic artifacts were associated with human remains; however, if they were, this area of the site was not as prominent or as large as the historic Cemetery D.

On his first day of excavations on Mescalitan Island, Yarrow went to the ranch of T. Wallace More, on the western side of the Goleta Slough (Putnam et al. 1879). Yarrow and his team conducted limited excavations in two cemeteries near the More ranch house that day (Putnam et al. 1879:34–35). One of these cemeteries was historic. Finding very little in the area, the team moved to the historic cemetery on Mescalitan Island, where most of Yarrow's excavations at Goleta (identified by them as La Patera) occurred. After a number of days of excavation on Mescalitan Island, the Yarrow expedition returned to the historic cemetery near More's house, where limited work was again conducted.[48] Fortunately, Yarrow's field notes from the excavations at these sites have been published, and they include a rough accounting of the artifacts that were recovered from the Mescalitan Island excavations (Putnam et al. 1879:35–40).

During the course of several different visits to the Smithsonian Institution, I examined the artifacts recovered from Yarrow's 1875 Mescalitan Island excavations (table 20). In this table, I only included artifacts that probably were from Mescalitan Island. I have also included the artifacts that Olson recovered in the historic cemetery at Mescalitan Island in table 20. This information is based on the notes taken by King (n.d.) on the Cemetery D collections. Both Olson's and Yarrow's investigations occurred in the same historic cemetery, Cemetery D (Glassow et al. 1986; Orr 1943:Plate 1). The numbers of artifacts listed in table 20 are estimates, since occasionally fragments were the only remains recovered. The numbers of artifacts recovered by the Yarrow expedition are probably underestimated; if it was noted that several ollas were recovered, I counted these as two. Only the larger and fancier artifacts were quantified in Yarrow's

TABLE 20. Commonly Occurring Artifact Types Recovered from Yarrow's and Olson's Excavations in Cemetery D on Mescalitan Island

Artifacts	Yarrow	Olson	Total
Ollas: Catalina Island steatite	43	13	56
Comals: Catalina Island steatite	11	4	15
Schist/serpentine bowls, cups, or dishes	7	8	15
Pipes	8	9	17
Mortars	19	14	33
Small mortars	4	3	7
Pestles	14	6	20
Small pestles	3	–	3
Iron implements	9	28	36
Glass beads	Many	2501	2501+
Shell beads	Many	1156	1156+

SOURCE: Compiled from King (n.d.) and Putnam et al. (1879).

notes; therefore, the tabulation of objects presented in table 20 is not completely representative of all the artifacts recovered in these excavations.

Some of the artifact types recovered in the two excavations but not mentioned in table 20 (because they were not quantified by Yarrow) include cakes or lumps of ochre, bone whistles, *Haliotis* shell dishes, ornaments, pendants, bone implements, stone points, stone knives, and stone spear points. A few of the stone bowls and abalone dishes contained red ochre, seeds, or asphaltum skirt weights. Artifacts recovered from Olson's excavations that were not mentioned in Yarrow's notes include four *Mytilus californianus* tubular shell-bead blanks, four *Tivela stultorum* tubular shell-bead blanks, and a *Haliotis rufescens* ornament blank. There were several types of artifacts (in addition to a tin can and copper pan) that were recovered from Yarrow's excavations but not from Olson's. These include a miniature steatite canoe, two soap-root brushes with asphaltum handles (one asphaltum handle was recovered from Olson's excavations), and a six-inch-long stone implement.

The burial with the latter artifact was found inside a redwood canoe[49] (Putnam et al. 1879:38–39). However, the canoe planks were so fragile that only portions of them were preserved (Putnam et al. 1879:39–40). Yarrow described the artifacts associated with this burial as follows:

Near the head of the canoe were a large olla and mortar, the mouths northward. On removing the skeleton, which was lying on its back, the bones fell to pieces. In the canoe, alongside of the skeleton, were 3 pestles, 2 pipes, an iron knife or dagger blade that had been wrapped in seal skin or fur, and a stone implement of triangular form and about 6 inches in length, probably used as a file, or perhaps for boring out pipes. This skeleton was probably that of a chief, or a noted hunter or fisherman (Putnam 1879:38–39).

The suggestion that this skeleton probably was that of a chief apparently was based on the abundance and quality of burial associations. The stone implement described in the text as approximately six inches in length and apparently triangular in cross-section may be similar to or be the same drill illustrated in Figure 4.6 of the Putnam report (1879:66; see figure 45). This drill is purported to have come from Dos Pueblos, but matches the description of the one in Putnam's burial notes so closely that I cannot help but wonder whether it might be the one from the historic cemetery on Mescalitan Island, or possibly a drill that was very similar. The drill described and illustrated in figure 45 is of the type used to drill the holes in canoe planks (Gamble 2002). In addition to these burial associations, a canoe-shaped pot, approximately 20 inches in length and made from Catalina Island steatite, was found in "close contiguity" to the burial in the redwood canoe (Putnam 1879:109). This burial may be that of a canoe owner; it is similar to some of the burials at *Humaliwo* that were associated with plank boats.

Olson also noted redwood planks associated with several burials in the historic cemetery on Mescalitan Island. Wide redwood planks were found below and above one skeleton (KK5). In addition, two iron spikes, an iron adze, two iron knives, and many other artifacts were associated with this burial. Some of these iron tools may have been used to repair or build canoes. Other burials that had both iron tools and redwood planks were also found in this cemetery. Burial KK2 was in the same area of the cemetery as KK5 and was associated with two redwood planks. In addition, a large iron adze was under this individual's stomach,[50] along with a large iron jacknife, a set of flat iron pieces, and two straight steel knives. A 3-foot by 1.5-foot redwood board with a U-shaped section cut into it was recovered underneath another burial (LL2) in this cemetery. In a fourth burial pit (TT), a redwood board approximately one-half inch thick and six

FIGURE 45 Stone canoe drill from Yarrow's excavations at La Patera (Putnam et al. 1879:66)

inches wide was discovered, along with fragments of other boards and a shaped whale bone. Most of these boards were probably canoe planks. Other examples of redwood planks associated with burials have been recorded at the historic Chumash villages at *Humaliwo*, *Simo'mo*, Arroyo Sequit, and Medea Creek, and on San Clemente, Santa Rosa, and Santa Cruz Islands (Jones 1956; L. King 1969:487; Rick 2004).

In addition to the iron tools, other artifacts possibly associated with plank canoe construction and maintenance were found in the historic cemetery on Mescalitan Island. Large flat siltstone grinding slabs were in the same area where the redwood planks and adzes were recovered. These slabs appeared to have been used as sharpening stones, possibly for sharpening adzes. Lumps of asphaltum and shaped cakes of ochre were also present in the historic cemetery. Asphaltum was used in large quantities in the construction and the repair of canoes and red ochre was used as a pigment for painting the canoes (Gamble 2002; Hudson et al. 1978).

Iron implements were not consistently classified by type by Yarrow, although he mentioned that an axe was recovered in the cemetery. Other metal items recovered from La Patera (many of which I documented in the collections at the Smithsonian) included a copper pan, a tin can, a nail that was set in a lump of asphaltum and appeared to be an awl, five iron knives, an iron spike, a brass button, iron blades, and two iron axes. The only artifact associated with *vaqueros* was one brass *higo*. The metal implements from Olson's excavations consisted of 19 iron knives, an iron jackknife, a set of flat iron pieces, two iron adzes, three iron spikes, one iron nail, one iron hook, and two undifferentiated iron implements. This collection consists of tools made by the Spanish but then altered, probably by the Chumash, to meet other needs. Putnam (1879:274) remarked that some of the knives and blades appeared to have been made from hoop-iron. The alteration of scrap metal into utilitarian tools by the Chumash has been noted elsewhere in the Santa Barbara Channel region (Hudson and Blackburn 1987:76).

Most of the iron implements from the historic cemetery at *Helo'* are not items of ornamentation associated with vaqueros, but tools that were probably used in woodworking and other traditional activities. Although stone tools were still used and produced at the historic settlement of *Helo'*, woodworking stone implements appear to be replaced by iron implements (Bamforth 1993). The metal artifacts from the historic cemetery excavations at *Helo'* differ considerably from those found at *Humaliwo* in that there were almost no artifacts associated with *vaqueros* at *Helo'*. Instead, knives, axes, and other utilitarian items were common. This is probably a reflection of the different experiences with European colonization in the two areas.

In the more central portion of the Santa Barbara Channel region to the northwest of *Humaliwo*, only one land grant was awarded prior to 1822; it was *Nuestra Senora del Refugio*, bestowed provisionally in November 1794 and definitively in July 1834 (Gudde 1998:314). *Nuestra Senora del Refugio* was approximately 25 km. from *Helo'*, and it is unlikely that it exerted much influence as far as the Goleta Slough area. There is evidence that farming was practiced in the Goleta Valley in 1805; however, this was after the abandonment of *Helo'* in about 1804. These data indicate that the differences in subsistence remains and types of metal artifacts in the Santa Monica Mountain sites of *Humaliwo* and *Talepop* and those from *Helo'* may be a result of Spanish influences and not necessarily resistance to acculturation. Although the Chumash were significantly affected by European colonization, there is archaeological evidence that suggests that they continued to maintain their traditional political, economic, and religious systems until (and even after) they entered the mission system.

OTHER CHUMASH CEMETERIES

A number of other Chumash cemeteries have been excavated that date from various time periods, and some of them are relevant to this discussion. The cemetery at Medea Creek was in use from approximately AD 1300 to 1785; it was situated about 15 km. inland from *Humaliwo* in the Santa Monica Mountains, and was excavated in its entirety. Linda King (1969, 1982) conducted a thorough analysis of the mortuary remains from this Late period cemetery, and showed that spatial differences in the types and quantities of shell beads suggested a hierarchically organized society. King (1969:35) also observed that the children with more grave goods in the cemetery were clustered in one portion of it and were buried in deeper graves than the children with few or no grave goods. She proposed that the internal variability observed in the Medea Creek cemetery reflected family plots of differentially ranked groups. The portion of the cemetery where most of the wealth was concentrated was interpreted by King as the area where chiefs and their families were interred.

Two burials (and possibly four) in this portion of the cemetery were associated with canoe planks and are of considerable significance. The fact that Medea Creek is about 15 km. from the ocean makes the find all the more intriguing. King made the following comment about the presence of plank canoes at the site:

It is not surprising then to find canoe planks associated with the area of the cemetery allocated to chiefly personages; it is proposed that canoe ownership was consistently associated with wealth and possibly with chieftainship (King 1969:61).

Two deer bone tibia whistles similar to those illustrated in figure 46 were also found at the Medea Creek cemetery; these are associated with the membership in the *'antap* society and are another indicator of a highly-ranked individual (Corbett 1999, 2004; King 1982). Variability in the quantity and spatial distribution of beads and other artifacts at the Medea Creek cemetery is similar to the variability at the precontact and postcontact period cemeteries at *Humaliwo*, suggesting that ranking had considerable time depth.

Several cemeteries that were used during the Middle period in the Santa Barbara Channel region exhibit similar patterns to the ones described for the Late period. The Chumash interred individuals in the prehistoric cemetery at *Humaliwo*, which was used between Middle period 5a and 5c (AD 950–1150, according to King's chronology). The distribution of beads and other artifacts in the historic period cemetery was very similar to that in the Middle period cemetery at *Humaliwo* (Gamble et al. 2001). There were some individuals interred with substantial quantities of grave goods and others buried with few or no grave goods, although the proportion of people buried with very few beads in the prehistoric cemetery was higher than in the historic one. The proportion of subadults (under the

FIGURE 46 Deer bone tibia whistles from *Muwu* (CA-VEN-27) (photo by Lynn Gamble, courtesy of the Santa Barbara Museum of Natural History)

age of 12) buried with large quantities of beads was similar in both cemeteries; in fact, the largest bead lot from the Middle period cemetery (n=4564 beads and ornaments) was found associated with a child. In addition, the people that had the most beads were found in the central portions of both cemeteries and tended to be in deeper graves. Moreover, children and adults with the largest quantities of beads were interred close to each other in both cemeteries. These notable consistencies between the Middle period and historic cemeteries at Malibu suggest that a ranked hierarchical social system had emerged by the end of the Middle period.

A burial from a Middle period 5 (AD 900–1150; Glassow et al. 1986) cemetery on Mescalitan Island supports the existence of a social hierarchy at this time. Phil Orr (1943), who had excavated numerous Chumash burials, was so impressed with this grave that he named the individual the "Queen of Mescalitan Island." The individual was originally discovered in a downward-facing flexed position on top of a whalebone scapula that had its spine planed off. Elaborately decorated, the scapula has a large, incised perimeter groove containing hundreds of inlaid shell beads and ornaments. Other grave offerings included hundreds of other shell beads, a wide-mouthed sandstone bowl mortar with inlaid beads, a large stone tubular bead with inlaid shell disc beads, three other tubular stone beads, and at least five abalone ornaments (Orr 1943:1013). No other burial in the Chumash region is as visually elaborate as this one, although it did not have as many beads as some of the burials from *Humaliwo* dating from the same time period. This person must have been greatly respected by the Chumash and clearly differed from people who had few or no grave goods.

Religious Power

The types and spatial patterning of grave goods from another Chumash cemetery provide further evidence of a hierarchy that is reflected in mortuary behavior. Las Llagas (CA-SBA-81) is situated on the mainland coast to the northwest of *Helo'*. Artifacts from the cemetery at the site indicate that people were buried there during Middle period Phase 2a (200 BC–AD 200). King (1990:226–227) has shown that the distribution of stone pipes, charmstones, and effigies in this cemetery differs markedly from the distribution of shell beads and ornaments, indicating that 'religious' objects were associated with different individuals than were 'wealth' artifacts; the people with wealth were not necessarily the same as the people who had access to ceremonial objects.

A similar distribution of religious artifacts is evident at the Middle period Malibu cemetery, where eleven individuals were buried with stone effigies (figure 47), most of which were representations of fish (Gamble et al. 2001). These effigies were more often associated with women than with men, and (with the exception of one individual) were always interred with young adults between the ages of 17 and 30. Like the burials at Las Llagas, most of the individuals at *Humaliwo* who were associated with these effigies were not buried with large quantities of wealth objects like beads. If it is assumed that effigies were ceremonial objects, a pattern like the one at Las Llagas is apparent; people buried with objects that represent wealth were not consistently the same people who were buried with objects representing supernatural power. This suggests that political and economic power differed from religious power and was probably controlled by different people during this period.

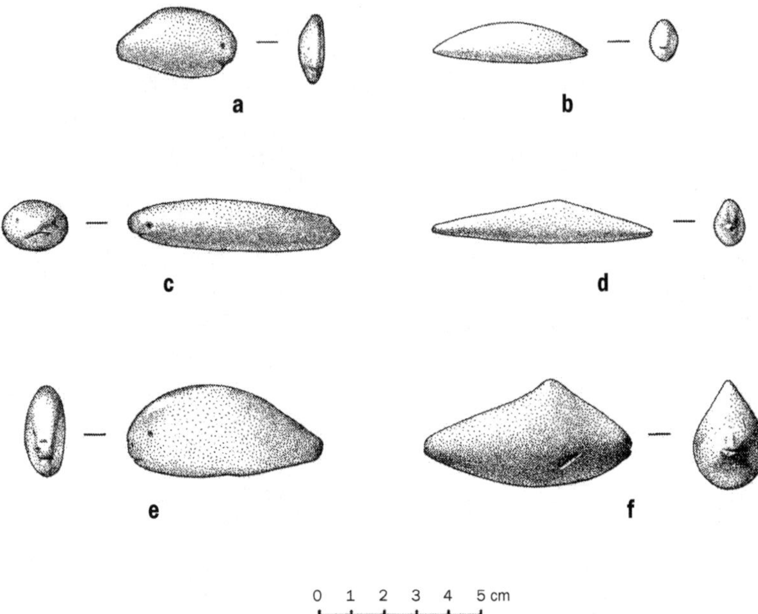

FIGURE 47 Stone effigies from Middle period cemetery at Malibu: (a) steatite fish effigy with mouth and eyes, #573-1737; (b) steatite fish effigy with mouth, #573-1750; (c) steatite fish effigy with mouth and eyes, possible shark, #573-1743; (d) siltstone fish effigy with mouth and dorsal fin, #573-1740; (e) steatite fish effigy with mouth and eyes, #573-1734; (f) siltstone fish effigy with mouth and dorsal fin, #573-1742. (artwork by Lisa Pompelli, courtesy of the Fowler Museum at UCLA)

The Chumash made use of European technology, especially iron tools, in order to maintain their production of traditional valued items such as redwood canoes, wooden bowls, beads, steatite vessels, and other objects. They persisted in their use of traditional foods, sometimes to the exclusion of introduced foods. Their complex exchange networks, although unquestionably affected by colonization, adapted to the new colonial system and took advantage of what might be offered within that system. Ceremonial practices, including the persistent use of traditional structures and shrine sites, endured even after the demise of the mission system. One clear example of a continuity of religious and economic practices after the secularization of the missions involved Mescalitan Island. Juan de Jesús Justo, a Barbareño Chumash consultant of Harrington's, described a shrine site on Mescalitan Island:

At *Helo'* (Mescalitan Island) there was a place for throwing things. Justo never saw it but heard there was a big square enclosure 35 feet or more square, made by tying bundles of feathers to tops of poles so stood three feet high. Poles were near together placed upright in the ground. Old men sat in there and made beads. They were very venerated. Not all knew very much. They were like interpreters, interpreting for god (King 1976:304).

Another reference from Harrington's notes also mentions a shrine site[51] on Mescalitan Island in the post-mission period:

Once Martina [niece of José *Kamuluyatset*] and Luisa [daughter-in-law of José *Kamuluyatset*] were clamming on this side of the water east of *Helo'* and Martina called Luisa's attention to some old weather-beaten *'isoyus* [shrine poles] . . . standing over at *Helo'*. There were several there, but at some other places only a single one was erected. The pole was about five feet tall, two or three inches thick, with bunches of feathers eight inches long, quill down, . . . at its top. Luisa thinks the feathers were all kinds of birds. [She] knows nothing as to whether the stick was painted or barked. [She] did not see it near to [it]. Indians used to pray at place (had their prayers) and threw on the ground. . . *shoxsh* [feather down] and seeds (Johnson 1990:5).

The ceremonial significance of *Helo'* can also be seen in the following narrative, again told by Juan Justo:

At a stop we [Juan Justo and Harrington] made when crossing the estero toward *Helo'*, Juan stated that he never explored around *Helo'* spring because the old people told him not to shout there, but to be quiet because of the occurrence of many *viboras* [rattlesnakes] there. When [Juan was] young, he believed this because his uncle told him the following story. When his uncle was a young man, he passed through *Helo'* with a companion. They saw a vibora, and Juan's uncle began to laugh and shout and make fun of the *vibora*, calling it *tetech shnoxsh* 'flat head.' The other man advised Juan's uncle to be quiet, telling him that it was very delicate there, but Juan's uncle made all the more noise. Then his friend again advised him to be quiet, telling him: "It is better for you to be quiet, you are going to see very extraordinary things." Juan's uncle paid no attention but continued to make all the more fun of the *vibora* and to shout harder than ever, whereupon the other man left him and went on alone. When he was alone, Juan's uncle looked around and saw a whole pile of *guicos* [alligator lizards] with their mouths open towards him and their tongues out. Juan comments that perhaps he really did not see them, that it may have been merely a delusion or hallucination. Juan's uncle shut his eyes and went jumping and climbing to break through the lizards, and when he opened his eyes there was nothing there—but now he believed what his companion told him about the *vibora* (Johnson 1990:5).

This cultural tenacity is indicative of the efficacy of the traditional economic, political, and religious organization of the Chumash.

Gender

The role of gender in the exercise of political and religious power was discussed in chapter 6 in relationship to subsistence activities, but has only been alluded to indirectly in this chapter. Most of the ethnohistoric and ethnographic references to chiefs indicate that Chumash chiefs tended to be males. There are some significant exceptions to this pattern that provide strong evidence that females were also sometimes chiefs. The earliest reference to a female chief was made by Cabrillo, who passed by Santa Barbara in 1542 and commented that an elderly female chief that he saw at *Syuxtun* was not only the chief of that town, but was recognized by communities between Point Conception and Santa Barbara as a paramount chief for the region (Wagner 1929:88). This is a particularly significant reference in that the existence of a female chief cannot be attributed to European colonization and the breakdown of traditional positions of authority. In another respect, the fact that a female was a 'big chief' or possibly a paramount chief of a major Chumash mainland region attests to the position of power that females could hold at this time.

Additional evidence for female chiefs has been found by Johnson in the mission registers (1988:Table 6.6): Maria Thomasa *Sagapueje* was identified in the records as the chief of *Shalawa*, which was located where Montecito is today. Two of Maria's sisters (one was a half sister), were married to the sons of chiefs from mainland coastal settlements (Johnson 1988:Figure 6.7), which is a clear example of chiefly families intermarrying.

A third example of a female chief among the Chumash was provided by Fernando Librado, Harrington's consultant, who described how Pomposa, the chief of *Muwu*, came to power:

> Mateo *Wataitset'* of *Muwu* was the son of Captain *Wataitset'* of that village. Mateo was offered the position of Muwu captain during a San Miguel Day fiesta in Ventura in 1862. He refused the position, though, since he was too poor to afford the expenses of the office. So at the house of José María Guadalupe, a Ventura Indian and former gran sacristan at Mission San Buenaventura, the various captains held a meeting to select a representative to be captain of *Muwu*. In the presence of Captain Justo of Santa Barbara, Captain Luis Francisco of *S'apwi*, Captain Marcelino of *Sohtonocmu'*, and Captain Rogerio at San Fernando, who was himself tied into the village of *Humaliwo*, Mateo *Wataitset'* appointed Pomposa as the captain to represent *Muwu*. Pomposa was of *Muwu* rancheria on her grandfather's side and still represented that village (Hudson et al. 1981:31).

Wataitset', who was in line to inherit the position of chief, was unable to assume the office because of poverty, yet Pomposa, who was the daughter of Captain Luis Francisco of Saticoy (Hudson et al. 1981:91), was entitled to become chief. In 1869, Pomposa hosted her first and last fiesta at the home of her father in Saticoy. Chiefs from numerous Chumash settlements came, as well as other Chumash and numerous Spanish people (Hudson et al. 1981:91–93). By the time of the fiesta, the missions had become secularized and Chumash society had changed drastically. The appointment of Pomposa as chief was undoubtedly affected by the dramatic changes that the Europeans brought. Nevertheless, as documented by Cabrillo, the position of chief was open to women, and although rare, there is evidence for women chiefs, including the more powerful position of paramount chief.

Women also held other powerful positions in Chumash society. Based on his analysis of Chumash oral narratives, Blackburn (1975:56–58) found that a Chumash woman's status could be independent of her husband's position in society. He suggested that although a woman was supposed to respect and obey her husband, women "were not totally subservient to men" (Blackburn 1975:56). Furthermore, women were described in the narratives as independently controlling or owning wealth or property. Blackburn also noted that females were often depicted as malevolent beings who were dangerous or potentially dangerous, reflecting a tension or antagonism that may have actually existed between men and women. Blackburn concluded that women had considerable influence in family life and over their own activities and lives.

Gender cannot be fully investigated without recognizing the significance of two-spirits (berdaches), who played an important role in Chumash society (Holliman 1997, 2000) and who possessed considerable power in their role as *ʾaqi* or undertakers. The *ʾaqi* were paid for their services, which included filling new baskets with the dirt that was excavated for the burial. Once the graves were filled, the *ʾaqi* received these baskets, which were very valuable items, as payment (King 1969:47). Presumably, the deeper the grave, the more baskets they acquired. Holliman (2000:181–182) suggests that the individuals that served as *ʾaqi* were sexually non-procreative, and could be considered a third gender composed of post-menopausal women and biological males who adopted women's attire and work. These individuals were occupational specialists who were probably integrated into the *ʾantap* society (Holliman 2000).

The idea that females were independently wealthy is confirmed in the archaeological record where we see that both females and males were buried with an abundance of wealth objects such as beads (Gamble et al. 2001; Hollimon 1990). In the historic cemetery at *Humaliwo*, richly endowed burials with over 1000 beads included both males and females, as well as people of all ages. Although males tended to have more associated beads than females, the ratio between the sexes did not differ significantly (Gamble et al. 2001:196–197). A similar pattern of beads associated with both sexes was noted in the Middle period Malibu cemetery (Gamble et al. 2001:200); however, a significant difference between male and female burial accompaniments was observed in the distribution of stone effigies at this Middle period cemetery (figure 47).

Effigies are known to have served as talismans throughout southern and central California (Hudson and Blackburn 1986:171–219; Walker and Hudson 1993). Many of the effigies at Malibu had carved anatomical features such as mouths, eyes, and dorsal fins, and were probably abstract representations of fish (Gamble et al. 2001:Figure 2). Female burials at Malibu were more commonly associated with effigies (78% [n=53] were buried with females) than were male burials or individuals of unknown sex (Gamble et al. 2001:202–203). All of the people with effigies whose age could be determined were young adults between the ages of 17 and 30 (with the exception of one six-year-old with an effigy).

Most of the individuals with effigies—who were clustered in the eastern portion of the cemetery—lacked substantial quantities of beads. One notable exception was Burial 35, a female who was approximately 17 years of age and was buried with 21 effigies and 962 shell beads (Gamble et al.

1996:Table 3). It is highly unlikely that the females who were buried with the effigies used these fish representations as talismans for good luck in fishing, since ethnographic and ethnohistoric data indicate that fishing was not a major subsistence activity of Chumash women (Gamble 1983); on the other hand, it is perhaps possible that they were used by women to ensure that male family members were protected when out at sea. It is also possible that these fish effigies were spirit helpers, placed by mourners in the female graves, or were used by females in rituals.

It is significant that these effigies were clustered in a restricted area of the cemetery (Gamble et al. 2001). King (1990a:226–227) found a similar pattern at the Middle period cemetery at Las Llagas (SBA-81), where effigies and other religious objects were buried with different people than were the wealth objects, and the people with religious paraphernalia were situated in a different portion of the cemetery than the people with wealth objects. Several scholars have noted that religious artifacts were less common burial accompaniments during the Late period (L. King 1969, 1982; King 1990a). King (1990a) has proposed that their decrease as burial associations during the Late period is a reflection of the institutionalization of religion at this time. Effigies and other religious artifacts that were used during the Late period have been found in caches in the Santa Monica Mountains (King n.d., Meighan 1969; Wallace 1987), adding credence to the idea that these types of objects were no longer owned by individuals. The presence of ritually powerful objects and items representing wealth in association with females in mortuary contexts corroborates ethnographic information that women were not only affluent but had considerable power in Chumash society.

Manifestations of Power

Many societies exert a considerable effort in building impressive monumental structures, plazas, and other public and private spaces that not only symbolize power, but also serve as communal ritual spaces for large numbers of people. The construction, maintenance, and reconstruction of monumental architecture requires large-scale and reliable labor pools (Pauketat 2004). Laborers who build and rebuild monumental structures need to be recruited and managed by centralized political authorities. Corporate societies that emphasize monumental ritual spaces tend to have a relatively even wealth distribution and balanced accumulation, practice a staple finance system of economics, and have shared power arrangements

(Feinman 2000; Feinman et al. 2000). The Chumash adopted a different tack that tended to emphasize network power (Blanton et al. 1996; Feinman 2000; Feinman et al. 2000).

It is clear from the information presented in this chapter that the Chumash had a ranked social system in which the elite were symbolically distinguished from commoners both in life and in death. The destruction of wealth and the ostentatious personal displays manifested in burial rituals are just one indication that the Chumash emphasized network power, or in Renfrew's (1974) terms, were "individualizing chiefdoms" that tended to emphasize personal wealth, prestige goods, and warfare. This pattern contrasts with that found in group-oriented chiefdoms, which tend to live in regions with limited regional ecological diversity, place little emphasis on technology, lack lavishly endowed burials, and which are characterized by monumental public architecture.

The Chumash did not differ significantly from other relatively complex societies in California in their emphasis on network power. The richly-endowed burials found in the former territory of the Patwin, Pomo, Yokuts, and other tribes are just one example (White 2003); one burial in a cemetery in central California (ALA-413) was associated with 28,287 shell beads (Milliken and Bennyhoff 1993). An excellent analysis and summary of political power among the Yokuts and Pomo can be found in Peter Kunkel's (1962) dissertation.

A brief review of Patwin sociopolitical organization provides a glimpse into the political and ceremonial life of this region. The Patwin lived in permanent settlements of varying size, some with over 1400 inhabitants. The Patwin were known for their complex set of ceremonies, some of which were restricted to members of a secret society with esoteric knowledge not available to non-members. The Kuksu religious system, practiced by the Patwin and several other tribes in central California, was the focus of both ritual and political organization. The Patwin recognized three levels of secret societies, whose members tended to be economically, socially, and politically superior to nonmembers (Bean 1978). Initiation into the Kuksu society had an element of danger, both in the ritual and in the acquisition of potentially dangerous knowledge. Chiefs and their families—which were often large because chiefs practiced polygyny—did not need to hunt, fish, or gather food. The chief could easily be distinguished from other people by the special apparel he wore every day, including fancy feathered headdresses, belts, and cloaks. The Patwin also used shell beads as a form of money, as did most groups in California.

As we shall see, the Chumash relied on shell beads as a medium of exchange and as a symbol of high rank and power. The elaborate exchange systems that existed between the Santa Barbara Channel Islands and the mainland, as well as outside the Chumash region, gave the Chumash relative stability in a region that had considerable ecological variability. Although there were many parallels with other regions of California that had systems of currency, the Chumash economy differed in its emphasis on free market exchange.

CHAPTER 8

Economics and Exchange

Manifestations of Wealth Finance

All these Indians are fond of trafficking and commerce. They trade frequently with the mountain people, bringing fish and beadwork and exchanging them for seeds, tápalos of foxskin, and a kind of blanket made of the fibers of a plant resembling cotton, preferring it to their own made of otter. In their trading they use beads for money. The beads are strung on long threads, arranged according to their value. The unit of exchange is a ponco[52] *of beads, which is two turns of the strings about the wrist and the extended third finger. The value of a ponco depends on the fineness and color of the beads, ours being held in the greatest of esteem; it also depends upon their abundance and their price relative to ours. In everything they keep as careful an account as the most scrupulous magnate does of all his money. Their currency is fashioned from a kind of snail shell, broken up and shaped one piece at a time into lentil-like beads, which they drill with our needles and then string, polishing them to the fineness they consider most desirable. The men wear strings of their beads and ours on their heads and around their necks, woven in various patterns. Each man displays his wealth on his head, from which he removes it for gambling or trafficking.*

José Longinós Martínez in 1792,
as translated by Simpson (1961:54–55)

Longinós Martínez was impressed with the Chumash proclivity for trade and the use of shell bead money. When the Spanish first encountered them, the Chumash practiced a system of wealth finance involving exchanges of prestige goods, a system that was partially supported by extensive marriage ties linking settlements in different ecological zones. Chiefs and other powerful individuals amassed considerable wealth in the form of prestige goods, large stores of food, feasting vessels, shell bead currency, and plank canoes. Chumash chiefs maintained extensive network systems that revolved around cyclical ceremonial feasts that were orchestrated with the help of a *paxa* or ceremonial leader. Through the ownership of seaworthy plank canoes, the chiefs and other wealthy individuals managed a critical resource in the form of the island/mainland exchange system that was flourishing at contact. Manifestations of this network system included the large ceremonial feasts that were hosted by chiefs in the mainland centers, elaborate mortuary rituals, and the production and use of shell-bead money. The Chumash economic system was one of the most complex to ever exist among hunter-gatherers. By the Late period, Chumash craft specialists were producing large quantities of shell bead currency. The bead-making industry was based on two different craft specializations; the well documented chert microblade drill industry, and the production of the beads themselves. In this chapter, the Chumash economic network and the accompanying organization of power that was integral to the system are examined.

Contexts of Exchange

One of the most important means of coping with an unpredictable environment involving variable ecological zones is through exchange of food, raw materials, and manufactured items between adjacent regions with varying resources (see King 1976; Gamble 2005). Chumash chiefs and other elite members of society orchestrated the redistribution of shell-bead money, subsistence goods, and other items. In addition, they were involved in cross-channel exchange in their role as canoe owners. Shell beads were an important medium in this system, functioning as a form of social storage when used in exchanges involving food, thus insuring that risks due to food shortages were minimized (Gamble 2005; O'Shea 1981; Rowley-Conwy and Zvebil 1989). Chiefs acted as agents in the storage and redistribution of subsistence goods and money, ensuring that their people were fed at feasts as well as in times of need.

REDISTRIBUTION AND RECIPROCITY

Chumash exchange was a complex affair. As in other regions in California, redistribution orchestrated by chiefs occurred at regular intervals during scheduled ritual events and trade feasts (Vayda 1967). Chiefs, with the help of the *paxa*, the poisoner, and other officials, organized these ceremonial events to which attendees were expected to bring food, money, or other resources to help fund the musicians, dancers, guests, and other individuals who participated in the ceremony. People from a wide geographical range,[53] including island, mainland, and interior villages, congregated in large centers along the mainland coast to attend these ceremonies. In preparation for such large feasts, chiefs spent months hiring dancers and singers and overseeing the gathering and preparation of foods. The dance grounds would have to be prepared, and the *siliyik* (the sacred brush enclosure) built. The chief needed to amass enough resources to pay participants for their services and provide the abundant meals that were served. Attendees also helped with payments:

> According to Fernando [Fernando Librado, Ventureño consultant] visiting captains at a festival would make donations on their arrival so that the host would have enough for the festival and the rest of the year. There was a pecuniary interest in having a festival in Indian times, for the captain would save some of the offerings so that when his subjects were in distress he would have something with which to assist them (L. King 1969:43).

As noted in chapter 7, individuals who did not contribute to a ceremonial gathering might be threatened by the poisoner or others (Blackburn 1976; Gayton 1930). If a chief refused to accept an invitation to a feast, it was grounds for war—presumably because refusal indicated a lack of peaceful intent (Harrington 1942; King 1969:43). These measures served to encourage chiefs not only to attend feasts, but to bring appropriate amounts of food, money, and other items so as not to insult a host chief.

The ability of chiefs to extract surpluses from people is well documented in the early descriptions by explorers in the Chumash region. The Spanish frequently noted that chiefs provided members of the expeditions, as well as other Chumash, with extensive provisions. The following account by Crespí provides an example of the chief's role in the distribution of food and beads:

> In the morning, on seeing we were going, they brought us a great many bowls of sage and gruel, and four or six ones with the aforesaid small raisins, before our setting out. They put a long beadwork around my neck like a rosary, and did the same also for our chief officers (Brown 2001:371).

It is assumed that the chief was distributing food and beads that had been collected previously from his constituents. The most detailed early description of the ability of Chumash chiefs to extract goods and provisions is the opening quotation in chapter 7 from Crespí, who described

El Buchón as a head chief, implying that he was more powerful than "lesser" chiefs. What is of interest here is the statement that *El Buchón* collected tribute from several villages, stored these foodstuffs in his community, and later redistributed these provisions to the people. Another statement by Crespí reveals that not only were food items provided to Chumash chiefs as "tribute," so were beads:

> Up to here, ever since the place called San Luis Rey on the Channel, we have been accompanied by a very imposing heathen man who is very bright and friendly. On his own initiative, he has come with us, bearing his own good-sized quiver of arrows and bow; on our reaching here, he was clasped by all of these heathens and well rewarded by each of them giving him a length of the beads that they made from shells. This heathen man dropped from our sight here, but on the way back we met him once more two days' march farther up, and he again accompanied us as far as his own country, and, the fact is, did us a very considerable favor by notifying the villages to bring us food, aware as he was of the want that we were in as we came. And, he being so bright and lively and a great talker, everyone called him El Loco, the Crazy Man (Brown 2001:467).

These accounts establish the role of the chief in reciprocity and redistribution, but also inform us about the extent of the power that chiefs possessed. Chiefs redistributed food and other items to people over a fairly wide region. *El Loco* was able to collect food for members of the Portolá expedition from people in each community between Gaviota and San Luis Obispo (Brown 2001; King 1984:1–38), even during the lean winter months, as Crespí noted on January 3, 1770, in this description of *El Loco's* actions:

> Having vanished from our sight at various points in these last days' marches, he would reappear along the way with villages that would appear with him by the wayside with gruel and mush, which, scarcely stopping at all, the officers would take from them and divide among everyone, thus considerably relieving the want that everyone was in (Brown 2001:647).

As these diaries demonstrate, a Chumash chief wielded considerable power over a regional network; a single chief was able to mobilize inhabitants from a series of villages and induce them to bring food and beads to the Spanish. The chiefs undoubtedly were also interested in impressing the Spanish with their wealth and power.

OTHER TYPES OF EXCHANGE

The ceremonial redistribution of resources did not preclude the more open (free-market) intervillage exchange described by C. King (1976).

During fiestas, gambling and trading also occurred, in addition to the redistributive activities. Of course, exchanges also occurred when fiestas were not taking place (C. King 1976). Shell beads served as a standardized medium of exchange in these transactions.

King (1978) has proposed that the shell bead exchange system in southern California was more monetized than it was elsewhere in California, where societies used types of shell beads that required a smaller investment of labor than the types used in southern California. He has suggested that the societies in Central California had economic systems that were both political and monetized, with neither aspect as developed as they were to the south or the north. However, Arnold (2001a) suggests that the Chumash system was more politicized: "The controlled release of shell-bead currency and the maintenance of its value would have been virtually impossible if dozens of production/distribution sites had been acting independently (and presumably competitively)" (Arnold 2001a: 296). How politicized was the exchange system of the Chumash? Were the principles of supply and demand present in Chumash transactions both within their boundaries and beyond? Were individuals free to exchange beads for goods that they needed and desired, or was the release of beads controlled? I first turn to some early ethnohistoric accounts to investigate these issues, then consider the particular environmental and geographical features that may have affected systems of exchange among the Chumash.

King (1976) has synthesized ethnohistoric and ethnographic evidence for exchange both within and outside the Chumash region. I will not review all the details of his work, but instead provide a summary with an emphasis on the types of economic interactions that occurred at the time of early European contact. King (1976) proposed that the Chumash maintained a market economy that relied on *Olivella biplicata* shell beads as a standardized and portable medium of exchange. He suggested that environmental variability within the Chumash area was a stimulus for increased economic activities in the region, and that the use of shell bead money enabled the Chumash to efficiently take advantage of and redistribute the plentiful resources in the different ecological zones.

According to early accounts, items that were traded from the islands to the mainland included shell beads, digging stick weights, and steatite ollas (King 1976); the latter came from Santa Catalina Island, not the northern Channel islands. In return, mainlanders exported seeds, acorns, bows and arrows, furs, skins, roots, and baskets to the islands. Trade items from the mainland to inland areas included fish and beads, while people living in the interior traded fish, game, seeds, fruits, and fox-skin shawls to the coast. Some of these exchanges were probably seasonally timed, as seasonally-available fish species have been documented as imported to or exported from the different regions. There is also evidence for exchanges directly between the islands and the interior: shells used in bead-making, otter skins, acorns, and islay were reported to have gone directly from the islands to the interior. Fernando Librado told Harrington that when it was time to harvest acorns and other wild foods that ripened in the fall, many people from the islands traveled to the mainland and then inland to gather acorns and other "wild fruit" (King 1976:293). Fernando also mentioned that the inhabitants of Santa Rosa Island would bring otter skins, because they were plentiful in the waters off this island, and trade them to the mainland people for acorns. As can be seen from Fernando's comments, the islanders went directly to the interior to gather acorns and other foods, and also traded with the people from the interior for these items. Fernando indicated that many exchanges took place on the mainland, presumably because of its central location between the islands and the interior:

> The coast of the mainland was where inland Indians, coast Indians, and island Indians mixed. That is why the *siliyik* (ceremonial enclosure used at fiestas) was used on the coast. There was commerce between inland and island Indians at *qasil* (Refugio). Exchanged otter skins. Shawa was not abandoned at large then. Refugio was a big village; it was a center for it was a port of the Santa Cruz Island Indians; a trail led to Santa Ines and there was much trade in acorns, wild cherry, etc., from Santa Ines when the Islanders came (Fernando to Harrington in King 1976:294).

Also noted by early explorers (and later by some of Harrington's consultants) was the proclivity that the Chumash had for exchange and commerce. The opening quotation by Longinos Martinez provides one example, as does this comment attributed to him: "The liveliness of these Indians makes them more given to thievery than those of the other parts, and to the possession of things of some value, the desire for which causes them to engage in commerce with soldiers and sailors" (Simpson 1939:45–46). In 1775, Fages also described Chumash exchange, and corroborated the fact that much of their commerce apparently took place outside of chiefly control:

> The Indians of all these villages are of good disposition and average figure; they are inclined to work, and much more to self-interest. They show with great covetousness a certain inclination to traffic and barter, and it may be said in a way

that they are the Chinese of California. In matters concerning their possessions, they will not yield or concede the smallest point (Priestley 1937:31).

Shell Beads as Indicators of Wealth and Rank

The Chumash emphasis on exchange outside of the context of reciprocity was unusual for a hunter-gatherer society, as was their reliance on shell-bead money. The inhabitants of villages on Santa Cruz and the other Channel Islands specialized in producing goods such as bead money as a way of gaining access to resources not available on the islands (Arnold 2001a, 2001b; King 1976; Kennett and Kennett 2000). In return for bead money, the Chumash on the mainland and in the interior of the Santa Barbara Coast region traded subsistence and status items to the Islanders. Sea-worthy plank canoes, which were expensive to build and maintain, provided a significant means of transport between the mainland and the islands.

Shell beads that were probably produced in the Santa Barbara Channel region were also exchanged outside of the Chumash region; they have been found in central California, Oregon, the Southwest, and the Great Basin (Bennyhoff and Hughes 1987; Earle 2005; King 1990a; Hughes and Milliken 2007). The different types of beads, their context, and their distribution are the focus of the following discussion.

Two types of craft specialization (Costin 2001) associated with the production of shell bead money have been identified for the Chumash. The first involved the drilling and shaping of shell beads at several sites on Santa Cruz, Santa Rosa, and San Miguel islands (Arnold 1987, 1992a; Kennett 1998:334–336; King 1976). Chumash bead-making specialists used *Olivella biplicata*, *Mytilus californica*, and *Haliotis rufescens* shells, among others, as materials for the production of shell beads. The most significant species for shell bead-making was *Olivella biplicata*. Different portions of the shells were used to make beads, with preferences changing over time. The hardest portion of the *Olivella biplicata* shell is the callus portion or whorl of the shell. This was the portion used for money beads. Although the callus portion of the shell was used prior to the Late period, it was only used at that time in combination with the wall sections of the shell, which were easier to drill than the thick, hard callus sections.

The second type of craft specialization associated with bead money was the manufacturing of the drills that were used to perforate the shell beads (Arnold 1987; King 1976). Small drills made from translucent Monterey Chert bladelets were standardized in form, although bladelet forms changed over time from trapezoidal to triangular with dorsal retouch, an indication that the drills became increasingly more efficient (Arnold 1987; Arnold et al. 2001:116–117). Numerous microblade cores at China Harbor, Prisoner's Harbor, and sites on the eastern end of Santa Cruz Island provide evidence for the specialized production of drills at these sites, which are situated fairly near the source of the semi-translucent blonde-to-brown cherts that are found in the "contact zone" where the Monterey formation adjoins the Santa Cruz volcanics at the eastern end of Santa Cruz Island. It should be emphasized that high quality chert was also available on the mainland, especially along the Purismeño coast near the present town of Lompoc. Nevertheless, specialized bead drill making was never a significant activity outside of the Northern Channel Islands. Arnold and her colleagues (Arnold 1987; Arnold et al. 2001) have suggested that a microlithic industry appeared on the northern Channel Islands about AD 900. By approximately AD 1150–1200, Arnold has suggested that craft specialization had developed, and that lithic specialists at Prisoner's Harbor, China Harbor, and sites on the eastern end of Santa Cruz Island were exporting numerous microblades to bead-making specialists elsewhere on Santa Cruz Island and on the other northern Channel islands, who then made them into drills and used them for perforating beads. Furthermore, Arnold et al. have proposed that the inhabitants of Prisoner's Harbor, China Harbor, and sites on the eastern end of Santa Cruz Island "appear to have begun to control use of the outcrops" (Arnold et al. 2001:113).

Prior to the Late period, most beads that included both wall and callus portions had holes drilled through the walls. At the onset of the Late period, "cupped" beads—beads made solely from the callus portions of Olivella shells—were used extensively for exchange (figure 48). These types of beads were common throughout the Chumash region during the Late period, and have been identified as 'money' beads on the basis of their distributions in cemeteries and in other contexts.

Certain beads types were highly restricted in distribution and have been identified with socially significant political positions (King 1990a); they include clam tube beads and tubular columella beads made from the hinge of the *Hinnites multirugosus* shell. Cupped beads tend to be more widely distributed, indicating that most individuals had access to them, although certain individuals in cemeteries were buried with hundreds or thousands of cupped beads while other people had significantly fewer. During the historic period, *Olivella* cupped beads ceased being used and were replaced by *Olivella biplicata* rough disk beads (figure 49), which were less costly to manufacture. *Olivella* rough disk beads frequently were referred to as money in J. P. Harrington's notes (King 1990a:60).

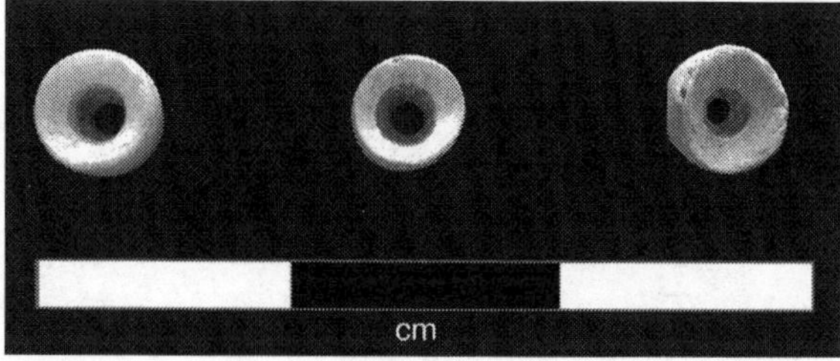

FIGURE 48 *Olivella biplicata* cupped beads from the Pitas Point Site (CA-VEN-27), #565-5913c, 565-3929a, 565-3929b (photo by Lynn Gamble, courtesy of the Fowler Museum at UCLA)

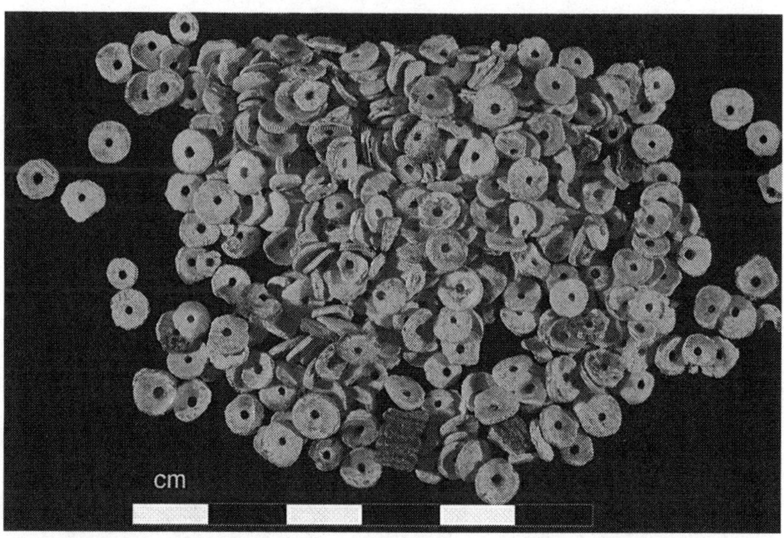

FIGURE 49 *Olivella biplicata* rough disc beads from *Humaliwu* (CA-LAN-264), #572-2440 3929b (photo by Lynn Gamble, courtesy of the Fowler Museum at UCLA)

Many early historic accounts and ethnographic accounts indicate that shell beads had standardized values, and some types were used as currency (see Hudson and Blackburn 1987:267–282 for detailed information on Chumash currency). In the quotation that opens this chapter, Longinós Martínez remarked on the value of shell bead money and described how strings of beads were measured. In the 1850s, Daniel Hill recorded the following information about the Chumash method of bead measurement:

These articles were exchanged for a species of money from the Indian mint of the Santa Barbara rancherias, called by them ponga. This description of money consisted of pieces of rounded shell, with a hole in the middle, made from the hardest part of the small, edible white mussel of our shores which was brought in canoes by the Barbarians from the island of Santa Rosa. The worth of a rial [real] was put on a string which passed twice and a half around the hand, i.e., from end of middle finger to wrist. Eight of these strings passed for the value of a silver dollar, and the Indians always preferred them to silver; even prior to 1833. This traffic the Padres encouraged, as it brought them into peacable intercourse with the tribes of the Tulare Valley (Woodward 1934:119).

Hill is probably confusing small white mussel shells with Olivella shells. It is noteworthy that the Yokuts from the Central Valley were interacting with the Chumash in the exchange of beads. Hill had this to say about the inhabitants of the Central Valley:

The Indians of the Tulare country generally came over once a year, in bands of from twenty to thirty, male and female, on foot, and armed with bows and arrows. They brought over panoche, or thick sugar, made from what is now called honey dew, and the sweet carisa cane, and put up into small oblong sacks made of grass and swamp flags; also nut pines and wild tobacco pounded and mixed with lime (Woodward 1934:119).

Hill's reference to once a year suggests that the Yokuts came over to the coast to attend regularly scheduled ceremonies.

After European colonization, the Chumash used iron needles to drill shells for bead making, and the exchange of beads continued, even when the Chumash lived in the missions (Gibson 1976). Iron needles became more common sometime after 1782, when the Santa Barbara Presidio and Mission San Buenaventura were founded. The Spanish maintained detailed invoices documenting the items that were shipped to the Santa Barbara Presidio; these records show that the number of iron needles in the region increased dramatically, with over 30,000 iron needles being shipped to Santa Barbara Presidio from San Blas, Mexico between 1788 and 1795 (Graesch 2001:279). Shell beads that were perforated with needle drills can be distinguished from beads drilled with stone drills because the perforations are straight instead of biconical or conical in cross-section.

Hammerstones, used to break shells into more manageable pieces, were another type of tool associated with bead making. Shells were usually set on stone or wooden anvils for various steps in the bead-making process, including drilling (figure 50) (Hudson and Blackburn 1987:128–130). Some

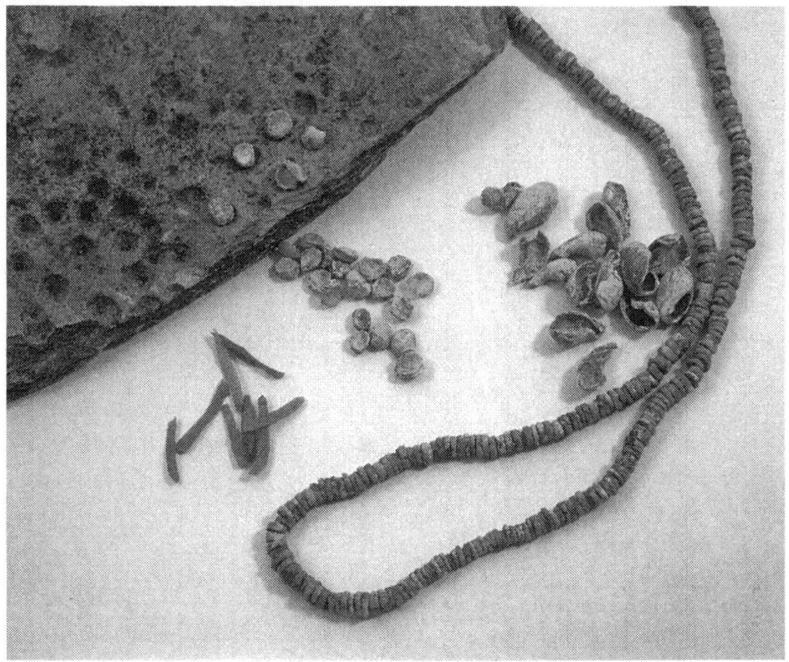

FIGURE 50 Beadmaking kit (courtesy of the Santa Barbara Museum of Natural History)

of the bead anvils made from stone exhibit evidence of grinding; they were probably used to smooth the edges of beads after they were strung. Harrington recorded the following information from Fernando Librado on bead making:

> They make the fine beads by stringing them when rough on a cord made of juncos and then rolling them on a thin slab or rock prepared for the purpose, until they make them nice and round (Hudson and Blackburn 1987:132).

Most cupped beads were traded within the Chumash region, although additional documentation on the distribution of shell beads both within and outside the Chumash region is needed to fully understand their role. Large quantities of Olivella rough disk beads have been found with burials at Tahquitz Canyon (CA-RIV-45) in the Cahuilla area (King 1995), as well as at the historic Kumeyaay site of *Amat Inuk* (C-144, CA-SDI-106) in San Diego County (Gamble and Zepeda 2002). The beads from these sites indicate that traditional exchange systems involving the Chumash and groups to the south and east continued for up to 80 years after Spanish colonization began (see also Earle 2005). The maintenance of traditional socioeconomic interactions between California Indian groups after Spanish colonization reflects the significance of these economic relationships, given Spanish efforts to destroy traditional Indian lifeways.

Theoretical Considerations Concerning Chumash Exchange

California Indian societies in general, and the Chumash in particular, were unique among hunter-gatherer societies because of the emphasis they placed on economic interactions. The ethnographic and ethnohistoric accounts of exchange and shell-bead money usage support King's (1976:289) characterization of the Chumash as a people that "maintained a market economy with standardized, portable mediums of exchange, frequently used to purchase subsistence materials, most manufactured goods, and some services." Beads made from *Olivella biplicata* shells served as this medium of exchange.

In a now classic work, Polanyi (1957) defined reciprocity, redistribution, and market exchange as economic modes of exchange that could be found in various combinations within non-western societies. Reciprocity, or gift exchange (Mauss 1967), refers to equal exchanges between individuals or groups that are symmetrically placed. Redistribution involves the movement of goods into a central place and their reallocation by authorities located at that place (Bohannan 1963; Polanyi 1957). The Chumash practiced both reciprocity and redistribution, especially in ceremonial contexts. Market exchange, as defined by Polanyi, is an exchange of goods at prices determined by supply and demand; money is often associated with market exchange. Dalton (1965:51–52) has identified three types of economic communities: (1)"marketless" communities that rely on reciprocity and redistribution for transactions; (2)"peripheral markets" that differ in the presence of market-place sites with a use of some "commercial" money; and (3)"market-dominated economies" where a large proportion of land, labor, goods, and service transactions occur in the marketplace. More recently, Smith (2004) has criticized Polanyi (1957) and Sahlins (1972) for their arguments against the application of capitalist ideas to noncapitalist societies. I believe that the Chumash in many ways were close to being a capitalist society despite the fact that they were nonagriculturalists and lacked a state-level political organization. In Dalton's terms, the Chumash had a peripheral market economy; money was used, but most people did not gain the majority of their income from market sales.

In his "distributional" approach to the identification of market exchange in the archaeological record, Hirth (1998) proposes that households are integral to market exchange in that they are both the primary suppliers and consumers of items. Chumash households on the northern Channel Islands specialized in the production of beads, although bead making was not an "attached" specialization in the sense that administrators controlled the behavior of the specialists (Arnold and Munns 1994; Brumfiel and Earle 1987; Costin 2001). Arnold and Munns suggest that bead makers were probably not monitored in their daily activities; although they believe that the distribution of beads probably was controlled by high ranked canoe owners who manipulated cross-channel exchanges (Arnold and Munns 1994:487).

In summary, the Chumash participated in a peripheral market economy that used shell beads as a medium of exchange. Shell beads had been used and produced in the Santa Barbara area for over 7000 years (King 1990a). The Chumash employed over 22 species of shell to make a variety of types of beads and ornaments. At approximately the onset of the Late period (or the Transitional period as defined by Arnold [1992a]), shell beads began to be used as a form of money in the Santa Barbara Channel regions (King 1990a), the scale of shell-bead production increased significantly, and "shell-bead making became a specialized craft occupation for many island villagers" (Arnold and Graesch 2001). The hypothesis that the release of beads was controlled by elites (Arnold 2001a:296) is difficult to test in the archaeological record. Before we consider this and other hypotheses about the nature of exchange between the islands and the mainland, the issue of the ownership and use of canoes must be explored.

Significance of Canoes

Plank canoes, which were expensive to build and maintain, were relied upon for exchanges between the mainland and the northern and southern Channel Islands; they also facilitated exchanges between settlements along the mainland coast. Chiefs or wealthy individuals paid for the materials needed and commissioned the necessary labor to have a canoe constructed. Once the watercraft was built, canoe owners probably had considerable control over the distribution of goods and food items between the islands and the mainland, and probably acted as intermediaries in economic transactions, taking a percentage of the profits. The question here is how much control they had. We know from ethnographic records that large ceremonial gatherings took place at Chumash centers, often on the mainland. These regularly scheduled ritual events drew people from the interior Chumash region, the islands, and the mainland coast, and provided opportunities for market exchange to occur, where people were free to buy and sell goods and services. Could canoe owners or their assistants have successfully kept people living on the islands from attending these festivals unless they paid a fee or were taxed based on the goods they were carrying? Given the restrictive nature of canoe ownership and canoe manufacturing knowledge, payment of a fee seems likely.

This idea is reflected in the ethnographic sources, which indicate that the Chumash had a strict craft guild called the Brotherhood of the *Tomol* (Blackburn 1975; Hudson et al. 1978:175). Only very wealthy individuals could afford to build and own a canoe. One of the important functions of the Brotherhood members was to operate as sea traders, transporting primarily manufactured goods from the Channel Islands to the mainland in exchange for subsistence items or other commodities available there. According to Harrington's notes, local members of the Brotherhood of the *Tomol* helped unload a canoe and received money for this role:

> They are met in the water by those waiting, for they have come to help unload the *tomol* there. These men belong to the Brotherhood-of-the-Canoe. . . . Those who unload the *tomol* are glad-hearted, for it is their duty to unload the boat. They receive a share in the profit for doing so, for it is theirs (Hudson et al. 1978:141).

Members of the Brotherhood reaped economic benefits from their role. Harrington's notes also provide information on the highly guarded knowledge associated with the building of a canoe:

> Only the canoemakers know how to build a canoe. They are called *'altomolich*, meaning "makers of canoes," for they have learned how to do it under older men. They are the ones that know how, and only they, for no one else was allowed to hang around. Only certain men in a village knew how. An old canoemaker would have his helpers and he would allow no one else around. There was much to know. The boards had to be fitted together well. Then the boards had to be tarred and tied. They used no iron in building a board canoe. They knew all the secrets in order to make a *tomol* which was agile on the sea. . . . They use their technical language in order to know how to put care in their work, and also to make good use of their tools (Hudson et al. 1978:40).

The secretive information and associated esoteric language of canoe-making served to limit the number of people that could build canoes. Harrington's consultants emphasized that a canoe had to be built properly, and that in the old days the Chumash did not care how long it took to build a canoe because they valued good safe canoes over hastily built ones (Hudson et al. 1978:41). The many stories about disasters at sea served to reinforce the idea that not just anyone could build a canoe. Fernando Librado related the following story about the perils surrounding seafaring:

> Canoe faring is dangerous, and drownings are frequent. There would be no coming home, for a wind or wave might capsize a tomol and a man could drown. Women were afraid to go to sea, for a rower might tip the boat over, and he alone would return to shore. Francisco *Kuliwit* once told me that he was one of 60 men who made a crossing of the channel from Cojo to San Miguel Island; only he and five others survived (Hudson et al. 1978:140).

This tragic crossing involved an event that occurred when Father José Señan ordered the "captain of all the Indians" to go to San Miguel Island in 30 canoes and bring all the Chumash that remained there to the mission. The group did not make the crossing from Port Hueneme to Anacapa, known as the safest crossing, but instead left from Cojo (near Point Conception), which required the voyagers to be farther away from land. Other oral traditions (Blackburn 1975; Hudson et al. 1978) emphasized the dangers encountered at sea and the possible loss of lives. Because of these dangers and the specialized knowledge needed to build a safe watercraft, it is unlikely that an untrained individual could easily build a safe craft. Among central California groups, both practical and esoteric ritual knowledge were necessary for success in occupations; usually inherited positions (Goldschmidt 1951; McKern 1922). The dangers at sea, in combination with the skills and esoteric knowledge needed to build a seaworthy watercraft, helped to insure that plank-boat building remained a restricted activity with highly guarded knowledge limited to a select few.

Additional descriptions from oral traditions fill in the gaps on the central role of canoe owners in the Chumash economy. In a Chumash narrative from one of Harrington's consultants, Momoy's[54] grandson wants to go to the islands across the channel, and is speaking with his grandmother Momoy about the trip:

> 'It would be best to talk to your uncle Hew [pelican]. He has a canoe and could take you over. He is the captain of the boat, and his companion, Mut [cormorant] is a sailor.'. . . 'Uncle, my grandmother said that you can carry me over to the other side of the channel.' Hew said, 'Yes, nephew, when do you want to leave?' 'Right

away,' replied the boy. 'All right, but first I have to deliver the fish I've brought,' Hew said. 'All right, uncle, but hurry' (Blackburn 1975:138).

Hew takes his nephew to Santa Cruz Island, where the nephew kills Hap, a dangerous supernatural being. Hew waits on the shore for his nephew, who returns to Hew and is taken back to the mainland. On their return, Hew said:

'Nephew, here we are, back in our own country.' 'Good,' said the boy. 'And how much do I owe you for your labor?' Hew said, 'Nephew, whatever you want to give me will be fine.' The boy took out his abalorio [shell-bead money] and began to measure it out. 'This is for you,' he said, 'and this is for your companion, Mut' (Blackburn 1975:139).

In this narrative, important aspects of the Chumash economic system are described. Apparently canoe owners took people out to the islands in exchange for money. The narrative also indicates that canoe owners imported fish from the islands, and then delivered the fish to the local families. Also aboard was a 'sailor' who, in addition to the captain of the boat, was paid by Hew. This narrative suggests that if an individual had the money, they could pay canoe owners or 'sailors' to transport them between the islands and mainland. The canoe owners and sailors made money on the deal, but were not actually controlling the merchandise. The early historic account by Font (see chapter 3) provides additional evidence that canoe owners received rewards; in this case some of the fish that were caught by the use of the canoe.

These accounts provide an incomplete but significant understanding of the nature of the Brotherhood of the *Tomol* and of the passage between the islands and mainland. The practical and esoteric knowledge of how to build a safe plank canoe was highly restricted to members of a hereditary craft guild who had a special vocabulary associated with the technology of building watercraft. Oral traditions and past misfortunes no doubt discouraged would-be entrepreneurs from taking on the task of building a plank boat or from making the crossing between the islands and the mainland without a plank canoe. This provided a distinct advantage to members of the Brotherhood, who built and navigated the canoes, and reaped the benefits associated with canoe ownership. In particular, islanders were beholden to canoe owners for transporting people and goods between the mainland and offshore islands safely. This created a situation where canoe owners, some of whom effectively owned several plank boats, had a monopoly on cross-channel transportation. By guarding and limiting the knowledge of canoe building and navigation to a select few, only a limited number of people could profit from the ownership of canoes. The existence of a craft guild with the esoteric knowledge of canoe building and navigation served to concentrate profits in the hands of a few. Archaeological evidence indicates that islanders as well as mainlanders made and owned canoes (Gamble 2002).

From the somewhat meager ethnographic accounts and oral traditions presented here, it appears that most people with wealth had access to canoes and could make the Channel crossing. There is no indication from these accounts, however, that canoe owners restricted the flow of beads that were exported to the mainland. Instead, it appears that the owners of the canoes and their associates reaped economic benefits when taking on passengers and trade goods.

Centers of Exchange

The concept of centrally located places as influential centers is well known, and is especially relevant to this discussion. In his seminal work on social organization in Native California, Bean (1976:102) observed that there was usually a central town in California Indian societies that served as a political, economic, and ritual center. Bean described exchange mechanisms associated with these centers: "Formal or informal trade feasts were set up between groups living in different ecological areas, so that goods from the mutually advantageous but politically separate areas were exchanged for those of others" (Bean 1976:120). In considering types of exchange systems, Lightfoot and Feinman (1982:67) pointed out that several locational studies have shown that certain centrally located settlements were much larger than other villages, and that these larger settlements usually were the residences of influential leaders. The authors noted that they were not surprised that villages of important decision makers were centrally located, since such locations would minimize the movement costs of goods and the processing of information. The term center is used here for a centrally located town that was larger than most of the settlements surrounding it. A center is where the chiefs and other important high ranked individuals resided.

The existence of centers should be reflected in the settlement patterns of a region. A center is likely to be located in an area where population density is high, resulting in diminished transportation costs in the economic exchange network. In the archaeological record, one would expect to see larger sites geographically closer to places identified as centers than to smaller sites. Larger sites should also contain a higher density of exchange goods than smaller sites. Site size would decrease as distance from the center increased, until another center was approached. Similarly, one would expect to find more houses in centrally located settlements and fewer houses in villages at a distance from the center.

The geographic context of the Santa Barbara Channel region is relevant to the placement of Chumash centers. The channel itself is a highly productive marine environment, with kelp forests and submarine canyons that host an abundance of fish and sea mammals. The offshore islands provide protection from the open seas between Point Conception and Ventura, where the south-facing coastline is much calmer than the turbulent surf to the north of Point Conception. Although the northern Channel Islands have a wealth of marine resources, they lack the abundance and variety of terrestrial resources that the mainland boasts. Conversely, the interior region has significant terrestrial staples, but not the significant marine resources that are present on the mainland coast. These circumstances place the mainland coastal settlements between Point Conception and Ventura in a strategically and economically advantageous location.

Site size is often used to determine site hierarchies in a region (Renfrew and Bahn (2004:182–186). The relationship of site size to population is complex and unclear in many areas of the world. In the Chumash area, site size is not an accurate measure of estimated populations. Many archaeological sites along the mainland coast were impacted by development before accurate measurements of site sizes were made. Another problem is that standard criteria were not used in determining site boundaries. Some archaeologists only included the area of the site where dense midden deposits were observed, while others included the area surrounding the higher-density portions of a site. Since only remnants of many of the significant sites in the Chumash area exist today (especially along the mainland coast), archaeologists cannot easily revisit archaeological sites to determine their spatial dimensions. Therefore, population estimates based on early historic accounts and mission records have been more commonly used.

Kennett (2005:108–110) conducted a rank-size analysis of Chumash settlements on the northern Channel Islands, the mainland coast, and in the interior based on baptismal tabulations by Johnson (1982, 1988). Kennett found that the rank-size distributions suggest that Chumash villages were relatively autonomous politically, with little political integration between historic period communities in the region. Kennett noted that the population figures derived from mission records represent only a small fraction of the total population, but does not discuss the problems arising from the use of a data set such as the mission records (Gamble 2006). One of the most significant difficulties with using the mission records is that they do not reflect village populations prior to colonization in the region. The deleterious effects of colonization on Chumash populations have been well documented (Cook 1976; Hornbeck 1983; Jackson and Castillo 1995; Johnson 1988; Lightfoot 2005); these include multiple deaths due to diseases.

Although it is difficult to reconstruct village populations just prior to missionization, the diaries that members of the 1769–1770 Portolá expedition maintained are excellent sources of information, but also are not entirely accurate for multiple reasons, including the effects of disease prior to contact (Erlandson and Bartoy 1995). Table 10 and figure 6 provide the population estimates made by Crespí and others prior to colonization. These estimates of population distributions along the coast differ considerably from the estimates based on mission records shown in table 11 and figure 7. It is probable that some of the more densely populated towns along the mainland coast may have suffered from higher death rates from introduced diseases than the settlements on the northern Channel Islands and in the interior, because the mainland populations were larger and more densely packed. In addition, settlements in the interior and on the northern Channel Islands were situated at much greater distances from the missions and may have been less affected by disease during the mission period.

The population estimates from the Portolá expedition (table 10 and figure 6) indicate that the largest populations along the Santa Barbara Channel mainland coast between Point Arguello and Ventura in 1769 were located in the geographic center of the Chumash region. When the population estimates from the mission records are examined (table 11 and figure 7), a different pattern is seen. Although the greatest populations are still on the mainland, people are more evenly distributed, with some of the populations in the interior settlements (such as *S'omis* and *Mat'ilha*) rivaling those of the coastal settlements. Nevertheless, large population centers are still found in several of the mainland regions. The four settlements around the Goleta Slough, *Helo'*, *'Alkash*, *S'axpilil*, and *Heliyik*, had 652 individuals who were baptized, compared with the approximately 1500–2000 people estimated by Crespí. The towns of *Mikiw* and *Kuya'mu* at Dos Pueblos had a total of 351 baptisms combined, compared with Crespí's population estimate of about 700, and *Syuxtun* had 201, compared with

Crespí's figure of approximately 600 (tables 10 and 11). Fewer than half the people who were estimated to have lived there in 1769 are accounted for in the mission records. In the case of *Syuxtun*, one-third of the people estimated to have lived there in 1769 were baptized. *Syuxtun* was situated close to Mission Santa Barbara and the Presidio, and probably was impacted more by European diseases than the settlements in Goleta and at Dos Pueblos. All of these settlements, with the possible exception of *Syuxtun,* remained population centers into the mission period.

Although the focus of this book is on the coastal mainland Chumash, some insight into how the mainland Chumash viewed the islanders is of relevance. Harrington noted that the mainlanders treated the island Chumash with condescension, considering them uncouth and their language as coarse (Johnson 2001:58–59). Apparently, the language of the island Chumash was unintelligible to the mainland Chumash (Klar 2000). Some of the diaries written by early explorers indicate that the island Chumash lived in tougher circumstances than did the mainland people. The earliest known account of the inhabitants of the Santa Barbara Channel Islands was penned by Cabrillo in 1542 and 1543. He commented that they were very poor on the islands, ate only fish, were dirty, and wore no clothes (Wagner 1929:90). He characterized the mainlanders very differently:

> They are in a good country with fine plains and many trees and savannas. The people go about dressed in skins and say that inland at three days distance there are many towns and much maize (Wagner 1929:86).

Cabrillo made a similar comment about them a few days later:

> They go dressed in skins and have very long hair tied up with some long cords. Inserted between the hair and these long cords are many daggers made of flint, bone, and wood. The country appears to be excellent (Wagner 1929:87).

Because Cabrillo was the first known European that passed through the Santa Barbara Channel, the differences between the island and mainland Chumash that he commented on cannot be attributed to the impact of European colonization. Of course, the consultants that Harrington spoke with had lived through colonization. By the time the island Chumash were brought to the missions, their bead-making industry was in severe decline, which no doubt affected them greatly.

Because of the Chumash reliance on watercraft for exchange between the mainland and the islands, south-facing beaches, on which most of the mainland towns were situated, served as excellent ports. The strategic locations of these towns for exchange between mainland and island settlements were no doubt envied by the islanders and the inhabitants of the interior, who were positioned in more peripheral areas for exchange. Mainlanders had the clear advantage over their neighbors on the islands and in the interior because all goods passing between the latter two regions had to be routed through the mainland coast. Moreover, coastal mainlanders were situated in a region that had a greater variety of subsistence resources. We do not know if the islanders could easily dock a canoe at a mainland town and then meet with trade partners in the interior without interacting with the inhabitants of the large mainland settlements.

It is probable that individuals in mainland settlements served as intermediaries in exchange interactions between the islanders and those dwelling in the interior. The fragmentary information that is available in the ethnographic, ethnohistoric, and oral traditions indicates that it is more likely that the Chumash from the interior and islands arrived on the mainland for fiestas, visited their relatives (we know there were numerous marriages between people living in the different areas), and then carried on market exchanges using shell-bead money. In addition, the Chumash participated in the more organized efforts of the chiefs and their associates in the redistributions that were usually associated with feasts. Regardless of the exact nature of the exchange transactions, wealthy and powerful Chumash individuals living in the mainland centers were undoubtedly involved in market exchange as a consequence of their strategically advantageous location on the coast. As market exchange, redistribution, and ritual congregations involved greater numbers of people from a wider geographic region, including people from outside the Chumash region, the elite in the mainland Chumash centers indubitably profited. As their wealth grew, the use of prestige goods as symbols of power and status became even more significant.

Prestige Goods and Wealth Finance

Prestige goods were produced by households in the interior, mainland, and island regions of the Santa Barbara Channel region and were then used by the Chumash elite to reinforce their social status. Some of these goods may have been made by the elite themselves, but others were probably produced by non-elites. Chiefs and other highly ranked individuals exchanged prestige goods with each other to maintain their alliances and reinforce their power and rank. In this section, types of prestige goods and their production, distribution, and consumption are investigated in order to better understand the system of wealth finance that existed among the Chumash.

The chiefs and other elite Chumash individuals were distinguished from commoners by their accoutrements, both in life and in death. The chief wore a full-length otter-skin cape and was accompanied by armed men who served as guards. Highly ranked individuals and chiefs wore long flint knives and bone pins with feathers in their hair, which was twisted and worn up, sometimes with false hair added (see chapter 7 for full descriptions). When Chumash chiefs and other elite individuals died, large painted grave poles decorated with feathers were erected. Poorer people could not afford these poles, which were costly and were apparently made by individuals who had the special knowledge and ability to produce them (Hudson and Blackburn 1986:76–83). Chiefs and their elite cohorts were also buried with more wealth. One of Harrington's consultants made these apropos comments:

> Putting a grave pole is a thing that used to cost much, not a mere ceremony. That is why the Indians are so poor, because they spent their property so freely at fiestas and also because they destroyed so much (Hudson and Blackburn 1986:80).

The destruction of wealth through burial or burning would tend to keep inflation in check and insure that prestige goods and bead money were always in demand. I suspect that this was the primary reason that shell-bead money maintained its value.

During ceremonies, the chiefs used ceremonial bone or wooden wands decorated with feathers and paint, and inlaid with shell or quartz crystals. One type of ceremonial staff was a "topknot wand" consisting of a yucca stalk decorated with eagle down feathers and quail topknots (Hudson and Blackburn 1986:252–253). The distribution of these is unknown, but they probably were used by the Ventureño Chumash, as well as by their neighbors the Gabrielino and Kitanemuk. I focus on these wands as examples of objects that were part of the political economy, because detailed descriptions of their use and worth were obtained from Harrington's consultants. They serve as an illustration of the kinds of paraphernalia that were used by the elite but were bought from other people, who not only knew how to make them but had access to the appropriate materials. This example is typical of many of the objects that are used by chiefs and other elite people to maintain their position and networks. According to Harrington's Kitanemuk consultants, these staffs were integral to inter-tribal ceremonies:

> Wands presented to visiting chiefs at the *wakacr* [major fiesta] placed on the *kutumic* poles [grave pole] were obtained by trade. . . . These wands were kept carefully stored away with other ritual gear in a huge basket; some chiefs might have to borrow some from others. . . . These sticks used to be sold at fiestas by men from outside villages who offered them for sale and consultant bought two of them. The fiesta was at El Monte here—the man was a Río Chiquito Indian. He had six of them and wanted $4 or $5 apiece. The captain gave one of these or a *mahivat* [inlaid wand] or both to each of the visiting captains when the fiesta was over. The visiting captain presented with these took them home with him, giving the captain fiestero other things to pay for the sticks, for they were very valuable. The K. [Kitanemuk] country was poor here. The *kakait* [Kitanemuk word for topknot wand] had to be gotten at Río Chiquito country where there were lots of quail and the *mahivat* could not be made here either, but they had to order them made from far away in advance (Hudson and Blackburn 1986:252–253).

Although these descriptions came from Kitanemuk consultants, the Ventureño Chumash (and probably other Chumash speakers) also used topknot wands. The staffs were made by individuals who had access to the appropriate materials and had the knowledge to produce these symbolic items. They were then sold at fiestas or through special order. Another artifact type associated with Chumash ceremonial activity was the small mortar used to pulverize tobacco (*Nicotiana* spp.), other medicinal substances, and pigments (Hudson and Blackburn 1986:133–136). One of Harrington's consultants made this comment about the exchange of the tobacco ground in the small mortars:

> The Tejon people brought coyote tobacco here on the coast on San Miguel day, to sell to the coast, or the coast people went over there to buy it (Hudson and Blackburn 1986:134).

This is another example of Chumash exchange involving items used for ceremonial purposes.

Elite families also used large decorated serving vessels and utensils for the preparation of food for feasts and special occasions. These included stone ollas, comals, mortars, and pestles, as well as large and elaborate baskets. All of this paraphernalia had to be produced for use by high-ranked families. Because feathers, otter skins, baskets, and other perishables are rarely preserved in the archaeological record, Chumash scholars tend to overlook their significance when considering production, labor organization, and exchange.

Although there is evidence for basket making at Pitas Point (Gamble 1983) and a few other sites (Braje et al. 2005), very little is known about the exchange of baskets and other perishables, with the exception of the few fragmentary historic accounts presented at the beginning of this chapter. Basket making is an exceptionally time-consuming activity that requires the basket maker to gather materials at the appropriate time, properly prepare them, and then weave the basket (McLendon and Holland 1979). Weaving baskets involved complex knowledge that was passed down by a master weaver. It is clear from the quality of Chumash baskets dating to the late 18th and early 19th centuries that their makers took exceptional care in producing finely woven baskets that far surpassed utilitarian needs (Gamble 2002b). Many were elaborately decorated with abstract and figurative designs (Hudson and Blackburn 1987:233–235). Dawson and Deetz (1965:208) have suggested that Chumash design elements were much more resistant to European influence than basket forms, which were greatly affected. The materials used to make baskets, however, persisted long after historic contact (Dawson and Deetz 1965). Continuity in the design elements and in the types of materials used reflects an emphasis on tradition. The European demand for baskets certainly increased their value and expanded their market. Scholars know little about the production of baskets prior to European colonization. Were special baskets made for elite families by master basket weavers, or were baskets directly produced by elite family members? The same types of questions can be asked about feather headdresses, wooden bowls, otter skin capes, and other items often associated with the elite.

Although very few of these types of items are preserved in archaeological sites, large decorated stone mortars (figure 40) and pestles, steatite vessels (figure 39), and other items, many of which were associated with elite households and feasting events, preserve well in archaeological contexts. Costansó wrote the following about large mortars:

> Some of these mortars are of extraordinary size, and as well formed as if the best tools had been used in making them. The patience, exactness and energy which they exercise in making these articles are well worthy of admiration (Hemert-Engert and Teggart 1910:47).

In addition to the serving and food preparation utensils used in feasting events, ritual paraphernalia such as smoking pipes, feather poles, whalebone markers, headdresses, effigies (figure 47), charmstones, quartz crystals, talismans, sunsticks, wands, bull roarers, rattles, and deer bone flutes were significant items used by Chumash ritualists. Other elite Chumash individuals were often distinguished from commoners by their personal adornments, which included special beads, ornaments, hairpins, and other items. King (1990a) has suggested that a number of bead types, including tubular clam beads, globular clam beads, other globular beads, columella tube beads, and purple *Hinnites multirugosus* beads, were associated with chiefs or high ranking individuals.

The objects associated with elite individuals, including personal adornments, ritual paraphernalia, and vessels used for feasting, can all be considered prestige goods involved in the Chumash system of wealth finance (D'Altroy and Earle 1985; Earle 1997). This system involved the exchange of valuables, many of which had established values, between political leaders both within and outside the Chumash region. Prestige goods were often produced by skilled craftspeople and then sold to political officials and other individuals who maintained the political economy. Wealth finance, combined with staple finance, fueled the Chumash dependence on beads and supported many people (at least on a part time basis) who helped maintain the economic system.

Network Power and Social Storage

The Chumash had a network system of power that was characterized by extensive marriage ties, abundant prestige goods, evidence of feasting, and elaborate burial rituals for the elite. Trade and a standardized medium of exchange were integral to the Chumash political and subsistence economy. The elite either bought lavish goods with shell-bead money from craftspeople who sold them at ritual congregations, or received them from other chiefs as part of an elaborate system of generalized reciprocity and redistribution. Power was manifested in ceremonial paraphernalia that could only be owned by chiefs and members of the *'antap* society. These same individuals owned plank canoes, had larger stores of food, ate higher quality foods, enjoyed lavish feasting vessels, and, generally possessed more wealth than others. In addition, chiefs practiced polygamy, thereby strengthening their role in the exchange system and enhancing their ability to host elaborate feasts. Not only did women produce the baskets used for processing, cooking, and storing foods, they managed most of the activities associated with both daily subsistence and elaborate feasting events. More wives meant more trading partners and greater economic opportunities.

The value of money was maintained, not because canoe owners controlled its release as Arnold (2001a:296) suggested, but because it was periodically destroyed. Shell bead money, feasting utensils, canoes, and sacred regalia were regularly destroyed when they were ceremonially buried with individuals or burned during mourning rituals; this practice insured that there would be a continued demand for these goods and at the same time kept inflation under control.

How did the complex economic system that was observed at the time of European contact develop? Why did the Chumash rely so heavily on shell beads as a medium of exchange? The Chumash used shell beads for at least seven millennia (King 1990a). Over time, the quantities and types of shell beads became more numerous and complex; then, about approximately 1000 years ago, some developed into a standardized medium of exchange. The emergence and use of 'money' beads did not preclude the use of other types of shell beads and ornaments that were symbols of social prestige, and which continued to be important even after European colonization. The elaborate exchange system that evolved in the Chumash region served to effectively minimize risks due to environmental variability and other calamities. Additional risk minimization strategies (Halstead and O'Shea 1989) that were utilized by the Chumash included diversification and storage (Gamble 2005). The use of prestige goods such as beads can be viewed as a form of social storage that served as an insurance against food shortages (O'Shea 1981; Rowley-Conwy and Zvelbil 1989).

The Chumash adapted to the environment and its uncertainties by effectively managing risks through strategies that were developed over thousands of years. They were able to adequately insure that individuals in the densely populated regions, as noted by the early explorers, were fed and in relatively good health. Chiefs and other elite persons who had access to more resources, including wealth in the form of bead money, prestige goods, large stores of food, and technological items such as the plank canoe, no doubt benefited during periods of favorable climatic conditions. During periods of climate-induced or culturally induced stress, chiefs and other elite persons were expected to share their stores of food and wealth, thus reinforcing their positions and maintaining societal stability. However, it is likely that some people's health still suffered during such difficult times. We know from archaeological, ethnohistoric, and ethnographic data that Chumash internal conflict existed and at times intensified. In the next chapter, competition and cooperation are examined as significant components of the network strategy chosen by the Chumash.

CHAPTER 9

Conflict and Social Integration

With us were two chiefs, the chief from the place we are going to, and the one belonging to this place here, with twelve other heathens belonging to this spot, most of them much painted and carrying bows and quivers full of arrows. To the scouts the heathens had reported that mountain heathens not long ago had destroyed two big villages, killing everyone, young and old, and afterward burning their houses as well. As we pursued our way, on going about a league we passed through the midst of the first village just mentioned, lying at the very edge of the shore, and from what we viewed of the ruins and the ashes, it must have happened two or three months ago. About two and a half leagues from setting out, we came upon the second village they had destroyed and burnt. Both had been at the shore's very edge, and are supplied with good running water; and this last one must plainly have been a very large village, as they give us to understand was indeed the case, with a great many people.

Crespí on August 18, 1769, in Brown 2001:411–413

Conflict among the Chumash was rife at the beginning of historic contact. Descriptions of the ravages of warfare,[55] such as the quotation above from Crespí, are prevalent in the early accounts written by explorers and priests. Recently, discussions about warfare in pre-state societies in North America have proliferated (Haas 1999, 2001; Keeley 1996; Lambert 1997, 2002; Leblanc 1999, 2003; Leblanc and Rice 2001; Walker 2001), and a large body of bioarchaeological data has now been examined in order to address questions concerning the causes and evolution of warfare. Despite this knowledge, warfare among the Chumash and in many other California and North American Indian societies is still poorly understood.

The study of conflict and warfare is relevant to understanding the development of sociopolitical complexity among the Chumash. The causes of Chumash conflict are of particular concern here. Many scholars working in the Chumash area have examined warfare and suggested that environmental instability and resource scarcity were closely tied to Chumash conflict (Johnson 1988, 2007; Kennett 2005; Kennett and Kennett 2000; Lambert 1994; Walker and Johnson 2003). Risk minimization strategies and mechanisms that serve to integrate society are closely tied to both conflict, and its avoidance. In this chapter, I first review selected early ethnohistoric and ethnographic accounts of conflict, and then summarize the available bioarchaeological data on conflict before and immediately after European contact. Finally, methods of social integration and the causes of warfare among the Chumash are examined in light of these multiple sources of data.

Evidence for Warfare in Ethnohistoric and Ethnographic Accounts

The earliest historic description of Chumash conflict consists of a brief mention in Cabrillo's diary of 1542, noting that the native inhabitants of the Santa Barbara Channel region "carry on great wars with each other" (Wagner 1929:116). Although this passage provides few details, it is significant in that it indicates that the Chumash were involved in battles prior to their first contact with Europeans.

Not until 1769 and 1770, when the Portolá expedition passed through the Chumash region, do we obtain more information about conflict. Crespí provided additional evidence of conflict when he was in the vicinity of Santa Barbara, just one day after he wrote the statement in the opening quotation:

> I had a report from the scouts that there were two running streams with good-sized flows of water about half a quarter-league off, and one of the two streams had a great amount of very large cottonwood trees along it; while close by this stream were to be seen the ruins of another big village destroyed by the mountain people at the time they burned the two others on the shore; and by what we understood from the good heathens here, they destroyed five villages at that time and also were about to put an end to that of San Joaquin that we have just left, but the latter being a large village fought back strongly. One of their companions was captured and killed by them. Another had his eye put out with an arrow and was given many other wounds by them; we saw him, and he was not entirely healed (Crespí on August 19, 1769, in Brown 2001:417–419).

The two burned settlements that the expedition passed through were *Shalawa*, near Montecito, and *Q'oloq'* (with 48 people in the mission registers), near Summerland (Brown 1967; Johnson 2007); both were situated on the coast to the east of Santa Barbara and were adjacent to one another (figure 6). Johnson has suggested that the burned village seen by the scouts was *Mismatuk*, near Santa Barbara, and that the other one was *Xana'yan*. The settlement that Crespí referred to as San Joaquin was *Syuxtun*, the large coastal town at Santa Barbara. The interior Chumash apparently attacked and burned the settlements surrounding *Syuxtun*, but were unsuccessful in taking the large town itself, which may have been their ultimate goal. Brown (1967:80–81) pointed out that the Spanish at this time regarded the coast range as one mountain chain filling the interior, and that the term "mountain people" could have referred to any of the Indian groups from the northeast or east, including the Chumash, Shoshoneans, or possibly Mohaves. Johnson (2007) however, concludes that the attack was launched by the Chumash, and that it therefore was an example of Chumash intergroup fighting. Given the many other incidences of internal conflict among the Chumash, his is the most likely interpretation. An attack of this magnitude, involving the successful destruction of five settlements on or near the coast and an attempt to destroy a sixth—the largest town in the vicinity with an estimated population of approximately 600 people—was a daring act indeed. We will return to this incident later in this chapter.

One of the most memorable Chumash chiefs that Crespí encountered anywhere in California was *El Buchón*, or "The Goiter" (see opening quotation in chapter 7). Brown (2001:61) noted that Crespí made numerous references to *El Buchón* and clearly was impressed with his political power. Crespí even suggested that *El Buchón* "might be a potent means of gaining converts" (Brown 2001:61). *El Buchón* was usually described as being accompanied by "body guards," or heavily armed men. As can be seen in the following statement made by Crespí, he was known and feared by the Chumash over a large geographic region:

> Great is the fear and awe in which he is held in all the surrounding parts. This Goitre's fame reaches as far as the Channel and the Santa Lucia Mountains; they designate him by making signs for his tumor (Crespí on September 4, 1769, in Brown 2001:477–479).

The next time that Crespí mentioned *El Buchón* was May 8, 1770, when the expedition marched north for the second time and was in the vicinity of what is now Vandenberg Air Force Base:

On going about three hours we came to the large spring-fed pool about eighty yards in length, and it must not be under some twenty wide, and very deep, with a great deal of tule rushes round about. This time we did not meet with the small-sized village of very fine heathens that had been close to this pool on the first occasion. . . . I have learned that the reason for the village's having abandoned this spot is that there is a heathen not very far from here who must be a petty king, for he is much feared in all his neighboring districts and others are a great deal in awe of him. He has been dubbed The Goitre, *El Buchón*, among the soldiers; we have only a few marches left before reaching his village, and he dealt very splendidly with us the other times, producing for us a great plenty of mush and gruels (Crespí on May 8, 1770, in Brown 2001:713).

Crespí implied that *El Buchón* was instrumental in this village's abandonment, and that it was a result of warfare or the threat of force. Two days later, after passing through a settlement of about 12 houses, the expedition arrived in the vicinity of *El Buchón's* home village where 14 people brought the expedition fish; the following day, approximately 60 people brought more food, including gruel, mush, deer meat, and fish (Brown 2001:715). Again Crespí reported that *El Buchón* was "feared in all these surroundings" (Brown 2001:713–715). Later in the day the expedition arrived at *El Buchón's* village, where Crespí made the following observation: "We have discovered nothing in the whole distance traveled that is anything like the way the Goitre here is feared, held in awe and obeyed" (Crespí on May 12, 1770, in Brown 2001:717). Although *El Buchón* was feared over a large area, his village was not as large as those along the Channel coast, as reflected in this statement by Fages upon seeing *El Buchón's* village: ". . . and in the whole of it we came upon only one small village of very poor, ill-conditioned Indians" (Priestley 1937:38–39).

The earliest and most detailed description of Chumash conflict that was observed firsthand is again from Crespí, when a couple of days after leaving *El Buchón's* village he witnessed the following incident:

At about sunrise today, before we set out, eight or ten heathens came to the camp, heavily painted, wearing their feather headdresses, and all of them heavily laden with their usual good-sized quivers full of arrows and their bows. . . . They stayed in order to accompany us to their village, and their chief said that he would turn two of the three aforesaid Indians over to us, as the third had died while out fishing. Thus in company of the ten fine heathens we set out along the shore. On going about a quarter-league, they became upset and refused to go on, giving us to understand that The Goitre with his village was coming up behind us in order to fight. We told them not to turn back and not to be afraid, as it must not be true; we had not even seen this Goitre. On going about a league, we had a message from the men in the rear with the pack train, reporting that [The] Goitre had just arrived with his village, looking for these other heathens; for they had fought with him not long before and had shot The Goitre himself in the body with two arrows, as our Governor and Don Pedro Fages explained to me, telling me that The Goitre showed them his two wounds himself when we passed through his village. I myself knew nothing of it while there. Our ten heathens commenced to scatter on hearing the news verified, and shortly we saw six of Goitre's men going by. He was coming up behind, and they said they were on their way to fight them. The fact is that the ten then clashed with Goitre's six within view of us, with those on each side shooting off a good many arrows, and there is no denying they must be great warriors and very skillful. Goitre's six men at once turned and ran back, since no more of their people had come than the aforesaid six, whereas there were ten of the others. We continued on our way, and left them to this entertainment; no telling what may have happened to the poor wretches. There was no way we could stop their warfare, which our people attempted to do; they paid no attention, however. On going three leagues we came to the Santa Serafina hollow, close to the point at the north side of the aforesaid embayment. At five leagues we reached the San Benvenuto pinewood, from which the ten above-mentioned heathens came. We reached this spot at one o'clock in the afternoon, having gone six hours and five leagues beyond San Adriano. About an hour after we had come to the pinewood here, the ten heathen warriors we had left on the way arrived and told us they had hit The Goitre with an arrow; however, we did not believe them, as we knew he had been coming with thirty or forty of his people, and these ones must have taken flight at a quick run as soon as they had seen the situation. They told us they were on their way to their village, a way off from where we stopped, but they would come back early in the morning and bring us gruel and our own two Indians (Crespí on May 14, 1770, in Brown 2001:721–723).

The following day, the Chumash men who had promised the expedition that they would return in the morning with food did not come back. Shortly after the expedition headed northwest along the shore, they encountered "a great many heathens" (Crespí on May 15, 1770, in Brown 2001:723) who had a float and were gathering mussels. The group greeted the Spanish and took them to their village, which was next to a creek. Crespí reported the following: "Their chief at once came out onto the shore and it proved to be our heathen warriors" (Crespí on May 15, 1770, in Brown 2001:723). Presumably these were the individuals whom the expedition had encountered the previous day. The Chumash at this village gave them gruel and fish; in return, the Spanish provided them with beads, which Crespí noted pleased the inhabitants. Members of the expedition then inquired about the two Indians that were to accompany them, and were told that they were "at another village farther down" (Crespí on May 15, 1770, in Brown 2001:723). The expedition proceeded for approximately three and a half hours, at which time they encountered some frightened women at the village where the two men were supposed to be. They were told that the men were fishing along the shore. However, when a soldier and two "heathens" went to search for them, they could not be found.

Although the details surrounding this incident provide context, the cause of the skirmish is not entirely clear. Brown has proposed that an amicable discussion among *El Buchón*, Captain Portolá, and Lieutenant Pedro Fages (the latter two being soldiers) two days preceding the event may have, at least in part, caused the skirmish:

> They exchanged their respective battle experiences through sign language (it must have been through signs, since they did not know each others' languages and there were no interpreters), and showed each other their wounds—Portolá had an old one from fighting in Italy during the War of the Austrian Succession. Apparently this conversation was a mistake. Father Juan only heard of this exchange two days later (14 May 1770) when in his presence The Goitre's warriors, probably trying to impress the foreigners with their prowess, attacked some friendly natives who had just been assured by the Spanish party that there was no danger (Brown 2001:47).

Brown clearly thinks that the battle was linked to the presence of the Spanish. Johnson has diverged from Brown in his interpretation of the battle's cause, stating that *El Buchón* raided this group as a "reprisal for previous injuries suffered by members of his town at the hands of the Cambria group" (Johnson 2007:86). Although Johnson does not provide further details supporting his interpretation, he identifies *El Buchón*'s village as *Chiliqin*, situated east of the modern town of Pismo, and the defenders' village as *Tsitkawayu*, located along the boundary shared by the Northern Chumash and the Salinan in modern Cambria. Johnson suggests that the latter village may have been Salinan, and if so, the battle was inter-tribal. As Ferguson (1992, 2006) and others (Blick 1988; Ferguson and Whitehead 1992) point out, however, colonization often altered traditional practices and had a considerable impact on indigenous groups. In some cases, European colonization increased the level of violence among traditional groups; I will return to this point later.

Another important ethnohistoric source of information on Chumash violence comes from Fages, who not only served as second-in-command under Portolá on the 1769–1770 expedition, but also made various official excursions to the San Luis Obispo area and elsewhere in Alta California before he wrote his description of California in 1775. Fages, unlike Crespí, was a soldier, and therefore was particularly interested in armed struggles among the California Indians. Fages (Priestley 1972:32) noted that the most important function of a chief in the area between Carpinteria and Punta de los Pedernales (the latter is in the vicinity of Vandenberg Air Force Base) was as a military commander. Fages' remarks are not a surprise, as this was the region where he met *El Buchón*, a Chumash chief who clearly adopted the role of military commander. Fages provided the following details about Chumash conflict in the San Luis Obispo region:

> The men do not often sleep in their houses at night; but, carrying with them their arms, bow and quiver, they are accustomed to congregate in numbers in great subterranean caves, where they pass the nights in sheer terror; (if they stayed at home) they might be surprised in their beds by the enemy whilst defenseless on account of the presence of their wives and children. They also congregate thus in order to keep watch, spy upon, set traps for and surprise those who may be taken off their guard, for they are a warlike people, always roaming from village to village at odds with everyone (Priestly 1972:48).

The great subterranean caves that Fages noted were undoubtedly the semi-subterranean earth-covered sweatlodges; ethnographic sources corroborate the suggestion that Chumash men slept in sweatlodges for defensive purposes, as does a statement made by Fr. Lasuén in 1775, quoted in Brown (1967:25), in which he "gives an eyewitness account of a fight in which Spanish soldiers, attacked by Indians, entrenched in their houses, killed six natives at the place called Los Dos Pueblos."

In the following passage (Priestley 1972:31), Fages implies that one possible cause of warfare was the defense of possessions: "In matters concerning their possessions, they will not yield or concede the smallest point. They receive the Spaniards well, and make them welcome; but they are very warlike among themselves, living at almost incessant war, village against village."

The diary of Fernando de Rivera y Moncada, a veteran soldier in Baja California who had served in the Californias since 1742 and was the military governor of California between 1774 and 1777 (Beebe and Senkewicz 2001; Johnson 2007), provides two accounts of Chumash violence that were witnessed by Spanish travelers and that involved the villages at Dos Pueblos. The first of these describes the burning of a relatively large settlement along the Santa Barbara Channel coast:

> Those gentiles [from Dos Pueblos] are troublemakers. I will relate two cases. Three or four leagues from this place [Dos Pueblos] there is a neighboring village, which is one of the largest of the [Coastal Chumash] settlements. I have counted the huts [at the latter], and including the two that serve as sweatlodges, there were more than 90. One night, [the Indians from Dos Pueblos] went out and put fire

to them, and no one knows the number they killed [Rivera (1775) in Johnson 1988:123.]

Crespí identified a settlement at Tajiguas that had 79 houses in August of 1769. However, this same settlement was abandoned six years later when Anza passed by the area. Rivera's account is of particular interest because it provides yet another example of the Chumash setting fire to a neighboring town during the historic period. In addition, it suggests that conflict between Dos Pueblos and other Chumash settlements was relatively common. The second account of Chumash warfare along the Santa Barbara Channel, also written by Rivera in 1775, further implicates the inhabitants of Dos Pueblos as aggressors:

> Two and a half leagues to the south or southeast [from Dos Pueblos] are three very large villages [at the Goleta estuary], one of which is isolated by water that enters inland from the sea [*Helo'* on Mescalitan Island]. When I dispatched a guard to guide some families [of settlers from Mexico], they encountered [some Indians from Dos Pueblos], returning from these [Goleta towns] to their own villages. They had been fighting [and were] carrying one or more caballeras [scalps], which is the skullcap with the hair that they cut from those they kill. One [of their number] has been wounded [Rivera (1775) in Johnson 1988:123].

The towns at the Goleta Slough and at Dos Pueblos were the most populous along the Santa Barbara Coast, according to the estimates provided by Crespí and other members of the Portolá expedition (table 10). The Santa Barbara Channel region had not as yet been fully affected by European colonization when Rivera penned these accounts in 1775. Furthermore the presidio at Santa Barbara and the mission at Ventura were not established until 1782. Four years later, the mission at Santa Barbara was established; the next year, Mission de la Purísima Concepción was built, followed by Mission Santa Inés in 1804. The Chumash area northwest of Ventura, the northern Channel Islands, and the interior Chumash regions were not affected by colonization as early as the Chumash region southeast of Ventura. Based on an account written by Governor Felipe de Neve, Rivera's successor in 1782, Johnson (2007) has suggested that the fighting between the Goleta towns and Dos Pueblos was not an isolated event. Before the Santa Barbara Presidio was built, de Neve proposed that it might be placed between Dos Pueblos and the Goleta region to control the warfare between these two centers, the inhabitants of which were, in his words, "declared enemies" (Johnson 2007).

Although written later in time and somewhat subjective in nature, Spanish mission period documents provide additional insight into the causes and nature of conflict in the Chumash region. One significant incident that involved Dos Pueblos occurred in 1795, when a group of Indians from Mission San Buenaventua joined forces with some unconverted Chumash from inland settlements and attacked Dos Pueblos, killing two chiefs there (Brown 1967:48; Johnson 2007). A subsequent confrontation that occurred in April of 1801 involved seven Chumash individuals from three inland Chumash villages, led by Lihuiasu, who formed an alliance and attacked the small settlement of *He'lxman*. The incident is described in the following passage written by Father Tapis in 1803:

> He [Lihuiasu] killed five persons and wounded two others, solely because the Gentiles of Eljman were relatives of Temiacucat, the chief of the Cuyamu Rancheria belonging to Dos Pueblos on the seashore, whom they regarded as the author of the epidemic of the *dolor de costado*, which at the time took the lives of many Indians (Engelhardt 1932:7).

Relying on extensive mission register analyses, Johnson (2007) has proposed that a federation of interior Chumash settlements, including the three that attacked *He'lxman*, recognized *Syuxtun* as their political center and were allied with the Goleta towns. Furthermore, Johnson suggests that the *Syuxtun* federation was opposed to the Dos Pueblos settlements and their one (*He'lxman*) or more allies in the Santa Ynez Valley.

The responses that the Franciscan missionaries provided in 1813–1815 to a Spanish questionnaire about the customs of the native people living in their New World colonies are also significant (Geiger and Meighan 1976:1). Fray José Señan, who was president of the California missions, was a priest at San Buenaventura for 17 years, and was fluent in Ventureño, was the last to complete his reply. His responses, however, were more detailed than those of the other missionaries (Geiger and Meighan 1976:1). In response to a question about the use of weapons among the Chumash, Fr. José Señan wrote:

> They had some sort of knowledge of warfare but almost always they would kill their adversaries, take vengeance on them in cold blood by coming upon them unawares or when enemies were in smaller numbers by employing cunning and malignant tricks like cowardly men without bravery (Geiger and Meighan 1976:139).

Fr. Señan commented about the causes and consequences of Chumash warfare when asked if the native populations were irascible or cruel:

> For although they frequently waged war and at times were somewhat harsh on their enemies they were driven to it through the necessity of defending their wives,

their right to the territory where they harvested their acorns and seeds upon which they depended for their subsistence, or also because the enemy had mentioned any one of their dead by the proper pagan name which with them is regarded as the most grievous injury and crime. Public vengeance for the curbing and punishment of excesses committed by individuals and for maintaining peace was not known among the pagan Indians. The consequence of this was that anyone who considered himself injured would himself take satisfaction and revenge. Sometimes he would enlist relatives in his cause. In some cases it was made a common cause. The chief and the whole rancheria with other friendly and allied rancherias would then plan revenge (Geiger and Meighan 1976:113–114).

Fr. Señan gives several motives for Chumash warfare, including the defense of wives and resources or taboos against speaking the name of a dead person. In response to a question about subsistence and tribute, Frs. Luís Martínez and Antonio Rodríguez, Franciscan missionaries at Mission San Luis Obispo, confirmed that one reason for Chumash conflict was the stealing of resources:

Notwithstanding that the Indians in their pagan state hold lands by families they have no need for agreements to plant for they live on the products bestowed by nature; yet it is a weighty matter that produces not a few wars if anyone has the effrontery to go and gather fruits without previously paying and notifying the legitimate owner. Such is the case in their pagan state (Geiger and Meighan 1976:110).

Although the Chumash did not own land in the sense that we do today, they owned the usufruct rights to resources within their territory, and an infringement on these was apparently a serious offense. Martínez and Rodríguez also noted that refusing an invitation to a feast was a serious affront:

These headmen summon to the pagan feasts all that assemble who happen to be his friends. If perchance anyone of them refuse the invitation, he distributes arms and after notifying his people, he sets out to avenge the injury done to him by refusal of the invitation. He takes the life not only of the chief but of as many as are together with him. For all these services they have no other recompense than the privilege of admiring as a public person him who had the good fortune of killing someone else (Geiger and Meighan 1976:122).

Linda King (1982:167–168), in her review of the evidence, noted that there was an increase in Spanish correspondences concerning aggression in the Santa Barbara Channel region in the 1790s; this may reflect an increase in violence toward the Spanish or simply indicate that the padres were taking the time to record these types of incidents in greater detail. Whatever the reasons, the mission records corroborate earlier descriptions of Chumash warfare and hypotheses about some of its causes.

In summary, historic documentation of Chumash violence indicates that the Chumash were frequently involved in inter-village conflict. Johnson, in his thorough analysis of Chumash warfare during the historic period (2007), has suggested that hostilities between Chumash federations of allied settlements may have persisted for decades and crosscut ecological boundaries, especially in a coast/inland direction. Chester King (1984:1–44), based on his synthesis of ethnohistoric documents for the northern Chumash, noted that networks that included politically powerful families probably helped mitigate the intensity of warfare between settlements, though not enough to totally prevent war. King (1984:1–45) also suggested that changes in polygynous men's marriage partners probably reflected changes in political alliances that were possibly initiated by warfare. In particular, the capture of wives may have affected alliances. King pointed out that there is documentation for the stealing of another man's wife by the first Alcalde at Mission San Luis Obispo.

Ethnohistoric research has provided some of our best data on the type of Chumash warfare that occurred at and immediately after contact. Surprise raids, ambushes, and sudden attacks were relatively common. Some of these attacks involved mobilizing alliances of warriors from several settlements, and often chiefs were targets (Johnson 2007). The burning of whole towns is of particular significance. The Crespí journal account of the burning of five villages in 1769, in addition to other descriptions of burned settlements, indicates that destruction by fire was not a rare occurrence. Exactly how settlements came to be burned is significant when trying to understand the motivations related to warfare. Did the invaders initiate the fires in order to surprise the inhabitants, or did they enter a town, seize its goods and valuables, and then set fire to the houses? One clue comes from King's ethnohistoric analysis of the northern Chumash region:

> On November 29, 1776 an arrow with firebrand was shot into the tule roof of a building behind the priests' house. This fire resulted in the destruction of the book of marriages which was reconstructed by the priests from the padrón and baptismal register (King 1984:1–5).

The use of flaming arrows to ignite houses was a technique that undoubtably predated Spanish arrival. There is no reason to believe that the Spanish introduced this concept, since they relied on firearms versus bows and arrows for weaponry. The advantage of using a firebrand on an arrow is that it would have allowed the attackers to launch a surprise assault that could seriously debilitate their enemies. It would also have allowed the attackers to maintain a safer distance from the people being attacked. The primary disadvantage of this approach is that very few goods and valuables, except perhaps women who fled, could have been acquired if entire settlements were burned in this manner. If a firebrand was attached to an arrow, it is unlikely that it could have traveled more than the approximately 30 yards that Librado mentions (see below). It would have been difficult to successfully attack settlements on Mescalitan Island using this technique, since it was surrounded by water. It may have been difficult to launch sneak attacks on other Chumash settlements as well.

The Chumash used both sinew-backed bows and self bows with stone-tipped cane arrows, wooden-tipped cane arrows, and self arrows (Hudson and Blackburn 1982:97–124). According to Fernando Librado, one of Harrington's Ventureño consultants, stone-tipped cane arrows were divided into two types, one for hunting and the other for war:

> *Ya 'axi'cahac* was the name for the war arrow. It was never made from *sax* Carrizo, but from *topo*. You could also call this arrow *ya topo*. These arrows were longer than the *sax* ones. They resembled the *sax* arrow, but the joints of the cane were left rough so as to prevent removal. The butt end of the *topo* cane is also made for the point of the arrow so that the arrow will not pull out easily (Hudson and Blackburn 1982:121).

However, Fernando Librado made another remark to Harrington that contradicted the statement that the war arrow was the longer type: "The Indians used shorter arrows for war than for hunting. These arrows shot only 30 yards, but with sure aim" (Hudson and Blackburn 1982:121–122). In any event, Librado's testimony suggests that war and hunting arrows were different. Harrington consultant Luisa Ygnacio also referred to short war arrows (Hudson and Blackburn 1982:127). DuBois (1935) noted that among the Wintun, tightly-hafted side-notched points were used for hunting whereas stemmed points were used in war, because the latter were more likely to stay in the individual (see also Keeley 1996:52).

Warriors were not a topic of great interest in the oral traditions of the Chumash, and warfare is infrequently alluded to in the narratives (Blackburn 1975:53–54). Blackburn observed that warfare usually involved only a portion of the people of two feuding villages, and only occasionally were a number of people from widely scattered settlements involved in conflict (Blackburn 1975:54). When a battle was planned, the time and the place were scheduled, and smoke signals were used to communicate information about the event. We now turn to bioarchaeological data and their significance in understanding Chumash warfare.

Bioarchaeological Evidence of Violence among the Chumash

Outstanding osteological and archaeological data on Chumash conflict exist for the mainland and Northern Channel Islands (Lambert 1994, 1997, 2002; Lambert and Walker 1991; Walker 1989, 2001). Unfortunately, no data from sites in the inland Chumash area have been analyzed, in part because few intact collections are available. One of the most thorough investigations of conflict in the Santa Barbara Channel region was completed by Lambert (1994, 2002), who analyzed skeletal remains and burial records for over 1700 individuals from 30 archaeological sites for evidence of violent conflict (table 21). Lambert documented the fact that lethal projectile wounds increased in frequency in the Channel area after AD 580, about the same time that the bow and arrow was introduced to the region. Prior to this time, evidence of conflict was most commonly seen in the form of cranial vault injuries, many of which healed so that the victim survived (Lambert 1994). Between about AD 580 and 1350 (primarily Lambert's late Middle period), approximately 10% of the individuals examined—

TABLE 21. Number of Burials or Burial Records Analyzed by Lambert from the Santa Barbara Channel Region

Time Period			Location		
Lambert (1994)	King (1990a)	Kennett (2005)	Mainland	Santa Cruz Island	Santa Rosa Island
EE	6000–3500 BC	6120–3590 BC	7	47	67
LE	3500–1400 BC	3590–490 BC	151	127	5
EM	1400 BC–AD 300	490 BC–AD 660	299	67	148
LM	AD 300–1150	AD 660–1380	264	138	0
L[a]	AD 1150–1804	AD 1380–1804	156	157	111
TOTAL			877	536	331

SOURCE: Based on Lambert (1994).

[a]This includes only 1 burial that was examined from King's (1990a) L1 (AD 1150–1500) context on the mainland, and no burials that clearly date to King's L1 on Santa Cruz Island were examined.

many of whom were from the mainland, not the Northern Channel Islands—suffered from projectile wounds (Lambert 1994, 2002). When the numbers of burials from the mainland with projectile wounds from Lambert's late Middle period are compared with those from the two Island samples combined (Lambert analyzed them separately), no significant difference was found ($x^2 = 1.45, p \leq 1.0$) (table 22). A similar pattern was observed when the number of individuals with projectile wounds on the mainland from Lambert's Late period was compared with the number of individuals on the Islands during the same period ($x^2 = .03, p \leq 1.0$; table 22).

Lambert (2002) concluded that there was a decline in warfare on the islands and mainland after AD 1350, which she attributed to improving climatic conditions and less resource stress. When numbers of individuals with projectile injuries on the mainland during the late Middle period are compared to numbers of individuals with projectile injuries in the Late period, a significant difference in the samples is observed ($x^2 = 13.50, p \leq 0.001$). A similar pattern is observed when numbers of individuals from the late Middle period with projectile injuries are compared with numbers of individuals with projectile wounds in the Late period on the Islands ($x^2 = 9.06, p \leq 0.001$). These data indicate that the frequency of individuals with projectile wounds on both the mainland and the islands was greater in the late Middle period than in the Late period. However, the evidence suggests that there were no significant differences between the islands and the mainland during these periods. In summary, there is greater evidence for violence associated with the bow and arrow during the late Middle period on both the islands and the mainland, with a decrease in both regions during the Late period.

Although the osteological data on conflict are relatively abundant in the Chumash region, they are not as complete as many researchers imply

TABLE 22. Number of Individuals with/without Projectile Wounds

Time Period (Lambert 1994)	Mainland	Islands
EE	0/7	1/113
LE	4/147	1/131
EM	1/298	6/209
LM	29/235	10/128
L	2/154	4/264
TOTAL	36/841	22/845

SOURCE: Based on data in Lambert 1994:Table 6.19.

(see Gamble 2005 for a discussion of this point). Only twenty-seven skeletons (only one of which has a burial record) from the mainland cemeteries were part of Lambert's (1994:Table 5.1) sample from King's (1990a) Late period, Phase 1 (AD 1150 to 1500, or as calibrated according to Kennett [2005], AD 1380–1670). This period overlaps with Arnold's Transitional period (table 1) and is of critical significance when addressing resource stress and violence during a period of time when many scholars (e.g., Arnold 1992a, 2001a; Johnson 2000; Kennett 1998, 2005; Kennett and Kennett 2000; Lambert 1994, 2002) propose that rapid cultural and environmental changes occurred on the Channel Islands.

The sample sizes of burials from the different phases of the Middle period on the mainland are larger than those from the Late period, Phase 1. In these samples, Lambert (1994:131–132) discovered particularly high numbers of victims with multiple projectile wounds in two cemeteries on the mainland (SBA-46A, and 46C), both of which are on Mescalitan Island. She also noted that the frequency of projectile wounds in individuals from these two cemeteries was higher than in samples from any time periods on the mainland or the islands. At SBA-46A (Middle 4 and 5a cemetery), eight out of 37 individuals or 21.6% had projectile point wounds, and at SBA-46C (Middle 5b and 5c cemetery), 10 out of 51 or 16.4% had evidence of projectile wounds (Lambert 1994:Table 6.21).

The Mescalitan Island site was situated on a small but prominent island in the middle of the Goleta Slough, which was a Chumash population center. Although Mescalitan Island could only be reached by watercraft, it and the other Goleta Slough towns were located in the geographic center of the Chumash region: on the mainland coast, in the middle of the Santa Barbara Channel, part way between the population centers of Dos Pueblos and *Syuxtun* and in between the ecological zones of the Islands and the interior Chumash region. This location was also centrally situated in relationship to the active Chumash exchange network. The high rate of projectile injuries in victims buried on Mescalitan Island is even more intriguing because of its naturally defensive location. If the population of Mescalitan Island was relatively high during the late Middle period, it would have been rather daring to attack this centrally located settlement.

It is also surprising that the level of violence was not more pronounced on the offshore Channel Islands than on the Mainland during the late Middle and Late periods. Lambert (1994, 2002) and others (Arnold 1992a, 2001a; Kennett 1998, 2005; Kennett and Kennett 2000) maintain that this was a time of resource stress and increased violence, especially on the islands.

Why then was the level of violence apparently about the same in both regions? This and other questions will be addressed after we investigate strategies of cooperation among the Chumash.

Mechanisms of Social Integration

A number of important mechanisms existed that promoted social integration and reduced hostilities among the Chumash. The first of these were the ritual gatherings, such as the winter solstice ceremonies, that were scheduled at regular intervals in the larger Chumash towns. These events brought together hundreds (sometimes thousands) of people from both within and outside the Chumash region. Large ceremonial feasts were hosted by chiefs who were members of the *'antap* society, a formal association of elites and ritual specialists. Most major settlements had *'antap* societies involving at least 12 individuals; members of the *'antap* society were also organized at the provincial level (Hudson and Underhay 1978). The *'antap* society served as a social and integrative mechanism that linked people throughout the Chumash area (Blackburn 1976).

Large ceremonial events were not only a time for chiefs, religious specialists, and other elite to interact, but were also an opportunity for others to conduct business and socialize. In addition to the performance of and participation in rituals, these ceremonial congregations provided an occasion for people to find mates, buy and sell goods, and exchange information. For chiefs, whether they were hosts or guests, ceremonies served as an arena in which they could display their generosity by providing wealth and goods through redistribution. Ritual occasions, such as the winter solstice, could also be the setting for conflict; for example, the refusal to attend a feast when invited was a cause for warfare. However, it was probably more likely that in these ceremonial contexts, people were united in their common beliefs and that they anticipated feasts as an occasion to socialize, demonstrate their devotion, communicate important information, and celebrate. These feasts were characterized by ritual dances, cycles of songs, the repaying of debts, and other prescribed ceremonies. The ritual specialists, *'antap*, and others with esoteric knowledge of religious observances undoubtedly reinforced their power at these events.

A second important mechanism that served to unite the Chumash was intermarriage, especially when it involved the common practice of chiefs and their families intermarrying with other chiefly families (Johnson 1988:174–179; King 1984). This practice would have served to unite families from different settlements and maintain the high status of elite families. In addition, chiefs had the prerogative to marry two or more women; Johnson (1988) and King (1984) have documented polygyny among chiefs in the mission registers. This practice allowed chiefs to establish even stronger ties between settlements, especially when matrilocality was usually practiced. Johnson (1988:173) has shown that Chumash postmarital residence tended to be matrilocal (the ratio of patrilocal to matrilocal residence was 1:3); however, among chiefs patrilocal residence was more common (the ratio of patrilocal to matrilocal residence among chiefs was 3:2). Interestingly, most matrilocal residence among chiefs involved the second or third wives. Chiefs probably needed their first wives to live with them so that they could help in hosting large feasts and in other tasks associated with entertaining people. With additional wives living in their native villages, powerful alliances and coalitions between a chief's settlement and the villages where his wives and children lived could have been more readily built and maintained. Intermarriage between commoners in different settlements, although not polygynous, also occurred and probably served to reduce hostilities between groups.

A third mechanism that fostered cooperation among the Chumash was exchange. Trade partnerships developed over thousands of years between island and mainland settlements. The existence of variable ecological zones within the Chumash region encouraged exchange, especially as populations increased and the demand for foods not readily available grew. Shell beads eventually became a common currency (circa AD 1000) among the Chumash, and the currency system allowed them to more efficiently take advantage of resources found in different ecological zones instead of relying simply on barter. A maintenance of alliances for the purpose of trade was most likely significant for both elite and commoners, all of whom were able to participate in the Chumash exchange system.

Based on ethnohistoric analyses, it is likely that all classes of Chumash people formed alliances at ritual congregations and through marriage. More formal coalitions between elite individuals both within and between settlements were also established through guild memberships, especially in the *'antap* society. Without exchange and storage (both physical and social), the densely populated towns observed by the early explorers could not have been supported. It is not surprising that a great deal of both time and effort were invested in the manufacture of beads; currency was essential to the maintenance of Chumash systems of exchange once population density reached the high levels observed during the initial period of European contact. Also significant for both the producers and the consumers were the prestige goods that were used to reinforce the legitimacy and the power of chiefs and other highly ranked individuals. Producers of feather headdresses, ceremonial staffs, feasting vessels, rare beads, and other prestige goods sought by political and religious leaders played a critical role in the Chumash system of wealth finance. Networks of exchange associated with ceremonial events were one means of distributing both prestige and subsistence goods.

Although these mechanisms promoted positive interactions between groups, they did not completely curtail all conflict. Keeley (1996:121–126) provides numerous examples of societies that maintained trade relationships and commonly intermarried, yet still conducted wars against each other. Alliances are dynamic relationships that can easily shift over time, sometimes rather suddenly. Cultural pressures, such as feuds, boundary violations, wife-stealing, abusive marriages, and a myriad of other forces can create conflict where peace once existed. Natural forces, including extended droughts, warm-water events, and other climactic changes, could have exerted pressure on societies and caused social disruptions (such as those listed above) that eventually could have erupted into violence and warfare. It is likely that both internal and external pressures affected the Chumash. Before we examine causes and motivations for Chumash warfare, methods of social control need to be reviewed, especially those that might be misinterpreted as evidence for warfare in the archaeological record.

Methods of Social Control

The Chumash chose to live in densely packed settlements, some with many hundreds of people. During ceremonies, thousands of people might be congregated in these settlements. In order to maintain social order on a daily basis, as well as during ritual congregations, the Chumash had developed numerous means of societal control. The Chumash had both informal and formal sanctions that served to reduce the frequency and effects of disruptive or unsociable actions. Informal sanctions, such as criticism, gossip, ostracism, fear of witchcraft, and apprehension about supernatural forces served as effective restraints on inappropriate behavior among the Chumash, as they do in many societies. Among the Chumash and many other California Indian groups, shamans were often feared because of their potentially malevolent power, and were an important source of social control. Chumash oral traditions provide useful insights into the power of shamans and their influence on society.

The Chumash had mixed emotions about shamans, who on the one hand cured people and possessed magical powers used to benefit the populace, but on the other hand were sometimes dangerous and caused illness or death. The Chumash recognized a dichotomy between acquired and innate supernatural power (Blackburn 1975:39); shamans with innate power were generally considered more malevolent than those with acquired power. Many Chumash kept an *'atishwin* or sacred talisman to deter malevolent supernatural forces. Shamans usually possessed several *'atishwin*, as well as a variety of herbs, medicines, and other items that empowered them (Blackburn 1975:38–40). Shamans served a significant function in a society that was filled with uncertainty, and they were part of a coterie of powerful individuals within Chumash society that deterred antisocial behavior.

The chief and the *paxa* were important in regulating behavior, particularly during large ceremonial gatherings. Other officials who helped people conform to the protocol at festivals were the *'altipatishwi*, or poisoner, and judges. When Juan Pico was questioned in 1891 about the term for Superior Judge, he responded:

> Those who I shall call judges are the ones that determine the feasts, how many days they are to last, and in honor of what thing or object. In case of greater crime they also pass sentence by order of the chieftain, and in the name of the people, and first of all the plaintiffs (Heizer 1955:189).

Pico was part Ventureño and was a consultant for H. W. Henshaw, who compiled data on mission Indian vocabularies. Pico recorded the term *Ca canay y al jilicnash* for judges. Apparently the Chumash had formal sanctions that were dictated by the chief and carried out by "judges," at least during ceremonies. Blackburn (1975:54), in his analysis of Chumash narratives, noted that many crimes were settled between the victim and the perpetrator. He also found that the chief might become involved in disputes:

> However, the chief as community spokesman can become involved in a conflict situation, and seems capable of applying both formal (nos. 29, 35, 45) and informal (no. 29) sanctions to the nonconforming individual. Anyone who commits a serious crime risks death unless he leaves the community at once—and other members of his family may still be held liable for his actions (no. 25) (Blackburn 1975:54).

Apparently chiefs had significant power in determining if someone was to be put to death.

An ethnographic account from Fernando Librado corroborates Chumash oral traditions. At the site of *Muwu*, the chief ordered a woman shot for adultery. She was shot with a bow and arrow by the executioner, who "did nothing but execute people" (Hudson et al. 1981:13).

> If a woman was unfaithful, she was sentenced to be shot three times with arrows by an executioner. On such occasions they would seat the woman down before the people and execute her. This would be done about three o'clock in the afternoon (Hudson et al. 1981:13).

The execution at *Muwu* was reportedly the basis for a war between the inhabitants of the Tejón region and the Chumash at Muwu (see Johnson [2007] for a recent analysis of this event).

According to Fernando, the formation of the *siliyɨk*, "a body like our congress" (Hudson et al. 1981:17), was a result of the concern over this war and the use of capital punishment. Fernando noted the following about the *siliyɨk*:[56]

> Narciso told Fernando that here on the mainland coast the Indians never knew hunger or need. It was a rich coast. They therefore formed the *siliyɨk* so that no outsider could come here and share rancherias. All newcomers would be required to appear before the *siliyɨk*. The name *siliyɨk* means "a council of officials" and "the whole world" (Hudson et al. 1981:17).

It is clear from this quotation that the mainland region was viewed by the Chumash as a desirable place to live because of its wealth of resources.

Additional evidence for social control comes again from Fernando, who noted the use of a search party during a fiesta held in Ventura:

> The search party consisted of a *paha*, the twelve *'antap* ministers of the *siliyɨk*, and an *'alaqtsum* who was the captain of the searching party; his title means "he who kisses," for he would make such a sound with his lips when he aimed his bow and arrow at the neck of the captain. He would not say a word, just point his bow-drawn arrow at the captain's neck and make this kissing sound while the rest of the group searched everything. They placed this arrow at the neck of rancheria *wots* only, while everything around the *wot* was searched, no matter to whom it belonged. If anything stolen was found, the *paha* called it to the attention of the local *wot* holding the ceremony, while the *paha* took the thief to his *wot*, where the thief was then seated to the right of the *wot*. Fernando does not know how the *wot* would punish the man, but he says that from childhood the Indians teach their children against stealing. The only punishment from heathen times Fernando recalls is killing a woman for adultery (Hudson et al. 1981:41).

This passage corroborates earlier evidence that the chief was instrumental in determining sanctions against individuals who committed crimes. It also underscores the fact that one of the more serious crimes among the Chumash was adultery, particularly for a woman. It is difficult to know whether or not this harsh sanction against adulterous women was a result of Spanish morality being imposed on the Chumash. It may have been a relatively common cause of war. In an attempt to curtail feuds and conflict, chiefs may have imposed such harsh sanctions to reduce the incidence of warfare. Whether the crime was theft or adultery, the bow and arrow was often the weapon used to threaten or carry out force among the Chumash. Poison has also been mentioned as a means of inducing illness or death in a person. It is certainly possible that some of the projectile point injuries observed in skeletal collections from the Chumash region may have resulted from capital punishment and not warfare.

Theoretical Perspectives on Chumash Warfare

Descriptions from historic sources allow a more complete understanding of the nature and causation of conflicts among hunter-gatherer societies which have left only ephemeral archaeological remains. Alternatively, such data can be problematic because of the difficulty in distinguishing the effects that culture contact can have on indigenous patterns of conflict (Ferguson 1992, 2006; Ferguson and Whitehead 1992). European contact often intensified and transformed warfare among traditional groups. Brown (2001:47) has suggested that the battle that Crespí and other members of the Portolá expedition observed in the northern Chumash region may have been a direct result of *El Buchón's* warriors demonstrating their valor to the Spanish after an exchange of war stories. I agree with Brown that this may have been part of the cause, but suspect that the motivations for this battle were more complicated. The presence of the Spanish in southern California and their economic interactions with the Chumash probably had a significant effect on traditional Chumash exchange networks.

Upon their arrival, the Spanish inundated the region with glass beads, metal tools, and other western goods not previously available to the Chumash. These types of goods no doubt were in demand, and many probably were considered prestige goods. The distribution of these Spanish items was highly dependent on where the expedition stopped and who provided them with provisions. This allowed some of the smaller settlements to become more significant players in the already established exchange networks. As a result, new networks of exchange may have been created, especially if one group had Spanish goods that were in demand by others.

A reallocation of power among Chumash exchange partners probably occurred after European colonization, creating conflicts with those who lost power. Some Chumash settlements may have competed with others to gain access to Spanish goods, while some may have eschewed these new items and those seeking them. Individuals who might have been marginalized in traditional Chumash society could have found new avenues for gaining wealth and perhaps prestige. These types of power shifts introduced all kinds of possibilities for disagreement and conflict. I suggest that at least some of the conflict documented during the historic period may have resulted from these types of disruptions in traditional networks. These interferences may have mimicked traditional disruptions in exchange networks, and the types of battles and skirmishes between groups were probably amplified or slightly distorted, but may have remained essentially the same. Certainly, the continued use of the bow and arrow well after European colonization supports this premise.

Some of the conflict among the Chumash, such as that observed by Crespí in August of 1769 when the Portolá expedition first entered the Chumash region, may have been less susceptible to European influences than clashes that occurred later in time. There is strong bioarchaeological evidence that conflict occurred hundreds, even thousands of years before Europeans entered the New World (Lambert 1994, 2002). The burned Chumash settlements observed by Crespí and others in mid-August 1769 probably reflect traditional patterns of Chumash warfare. What were the causes of these hostilities prior to European contact?

Lawrence Keeley (1996) has suggested that armed conflict was present in all societies in the past, regardless of level of social complexity or population densities. He has examined the motives and causes of warfare in non-state societies and has effectively debunked theories that suggest that conflict was relatively benign among "bands," "tribes," and "chiefdoms." In his review of the ethnographic literature on the causes and motives of warfare, Keeley observed that the major motives for prestate warfare fall into two categories: (1) revenge for homicides, and (2) assorted economic concerns. In California, Keeley found that conflicts over resource poaching were common. Counter to what many researchers (Carneiro 1990; Redmond 1994) have proposed, the urge to increase prestige or other personal motives—an often-cited characteristic of "primitive" war—was relatively uncommon at all levels of social organization.

In addition, Keeley noted that disputes over women often had an economic element; he suggested that it is important to distinguish proximal causes of warfare from the underlying motives.

Steven LeBlanc (1999) concurs with Keeley on many levels, and also suggests that causes of warfare can be broken into two categories: (1) competition for scarce resources; and (2) non-materialistic motivations, including vengeance and ritual. Many others have noted correlations between environmental instability, scarce resources, and warfare (Allen 2006; Arnold 1992a; Ember and Ember 1992; Haas 1990; Johnson 2000, 2007; Kennett and Kennett 2000; Lambert 2002; LeBlanc 2003; Lekson 2002). Allen and Arkush (2006:3), in their recent volume on the archaeology of warfare, have noted that some archaeologists tend to neglect ideological and social issues because they are more difficult to document archaeologically than are material factors such as environmental change.

A synthesis of the data presented in this and earlier chapters suggests that conflict among the Chumash was more complex than previously thought. Strictly materialistic approaches to the interpretation of warfare among hunter-gatherer societies may be too simplistic for explaining conflict among the Chumash. Many scholars (Arnold 1992a, 2001a; Johnson 2000, 2007; Kennett 2005; Kennett and Kennett 2000; Lambert 1994, 2002) working in the Chumash region have suggested that ecological variables played a significant role in cultural change and conflict. In a recent discussion of conflict among the Chumash, Johnson (2007) comments that it is tempting to view Chumash conflict solely in cultural ecological terms, but notes that from the perspective of the Chumash, economic motives were seldom perceived as causes for conflict. Instead, revenge was viewed as a primary motive. He also suggests that alliances, which took form as a defense against raids, appear to have led to the emergence of federations.

While this may be partly true, I propose that alliances were established for many reasons among the Chumash and that they had great antiquity. The *'antap* society, marriage practices, exchange networks, and other cultural traditions of the Chumash all required the formation of regional alliances. Brumfiel (1994) has pointed out that the intensity and organization of coalition building is visible in the distribution and frequency of highly crafted or exotic wealth items and feasting paraphernalia in sites. The extensive Chumash exchange system encompassed the trade of a wide range of artifacts, including prestige goods, and evolved over a long period of time (King 1990a). Shell beads, obsidian artifacts, red ochre, stone bowls, finely crafted pestles, and a multitude of other items have been documented far from their sources throughout the Middle and Late periods, indicating that exchange had occurred for thousands of years in southern California (Jackson and Ericson 1994; King 1990a). Alliance networks were associated with these exchange systems. In addition, large feasts created not only economic benefits, but also generated cooperative alliances among those in attendance. Extravagant food preparation vessels used in feasting, such as the sizeable mortar found at the Mescalitan Island site (see chapter 6), appeared approximately 2000 years ago in the Chumash region, suggesting that ceremonial gatherings that attracted large groups of people had been occurring for at least two millennia.

Coalitions were probably continually shifting, depending on the particular context of their formation and their ongoing management. Parallel and overlapping alliances were often formed by chiefs who attempted to maintain friendly relationships within their coalitions, while at the same time endeavoring to retain power, resources, territory, and partnerships. To accomplish this, they had to keep their communities happy. Any discord between individuals within these alliances could upset the balance and set off a series of discordant reactions, with some ballooning into revenge and warfare. When resources were unreliable or scarce, the likelihood of factional competition, conflict, and warfare was greater.

The historic period serves as an example. In their reconstruction of climatic conditions for the coastal Chumash during the mission period, Larson and his colleagues (1994:280–281) found that there were several severe droughts between 1752 and 1756, in 1782, between 1794 and 1795, and from 1805 to 1813. The years 1769 and 1770 were not identified as a period of severe drought, yet the Crespí journals indicate that the Chumash were involved in intertribal warfare during this period. In fact, the Chumash had large enough stores of food to feed the Portolá expedition throughout most of their journey. This suggests that some of the conflict documented by Crespí and others was affected by the Spanish presence and by the disruption of traditional exchange networks, or by other factors not related to climate.

During the protohistoric period (1542–1769), the Chumash had several contacts with well documented maritime voyages; only two of these contacts were extensive (Erlandson and Bartoy 1995). These contacts may have been sources for European diseases. It has also been suggested that disease may have entered North America before direct first contact occurred. Dobyns (1983:49–50, 1992) has suggested that European diseases may have followed trade routes from central Mexico into northern Mexico, and then to the American southwest. Walker and his colleagues (2005), as well as Erlandson and Bartoy (1995), point out that these European diseases could then have reached the Chumash in southern California through trade routes. Walker and his colleagues have proposed that a new, European form of syphilis may have been introduced during the protohistoric period in California, as seen in two unusual skeletons from Skull Gulch on Santa Rosa Island (Walker et al. 2005). If European diseases were introduced at this time, some of the violence that Crespí and others on the Portolá expedition noted in the Chumash region may have resulted from the social disruption caused by introduced diseases, as death and sickness were often blamed on witchcraft (Walker et al. 1989:359). Although this is possible, we do not know if the impact of European diseases was the cause of the violence noted by Crespí in 1769.

It is also possible that disease had had little effect on the population when the Portolá expedition first entered the Chumash region. Although the expedition itself may have triggered the battle that Crespí described in May 1770, the burned villages they noted approximately nine months before may have been typical of traditional patterns of Chumash conflict and not a result of the Spanish presence.

If this was the case, why then did Chumash from the interior come to the mainland coast, burn all of the structures in several coastal settlements, and attempt to destroy one of the largest Chumash towns on the coast? I propose that the Chumash were protecting and trying to expand their powerful exchange networks. The economic system played a prominent role in the ritual, political, and social lives of the Chumash. Chiefs had a tremendous investment in the exchange networks; they owned the plank canoes, massive amounts of beads, the ritual paraphernalia, and the prestige goods that fueled the economic system and made it function on such an expansive scale. They did not take these investments lightly, but instead ensured that their exchange networks were not only maintained, but were also expanded and intensified. Chiefs and the Chumash people protected these networks, as they did their collecting areas and other resources, and if necessary fought over them. Although mechanisms that encouraged cooperation, such as regularly scheduled feasts and intermarriages, frequently were effective in controlling disputes and warfare, they were not infallible.

I suggest that the root cause of many of the conflicts that have been described in this chapter were related to shifting exchange networks and the uneven distribution of resources, and that the available information on Chumash conflicts in ethnohistoric sources supports this hypothesis. Fages suggested that one reason that the Chumash conducted war was to defend their possessions, while Father Señan stated that it was to defend their wives and rights to their territory. The refusal of a chief to attend a feast was considered a reason for warfare. The Chumash on the mainland were situated in ideal locations for both obtaining resources and mediating exchanges. The burning down of entire villages probably destroyed many of the stored resources and much of the wealth present in these villages, but was effective in opening up strategically located places for others to possibly invade, or to disrupt the exchange networks. It is likely that chiefs attempted to maintain their ideal geographic positions with allies and vied with other chiefs if their "territories" were impinged upon.

When the Spanish entered the region and distributed beads, metal tools, cloth, and other items in exchange for food and services, they transformed the Chumash system of exchange. Individuals who may have lacked political power and wealth suddenly had a new avenue to gain these resources. The battle described by Crespí in May of 1770 may have been similar to Chumash warfare prior to European contact, but it is fully possible that Chumash chiefdoms were vying for access to the Spanish and their resources.

CHAPTER 10

The Chumash, Pomo, and Patwin

Comparative Analysis and Final Thoughts

The coast along the entire Channel, between the first town, La Asunta, and Point La Concepción here, runs due east and west, while on passing this point it once more runs northwestward until past the Santa Lucia Mountains. How fine all the land here on the Channel is, it is a joy to see: how grass-grown everything is; how many watering places there are and how plenteous; how many towns, with so many people, regularly laid out, with such good-sized grass lodges, some that I have been inside so large that they can, no doubt at all, hold sixty persons. A folk all of whose towns have entertained us and presented us with a vast amount of fish, gruels, and mushes made from their seeds, the three times that we have passed along the Channel here. I trust in God that there shall soon be missions here and all these thousands of souls won over to our holy faith, and that the knowledge of the true God shall come among them. There are various embayments upon this Channel and a very peaceful sea all along it.

Crespí in Brown 2001:707

The Chumash along the Santa Barbara Channel mainland coast were thriving and prosperous when first encountered by the Spanish. Although cyclical droughts and El Niño events repeatedly challenged them, they had developed successful coping strategies after living in an unpredictable environment for thousands of years. In this final chapter, I briefly review the evidence that clearly characterizes the Chumash as complex hunter-gatherers (Ames and Maschner 1999). This will serve as background for a discussion of the relationship between resource abundance, adaptive mechanisms that cope with environmental stresses, and the emergence of social complexity. Finally, I address two fundamental issues raised in the current study—the nature of power and the significance of centrally located places.

Complex Hunter-Gatherers: The Chumash Example

The Chumash exhibited numerous traits of sociopolitical complexity as outlined by Ames and Maschner (1999). These traits include sedentism, possession of large quantities of stored and processed foods, environmental manipulation to increase productivity, complex technologies, a social hierarchy, high population densities, and occupational specialization. The evidence for these traits is briefly reviewed in this section and provides the foundation for the remainder of the chapter.

At the time of European contact, the Chumash on the Santa Barbara Channel mainland coast lived in sedentary settlements, some with over 700 inhabitants. Crespí estimated that there were 100 houses in the historic town of *Helo'* on Mescalitan Island. The houses at *Helo'* and at other towns on the mainland coastline were described in the early accounts as being closely packed together in rows, with streets running between them. Other indications of sedentism include the large quantities of goods that accompanied some individuals after death.

There is strong evidence in the archaeological, ethnohistoric, and ethnographic records that the Chumash processed and stored large quantities of food. The best evidence for storage comes from ethnohistoric accounts, particularly that of Crespí, who noted that the Chumash had vast quantities of dried fish on their roofs, in addition to stored seeds and other processed foods, that they shared with the Portolá expedition. The Chumash also had a well developed system of social storage; shell beads could be exchanged for food during times of need, and thus served as an insurance against localized shortages of food (Rowley-Conwy and Zvebil 1989). The manufacture and exchange of shell beads by the Santa Barbara Channel islanders helped them get through periods of food shortages in an environment less richly endowed with resources than the mainland.

The Chumash also managed their environment to increase the yield of certain foods. The best example of this involved their use of fire to promote the growth of seed-bearing plants, discourage the growth of other, undesirable plants, and create habitats that were more favorable for deer and other game animals (Timbrook et al. 1982). Other practices, such as the use of careful gathering processes and the pruning, tilling, weeding, and coppicing of plants, also increased the yield of seeds, bulbs, tubers, and other foods (Anderson 1993, 2005).

The Chumash had developed a specialized and complex technology that facilitated fishing, hunting and gathering, and regional exchange. The most notable technological innovation that served to intensify fishing and exchange was the plank canoe. Occupational specialists were members of a craft guild—collectively known as the "Brotherhood of the *Tomol*" (Hudson et al. 1978)—that had the knowledge and expertise to build these seaworthy vessels. Most other manufactured goods were also produced by occupational specialists who belonged to sodality-like organizations. The Chumash had a monetized market economy, with shell beads that were used as a currency for the exchange or purchase of manufactured goods, food, and some services.

Chiefs inherited their positions and belonged to an elite organization, the *'antap* society, whose members organized and conducted rituals at large ceremonial gatherings. They owned and used all ritual paraphernalia and were distinguished from commoners by their dress. The chiefs and ceremonial leaders among the Chumash worked closely together during rituals, collecting and redistributing shell bead money and other items. The Chumash clearly had a social hierarchy, with permanent leadership positions characterized by considerable prestige and power.

Resource Abundance and Sociopolitical Complexity

The Chumash lived in an environment rich in terrestrial and maritime resources and with pronounced geographical and ecological diversity. Raab and Jones (2004:210–211) have proposed that the idea that California Indians lived in an environment with abundant resources is a myth; in reality, they suggest, California Indians struggled with environmental challenges. It is, however, important to consider the environmental variability across California in order to better understand the nature and responses of California Indian societies to the challenges that they faced. If the environment in the Santa Barbara Channel is compared to that in much of the desert west, for example, considerable differences are evident. The climate in the interior desert areas is quite severe, and the California Indian groups who lived there faced significant challenges. Many more subsistence resources were available along the Santa Barbara Channel mainland than were present further inland. This does not mean that the Chumash never faced significant challenges from environmental stresses, such as extended droughts and cyclical El Niño and La Niña events, which posed considerable risks to the relatively dense populations in the region. However, when adverse climatic changes occurred, the Chumash were able to employ numerous strategies to minimize the risks associated with these events (see Gamble 2005). These coping mechanisms included an elaborate economic system, partly based on a shell-bead currency, the exchange of items between different ecological zones, physical and social storage, subsistence diversification, regularly scheduled ceremonial gatherings attended by people from a broad geographical area, intercommunity marriage ties, and loosely organized federations overseen by paramount chiefs. Sociopolitical complexity emerged in part as a result of the interplay between resource abundance and a highly developed set of risk minimization strategies.

Many scholars (e.g., Arnold 1992a, 2001a and b; Glassow 1996; Johnson 2000; Kennett 2005; Kennett and Kennett 2000; Lambert 1997; Raab and Larson 1997) have at least in part linked the emergence of political and economic complexity in the Chumash area to paleoclimatic changes that took place sometime between AD 450 and 1300 (see Gamble 2005 for a review of these hypotheses). I agree with my colleagues that environmental change affected Chumash sociopolitical and economic strategies, but differ from many of them in that I do not see evidence for punctuated change. Instead, I propose that the Chumash, by developing a series of risk management strategies, adapted to their fluctuating environment through economic and sociopolitical means, and that change was rather gradual.

As King (1976) showed decades ago, the use of shell-bead money allowed the Chumash to effectively regulate and mobilize resources from different ecological zones throughout the year. Despite the relatively lush environment, especially in the Santa Barbara Channel region, southern California is plagued by a variable climate. The Chumash, who had lived in the area for over ten millennia, had successfully adapted to the environmental conditions that characterize the region. Although they most certainly knew about horticulture, they chose not to grow crops, probably because the acorn economy, along with abundant marine resources and other foods, sufficed to support their relatively dense populations. Moreover, at least during most of the Late Holocene, rainfall tended to be highest during the winter months, not in the summer months when most crops are easier to grow (Bean and Lawton 1976). Although not as vulnerable to droughts as agriculturalists, the Chumash probably were affected by the consequences of extreme climatic change, such as massive food shortages (Johnson 2000; Larson et al. 1994).

Power Strategies of the Chumash

Chumash chiefs, in conjunction with other prestigious individuals, had numerous sources of power. One major source of power was certainly economic in nature. Earle (1997) has identified economic power as an important source of chiefly influence, and suggested that control over wealth creates a basis for political power. The Chumash differed from other California Indians (except the neighboring Tongva) in the fact that their cross-channel exchanges required seaworthy watercraft. Individuals who owned plank boats had a distinct advantage over others in the distribution of shell beads and groundstone items made on the islands, and in the flow of mainland goods to the islands and between mainland settlements. Without the plank canoe, or other seaworthy watercraft, it would have been very difficult to maintain the intense level of exchange that was observed in the Chumash region at the time of European contact.

Plank canoes required specialized knowledge and materials for their construction, and the materials were costly, as was the labor. Because of their cost and relative rarity, only chiefs and other wealthy individuals owned them. Plank canoes were not only critical for exchanges between the islands and the mainland, they were also important for trade between the coastal mainland settlements and for the acquisition of fish, especially large pelagic fish. Chumash chiefs and other wealthy individuals had the means to control the distribution of both the manufactured goods that were exported from the Channel Islands and the food and other materials that were imported to the islands. However, at the time of European contact, there is no clear evidence that boat owners actually restricted access to watercraft. Nevertheless, the fact that they had such a source of power placed them in an economically advantageous position. Boat owners received a portion of the catch when their watercraft were used for fishing, and they probably charged a fee for transporting people and their goods across the channel.

There is also evidence that Chumash chiefs, ceremonial leaders, and others worked closely together in the redistribution of money and goods during the context of regularly scheduled ritual feasts. Dancers, singers, and other specialists who participated in ceremonial gatherings were paid in shell beads by host chiefs, who collected funds from attendees with the help of the *paha* and poisoner (Blackburn 1976; Gayton 1930). In return, those who were invited to the ceremonies were feasted, entertained, and presented with gifts. These ritual events served to enhance the prestige and reputation of the chiefs, who were looked upon as generous providers; at the same time, the chiefs and their assistants reaped economic benefits from these transactions. In addition, the chiefs and other members of the *'antap* society owned all of the ritual paraphernalia that were part of the wealth finance system of the Chumash.

In summary, chiefs (and some of the elite associated with them) had two major sources of economic power. The first source involved the ownership of a major means of transport (Earle 1997), and therefore control of an important means of distribution. Owners of plank canoes in effect had some level of control over the cross-channel exchange system. Chiefs in the large population centers along the mainland coast dominated trading routes because of their strategic, central location between the islanders and groups in the interior. A second source of economic power involved a chief's role in redistribution. Most items that were redistributed, as well as many of the other goods that were exchanged in the Chumash region, were part of the Chumash system of wealth finance. Earle (1997:74) has argued that "control over the ideology of social ranking rested on control over the system of wealth finance." By commanding certain aspects of the Chumash economic system and controlling wealth finance, Chumash chiefs gained control over the ideological basis of their social positions.

Network Power

Chumash society at historic contact varied considerably in form from that characteristic of many hunter-gatherers, and therefore never fit into such unilinear models of progressivist typological frameworks as those proposed by Service (1971) or Fried (1967). This has been frustrating for scholars trying to understand the development of sociopolitical complexity in the area. Until the publication of Price and Brown's (1985) significant volume on cultural complexity among hunter-gatherers, the recognition that some hunter-gatherers had complex societies or simple chiefdoms was generally disregarded, and such societies were viewed as being exceptional rather than as indicative of an alternative route to organizational complexity and inequality (see Feinman 1995). Unfortunately, many introductory archaeology and anthropology textbooks still do not recognize that some hunter-gatherers can be classified as "chiefdoms" or "tribes" (e.g., Price 2006; Thomas and Kelly 2006). Feinman (1995, 2000) and others (Blanton et al. 1996; Earle 2001; Feinman et al. 2000) have proposed that there are two pathways toward inequality, one corporate-based and the other network-based. This is a heuristically useful distinction for examining any group's route to becoming a ranked society. It should be emphasized that networked-based power and corporate-based power should not be considered as alternatives, but as strategies that are followed to varying degrees (Blanton et al. 1996; Earle 2001; Feinman 1995; Peregrine 2001).

Over thirty years ago, Renfrew (1974) identified similar strategies in prehistoric Europe, involving what he called "group-oriented chiefdoms" and "individualizing chiefdoms." Renfrew recognized "group-oriented chiefdoms" as societies that frequently had limited ecological diversity, built large public works, placed little importance on technology, and lacked opulent burials. These types of chiefdoms were similar to the societies described by Feinman (1995) and Blanton et al. (1996) that emphasized corporate power. Material manifestations of corporate power often involve monumental public architecture, with plazas and other areas for large group-based ceremonies, as well as corporate labor projects such as roads or large irrigation projects (Blanton et al. 1996). A corporate emphasis always involves a cognitive code that stresses corporate solidarity. It follows, then, that a corporate strategy tends to produce relatively few royal tombs or wealthy burials, as that type of ostentatious individualism in life and death is discouraged. Leaders in corporate societies tend to be harder to identify in the archaeological record than leaders in network-based societies, in part because power was shared. Blanton and his colleagues have proposed that the Teotihucuan polity that existed between AD 300 and 750 in Mesoamerica was an example of a corporate strategy in operation. Another example of corporate, or group-oriented power, involved the Chaco Canyon chiefdom (Earle 2001), which had carefully planned great houses, plazas, and kivas, as well as an extensive and complex system of roads. That system was partly supported by staple-finance involving the storage of agricultural products.

Networked-based power, in contrast to corporate power, tends to accentuate individual prestige and wealth. Renfrew (1974) characterized "individualizing chiefdoms" as societies that emphasized personal wealth and prestige goods (which were often found as burial associations). Renfrew also suggested that "individualizing chiefdoms" often lacked large public works, except for tombs and chiefly residences, and were frequently plagued by conflict. Earle (2001) has elaborated on the insights of Renfrew and others (Blanton et al. 1996; Feinman 1995), and noted that individuals and their interrelationships across the landscape are important in groups that stress network power. The following traits are characteristic of societies employing a network strategy (see Blanton et al. 1996; Earle 2001; Feinman 1995, 2000):

- Emphasis on personal wealth
- Ostentatious personal displays in life and after life in the burial ritual
- Wealth finance manifested in the exchange of prestige goods
- Extralocal networks with differential access to prestigious marriage partners, prestige items, and specialized knowledge
- Long distance trade networks
- Ceremonial displays accompanied by lavish feasts
- Chiefly control over the production or distribution of valuables and prestige goods
- Frequent or heightened conflict
- Regional ecological diversity

Societies that stress network power tend to lack constructed landscapes involving such things as large public monuments, large-scale irrigation canals, and roads, in part because the use of communal projects to build group solidarity is not a high priority.

I propose that the hunting-gathering Chumash were able to succeed and prosper in part because of a network strategy that they had developed to cope with the variable ecological and climatic conditions in the Santa Barbara Channel region. The risks associated with the regional ecological diversity of the region were managed through exchanges of raw materials, manufactured items, and food (facilitated by a well-developed system of currency), between regions with varying resources. Although long distance exchange was not as common as trade within the Chumash region, exchanges involving great distances in the area did exist (Earle 2005; Jackson and Ericson 1994; King 1990a). The Chumash emphasized egocentric exchange systems that were reinforced by extensive marriage ties between trade partners. Chiefs and other elite persons gained recognition and power through the control of esoteric knowledge, reinforced by the ownership of prestige goods. The Chumash elite were buried in canoes and often were accompanied by hundreds or even thousands of beads. Their power was also evident in the lavish feasts they orchestrated. The abundant amounts of food consumed at these feasts were prepared and served in large, highly decorated vessels, some made of rare materials.

Blanton and his colleagues (1996:4) have noted that among societies that stress network-based power, any household or individual theoretically could strive to establish network ties. This situation could cause rivalry between people with overlapping networks. Among the Chumash, much of this competition was mitigated through traditional channels, such as regularly scheduled ceremonial feasts, but the potential for conflict was probably higher when mechanisms for cooperation failed. Archaeological, ethnohistoric, and ethnographic data suggest that Chumash internal conflict was relatively frequent during certain periods of time. Unfortunately, chronological data for the region lack the resolution necessary to link cultural shifts to the paleoclimatic record. This is a significant problem which continues to undermine the various studies that have attempted to link the emergence of sociopolitical complexity to paleoclimatic change.

The mechanisms that were in place during the Late period to reduce conflict and warfare were not effective enough to put a complete stop to disruptive behavior. A scarcity of resources, engendered by climatic changes, may have been an important cause of warfare; but in light of oral traditions, ethnohistoric sources, and ethnographic documentation on the subject, and given the complexity of Chumash society, the reasons for conflict were probably much more complicated, and included such factors, for example, as chiefs vying for territories and exchange networks. The Chumash lived in a rich environment with variable climatic conditions and resources, and for thousands of years managed risks well, although they certainly were not invulnerable when severe droughts or other climatic disasters hit. The protection of networks associated with exchanges, political and ritual positions, and social relationships was a high priority. This is typical of societies that emphasize network power, where there is a tendency for abundant prestige goods, increased feasting, and heightened conflict to exist (Blanton et al. 1996; Feinman 2000).

Emergent Complexity and the Relationship of the Island and Mainland Chumash

A wealth of research-oriented archaeological data has been collected on the northern Santa Barbara Channel Islands, where an absence of burrowing rodents and limited development have contributed to a much better preservation of cultural remains than is found on the Channel mainland. This has resulted in a skewed picture of the past and of the factors that led to the political and economic complexity documented for the historic Chumash. Modeling political elaboration on the islands, with little consideration given to the role played by the mainland Chumash in that elaboration, can only lead to an incomplete and imperfect picture of the nature of Chumash social complexity. One goal of this book has been to develop a more complete understanding of Chumash society by analyzing the sociopolitical and economic practices of the people who lived along the mainland coast, and to then suggest how those practices were relevant to the entire Chumash region. I believe that the data presented here strongly support the view that island Chumash political complexity did not develop in isolation, but in fact was integrally related to (and perhaps dependent upon) the emergence of political complexity on the mainland.

Jeanne Arnold (2001a) has proposed a number of hypotheses concerning the development of political complexity on the islands that are relevant to the present discussion. In a discussion of the Chumash use of shell-bead currency, for example, she has made the following comments:

> When the currency emerged, control over its production and/or release was likely economically and politically essential. A currency simply cannot hold its value if counterfeiting is rampant or even a serious threat. Some form of centralized leadership is implicated in this development. Indeed, organizational changes 3, 4, and 5 [the origins of specialized craft production, greatly accelerated exchange, and the origins of Chumash currency] listed here all developed simultaneously and may have been stimulated by emerging elites to finance their political aspirations. It may be somewhat surprising that Olivella callus bead manufacturing was not controlled by means of confinement to a very small number of communities. Instead, and quite important for us to recognize, the distribution of finished island-made beads to cross-channel consumers was apparently controlled by means of elite plank canoe ownership (Arnold 2001a:289).

Certainly, counterfeiting could limit the value of a currency, but this was probably not as relevant to centralized leadership as Arnold has suggested. Counterfeiting can only occur when some social entity controls either the raw materials or the manufacturing processes necessary for producing the currency, or has the sole socially recognized right to make it. None of these factors applied in the Chumash example. Shell-bead money could easily have been made on the mainland, and in fact was. *Olivella biplicata* shells were readily available there, as were chert and other cryptocrystalline materials suitable for making bead drills. We know that beads were made on the mainland, albeit not generally in great quantities. A considerable quantity of shell bead detritus, for example, was found on the mainland at the Corral Canyon site (SBA-1731). The 1,460 fragments of *Olivella biplicata* shell that were discovered there indicate that the inhabitants were making cup beads from the callus portion of the shell (Erlandson and Rick 2002b). Although the density of shell bead detritus was not as great as that occurring at many of the sites on Santa Cruz Island, the density overlapped the lower range of densities found in sites on the northern Channel Islands (Arnold and Graesch 2001; Erlandson and Rick 2002b).

We can state with some certainty that the centralized leadership on Santa Cruz Island had no practical means of controlling the production of shell beads on the mainland. Therefore, although 'counterfeiting' was possible, it probably was not an important issue; the people living along the mainland coast presumably chose *not* to spend their time and effort making shell beads because it was not cost effective. They instead chose to exchange their abundant and diverse food resources and other goods for the shell beads that were produced on the islands, as King (1976) suggested over thirty years ago. The reason that shell beads maintained their value was because they were periodically destroyed during death and mourning rituals—a factor attested to by the many Chumash burials interred with beads (Gamble et al. 2001; King 1990a)—not because island leaders were controlling their production or distribution. Beads were also removed from local circulation among the Chumash by being 'consumed' by inland groups like the Yokuts.

Arnold (2001a) has also noted that shell bead making was not controlled by confining manufacture to a few specialized communities on the islands; instead, she has suggested, the cross-channel distribution of beads was controlled by island canoe owners. But what evidence exists for this? How do we know? Many plank canoes were built, owned, and used along the mainland coast, not just on the islands. Presumably, mainland residents could cross the channel without any impediment when they chose to visit relatives and friends on the islands. Mission records show that numerous marriages occurred between islanders and mainlanders. I suspect that if mainland chiefs or others chose to visit the islands, they were able to do so easily, even though it was more likely that the islanders came to the mainland to attend the large feasts or obtain foods or other resources not readily available on the islands (see chapter 6).

Arnold has made another statement about the Island Chumash that is relevant to this discussion:

> Ultimately, the factors stimulating political elaboration in the Island Chumash case were changes in the organization and manipulation of labor associated with technological innovation, specialized production, and control over intensified

> middle-distance exchange early in the second millennium. A small group of privileged leaders, canoe owners, and traders was able to begin to control and differentially distribute many goods and considerable information about regional political, economic, social, and ecological conditions (Arnold 2001a:295).

This is an intriguing proposal, but again it fails to consider the role of the mainlanders. Did the privileged island leaders, canoe owners, and traders have considerable information that was not available to their counterparts on the mainland? Or does the statement pertain to both the island and mainland Chumash? Arnold's suggestion is not entirely clear.

As a result of the evidence presented here, and after considering alternative explanations and data proffered by Arnold (2001a and b), Johnson (1982, 1988, 2001), Kennett (1998, 2005), King (1990a), Rick (2004, 2007), and others, I would like to propose an alternative explanation for the emergence of political elaboration among the Chumash, one involving both islanders and mainlanders. The production of beads was in response to a demand for beads. The key factor was *not* the control of production or distribution by chiefs on the islands, but rather the demand for beads and the control of exchange by chiefs on the mainland. There are allusions in Chumash oral traditions and elsewhere to the fact that canoe owners apparently took a cut of the items that were transported in canoes or charged a fee as payment for this service; however, they probably seldom refused to take people or goods across the channel, except under unusual circumstances or during periods when dangerous seas were running.

The Chumash invested enormous energy in their economic system, a system that was characterized by the use of currency; a complex and wide-flung exchange system that included prestige goods and food in addition to money; regularly scheduled feasts that provided opportunities for an exchange of knowledge, food, and goods; innovative technological items such as the plank canoe; free market exchange; and redistribution. The Chumash fought to maintain their trade partners and their network system of political control. Power was held by chiefs and their associates, who benefited politically, economically, and ideologically from cross-channel exchanges, ceremonial gatherings, redistributive efforts, and trade partnerships that were likely to have been established through centuries of inter-village marriages. The Chumash exchange system, in part, allowed Chumash society to reach the level of population density and sociopolitical complexity outlined here. The ecological diversity in the Chumash region was managed and exploited through exchange and the use of currency. Chumash leaders had devised methods that served to keep large populations fed without agriculture, and which also served to reinforce their own entitlement to surplus food, goods, money, and power.

Sociopolitical Complexity among Hunter-Gatherers in California

The Chumash were only one among a number of hunter-gatherer societies in North America that had a relatively complex political structure, but did not rely on fully domesticated foods. Other hunter-gatherer societies that attained unusual levels of sociopolitical complexity in North America were the Calusa in southwest Florida; a number of groups on the Northwest Coast and in Alaska; the Yokuts in central California; and the Pomo, Patwin, and other groups in north-central California. Most of these societies relied heavily on marine resources and had large, sedentary settlements; most apparently also had hereditary chiefs, social ranking, craft specialization, and political, economic, and religious complexity. Arnold (2001c:6–10) has provided a useful summary concerning sociopolitical complexity among some of these groups that I will not duplicate here. Instead, I will focus on the Patwin and the Pomo in north-central California and compare these groups to the Chumash; I will also expand upon Arnold's, Beaton's (1991), and others' conclusions concerning Patwin sociopolitical complexity. This brief comparison will illustrate how power strategies differed in two socially complex California Indian societies located in different environmental settings. Many of the data presented here on the Patwin are derived from ethnohistoric and ethnographic sources. Greg White (2003) has recently synthesized a large body of archaeological information that generally supports the ethnographic information presented below.

THE PATWIN

The Patwin Indians, who lived along the river in the southern Sacramento River Valley region, on the surrounding plains, and in the lower hills of the eastern Coast range, shared many cultural traits with the Pomo, Nisenan, Miwok, and Nomlaki, among others. Patwin Indian towns along the lower Sacramento River during the historic period included some of the largest settlements to be found anywhere in aboriginal California. Cook (1976), who based his conclusions on a synthesis of early historic documents, developed estimates of population numbers for the Patwin region; he noted that several settlements, each containing over 1400 individuals, could be found along the Sacramento River, and estimated that an average of 1280 inhabitants were present in each of the five main River Patwin settlements. This represents a considerable number of people who needed to be fed, cared for, and managed. The largest centers of population for the Patwin were the settlements between the present-day towns of Colusa and Knight's Landing along the Sacramento River.

Patwin settlement patterns involved a two-level hierarchy, with principal settlements surrounded by minor settlements that shared a place name. The larger settlements had at least one sizable earthen dance house, often occupied by the chief, that was situated in the principal town (Kroeber 1932). According to Captain Luis Antonio Argüello, who traveled in the region in 1782, some of these lodges were 125 to 150 feet in diameter and served as ceremonial structures for hundreds, if not thousands, of people in the surrounding region (Fisher 1992). Within the dance house, rules were followed regarding seating arrangements, with chiefs and other highly-ranked individuals assigned specific places (Kroeber 1932). Political and religious power was closely linked among the Patwin.

The Patwin and surrounding tribes differed from the Chumash in their heavy reliance on anadromous (spawning) fish such as salmon. Fish weirs (also known as dams or fences) were erected at the largest settlements across a shallow part of the river, enabling the Patwin to capture vast quantities of salmon and other anadromous fish (Kroeber 1932; McKern 1922). The construction of these weirs required the coordination of a large labor pool consisting of all of the men in a settlement. The chief orchestrated the necessary labor and decided when the weirs were to be built. Large posts had to be driven into the stream bed, and smaller poles of willow were set between and secured the posts. Finally, a framework was added to this foundation to make an insurmountable barrier, with gateways that were spaced approximately three feet apart. Conical basket traps were then placed in these gateways to capture the fish. Some gateways were left open so that fish could swim through. The chief supervised the entire process.

Patwin chiefs, who were almost exclusively males, inherited their positions through the male line (Kroeber 1932; McKern 1922). Chiefs not only regulated the construction and operation of fish weirs, but were also responsible for the storage and redistribution of food and wealth. Meat products of sufficient quantities, including fish, were brought to the chiefs, who then stored them until the food was distributed to needy households or during ceremonies. Fish and meats were dried and sometimes pulverized to help in their preservation. Seeds, acorns, dried and powdered salmon, and dried meat were stored in layers separated by mats in very large woven bins. Chiefs' families, which could be quite large because chiefs had more than one wife, did not need to hunt, fish, or gather food, but were supplied with most necessities, including firewood and baskets. The chief could easily be distinguished from other people by the special apparel that he wore on a daily basis, including fancy feathered headdresses, belts, and cloaks. Some towns had multiple chiefs, one of whom was identified as the head chief (Kroeber 1932:273).

The Patwin observed numerous ritual events throughout the year, in addition to the specific ceremonies associated with the Kuksu religion (Bean 1978; Kroeber 1932). The Kuksu religious system was the focus of both ritual and political organization and was found among numerous tribes in central California. The Kuksu religion could be distinguished from others in California because of its formal organization and its complexity (Bean and Vane 1978). Its most elaborate manifestation was present among the Patwin, who recognized three levels of secret society membership; in addition, the members of these societies tended to be economically, socially, and politically superior to non-members (Bean 1978). In general, women were excluded from membership, although upper class Patwin women were allowed to become members of some of the societies. Initiates paid for the privilege of membership and were required to make repeated payments as they advanced through the different levels (Bean and Vane 1978). A strict seating arrangement was maintained in the dance house during the initiation ceremonies associated with the Kuksu religion (Kroeber 1932). Initiation into the Kuksu cult had an element of danger, both in the ritual itself and in the acquisition of potentially dangerous knowledge. Initiates did not take hallucinogens, as they did in rituals in southern California, but were subjected to physical and mental challenges that resulted in the initiates appearing to go insane and die, only to then be revived. The Patwin used shell beads as a currency, but relied more heavily on clamshell (*Saxidomus* spp. and *Tresus* spp.) disk beads than on beads made from the callus portion of *Olivella biplicata* shells (King 1978:61).

THE POMO

Ethnographic and historical information indicates that the Pomo, and possibly the Miwok, manufactured clamshell disk beads that were used as currency, buried with the dead, and traded to the Patwin and other groups in the region. The best ethnographic information about the production of beads involves the Pomo, who made clamshell disk and magnesite tubular beads, and were known as "great counters" and the "principal purveyors of the standard disk currency to north-central California" (Kroeber 1925:256–257).

The Pomo, a diverse collection of indigenous speakers of seven distinct Pomoan languages, lived north of San Francisco Bay and comprised more than 75 "distinct politically autonomous village-communities" (McLendon 1993:49) when they were first encountered by non-Indians. Many of the relatively early ethnographic accounts state that a number of Pomo groups traveled considerable distances to Bodega Bay, an area occupied by the Coast Miwok, to gather clam shells (*Saxidomus* spp.). Once the shells were collected, they were carried back in large conical baskets and made into disk beads. Selected ethnographic accounts that identify which groups made the beads and how the raw materials were acquired are summarized in table 23. As can be seen, many Pomo groups made both shell and magnesite beads, but a few did not. Curiously, clam shells were often carried inland 85 miles or more from Bodega Bay, which was their source, yet were not made into beads locally at Bodega Bay. Isabel Kelly noted the following about the clam beds: "The Coast Miwoks owned the clam beds that provided all neighboring peoples with shell, yet seem not to have derived any particular advantage from such potential monopoly" (Kelly 1978:418). Gifford provided additional information on the conveyance of clam shells in the following statement:

> The Eastern Pomo currency consisted of discs of shell of the large clam *Saxidomus nuttali*, which is particularly abundant at Bodega bay, Sonoma county. Every man manufactured the discs, but some were able to devote more time to the occupation than others. So far as the informant knew, the Eastern Pomo themselves went to Bodega bay for the shells; they did not merely obtain them through trade from intervening peoples.
>
> The Cigom [an Eastern Pomo village situated on the eastern shore of Clear Lake] informant had himself been six times to Bodega bay to obtain the clams. The customary load borne home on the back weighed about one hundred pounds. The journey from Cigom to Bodega bay took three and one-half days, the route being by way of Cloverdale and Sebastopol. At Sebastopol the last night camp was made. The final leg of the journey required all of the following day. The Miwok at Bodega bay neither charged for the clams nor objected to the Pomo digging them. Digging sticks were used to dig the clams. The mollusks were eaten at the camp and only the shells brought home to Cigom.
>
> The Southeastern Pomo informant Wokox said that anciently clam shells for money manufacture were obtained mostly through trade. Individuals seldom went for the shells for fear of trouble with peoples along the route. The Coast Miwok of Bodega bay sold the shells to the Russian River people, who in turn sold them to

TABLE 23. Shell and Magnesite Beads among the Pomo

Source of Raw Materials/ Site of Manufacture	Pomo Community	Modern Community	Region	Reference	Comments
Clamshells from Bodega Bay/ Made locally	Shanel (Shenel)	Hopland	Central	Gifford and Kroeber 1937:186	
Infrequently traveled over 100 mi. to Bodega Bay for clamshells/conflicting data on site of manufacture	Xowalek	Upper Lake	E	Stewart 1943:43	Shell beads obtained in exchange for magnesite.
Obtained or traded clamshells from coast/made locally	Kalekau	Sherwood Valley	N	Gifford and Kroeber 1937:186	Used flat slab for grinding beads.
Traveled 85 mi. to Bodega Bay to obtain clamshells/made locally	Masut	Forsythe or Walker Valley	N	Stewart 1943:39	
Two informants stated that traveled to Bodega Bay to obtain clamshells/conflicting data on site of manufacture	Mato Poma	Sherwood Valley	N	Stewart 1943:36	Two informants stated clamshell beads were made in Sherwood, two others said that no shell bead money was made at Sherwood, but all money was traded for, including magnesite, with Ukiah Indians.
Regularly traveled to Bodega Bay to get clamshells. Dangerous trip because of hostile tribes on the way/made locally	Canel (Shenel)	Hopland	N	Stewart 1943:46	Special craftsmen who lived from the sale of their products, were highly developed in Hopland.
Source of clamshells not mentioned/made locally	Mukano	Near Santa Rosa	S	Gifford and Kroeber 1937:187	Continually made, traded to Indians in Lake Co. for baskets and magnesite.

(*continued*)

TABLE 23. (continued)

Source of Raw Materials/ Site of Manufacture	Pomo Community	Modern Community	Region	Reference	Comments
Traveled to Bodega Bay for clamshells/made locally	Makamot-cemei	Cloverdale	S	Stewart 1943:52	The Kacia (Kashia) allowed anyone who gathered them to take ocean products.
Traveled to Bodega Bay for clamshells/presumably made locally	Bitakomtara	Santa Rosa	S	Stewart 1943:53	
Clamshell beads were imported from the South.	Meteni	Fort Ross	SW	Gifford and Kroeber 1937:186	Used for necklaces.
Magnesite cylinders were bought ready made.	Icheche	Pt. Arena	Central	Gifford and Kroeber 1937:187	
Obtained magnesite from Cache Creek of Clear Lake/ made locally	Shenel	Hopland	Central	Gifford and Kroeber 1937:187	
Mined magnesite on Cache Creek/ presumably made locally	Shigom (Cigom)	Lucerne	E	Gifford and Kroeber 1937:187	Deposit not owned by any one group. Various people went there for stone.
Obtained magnesite by going across lake/presumably made locally	Xowalek	Upper Lake	E	Stewart 1943:43	Green chert used for drills.
Traveled 55 mi. to obtain magnesite in Lake County/magnesite cylinders made locally	Masut	Forsythe or Walker Valley	N	Stewart 1943:39	No payment made to obtain magnesite.

Obtained unbaked magnesite by going to Lake County. No payments given/presumably made locally	Canel (Shenel)	Hopland	N	Stewart 1943:46	
Magnesite cylinders imported from Lake Pomo	Salt Pomo	Stonyford	NE	Gifford and Kroeber 1937:187	
Magnesite cylinders imported ready made	Mukano	Near Santa Rosa	S	Gifford and Kroeber 1937:187	
Magnesite cylinders were bought ready made	Makahmo	Cloverdale	S	Gifford and Kroeber 1937:187	
Magnesite cylinders were bought ready made	Bitakomtara	Santa Rosa	S	Stewart 1943:53	
Traveled to Lake County to obtain magnesite/magnesite cylinders made locally	Makamot-cemei	Cloverdale	S	Stewart 1943:52	
Source of magnesite not mentioned/magnesite cylinders made locally	Koi	Lower Lake	SE	Gifford and Kroeber 1937:187	
Magnesite cylinders imported ready made from the east	Meteni	Fort Ross	SW	Gifford and Kroeber 1937:187	Called "gold money."

the Wappo of the Middletown region, they to the Lake Miwok of Coyote valley, and the Lake Miwok sold them to the Southeastern Pomo (Gifford 1926:377–378).

Gifford gathered this information in 1919 when he collected census data on *Cigom* (also written as *Shigom*). This evidence reinforces other ethnographic sources that specify that the Coast Miwok did not take payment from others who used the clam beds. The account by Wokox is especially interesting in that he described a very different situation in "ancient" times, when the shells were traded down the line to the beadmakers instead of being directly accessed by them. Gifford and Kroeber (1937:186) stated that the Pomo from Sherwood Valley traded for the shells from the coast, but most other references indicate that the beadmakers carried the shells back themselves (table 23).

Magnesite beads, known as "Indian gold" (McLendon and Lowy 1978:311), also were highly valued in the region. According to Alfred Kroeber (1925:249), magnesite was mined at White Buttes on Cache Creek near Clear Lake; Sally McLendon and Michael Lowy (1978:311) note that the mine was in the Southeastern Pomo region. It is interesting to note that the area near Cache Creek and Lower Lake is where the Southeastern Pomo, the Patwin, and the Lake Miwok territories joined, according to maps in the California volume of the *Handbook of North American Indians* (1978). Some indigenous groups went to the region to mine magnesite themselves, whereas others exported it from the region in both raw form and as finished beads (Gifford and Kroeber 1937:187; table 23).

John Hudson, a medical doctor who arrived in Ukiah in 1889 and married Grace Carpenter the following year, wrote an early account of Pomo bead making in the *Overland Monthly* in 1897 (Hudson in Heizer 1975:15–17) that was probably based primarily on his contacts with Pomoan speakers in Potter Valley, north of Ukiah, where his wife had numerous ties to the local indigenous peoples (McLendon 1993:51). The lengthy process of making the beads from raw magnesite involved several steps. First, the Pomo baked magnesite nodules in a pit for about four hours, causing the white or dull grey color to turn into buff, salmon, or red colors that were often shaded and streaked (Hudson in Heizer 1975:15–17; Kroeber 1925:249). The nodules were then chipped into cylindrical shapes, ground on a slab of stone, and finally drilled using a green chert drill (Stewart 1943:43) attached to a stick that was twirled between the hands. Hudson estimated that it took about 12 hours to shape and drill each stone bead by a "skilled white" laborer (Hudson in Heizer 1975:15–17). This did not include the time required for acquisition and baking of the magnesite. It is noteworthy that no charge was exacted from the people who came to the Clear Lake area to mine the magnesite (table 23). Although the value of the clamshell disk beads (known as "silver" among the Indians of the region) was generally less than that of the magnesite beads, their distance from their source also had a significant effect on their value (Hudson 1897 in Heizer 1975; Kroeber 1925:249).

One question that needs to be considered before these ethnographic sources are interpreted is what effect colonization may have had on beadmaking activities in the region. Kent Lightfoot (2005:149–150) has synthesized what is known about the effects of the exploitation of indigenous laborers in the North Bay region, and has noted that several lethal epidemics occurred there between the late 1810s and the 1830s. Most noteworthy was the smallpox epidemic at Fort Ross in 1838, which spread to the surrounding region and was rumored to have killed off substantial numbers of Indians (Lightfoot 2005:149–150). Epidemics and other effects of colonization may have changed the nature of traditional beadmaking activities, especially in areas where colonial encounters were the most intense, such as the coastal region near Fort Ross. The comment made by Wokox about ancient times, when the shells were traded out from Bodega Bay, is particularly interesting. It implies that the native populations that lived near the clam beds were more active in the exchange process at one time and probably benefited directly from it.

If we turn to the archaeological record, there are some clues that clarify the issue of the precontact manufacturing and trading of beads in north-central California. In a recent publication, Randall Milliken and his colleagues provide a summary of the archaeological evidence for clamshell bead manufacture in the San Francisco Bay region:

> Clam beads were not manufactured in volume on the coast. Some manufacture did occur at Point Reyes (King and Upson 1970:131), but at Bodega Bay, known ethnographically as a collection point for clamshells, only one bead blank and several drills were recovered during controlled-volume sampling at five separate sites (Kennedy 2005). Evidence of a thriving clam disk manufacturing industry does appear on the Santa Rosa plain some 30 kilometers inland (Keswick 1990; Wickstrom 1986), as well as at NAP-539 80 kilometers inland in the Berryessa Valley (Hartzell 1991), and YOL-69 (Wiberg 2005), 115 kilometers inland in the lower Sacramento Valley (Milliken et al. 2007:117).

These archaeological data corroborate many of the ethnographic sources cited (table 23); there is very limited archaeological evidence for clamshell bead manufacture at Bodega Bay, and relatively little evidence elsewhere along the coast. Clamshell disk beads and magnesite cylinder beads appear along with a number of other innovations in the North Bay during the Late 2 Horizon (cal AD 1500 or 1550 to AD 1700) (Milliken et al. 2007:117).

Before we return to the Chumash region, however, I would like to turn first to a discussion of the use of beads in the Bay area and central California. Beads were often used in redistribution, which was common among the Patwin, Pomo, and other north-central California Indian groups. A good description of such redistribution, based on ethnographic accounts, can be found in Vayda's (1967) essay on Pomo trade feasts. During these trade feasts, surpluses of acorns in the fall or of fish in the spring were redistributed between inhabitants of different ecological zones, with shell beads used as the medium of exchange between trading sides. Vayda took a functionalist approach to these feasts, noting that the Pomo lived in an area that was environmentally diverse, and that the trade feasts served to redistribute resource surpluses; they also allowed members of the host group to convert these excess resources into durable wealth—a form of social storage. Since chiefs often took extra or excess portions of the bead strings used in the exchange, they were able to accumulate wealth. This is a classic example of shell beads representing a form of social storage. Lowell Bean and Dorothy Theodoratus, in their summary of information on the Western and Northeastern Pomo, made the following comments about trade:

> In addition to trade feasts, individuals and groups went on trading expeditions, not only to other Pomo groups but also to other tribes. The Central groups acted as middlemen between the Eastern and Northern, and Southern groups in the traffic of foods, manufactured goods, and raw materials. They became the market places for goods and were able to amass greater "wealth" than other groups (Aginsky 1958). By and large this wealth took the form of possession of beads, beads being a sign of position and status. One amassed beads through individual and collective efforts in the context of trading and trade-feasts (Bean and Theodoratus 1978:298).

Beads also figured prominently in burial ceremonies among the Pomo, Patwin, and other north-central California indigenous groups. Milliken et al. (2007:110) note that thousands of beads were buried as mortuary offerings in the San Francisco Bay area during most time periods. One of the most spectacular examples of this was the internment of approximately 30,000 *Olivella* saucer beads with a Middle Horizon 1 burial of a 30-year-old male in the Livermore Valley (ALA-413); this is the largest documented bead lot found in California so far (Milliken et al. 2007:116). Hudson made the following remark many years ago about mortuary practices during the historic period: "Despite the ancient coiner's continued activity, the supply is steadily and rapidly decreasing. The explanation is the lavish devotion bestowed by the Indian upon his dead" (Hudson 1897, in Heizer 1975:20). The adherence to mortuary protocols that had developed over the course of hundreds of years in the region in part drove this remarkable demand for traditional beads. In order to maintain a system that entails this magnitude of bead destruction, intensive bead manufacture is required.

The demand for beads probably fluctuated as a result of social, symbolic, and environmental interactions. Paradoxically, although the traditional practice of making clamshell disk beads persisted after historic contact, the social relationships, trade networks, and technology changed drastically. According to William Henry Holmes, who published an essay entitled "Anthropological Studies in California" in the U.S. National Museum Annual Report for 1900, a Spaniard introduced the pump drill into the Ukiah Valley in the early 1870s (Holmes 1902, in Heizer 1975: 21–23). An early article on bead making, published in 1877 by Lorenzo Yates (in Heizer 1975:5–7) described the use of a pump drill at about this time, thereby providing supporting evidence for its introduction by the 1870s. It is interesting that the foot-powered grinding wheel was not mentioned by Yates; instead a traditional grinding slab was noted as being used. Before this, the Pomo hafted a stone drill to a straight shaft of wood that was twirled between the hands. Once these innovations were introduced, the production of massive quantities of beads became much easier. These innovations, then, served to preserve cultural practices in north-central California: traditional mortuary observations, bead manufacture, trade routes, economic customs, and social networks persisted.

Although the archaeological record is replete with examples of glass beads also being associated with burials in the region (Lightfoot 2005), they were not always accepted as replacements for traditional shell and magnesite beads. Hudson (in Heizer 1975:17–18) collected an intriguing story about an attempt by the Russians to introduce a glass bead similar in appearance to the magnesite cylinder beads. It was reported that the indigenous people not only rejected these "counterfeit" beads, but viewed them as evil. "Tradition confirms the record with added details of how three Russian traders of *charlil kol* (devil's beads) [the glass beads that resembled magnesite cylinders] were taken unawares and their heads burnt with the beads" (Hudson 1897, in Heizer 1975:17–18).

I think it is worthwhile asking why the Pomo placed such an emphasis on beads during the early historic period that they carried heavy baskets filled with clam shells over long distances, sometimes 85 miles or more. In part, it was so that they could continue to follow their traditional spiritual beliefs and maintain their economic and social relationships. But why did they go to such great efforts? Pomoan speakers, at least in some regions, shunned the use of glass beads; their behavior during this early historic period defies easy explanations, including those stemming from such recent theoretical approaches as human behavioral ecology, a perspective grounded in neo-Darwinian principles (Kennett 2005:11).

In addition, other questions come to mind. Was this behavior adaptive? What were the bead-making activities in north-central California like prior to contact with Europeans? Did they always haul the shells inland to make beads, or did the north-central California indigenous people use the water routes in the Miwok region to transport heavy goods such as clam shells? Did the people who once inhabited the regions where significant sources of bead-making materials were found once take a more active role in the process of bead-making? Did they gain economically or socially from this industry? Did chiefs and other people in powerful positions gain from the process in the pre-contact period, as they apparently did during post-contact times? Were the *Olivella* saucers so common in the Middle Period in north-central California (and so similar to the *Olivella* saucers in the Chumash region) traded from the Chumash region to north-central California, or were they made more locally? Was the distribution of beads subject to redistribution and chiefly involvement more frequently in north-central California than was the case in southern California, as King (1978) suggested? Although these and many more questions relevant to indigenous economic practices have not yet been answered, more data have become available in the last 25 years, which in turn allowed us to formulate and at least partially address these questions.

COMMONALITIES AND DIFFERENCES

We can currently affirm that the Patwin and Pomo shared many traits with the Chumash; these would include the ability to acquire large quantities of food, some of which could be stored for a period of years; the existence of hereditary chiefly power, secret societies with restricted membership, and trade feasts marked by redistribution; the use of shell beads as money; the burial of wealth at funerals; a heavy reliance on wealth finance; and densely populated settlements. However, there are a number of significant differences between the Chumash and Patwin/Pomo. Religious practices in north-central California were apparently more complexly organized than those of the Chumash, as reflected in the three levels of secret societies found among the River Patwin. The Pomo and Patwin also had more substantial structures used for religious purposes, such as the large, earth-covered dance houses, which required a considerable amount of effort and resources to build.

However, one of the most significant differences between the two areas involved the technology associated with the capture of fish. Although both regions relied heavily on fish, the Patwin techniques for capturing them entailed a group effort that required coordination by the chief. If a weir was built too early in the season, or used for too long, it could have severely affected groups living upstream who relied on the spawning fish for subsistence. The building of the weir next to one of the major towns along the Sacramento River was not a solitary effort or even one that could have been completed by a few individuals. Instead, it required a major labor investment that had to be coordinated by a strong leader. Nothing quite comparable existed among the Chumash. The Chumash had the plank canoe, but the building of the watercraft did not normally involve a large labor force.

Another significant difference between north-central California native peoples and the Chumash involved their exchange systems. King (1978) has proposed that the Chumash use of shell beads was more monetized than it was among the north-central groups in California, in that shell bead types requiring a smaller investment of labor were utilized. He has suggested that the societies in north-central California had economic systems that were both political and monetized, and implied that there was a greater reliance on redistribution for economic transactions in that region. Although the Pomo were a coastal group, exchange along the coast was very different from that found among the Chumash, in part because there were no offshore islands that were inhabited year round. The Patwin were not a coastal group and there were, of course, no offshore islands where people made and traded shell beads. This, and the centrality of the plank canoe in the Chumash exchange system, created a very different set of parameters in the exchange system of the Chumash compared with that present in north-central California. A cursory comparison suggests that the Pomo and Patwin may have relied on network power like the Chumash, but perhaps also emphasized corporate power more during the Late Period.

It should be noted that there are many problems inherent in the use of ethnographic and ethnohistoric information involving the Pomo and Patwin. Significant changes may have occurred after European contact.

Marquardt (2001), for example, has proposed that the historic Calusa of Florida may have differed greatly from the precontact Calusa, and has suggested that hierarchy, tribute, and political power may have become much more complex after the Spanish invasion as a consequence of that profound impact. This may have also been the case with the Patwin and the Pomo. Without a more detailed analysis, such as the one I have presented here for the Chumash, it is difficult to fully assess the precise nature of Patwin sociopolitical organization and of Pomo economics. Nevertheless, a comparison of the Patwin, Pomo, Yokuts, and other complex California hunter-gatherer societies with the Chumash would undoubtedly help to clarify the nature of power and complexity in both areas.

The emergence of sociopolitical complexity among the Chumash has received much greater theoretical scrutiny in the last twenty years than that afforded many other indigenous groups in California. This is true despite the fact that several groups in California, including the Pomo, the Patwin, and the Yokuts, had levels of sociopolitical and/or economic complexity similar to that achieved by the Chumash. That complexity becomes of even greater interest if we also consider the very different ecological, cultural, and geographical contexts in these regions. As we amass more archaeological data, we can begin to move from a rather focused analysis of sites to syntheses of large regions, and then hopefully to cross-cultural comparisons.

One commonality among the Chumash, Pomo, Patwin, Yokuts, Yurok, and other groups in California was their reliance on shell beads. Chester King (1990a), and James Bennyhoff and Richard Hughes (1987), among others, have demonstrated that shell beads were used and buried with the dead in California for over 5000 years. Although shell beads have been used in many other parts of the world, the amount of energy invested in their manufacture and use in California was perhaps greater than that expended by any other hunter-gatherers in the world. The reasons for this phenomenon are well worth further investigation. The time and energy spent in the production and pursuit of beads could have been invested in other activities, such as the construction of monumental architecture. However, such was not the case. Instead, extensive trade networks were developed. In north-central California, where redistribution may have been emphasized more than in southern California, chiefs figured prominently in these networks. Strategic locations related to the movements and exchanges of beads undoubtedly were also an important variable in these trade networks. For example, individual Pomo noted on a couple of occasions that the trip to the coast to collect clam shells was dangerous because of the existence of hostile tribes along the route.

Future Studies of Complex Hunter-Gatherers

In summary, I suggest that in both north-central California and in the Chumash region, these networks were highly valued and guarded. Beads were an important symbolic element in burial rituals, and were vital in establishing, maintaining, and marking the social status of chiefs and other elites; perhaps even more significantly, they were an integral part of subsistence practices, and were vital to the associated maintenance of relatively dense populations in regions where environmental diversity and fluctuations were relatively common. Beads, in fact, were inextricably intertwined with all aspects of social life among these groups. Beads were a cornerstone of the secret religious organizations of the Patwin, Pomo, and Chumash—only individuals who possessed adequate wealth in the form of shell-bead currency were accepted into these societies. Eventually, initiates learned a special language that was only understood by other members of these socially restrictive organizations. Beads were used in displays during ceremonies and at other times as signifiers of wealth and power. They were used to show respect for the dead and to help those who had departed on their journey to the other world. Beads were sacrificed in ceremonial hearths and in sacred places to recognize the power inherent in these spaces and events and to elicit favorable results in future activities. Beads were used in exchanges of resources, especially in regions where such resources were not evenly distributed in either time or place. They were used to purchase fancy cooking and serving vessels, special foods, and ceremonial regalia, and were often exhibited during feasts. They were used to pay entertainers and others who were involved with feasts or other ceremonial or public activities. Beads were used to settle debts, pay for labor, and—in the case of the Yurok and other northwest coast groups—to buy a wife. In other words, beads were vital to the maintenance of many different kinds of social relationships in California Indian societies, and in fact played a critical role throughout the religious, political, and economic realms. Beads were a material manifestation of the networks that were integral to indigenous societies in California. It is no wonder that chiefs, elites, traders, and others carefully guarded and maintained the exchange networks, settlement locations, and methods of transportation that were critical to these different realms. Battles were waged and lives were lost over them. Even after Europeans drastically disrupted the traditional lives of people in indigenous societies, the California Indians persisted in producing and exchanging beads, in an attempt to maintain their traditional networks.

In closing, I would like to see scholarly research on complex hunter-gatherers go beyond the environmental explanations that have been emphasized to date, and instead—through the use of cross-cultural comparisons and other methods of anthropological investigation—attempt to understand better the cultural practices that developed over centuries in these societies.

Notes

Chapter 1

1. The term 'town' is used throughout this book in accordance with Webster's definition: "A compactly settled area as distinguished from surrounding rural territory." I realize that the term town is used to denote much larger settlements by archaeologists working in other parts of the world.

2. Two-spirit is synonymous with the term 'berdache,' which is not used here because of its negative connotations. Two-spirit can refer to a third gender or a person who dresses and behaves like a member of the opposite sex.

Chapter 2

3. Rivera, the military governor of California, apparently referred to only the island when he described Mescalitan Island on April 24, 1776, just two months after Font visited the area: "I passed near the place called Mezcaltitlan by the soldiers. It is the part of the Santa Barbara Channel that is most populous. It is an island town and the two other towns are in sight and the three are adjacent." (This translation was provided by Chester King, personal communication 1991.) John Johnson (personal communication 1995) has a somewhat different translation, which gives a slightly different interpretation of this important sentence: "There is an isolated town and two others in view and the three are contiguous." If Rivera was referring to *Helo'* when he commented that it was the part of the Santa Barbara Channel that is most populous, then he appears to contradict the comments made by Font, also in 1776. Johnson states in a recent ethnohistory on *Helo'* that *S'axpilil*, rather than *Helo'*, came to be synonymous with the name Mescaltitlán during mission times (1990:2–4). It is not clear exactly when the name Mescaltitlán actually came to be used to refer to an area besides *Helo'* and the island itself.

4. The first of these maps was discovered at the Santa Barbara Airport archives, the second at the Goleta Sanitary District map room, and the third was found

over a year later in files pertaining to Orr's (n.d.) 1941 excavations at Mescalitan Island housed at the Santa Barbara Museum of Natural History (File # (D)NA-CA-46-9). The third map provided topographic information on the western portion of the island, the portion that was missing in the first two maps.

5. Fages is referring to his description of the Indians near San Gabriel. In this account, he mentions the following animals: "Besides deer, antelope (which is a kind of mountain goat), coyote, wolf, fox, cony, hare, squirrel, and skunk, there is here another land animal just like a suckling pig, which they call *mantugar* and the flesh of which they eat, just as they do that of the other animals mentioned" (Priestley 1972:22).

Chapter 4

6. Coastal settlements to the north of *Noqto* are not included in this discussion because they lie outside the Santa Barbara Channel region. It could be argued that *Noqto* and *Shilimaqshtush* lie outside the Santa Barbara Channel because they are situated north of Point Conception. I have included both in this discussion because their inhabitants were actively involved in the exchange system in the Santa Barbara Channel region and Crespí identified both as Santa Barbara Channel settlements.

7. The place names in parentheses are alternative spellings.

8. Many marriage ties between *Helo'* and *S'axpilil* were noted by Johnson (1988, 1990) in the mission records.

9. According to the American Heritage Dictionary of the English Language, Fourth Edition (2000), this is "a unit of weight in the U.S. Customary System equal to 100 pounds (45.36 kilograms)."

Chapter 5

10. See also Hudson and Blackburn (1986:51), who believe that this may be referring to a dance area.

11. This evidence for separate cemeteries for men and women is not borne out by recent studies of human remains from Chumash cemeteries.

12. The ethnographic reference for the use of this structure is from one of Harrington's Kintanemuk consultants, Magdelena Olivos. It is assumed that the Chumash also used this structure, although there are no direct references to the Chumash use of a male puberty hut.

13. A drawing in Hudson and Blackburn (1986:Figure 301-1) indicates that four posts and a ladder pole were situated near the perimeter of the structure.

14. A portico or colonnade is defined as a series of columns set at regular intervals. The reference to porticos indicates that there were probably posts in the interior of the sweatlodges.

15. In Harrington's review of houses, he does not give the diameter of the larger houses.

16. There is a contradictory statement in another document of Harrington's at the National Anthropological Archives in Washington. This was to be published under the title "Life and Manufactures of the Santa Barbara Mission Indians" in a pamphlet by A. P. Ousdal, entitled "Geology and Archaeology of the Santa Barbara Region." In this article, Harrington states that the fireplace was toward the door from the center of the house. He also comments that cooking occurred on outdoor fires.

17. Kelsey (1998) believes that Santa Catalina Island is the island referred to, not San Miguel Island. Santa Catalina Island was occupied by the Gabrielino/Tongva at this time.

18. This is how Wagner's translation reads; however, in a footnote, Wagner commented: "The 'no' seems from the context to be an error, but some of the Channel Island Indians are said to have had a kind of bed or bunk, so perhaps this bald statement is as originally reported by Cabrillo" (Wagner 1929:336). In the Bolton translation, the text reads: "They sleep on the ground" (Bolton 1916:34). There is no footnote or explanation as to why this passage was translated in this manner by Bolton.

19. Dugouts refer to house depressions.

20. This identification is unclear. It is possible that this village was on Santa Catalina Island.

21. This was probably a feathered pole.

22. Twenty yards refers to Spanish yards; these 20 yards equate to about 54 or 55 feet (16.5 or 16.8 m) (Brown 1967:4).

23. The criteria that Bowers used to distinguish house sites from the remains of other structures are not entirely clear.

24. The enclosures that Bowers observed were somewhat unusual, particularly the larger one, which he interpreted as an area probably used for games or religious rites (Benson 1982:166–167). This larger enclosure is probably a natural landform (John Johnson, personal communication, 2005).

25. Tainter mapped some structures at SBA-865, although he did not discuss them (Tainter 1971:50).

26. Perhaps Bowers meant outlined instead of paved, since the boulders were set on edge.

27. Claude Warren and Tom King conducted excavations at this site in the 1960s. During their excavations, they encountered a small structure with a feature in the center. The results of these excavations were not reported at the time, but a master's thesis by a student that worked with Warren was completed in 1992 (DuBarton 1992).

28. In a 1966 letter written to Donald Miller by Leif Landberg, Landberg commented that a "deer rib sweat scraper" was found in this structure. I have found no further documentation of the presence of this artifact in the "*temescal*." Strigils or sweat scrapers were used inside sweatlodges to scrape perspiration from the skin (Hudson and Blackburn 1986:107–109). Landberg also commented that the structural remains identified as a "*temescal*" were totally different from the rest of the house types at Muwu, according to Woodward (1932).

29. The notes used for this section were obtained from Patricia Martz. Her copy was transcribed from microfilm on file at the Smithsonian Institute (Ms. 6042-Archaeology of California). Most of the photographs from the site are available from the Los Angeles County Museum of Natural History, although one was obtained from Jeff Rigby, who acquired photographs from Woodward when he was residing in Patagonia, Arizona.

30. Lathrap and Hoover's descriptions of the features found at the site are confusing and difficult to follow, probably in part because the monograph on this site was published twenty-five years after the completion of excavations (Glassow 1980). Nevertheless, the features that were recorded are some of the best examples of storage facilities along the Santa Barbara Channel coast.

31. The site is situated on a Holocene sand dune complex (Rockwell and Gamble 1990).

32. The excavations of the site were part of a cultural resource mitigation program. The UCSB archaeologists had agreed to excavate the areas of the site that were slated for destruction. Because of this agreement, only portions of the floors were excavated. The one-meter unit in the floor area was excavated through the floor (see figure 18). After careful examination, the team realized that it had inadvertently removed a compacted clay floor.

33. Because some of the squares were not processed (figure 20), the remaining squares were left with unknown values. The unknown values for each class of cultural remains were given an expected value based on the values of the adjacent cells. The cells that were diagonally adjacent to the cells with the unknown value were not included in this analysis. The average of the adjacent cells was computed and this average was used as the expected value. This decision was made under the assumption that the unknown amount would be most similar to those in the physically nearest squares. If no floor was present in the adjacent square, then an expected value was not assigned.

34. The minimum column in table 12 indicates that non-fish bone was the only class of remains that was not present in every square and the maximum column indicates that there was not an abundance of non-fish bone in any of the squares, but there was an abundance of shell in at least one of the squares. The mean values indicate that there was a considerable amount of shell by weight compared to the bone or charcoal. It is possible that the variation in the shell and the other cultural remains is affected by the fact that different amounts of soil were processed in different areas of the floor.

35. The variance-mean ratio (or the Poisson method) and the problems with this statistic are discussed at length by Carr (1984:140–144). Despite Carr's criticisms, I thought it would be helpful to present this statistic in my analysis and to remain consistent with Spencer and Flannery's analysis (1986:331–333).

36. Errors resulting from non-standardized recovery, or from catalogue errors, could cause non-random distributions, or clustered distributions that are not real patterns.

37. Only a sample of flakes was pulled during the sorting process; therefore, the counts of flakes in the 8-mesh and 16-mesh per inch were adjusted to reflect the expected amount if all of them were sorted (for a more complete explanation

of the sampling procedures, see Gamble 1991:199–206). The counts of beads and otoliths in the 8-mesh per inch and 16-mesh per inch sizes did not require adjustments because all residues in these size categories were scanned for these classes of artifacts.

38. A more thorough discussion and additional maps can be found in Gamble 1991:366–380.

39. Aggregates are clumps of a single type of pollen. Cummings (1991) suggests that the presence of aggregates probably indicates that a portion of the plant was introduced into the archaeological setting.

40. This is considerably different than at the village of *Talepop*, which was also historic, but located in the Santa Monica Mountains. *Talepop* had evidence of fairly intensive point production (Gamble 1982).

41. Cow-bone fishhooks indicate a later historic occupation of the site; therefore this hook is most likely intrusive, since Floor 2 was used prior to this time.

42. The beads from both floors indicate that Structure 1 may have been built almost immediately after the abandonment of Structure 2. In all likelihood, not enough time elapsed between the abandonment of Structure 2 and the construction of Structure 1 for the infrastructure of Structure 2 to have naturally collapsed and decomposed.

43. There is also evidence that structures became smaller in the historic period in the overlapping house depressions at *Muwu* (see chapter 5): the smaller house was from the later historic occupation.

Chapter 6

44. Poaceae was formerly known as Gramineae. Cummings used the term Gramineae in her 1991 report. I have chosen to use the more recent nomenclature of Poaceae.

45. I examined collections at the Smithsonian Institution associated with the Yarrow expedition's excavations at La Patera, and much of the information here is taken from my notes on the artifacts from the historic cemetery at Mescalitan Island.

46. The term "La Patera," which refers to Goleta, was used in this context to refer to three cemeteries excavated in the Goleta area. Two of these were on T. Wallace More's ranch, on the western side of the Goleta Slough (Putnam et al. 1879), where Yarrow and his team conducted limited excavations. One of these cemeteries was historic. Most of the artifacts that were labeled "La Patera" were from the historic cemetery on Mescalitan Island, when *Helo'* was occupied.

Chapter 7

47. The historic cemetery had 140 burials; however, for some of the analyses, only 112 burials were used in the sample because the rest were too fragmentary or disturbed to determine age or sex, lacked detailed provenience information, or were too fragmentary or disturbed to determine if they had grave associations (Gamble et al. 2001).

48. From Yarrow's (Putnam 1879) and Bower's notes (Benson 1982:55–56), the Yarrow expedition excavated a total of ten days in the historic cemetery on Mescalitan Island, and apparently less than a day when they returned to this first historic cemetery near More's house (Putnam 1879:40). In summary, less than two days were spent in excavations at the historic cemetery near More's Ranch.

49. It is not clear if this was a whole canoe or part of one.

50. I have used Hoover's transcriptions of Olson's notes. The diagram he drew with the planks appeared to be associated with the burial associated with the adze, although his notes are somewhat unclear.

51. Many Chumash towns probably had shrine sites associated with them.

Chapter 8

52. The term *ponco* or *ponko* is a Gabrieleño term used for a certain measured amount of beads (Kroeber 1925:565).

53. Blackburn (1976:231) notes that "an important Ventureño fiesta, for example, might be attended by sizeable numbers of people from as far west as Gaviota or the Santa Ynez Valley, as far east as Malibu or the San Fernando Valley, and as far north as Tejon, while performances by Yokuts dancers were not uncommon on such occasions."

54. *Momoy* is the Chumash word for Jimsonweed (*Datura wrightii*), used as a hallucinogen by the Chumash.

Chapter 9

55. Warfare is defined here as a state of armed hostility (see Lambert 2002:209).

56. The term *siliyik* is also used for the ceremonial enclosure that was erected on the dance grounds during ceremonies. See chapter 5 for a more thorough description.

References

Abbott, C.C.

1879. Textile Fabrics, Basket-Work, etc. In *Geographical Surveys West of the One Hundredth Meridian, in charge of George M. Wheeler*, edited by Frederick W. Putnam, pp. 239–250. Government Printing Office, Washington, D.C.

Allan, Robert J.

2000. ENSO and Climate Variability in the Past 150 Years. In *El Niño and the Southern Oscillation*, edited by Henry F. Diaz and Vera Markgraf, pp. 3–55. Cambridge University Press, Cambridge.

Allen, Mark W.

2006. Transformations in Maori Warfare: Tao, Pa, and Pu. In *The Archaeology of Warfare: Prehistories of Raiding and Conquest*, edited by Elizabeth N. Arkush and Mark W. Allen, pp. 184–213. University Press of Florida, Gainesville.

Allen, Mark W. and Elizabeth N. Arkush

2006. Introduction: Archaeology and the Study of War. In *The Archaeology of Warfare: Prehistories of Raiding and Conquest*, edited by Elizabeth N. Arkush and Mark W. Allen, pp. 1–19. University Press of Florida, Gainesville.

Ames, Kenneth M.

1994. The Northwest Coast: Complex Hunter-Gatherers, Ecology, and Social Evolution. *Annual Reviews of Anthropology* 23:209–229.

1995. Chiefly Power and Household Production on the Northwest Coast. In *Foundations of Social Inequality*, edited by T. Douglas Price and Gary M. Feinman, pp. 155–187. Plenum Press, New York.

Ames, Kenneth M. and Herbert D.G. Maschner

1999. *Peoples of the Northwest Coast: Their Archaeology and Prehistory.* Thames and Hudson, London.

Anakouchine, Natalie

1990. Mescalitan Island Fauna (Exclusive of Fish, Shellfish, and Bird). In *Archaeological Investigations at Helo' on Mescalitan Island*, edited by Lynn Gamble, pp. 15-1 to 15-15. Department of Anthropology, University of California, Santa Barbara.

Anderson, Kat

1993. Native Californians as Ancient and Contemporary Cultivators. In *Before the Wilderness: Environmental Management by Native Californians*, compiled and edited by Thomas C. Blackburn and Kat Anderson, pp. 151–174. Ballena Press, Menlo Park.

2005. *Tending the Wild: Native American Knowledge and the Management of California's Natural Resources.* University of California Press, Berkeley.

Applegate, Richard

1975. An Index of Chumash Placenames. Papers on the Chumash. *San Luis Obispo Archaeological Society Occasional Paper* 9:21–46.

Arnold, Jeanne E.

1987. *Craft Specialization in the Prehistoric Channel Islands, California.* University of California Publications in Anthropology, Volume 18. University of California Press, Berkeley.

1990. An Archaeological Perspective on the Historic Settlement Pattern on Santa Cruz Island. *Journal of California and Great Basin Anthropology* 12(1):112–127.

1992a. Complex Hunter-Gatherer-Fishers of Prehistoric California: Chiefs, Specialists, and Maritime Adaptations of the Channel Islands. *American Antiquity* 57:60–84.

1992b. Cultural Disruption and the Political Economy in Channel Islands Prehistory. *Essays on the Prehistory of Maritime California*, edited by Terry L. Jones, pp. 129–146. Center for Archaeological Research, University of California, Davis.

1995. Social Inequality, Marginalization, and Economic Process. In *Foundations of Social Inequality*, edited by T. Douglas Price and Gary M. Feinman, pp. 87–103. Plenum Press, New York.

2001a. Social Evolution and the Political Economy in the Northern Channel Islands. In *The Origins of a Pacific Coast Chiefdom: The Chumash of the Channel Islands*, edited by J. E. Arnold, pp. 287–296. University of Utah Press, Salt Lake City.

2001b. The Chumash in World and Regional Perspectives. In *The Origins of a Pacific Coast Chiefdom: The Chumash of the Channel Islands*, edited by J. E. Arnold, pp. 1–19. University of Utah Press, Salt Lake City.

2001c. The Channel Islands Project: History, Objectives and Methods. In *The Origins of a Pacific Coast Chiefdom: The Chumash of the Channel Islands*, edited by Jeanne E. Arnold, pp. 21–52. University of Utah Press, Salt Lake City.

Arnold, J. E. and A. P. Graesch

2001. The Evolution of Specialized Shellworking among the Island Chumash. In *The Origins of a Pacific Coast Chiefdom: The Chumash of the Channel Islands*, edited by J. E. Arnold, pp. 71–112. University of Utah Press, Salt Lake City.

Arnold, J. E. and A. Munns

1994. Independent of Attached Specialization: The Organization of Shell Bead Production in California. *Journal of Field Archaeology* 21(4):473–489.

Arnold, Jeanne E., Amy M. Preziosi and Paul Shattuck

2001. Flaked Stone Craft Production and Exchange in Island Chumash Territory. In *The Origins of a Pacific Coast Chiefdom: The Chumash of the Channel Islands*, edited by J. E. Arnold, pp. 113–131. University of Utah Press, Salt Lake City.

Arnold, J. E. and B. Tissot

1993. Measurement of Significant Marine Paleotemperature Variation Using Black Abalone Shells from Prehistoric Middens. *Quaternary Research* 39:390–394.

Arnold, Jeanne E., Michael R. Walsh and Sandra E. Hollimon

2004. The Archaeology of California. *Journal of Archaeological Research* 12(1):1–73.

Bamforth, Douglas B.

1990. The Flaked Stone Assemblage from SBA-46. In *Archaeological Investigations at Helo' on Mescalitan Island*, edited by Lynn Gamble, pp. 10-1 to 10-115. Department of Anthropology, University of California, Santa Barbara.

1993. Stone Tools, Steel Tools: Contact Period Household Technology at Helo'. In *Ethnohistory and Archaeology: Approaches in Postcontact Change in the Americas*, edited by J. Daniel Rogers and Samuel M. Wilson, pp. 49–72. Plenum Press, New York.

Bean, Lowell John

1976. Social Organization in Native California. In *Native Californians: A Theoretical Retrospective*, edited by Lowell John Bean and Thomas C. Blackburn, pp. 99–123. Ballena Press, Menlo Park.

1978. Social Organization. In *Handbook of North American Indians, Vol. 8, California*, edited by Robert F. Heizer, pp. 673–682. Smithsonian Institution, Washington, D.C.

Bean, Lowell John and Harry Lawton

1976. Some Explanations for the Rise of Cultural Complexity in Native California with Comments on Proto-Agriculture and Agriculture. In *Native Californians: A Theoretical Retrospective*, edited by Lowell John Bean and Thomas C. Blackburn, pp. 19–48. Ballena Press, Menlo Park.

Bean, Lowell John and Katherine Siva Saubel

1972. *Temalpakh: Cahuilla Indian Knowledge and Usage of Plants.* Malki Museum Press, Banning, CA.

Bean, Lowell John and Sylvia Brakke Vane

1978. Cults and Their Transformations. In *Handbook of North American Indians, Vol. 8, California*, edited by Robert F. Heizer, pp. 662–672. Smithsonian Institution, Washington, D.C.

Bean, Lowell John and Dorothea Theodoratus

1978. Western Pomo and Northeastern Pomo. In *Handbook of North American Indians, Vol. 8, California*, edited by Robert F. Heizer, pp. 289–305. Smithsonian Institution, Washington, D.C.

Beaton, John M.

1991. Extensification and Intensification in Central California Prehistory. *Antiquity* 65:946–952.

Beebe, Rose Marie and Robert M. Sencewicz (editors)

2001. *Lands of Promise and Despair: Chronicles of Early California, 1535–1846*. Heyday Books, Berkeley.

Bennyhoff, James A.

1950. California Fish Spears and Harpoons. *University of California Anthropological Records* 9(4):295–338. Berkeley.

Bennyhoff, James A. and Richard E. Hughes

1987. Shell Bead and Ornament Exchange Networks between California and the Western Great Basin. *Anthropological Papers of the American Museum of Natural History* 64:2. The American Museum of Natural History, New York.

Benson, Arlene Svea

1997. *The Noontide Sun: The Field Notes and Unpublished Manuscripts of the Reverend Stephen Bowers, Pioneer California Archaeologist.* Ballena Press, Menlo Park.

Bernard, Julienne

2004. Status and the Swordfish: The Origins of Large-Species Fishing among the Chumash. In *Perspectives in California Archaeology, Vol. 7, Foundations in Chumash Society*, edited by Jeanne E. Arnold, pp. 25–51. Cotsen Institute of Archaeology, University of California, Los Angeles.

Bickford, Virginia

1982. *European Artifacts from a Chumash Cemetery, CA-LAN-264*. Unpublished Masters Thesis, Department of Anthropology, California State University, Long Beach.

Blackburn, Thomas C.

1975. *December's Child: A Book of Chumash Oral Narratives.* University of California Press, Berkeley.

1976. Ceremonial Integration and Social Interaction in Aboriginal California. In *Native Californians: A Theoretical Retrospective*, edited by Lowell J. Bean and Thomas C. Blackburn, pp. 225–244. Ballena Press, Ramona.

Blackburn, Thomas C. and Kat Anderson

1993. Introduction: Managing the Domesticated Environment. In *Before the Wilderness: Environmental Management by Native Californians*, compiled and edited by Thomas C. Blackburn and Kat Anderson, pp. 15–25. Ballena Press, Menlo Park.

Blanton, Richard E., Gary M. Feinman, Stephen A. Kowalewski and Peter N. Peregrine

1996. A Dual Processual Theory for the Evolution of Mesoamerican Civilization. *Current Anthropology* 37(1):1–14.

Blick, J.

1988. Genocidal Warfare in Tribal Societies as a Result of European-Induced Culture Conflict. *Man* 23:654–670.

Bloomer, William W.

1982. Analysis of Shellfish Remains at LAN-229. In *Archaeological Investigations at Talepop, (LAN-229)*, by Chester King, William W. Bloomer, Eric Clingen, Bob E. Edberg, Lynn H. Gamble, Julia E. Hammett, John R. Johnson, Truus H. Kemperman, Christopher D. Pierce, and Eric Wohlgemuth, pp. 10-1 to 10-57. Office of Public Archaeology, University of California, Santa Barbara.

Bohannan, Paul

1963. *Social Anthropology*. Holt, Rinehart and Winston, Inc., New York.

Bolton, Herbert E.

1916. *Spanish Explorations in the Southwest*, 1542–1706. Scribner's, New York.

1927. *Fray Juan Crespí. Missionary Explorer on the Pacific Coast 1769–1774*. University of California Press, Berkeley.

1930. *Anza's California Expeditions*. University of California Press, Berkeley.

1931. *Font's Complete Diary: A Chronicle of the Founding of San Francisco*. University of California Press, Berkeley.

Braje, Todd J., Jon M. Erlandson and Jan Timbrook

2005. An Asphaltum Coiled Basket Impression, Tarring Pebbles, and Middle Holocene Water Bottles from San Miguel Island, California. *Journal of California and Great Basin Anthropology* 25:207–213.

Brandoff, Joan

1980. *Plant Foods of the Goleta Slough*. Manuscript on file, Department of Anthropology, University of California, Santa Barbara.

Brown, Alan K.

1967. The Aboriginal Population of the Santa Barbara Channel. *University of California Archaeological Survey Reports* 69:1–99. Berkeley.

Brown, Alan K., Editor and Translator

2001. *A Description of Distant Roads: Original Journals of the First Expedition into California, 1769–1770 by Juan Crespi.* San Diego State University Press, San Diego.

Brumfiel, Elizabeth M.

1994. Factional Competition and Political Development in the New World: An Introduction. *Factional Competition and Political Development in the New World*, edited by Elizabeth M. Brumfiel and John W. Fox, pp. 3–13. Cambridge University Press, Cambridge.

Brumfiel, Elizabeth M. and Timothy K. Earle

1987. Specialization, Exchange, and Complex Societies: An Introduction. In *Specialization, Exchange, and Complex Societies.* Edited by Elizabeth M. Brumfiel and Timothy K. Earle, pp. 1–9. Cambridge University Press, Cambridge.

Bryan, Bruce

1931. Excavations at Mishopsnow. *Art and Archaeology.* 33(3):176–185.

Burnett, E. K.

1944. *Inlaid Stone and Bone Artifacts from Southern California.* Contributions from the Museum of the American Indian Heye Foundation, Vol. XIII. New York: Museum of the American Indian Heye Foundation.

Carneiro, Robert L.

1990. Chiefdom Level Warfare as Exemplified in Fiji and Cauca Valley. In *The Anthropology of Warfare*, edited by Jonathan Hass, pp. 190–211. Cambridge University Press, Cambridge.

Carr, Christopher

1984. The Nature of Organization of Intrasite Archaeological Records and Spatial Analytic Approaches to their Investigation. In *Advances in Archaeological Method and Theory*, Volume 7, edited by M. B. Schiffer, pp. 103–222. Academic Press, Orlando.

Chartkoff, Joseph L., and Kerry K. Chartkoff

1984. *The Archaeology of California.* Stanford University Press, Stanford.

Clay, Vickie L. and Kevin J. Peter

1985. Stratigraphy, Disturbance Processes, and Cultural Deposits. In *SBA-46 Test Program, Vol. II*, edited by Scientific Resource Surveys, Inc., pp. 129–202. Prepared for Goleta Sanitary District and Brown and Caldwell.

Coleman, Chris D. and Karen Wise

1994. Archaeological Field Research by Los Angeles Museum: Channel Islands Biological Survey 1939–1941. In *The Fourth California Symposium: Update on the Status of Resources*, edited by W.L. Halvorson and G.J. Maender, pp. 183–191. Santa Barbara Museum of Natural History, Santa Barbara.

Colten, Roger H.

1993. *Prehistoric Subsistence, Specialization, and Economy in a Southern California Chiefdom.* Unpublished Ph.D. Dissertation, Department of Anthropology, University of California, Los Angeles.

1995. Faunal Exploitation during the Middle to Late Period Transition on Santa Cruz Island, California. *Journal of California and Great Basin Anthropology* 17:93–120.

2002. Prehistoric Marine Mammal Hunting in Context: Two Western North American Examples. *International Journal of Osteoarchaeology* 12(1):12–22.

Colten, Roger H. and Jeanne E. Arnold

1998. Prehistoric Marine Mammal Hunting on California's Northern Channel Islands. *American Antiquity* 63:679–701.

Conlee, C. A.

2000. Intensified Middle Period Ground Stone Production on San Miguel Island. *Journal of California and Great Basin Anthropology* 22(2):374–391.

Cook, Sherburne F.

1960. *Colonial Expeditions to the Interior of California: Central Valley, 1800–1820*, University of California Press, Berkeley and Los Angeles.

1976. *The Population of the California Indians 1769–1770*. University of California Press, Berkeley and Los Angeles.

Cook, Sherburne F. and Robert F. Heizer

1965. The Quantitative Approach to the Relation Between Population and Settlement Size. *Reports of the University of California Archaeological Survey* 64. Berkeley.

Corbett, Ray

1999. *Chumash Bone Whistles: The Development and Elaboration of Ritual Activity and Ceremonial Integration in Chumash Society.* Unpublished Master's Thesis, Department of Anthropology, University of California, Los Angeles.

2004. Chumash Bone Whistles: The Development of Ceremonial Integration in Chumash Society. In *Perspectives in California Archaeology, Vol. 7, Foundations of Chumash Society*, edited by Jeanne E. Arnold, pp. 65–73. Cotsen Institute of Archaeology, University of California, Los Angeles.

Costin, Cathy Lynne

2001. Craft Production Systems. In *Archaeology at the Millenium: A Sourcebook*, edited by Gary M. Feinman and T. Douglas Price, pp. 273–327. Kluwer Academic/ Plenum Publishers, New York.

Craig, Steve

1966. Ethnographic Notes on the Construction of Ventureño Chumash Baskets: From the Ethnographic and Linguistic Field Notes of John P. Harrington. In *Annual Reports of the University of California Archaeological Survey* 8:197–214. Los Angeles.

1967. The Basketry of the Ventureño Chumash. In *Annual Reports of the University of California Archaeological Survey* 9:78–149. Los Angeles.

Crosby, Harry

2003. *Gateway to Alta California: The Expedition to San Diego, 1769*. Sunbelt Publications, San Diego.

Cummings, Linda Scott

1991. Pollen Analysis of a Floor at CA-SBA-46 (Mescalitan Island), Santa Barbara, California (Appendix 1). In *Organization of Activities at the Historic Settlement of Helo': A Chumash Political, Economic, and Religious Center.* Ph.D. dissertation, by Lynn Gamble. University of California, Santa Barbara.

Curtis, F.

1959. *Arroyo Sequit: Archaeological Investigation of a Late Coastal Site in Los Angeles County, California.* Paper no. 4, Archaeological Survey Association of Southern California.

1963. Arroyo Sequit, LAN-52: Archaeological investigations in Leo Carillo Beach State Park, Los Angeles Co., California. *Archaeological Report No. 9*. Sacramento: California Department of Parks and Recreation, Division of Beaches and Parks.

Dalton, George

1965. Primitive Money. *American Anthropologist* 67:44–65.

D'Altroy, Terence N. and Timothy K. Earle

1985. Staple Finance, Wealth Finance, and Storage in the Inka Political Economy. *Current Anthropology* 26(2):187–206.

Davenport, Demorest, John R. Johnson and Jan Timbrook

1993. The Chumash and the Swordfish. *Antiquity* 67:257–272.

Dawson, Lawrence and James Deetz

1965. A Corpus of Chumash Basketry. In *Annual Reports of the University of California Archaeological Survey* 7:193–275. Los Angeles.

Denardo, Carole

1990. Analysis of Marine Invertebrates at CA-SBA-46, Phase III. In *Archaeological Investigations at Helo' on Mescalitan Island*, edited by Lynn Gamble. Department of Anthropology, University of California, Santa Barbara.

Dietler, Michael and Brian Hayden, Editors

2001. *Feasts: Archaeological and Ethnographic Perspectives on Food, Politics, and Power.* Smithsonian Institution Press, Washington and London.

Dillon, Brian

1987. *Preliminary Summary of Archaeological Boundary Test Excavations on the Malibu Coast: CA-LAN-19, 210, 226, 264, and 1298, Los Angeles County, California.* Manuscript on file at the South Central Coastal Information Center, California State University, Fullerton.

Dobyns, Henry F.

1983. *Their Number Become Thinned: Native American Population Dynamics in Eastern North America*. University of Tennessee Press, Knoxville.

1992. Native American Trade Centers as Contagious Disease Foci. In *Disease and Demography in the Americas: Changing Patterns Before and After 1492*, edited by J. Verano and D. Ubelaker, pp. 215–222. Smithsonian Institution, Washington, D.C.

Drucker, P.

1981. Ronald Leroy Olson 1895–1979. *American Anthropologist* 83(3):257–272.

DuBarton, Anne Evelyn

1992. *From Hunters to Fisherman? Developing Marine Resource Specialization on the Santa Barbara Channel. Analysis of the Artifacts and Midden Constituents from CA-SBA-71 (California)*. Unpublished Master's Thesis, Department of Anthropology, University of Nevada, Las Vegas.

DuBois, Cora

1935. Wintu Ethnography. *University of California Publications in American Archaeology and Ethnology* 36(1) Berkeley.

Earle, David D.

2005. The Mojave River and the Central Mojave Desert: Native Settlement, Travel, and Exchange in the Eighteenth and Nineteenth Centuries. *Journal of California and Great Basin Anthropology* 25:1–37.

Earle, Timothy

1991. The Evolution of Chiefdoms. In *Chiefdoms: Power, Economy, and Ideology*, edited by Timothy Earle, pp. 1–15. Cambridge University Press, Cambridge.

1997. *How Chiefs Come to Power: The Political Economy in Prehistory*. Stanford University Press, Stanford.

2001. Economic Support of Chaco Canyon Society. *American Antiquity* 66: 26–35.

Eastwood, Alice, Editor

1924. Archibald Menzies' Journal of the Vancouver Expedition. *California Historical Society Quarterly* II(4):264–340.

Edberg, Robert and Clay Singer

1981. Solfateras, Fused Shale and Combustion Metamorphism. Paper presented at the 14th Annual Meeting of the Society for California Archaeology, Bakersfield, California.

Ember, Carol L. and Melvin Ember

1992. Resource Unpredictability, Mistrust, and War: A Cross-Cultural Study. *Journal of Conflict Resolution* 36(2):242–262.

Engelhardt, Zephryin

1927. *San Fernando Rey, The Mission of the Valley*. Herald Press, Chicago.

1932. *Mission Santa Inés.* Mission Santa Barbara, Santa Barbara.

Erlandson, Jon M.

1980. Environmental Setting. In *Cultural Resources Technical Report: Proposed Embarcadero Residential Development*, pp. 125–146. Office of Public Archaeology, Social Process Research Institute, Santa Barbara.

1991a. The Antiquity of CA-SMI-1: A Multicomponent Site on San Miguel Island. *Journal of California and Great Basin Anthropology* 13:273–279.

1991b. A Radiocarbon Series for CA-SBA-1 (Rincon Point), Santa Barbara, California. *Journal of California and Great Basin Anthropology* 13:110–117.

1994. *Early Hunter-Gatherers of the California Coast.* Plenum Press, New York.

2007. Sea Change: The Paleocoastal Occupations of Daisy Cave. In *Seeking Our Past: An Introduction to North American Archaeology*, edited by S. W. Neusius and G. T. Gross, pp. 135–143. Oxford University Press, New York.

Erlandson, Jon M. and Kevin Bartoy

1995. Cabrillo, the Chumash, and Old World Diseases. *Journal of California and Great Basin Anthropology* 17:153–173.

Erlandson, Jon M. and Roger H. Colten

1991. An Archaeological Context for Early Holocene Studies on the California Coast. In *Hunter-Gatherers of Early Holocene Coastal California*, edited by Jon M. Erlandson and Roger H Colten, pp. 1–10. Institute of Archaeology, University of California, Los Angeles.

Erlandson, J.M., D. J. Kennett, B. L. Ingram, D. A. Guthrie, D. Morris, M. Tveskov, G. J. West and P. Walker

1996. An Archaeological and Paleontological Chronology for Daisy Cave (CA-SMI-261), San Miguel Island, California. *Radiocarbon* 38:355–373.

Erlandson, J.M. and T.C. Rick

2002a. A 9700-Year-Old Shell Midden on San Miguel Island, California. *Antiquity* 76:315–316.

2002b. Late Holocene Cultural Developments along the Santa Barbara Coast. In *Catalysts to Complexity: Late Holocene Societies of the California Coast. Perspectives in California Archaeology* 6:166–182, edited by J.M. Erlandson and T.L. Jones. Costen Institute of Archaeology, University of California, Los Angeles.

Erlandson J., T. C. Rick and R. L. Vellanoweth

2005. *A Canyon Through Time: The Archaeology, History, and Ecology of the Tecolote Canyon Area, Santa Barbara County, California.* University of Oregon, Eugene.

Erlandson J., T. C. Rick, R. L. Vellanoweth and D. J. Kennett

1999. Maritime Subsistence at a 9300-Year-Old Shell Midden on Santa Rosa Island, California. *Journal of Field Archaeology* 26:255–265.

Erlandson, Jon M., Torben Rick, Douglas Kennett and Phillip Walker

2001. Dates, Demography, and Disease: Cultural Contacts and Possible Evidence for Old World Epidemics among the Island Chumash. *Pacific Coast Archaeological Society* 37(3):11–26.

Fagan, Brian

2004. The House of the Sea: An Essay on the Antiquity of Planked Canoes in Southern California. *American Antiquity* 69(1):7–16. Society for American Archaeology, Washington, D.C.

Farris, Glenn

1999. The Reyes Rancho in Santa Barbara County, 1802–1808. *Southern California Quarterly* 81(2):171–180.

Feinman, Gary M.

1995. The Emergence of Inequality: A Focus on Strategies and Processes. In *Foundations of Social Inequality*, edited by T. Douglas Price and Gary M. Feinman, pp. 255–279. Plenum Press, New York.

2000. Corporate/Network: A New Perspective on Leadership in the American Southwest. In *Hierarchies in Action, Cui Bono?*, edited by M.W. Diehl, pp. 152–180. Center for Archaeological Investigations Occasional Papers 27. Southern Illinois University, Carbondale.

Feinman, Gary M., Kent G. Lightfoot and Steadman Upham

2000. Political Hierarchies and Organizational Strategies in the Puebloan Southwest. *American Antiquity* 65:449–470.

Feinman, Gary M. and Linda M. Nichols

2004. Unraveling the Prehistoric Highland Mesoamerican Economy: Production, Exchange, and Consumption in the Classic Period Valley of Oaxaca. In *Archaeological Perspectives on Political Economies*, edited by Gary M. Feinman and Linda M. Nichols, pp. 167–188. University of Utah Press, Salt Lake City.

Ferguson, R. Brian

1992. A Savage Encounter: Western Contact and the Yanomami War Complex. In *War in the Tribal Zone: Expanding States and Indigenous Warfare*, edited by R. Brian Ferguson and Neil L. Whitehead, pp. 199–227. School of American Research Press, Santa Fe.

2006. Archaeology, Cultural Anthropology, and the Origins and Intensifications of War. In *The Archaeology of Warfare: Prehistories of Raiding and Conquest*, edited by Elizabeth N. Arkush and Mark W. Allen, pp. 469–523. University Press of Florida, Gainesville.

Ferguson, R. Brian and Neil L. Whitehead

1992. The Violent Edge of Empire. In *War in the Tribal Zone: Expanding States and Indigenous Warfare*, edited by R. Brian Ferguson and Neil L. Whitehead, pp. 1–30. School of American Research Press, Santa Fe.

Fisher, Vivian C. (translator)

1992. *The Diary of Captain Luis Antonio Argüello, 1821: The Last Spanish Expedition in California.* The Friends of Bancroft Library, University of California, Berkeley.

Fitch, J.E.

1969. Fish Remains, Primarily Otoliths, from a Ventura, California, Chumash Village Site (Appendix A). In *A Coastal Chumash Village: Excavation of Shisholop, Ventura County, California. Southern California Academy of Sciences Memoir*, vol. 8, edited by Roberta S. Greenwood and Robert O. Browne, pp. 56–71. The Academy, Los Angeles.

1972. Fish Remains, Primarily Otoliths, from a Coastal Indian Midden (SLO-2) at Diablo Cove, San Luis Obispo County, California. Appendix to "Nine Thousand Years of Prehistory" by Roberta Greenwood. *San Luis Obispo County Archaeological Society Occasional Papers, No. 7.*

Ford, Henry Chapman

1887. Notes on Excavations Made in Indian Burial Places in Carpinteria. *Bulletin of the Santa Barbara Society of Natural History* 1(1):11–18.

Forrester, Amy L.

1997. The Effects of El Niño on Marine Life. *Cambridge Scientific Abstracts*, Bethesda, MD.

Fried, Morton H.

1967. *The Evolution of Political Society: An Essay in Political Anthropology.* Random House, New York.

Gamble, Lynn H.

1982. Chipped Stone Production and Tool Use at Talepop (LAN–229). In *Archaeological Investigations at Talepop*, (LAN–229), by Chester King, William W. Bloomer, Eric Clingen, Bob E. Edberg, Lynn H. Gamble, Julia E. Hammett, John R. Johnson, Truus H. Kemperman, Christopher D. Pierce, and Eric Wohlgemuth, pp. 8-1–8-61. Office of Public Archaeology, University of California, Santa Barbara.

1983. The Organization of Artifacts, Features, and Activities at Pitas Point, A Coastal Chumash Village. *Journal of California and Great Basin Anthropology* 5:103–129.

1990. Appendix 3: Chipped Stone Tools and Tool Manufacturing Refuse from Talepop, CA-LAN-229. In *Archaeological Studies at Site CA-LAN-229: An Experiment in Inference Justification.* Prepared for Department of California State Parks and Recreation. Northridge Center for Public Archaeology, California State University, Northridge.

1991. *Organization of Activities at the Historic Settlement of Helo': A Chumash Political, Economic, and Religious Center.* Unpublished Ph.D. Dissertation, Department of Anthropology, University of California, Santa Barbara.

1995. Chumash Architecture: Sweatlodges and Houses. *Journal of California and Great Basin Anthropology* 17:54–92.

2002a. Archaeological Evidence for the Origin of the Plank Canoe in North America. *American Antiquity* 67(2):301–315.

2002b. Persistence of Traditional Baskets and Foods during the Historic Period among the Chumash Indians of California. Paper presented at the 67th Annual Meeting of the Society for American Archaeology, Denver, Colorado.

2002c. Fact or Forgery: Dilemmas in Museum Collections. *Museum Anthropology* 25(2):3–20.

2003. Culture and Climate: A Reconsideration of the Effect of Climatic Variability on Social Change among Southern California Hunter-Gatherer Societies. Paper presented at the 68th Annual Meeting of the Society for American Archaeology, Milwaukee.

2004. Mescalitan Island, CA-SBA-46: Anatomy of a Center. Paper presented at the 38th Annual Meeting of the Society for California Archaeology, Riverside, California.

2005. Culture and Climate: Reconsidering the Effect of Paleoclimatic Variability among Southern California Hunter-Gatherer Societies. *World Archaeology* 37(1):92–108.

2006. Book review, The Island Chumash: Behavioral Ecology of a Maritime Society, by Douglas J. Kennett. In *Journal of Anthropological Research* 62(2):279–282.

Gamble, Lynn, Editor

1990. *Archaeological Investigations at Helo' on Mescalitan Island.* With contributions by Natalie Anakouchine, Douglas B. Bamforth, Carole Denardo, John R. Johnson, Chester King, Thomas Rockwell, Phillip L. Walker. Report on file at the Information Center, University of California, Santa Barbara.

Gamble, Lynn H., Glenn S. Russell and Jean Hudson

1995. *Archaeological Site Mapping and Collections Assessment of Humaliwu (CA-LAN-264) and Muwu (CA-VEN-11).* Submitted to California Department of Parks and Recreation, Sacramento, California.

1996. *Distribution of Wealth and Other Items at the Malibu Site, CA-LAN-264.* Submitted to California Department of Parks and Recreation, Sacramento, California.

Gamble, Lynn H., P. L. Walker and G. S. Russell

2001. An Integrative Approach to Mortuary Analysis: Social and Symbolic Dimensions of Chumash Burial Practices. *American Antiquity* 66:185–212.

2002. Further Considerations on the Emergence of Chumash Chiefdoms. *American Antiquity* 67:772–777.

Gamble, Lynn H. and Irma Carmen Zepeda

2002. Social Differentiation and Exchange during the Historic Period among the Kumeyaay. *Historical Archaeology* 36(2):71–91.

Gayton, Anna H.

1930. Yokuts-Mono Chiefs and Shamans. *University of California Publications in American Archaeology and Ethnology* 24:361–420. Berkeley.

Geiger, Maynard and Clement W. Meighan

1976. *As the Padres Saw Them: California Indian Life and Customs as Reported by the Franciscan Missionaries, 1813–1815*. Santa Barbara Mission Library, Santa Barbara.

Gibson, Robert O.

1975. The Beads of Humaliwo. *The Journal of California Anthropology* 1:110–119.

1976. A Study of Beads and Ornaments from the San Buenaventura Mission Site (Ven-87). In the *Changing Faces of Main Street: Ventura Mission Plaza Archaeological Project*, edited by P. S. Greenwood, pp. 77–166. Report Prepared for The Redevelopment Agency, City of San Buenaventura, Ventura, California.

1987. *A Preliminary Study of Beads From Humaliwo, 4-LAN-264 at Malibu State Park, Los Angeles County, California*. Submitted to California Department of Parks and Recreation, San Diego.

Gifford, Edward W.

1926. Clear Lake Pomo Society. *University of California Publications in American Archaeology and Ethnology* 18(2):287–390. Berkeley.

Gifford, Edward W. and Alfred L. Kroeber

1937. Culture Element Distributions: IV Pomo. *University of California Publications in American Archaeology and Ethnology* 37(4):117–254. Berkeley.

Glassow, Michael A.

1980. Lathrap and Hoover: Excavations at Shilimaqshtush: SBA-205 and Hoover and Sawyer: Los Osos Junior High School Site 4-SLO-214. *Journal of California and Great Basin Anthropology* 2(2):315–318.

1992. The Relative Dietary Importance of Marine Foods through Time in Western Santa Barbara County. In *Essays on the Prehistory of Maritime California*, edited by Terry L. Jones, pp. 115–128. Center for Archaeological Research, University of California, Davis.

1996. *Purismeño Chumash Prehistory: Maritime Adaptations along the Southern California Coast.* Harcourt Brace and Company, Orlando.

1997. Middle Holocene Cultural Development in the Central Santa Barbara Channel Region. In *Archaeology of the California Coast during the Middle Holocene*, edited by Jon M. Erlandson and Michael A. Glassow, pp. 73–90. Institute of Archaeology, University of California, Los Angeles.

Glassow, Michael A., Lynn H. Gamble, Jennifer E. Perry and Glenn S. Russell

2007. Prehistory of the Northern California Bight and the Adjacent Transverse Ranges. In *California Prehistory: Colonization, Culture, and Complexity*, edited by Terry L. Jones and Kathryn Klar, pp. 191–213. AltaMira Press, Lanham, MD.

Glassow, Michael A., John R. Johnson and Jon M. Erlandson

1986. Mescalitan Island Archaeology and the Canaliño Period of Santa Barbara Channel Prehistory. In *A New Look at Some Old Sites*, Coyote Press Archives of California Prehistory No. 6. Coyote Press, Salinas.

Glassow, Michael A. and Larry R. Wilcoxon

1988. Coastal Adaptations Near Point Conception, California, with Particular Regard to Shellfish Exploitation. *American Antiquity* 53:36–51.

Glenn, Brian

1990. Fish Exploitation: Analysis of Vertebrae and Otoliths. In *Archaeological Investigations at Helo' on Mescalitan Island*, edited by Lynn H. Gamble. Department of Anthropology, University of California, Santa Barbara.

Glenn, Brian, Phillip Walker and Natalie Anakouchine

1988. Exploitation of Faunal Resources at SBA-46. Paper presented at the 53rd Annual Meeting of the Society for American Archaeology, Phoenix.

Goddard, Ives

1996. The Classification of the Native Languages of North America. In *Handbook of North American Indians, Vol. 17, Languages*, edited by Ives Goddard, pp. 290–324. Smithsonian Institution, Washington, D.C.

Goldschmidt, Walter R.

1951. Nomlaki Ethnography. *University of California Publications in American Archaeology and Ethnology* 42(4):303–436. Berkeley.

Gould, G.H.

n.d. Interview with Juan de Jesus. National Anthropological Archives, Smithsonian Institution, Washington, D.C.

Graesch, Anthony P.

2001. Culture Contact on the Channel Islands: Historic Era Production and Exchange Systems. In *The Origins of a Pacific Coast Chiefdom: The Chumash of the Channel Islands*, edited by J. E. Arnold, pp. 261–285. University of Utah Press, Salt Lake City.

Green, Terisa M.

1999. *Spanish Missions and Native Religion: Contact, Conflict, and Convergence*. Unpublished Ph.D. Dissertation, Institute of Archaeology, University of California, Los Angeles.

Greenwood, Roberta S. and Robert O. Browne

1969. A Coastal Chumash Village: Excavation of Shisholop, Ventura County, California. *Southern California Academy of Sciences Memoir*, Vol. 8. The Academy, Los Angeles.

Gudde, Erwin G.

1998. *California Place Names: The Origin and Etymology of Current Geographical Names.* University of California, Berkeley.

Guthrie, Daniel A.

1985. Appendix G: Avian Remains from Mescalitan Island, Site III. In *SBA-46 Test Program, Vol. III*, edited by Scientific Resource Surveys, Inc. Prepared for Goleta Sanitary District/ Brown and Caldwell.

Gutman, Theodore E.

1979. The Use of Asphaltum Sourcing in Archaeology. *Journal of New World Archaeology* III(2):32–43.

Haas, Jonathan

1990. Warfare and the Evolution of Tribal Polities in the Prehistoric Southwest. In *The Anthropology of Warfare*, edited by Jonathan Hass, pp. 171–189. Cambridge University Press, Cambridge.

1999. The Origins of War and Ethnic Violence. In *Ancient Warfare: Archaeological Perspectives*, edited by John Carman and Anthony Harding, pp. 11–24. Sutton Publishing, Stroud, UK.

2001. Warfare and the Evolution of Culture. In *Archaeology at the Millenium: A Sourcebook*, edited by Gary M. Feinman and T. Douglas Price, pp. 329–352. Kluwer Academic/Plenum Publishers, New York.

Halstead, Paul and John O'Shea

1989. Introduction: Cultural Responses to Risk and Uncertainty. In *Bad Year Economics: Cultural Responses to Risk and Uncertainty.* Edited by Paul Halstead and John O'Shea, pp. 1–7. Cambridge University Press, Cambridge.

Hammett, Julia E.

1991. *The Ecology of Sedentary Societies Without Agriculture: Paleoethnobotanical Indicators from Native California.* Unpublished Ph.D. Dissertation, Department of Anthropology, University of North Carolina, Chapel Hill.

Hammett, Julia and Eric Wohlgemuth

1982. Charred Plant Remains from Talepop. In *Archaeological Investigations at Talepop (LAN-229).* Office of Public Archaeology, Social Process Research Institute, Santa Barbara.

Harrington, John P.

1928. Exploration of the Burton Mound at Santa Barbara, California. In *44th Annual Report, 1926–1927*. Bureau of American Ethnology, pp. 23–168. Smithsonian Institution, Washington, D.C.

1942. Culture Element Distributions: XIX, Central California Coast. *University of California Anthropological Records* 7(1). Berkeley.

Harrison, William M.

1965. Mikiw: A Coastal Chumash Village. *Annual Reports of the University of California Archaeological Survey* 7:91–178. Los Angeles.

Hau, C.

1885. Nécrologie, Paul Schumacher. *Revue d'Ethnographie* 3:461.

Hayden, Brian

1995. Pathways to Power: Principles for Creating Socioeconomic Inequalities. In *Foundations of Social Inequality*, edited by T. Douglas Price and Gary M. Feinman, pp. 15–86. Plenum Press, New York.

2001. Fabulous Feasts: A Prolegomenon to the Importance of Feasting. In *Feasts: Archaeological and Ethnographic Perspectives on Food, Politics, and Power*, edited by Michael Dietler and Brian Hayden, pp. 23–64. Smithsonian Institution Press, Washington, D.C.

Heizer, Robert F.

1938. The Plank Canoe of the Santa Barbara Channel Region, California. *Ethnological Studies* 7:193–227.

1940. The Frameless Plank Canoe of the California Coast. *Primitive Man* 13:80–89.

1951. The French Expedition to California, 1877–1879. *University of California Archaeological Survey Reports* 12:6–13.

1955. California Indian Linguistic Records: The Mission Indian Vocabularies of H. W. Henshaw. *University of California Anthropological Records* 15(2):85–202. Berkeley.

1978. History of Research. In *Handbook of North American Indians, Vol. 8, California*, edited by Robert F. Heizer, pp. 6–15. Smithsonian Institution, Washington, D.C.

Heizer, Robert F., Editor

1975. Seven Early Accounts of the Pomo Indians and their Culture. *Miscellaneous Publications of the University of California Archaeological Research Facility*. Berkeley.

Heizer, Robert F. and William C. Massey

1953. Aboriginal Navigation off the Coasts of Upper and Baja California. *Bureau of American Ethnology Bulletin* 151:282–311.

Hemert-Engert, Adolph von and Frederick Teggart, Editors

1910. The Narrative of the Portolá Expedition of 1769–1770 by Miguel Costansó. *Publications of the Academy of Pacific Coast History* 1(4):9–159. University of California Press, Berkeley.

Hirth, Kenneth G.

1998. The Distributional Approach. *Current Anthropology* 39:451–476.

Hollimon, Sandra H.

1990. *Division of Labor and Gender Roles in Santa Barbara Channel Area Prehistory*. Unpublished Ph.D. Dissertation, Department of Anthropology, University of California, Santa Barbara.

1997. The Third Gender in Native California: Two-Spirit Undertakers Among the Chumash and their Neighbors. In *Women in Prehistory: North America and Mesoamerica*, edited by C. Claassen and R. Joyce, pp. 173–188. University of Pennsylvania Press, Philadelphia.

2000. Archaeology of the *'Aqi*: Gender and Sexuality in Prehistoric Chumash Society. In *Archaeologies of Sexuality*, edited by R. A. Schmidt and B. L. Voss, pp. 179–196. Routledge, London.

2001. Death, Gender, and the Chumash Peoples: Mourning Ceremonies as an Integrative Mechanism. In *Social Memory, Identity, and Death: Anthropological Perspectives on Mortuary Rituals*, edited by Meredith S. Chesson, pp. 41–55. Archeological Papers of the American Anthropological Association Number 10, American Anthropological Association, Arlington, Virginia.

Holmes, William H.

1902 [1975]. Pomo Reservation, Mendocino County. In *Seven Early Accounts of the Pomo Indians and their Culture*, assembled and edited by Robert F. Heizer, pp. 21–23. Archaeological Research Facility, Berkeley.

Hornbeck, David

1983. *California Patterns: A Geographical and Historical Atlas.* Mayfield Publishing Company, Palo Alto.

Howard, Virginia

2000. Santa Catalina's Soapstone Vessels: Production Dynamics. Paper presented at the Proceedings of the Fifth California Islands Symposium, Washington, D.C.

Huddleston, Richard W.

1988. Letter Report to Lynn Gamble. Manuscript in Possession of Author.

Hudson, John W.

1897 [1975]. Pomo Wampum Makers. In *Seven Early Accounts of the Pomo Indians and their Culture*, assembled and edited by Robert F. Heizer, pp. 9–20. Archaeological Research Facility, Berkeley.

Hudson, Travis and Thomas C. Blackburn

1982. *Food Procurement and Transportation: The Material Culture of the Chumash Interaction Sphere, Vol. I*, Ballena Press Anthropological Papers No. 25, edited by Thomas C. Blackburn. Ballena Press/Santa Barbara Museum of Natural History Cooperative Publication, Los Altos and Santa Barbara.

1983. *Food Preparation and Shelter: The Material Culture of the Chumash Interaction Sphere, Vol. II*, Ballena Press Anthropological Papers No. 25, edited by Thomas C. Blackburn. Ballena Press/Santa Barbara Museum of Natural History Cooperative Publication, Los Altos and Santa Barbara.

1985. *Clothing, Ornamentation, and Grooming: The Material Culture of the Chumash Interaction Sphere, Vol. III*, Ballena Press Anthropological Papers No. 25, edited by Thomas C. Blackburn. Ballena Press/Santa Barbara Museum of Natural History Cooperative Publication, Los Altos and Santa Barbara.

1986. *Ceremonial Paraphernalia, Games, and Amusements: The Material Culture of the Chumash Interaction Sphere, Vol. IV*, Ballena Press Anthropological Papers No. 25, edited by Thomas C. Blackburn. Ballena Press/Santa Barbara Museum of Natural History Cooperative Publication, Los Altos and Santa Barbara.

1987. *Manufacturing Processes, Metrology, and Trade: The Material Culture of the Chumash Interaction Sphere, Vol. V*, Ballena Press Anthropological Papers No. 25, edited by Thomas C. Blackburn. Ballena Press/Santa Barbara Museum of Natural History Cooperative Publication, Los Altos and Santa Barbara.

Hudson, Travis, Thomas Blackburn, Rosario Curletti and Janice Timbrook

1981. *The Eye of the Flute: Chumash Traditional History and Ritual as Told by Fernando Librado Kitsepawit to John P. Harrington.* Santa Barbara Museum of Natural History, Santa Barbara.

Hudson, Travis, Janice Timbrook and Melissa Rempe

1978. *Tomol: Chumash Watercraft as Described in the Ethnographic Notes of John P. Harrington.* Ballena Press Anthropological Papers No. 9, Soccorro.

Hudson, Travis and Ernest Underhay

1978. *Crystals in the Sky: An Intellectual Odyssey Involving Chumash Astronomy, Cosmology and Rock Art.* Ballena Press, Socorro.

Hughes, Richard E. and Randall Milliken

2007. Prehistoric Material Conveyance. In *California Prehistory: Colonization, Culture, and Complexity*, edited by Terry L. Jones and Kathryn A. Klar, pp. 259–271. AltaMira Press, Lanham, Maryland.

Jackson, Robert H. and Edward Castillo

1995. *Indians, Franciscans, and Spanish Colonization: the Impact of the Mission System on California Indians.* University of New Mexico Press, Albuquerque.

Jackson, Thomas L. and Jonathan E. Ericson

1994. Prehistoric Exchange Systems in California. In *Prehistoric Exchange Systems in North America*, edited by Timothy G. Baugh and Jonathon E. Ericson, pp. 385–414. Plenum Press, New York.

Johnson, Allen W. and Timothy Earle

2000. *The Evolution of Human Societies: From Foraging Group to Agrarian State.* Stanford University Press, Stanford.

Johnson, John R.

1980. Archaeological Analysis of Fish Remains from SBA-1, Rincon Point. In *Cultural Resources Technical Report: Rincon Tract No. 12,932*. Marcel Kornfield (assembler). Social Process Research Institute, Office of Public Archaeology, University of California, Santa Barbara.

1982. *An Ethnohistoric Study of the Island Chumash.* Unpublished Master's Thesis, Department of Anthropology, University of California, Santa Barbara.

1986. The Chumash History of Mission Creek. *Noticias* 32 (2):20–37. Santa Barbara Historical Society, Santa Barbara.

1988. *Chumash Social Organization: An Ethnohistoric Perspective.* Unpublished Ph.D. Dissertation, Department of Anthropology, University of California, Santa Barbara.

1990. Ethnohistory of the Village of Helo' on Mescalitan Island. In *Archaeological Investigations at Helo' on Mescalitan Island*, edited by Lynn H. Gamble. Department of Anthropology, University of California, Santa Barbara.

1997. *Native Americans on the Central Coast: A Photo Essay.* Black Gold Cooperative Library System, Ventura.

1998. Foreword: A Bibliographic History of Chumash Sites. In *The Chumash and their Predecessors, An Annotated Bibliography.* Compiled by Marie S. Holmes and John R. Johnson, pp. i–xi. Santa Barbara Museum of Natural History, Santa Barbara.

2000. Social Responses to Climate Change among the Chumash Indians of South-Central California. In *The Way the Wind Blows: Climate, History, and Human Action*, edited by R. J. McIntosh, J.A. Tainter, and S. K. McIntosh, pp. 301–327. Columbia University Press, New York.

2001. Ethnohistoric Reflections of Cruzeño Chumash Society. In *The Origins of a Pacific Coast Chiefdom: The Chumash and Channel Islands*, edited by J.R. Arnold, pp. 53–70. University of Utah Press, Salt Lake City.

2005. The Advent of 'Big Time Fishing' and the Polynesian Contact Hypothesis. Paper Presented at the 70th Annual Meeting of the Society for American Archaeology, Salt Lake City, Utah.

2007. Ethnohistoric Descriptions of Chumash Warfare. *North American Indigenous Warfare*, edited by Richard Chacon and Ruben Mendoza, pp. 74–113. University of Arizona Press, Tucson.

Johnson, John R. and Joseph G. Lorenz

2006. Genetics, Linguistics, and Prehistoric Migrations: An Analysis of California Indian Mitochondrial DNA Lineages. *Journal of California and Great Basin Anthropology* 26:31–62.

Johnson, John R., Claude N. Warren and Susan E. Warren

1982. Ethnohistoric Overview of Native American Culture in the Goleta Valley (1542–1835). In *Intensive Cultural Resources Survey for the Goleta Flood Protection Program, Santa Barbara County, California*, edited by Larry Wilcoxon. Archaeological Systems Management, Inc., San Diego. Submitted to the U.S. Army Corps of Engineers, Los Angeles District.

Jones, Philip Mills

1956. Archaeological Investigations on Santa Rosa Island in 1901. Edited by Robert F. Heizer and Albert B. Elsasser. *University of California Anthropological Records* 9(2):201–280. Berkeley.

Keeley, Lawrence

1996. *War Before Civilization: The Myth of the Peaceful Savage*. Oxford University Press, New York.

Kelly, Isabel

1978. Coast Miwok. In *Handbook of North American Indians, Vol. 8, California*, edited by Robert F. Heizer, pp. 414–425. Smithsonian Institution, Washington, D.C.

Kelsey, Harry

1998. *Juan Rodriguez Cabrillo*. Huntington Library, San Marino.

Kennett, Douglas J.

1998. *Behavioral Ecology and the Evolution of Hunter-Gatherer Societies on the Northern Channel Islands, California*. Unpublished Ph.D. dissertation, Department of Anthropology, University of California, Santa Barbara.

2005. *The Island Chumash: Behavioral Ecology of a Maritime Society*. University of California Press, Berkeley.

Kennett, Douglas J. and Christina A. Conlee

2002. Emergence of Late Holocene Sociopolitical Complexity on Santa Rosa and San Miguel Islands. In *Catalysts to Complexity: Late Holocene Societies of the California Coast*, edited by J.M. Erlandson and T.L. Jones, pp. 147–165. Cotsen Institute of Archaeology, University of California, Los Angeles.

Kennett, D. J., and J. P. Kennett

2000. Competitive and Cooperative Responses to Climatic Instability in Coastal Southern California. *American Antiquity* 65:379–395.

King, Chester D.

1967. The Sweetwater Mesa Site (LAN-267) and its Place in Southern California Prehistory. *Archaeological Survey Annual Report* 9:25–76. University of California, Los Angeles.

1975. The Names and Locations of Historic Chumash Villages (Assembled by Thomas Blackburn). *Journal of California Anthropology* 2:171–179.

1976. Chumash Intervillage Economic Exchange. In *Native Californians: A Theoretical Retrospective*, edited by Lowell J. Bean and Thomas C. Blackburn, pp. 289–318. Ballena Press, Ramona.

1978. Protohistoric and Historic Archaeology. In *Handbook of North American Indians*, Vol. 8, California, edited by Robert F. Heizer, pp. 58–68. Smithsonian Institution, Washington, D.C.

1980a. Prehistoric Background. In *Cultural Resources Technical Report: Rincon Tract No. 12,932*, edited by Pandora E. Snethkamp, pp. 3-1 to 3-20. Office of Public Archaeology, Social Process Research Institute, University of California, Santa Barbara.

1980b. Chapter 3: Prehistoric Background. In *Cultural Resources Technical Report: Proposed Embarcadero Residential Development.* Office of Public Archaeology, Social Process Research Institute, University of California, Santa Barbara.

1984. Ethnohistoric Background, Appendix I. In *Archaeological Investigation of the San Antonio Terrace, Vandenberg Air Force Base, California, In Connection with MX Facilities Construction*, edited by Chambers Consultants and Planners. Submitted to the Army Corps of Engineers, Los Angeles County District.

1985. Appendix B: Beads and Ornaments from CA-SBA-46, Site III. In *SBA-46 Test Program, Vol. III*, edited by Scientific Resource Surveys, Inc. Prepared for Goleta Sanitary District and Brown and Caldwell.

1988. Ethnohistoric Reconstruction of Subsistence-Settlement Systems in the Vicinity of Burton Mesa. In *Draft, Prehistoric Resource Use and Settlement in the Santa Ynez River Basin, Volume I: Analysis and Synthesis*, edited by URS Consultants Inc., Santa Barbara. Prepared for Unolocal Corporation.

1990a. Evolution of Chumash Society: A Comparative Study of Artifacts Used for Social System Maintenance in the Santa Barbara Channel Region before A.D. 1804. In *The Evolution of North American Indians*, edited by David Hurst Thomas. Garland Publishing, Inc., New York.

1990b. Beads from Helo'. In *Archaeological Investigations at Helo' on Mescalitan Island*, edited by Lynn H. Gamble, pp. 8-1 to 8-64. Department of Anthropology, University of California, Santa Barbara.

1993. Native American Placenames in the Vicinity of the Pacific Pipeline, Part 2: Gaviota to the San Fernando Valley. Ann Peak and Associates, Sacramento. Report on file at the Information Center, University of California, Santa Barbara.

1994. *Prehistoric Native American Sites in the Santa Monica Mountains.* Santa Monica Mountains and Seashore Foundation and the National Park Service.

1995. Beads and Ornaments from Excavations at Tahquitz Canyon (CA-RIV-45). In *Archaeological, Ethnographic, and Ethnohistoric Investigations at Tahquitz Canyon.* Palm Springs, California, pp. XIII-1–XIII-77. Report to Riverside County Flood Control and Water Conservation District, Riverside, from Cultural Systems Research, Menlo Park.

1996. Appendix I: Beads and Ornaments from Cemetery Excavations at Humaliwo (CA-LAN-264). In *Distribution of Wealth and Other Items at the Malibu Site, CA-LAN-264*, by L. Gamble, G. Russell, C. King, and J. Hudson. Submitted to California Department of Parks and Recreation, Sacramento, California.

2000. *Native American Indian Cultural Sites in the Santa Monica Mountains.* Santa Monica Mountains and Seashore Foundation and the National Park Service.

2005. Overview of the History of the American Indians in the Santa Monica Mountains. Ms in possession of the author.

n.d. Notes on Olson's Collections at the Phoebe Hearst Museum. Ms in Possession of the author.

King, Chester , William W. Bloomer, Eric Clingen, Bob E. Edberg, Lynn H. Gamble, Julia E. Hammett, John R. Johnson, Truus H. Kemperman, Christopher D. Pierce and Eric Wohlgemuth

1982. *Archaeological Investigations at Talepop (LAN-229)*. Office of Public Archaeology, Social Process Research Institute, University of California, Santa Barbara.

King, Chester and Steve Craig

1978. *Cultural Resources Technical Report No. 8: In Support of Point Conception LNG Project Environmental Impact Report.* Arthur D. Little, Inc., San Francisco. Submitted to California Public Utilities Commission.

King, Chester and Lynn Gamble

1979. Appendix IV: An Archaeological Surface Reconnaissance at Dos Pueblos Canyon, Santa Barbara County. In *Cultural Resources Technical Report for the Proposed Santa Barbara Health Center*, by Brian Haley, Marcel Kornfeld and Jeffery Serena. Social Process Research Institute, Office of Public Archaeology, University of California Santa Barbara.

King, Chester and John R. Johnson

1999. The Chumash Socio-Political Groups in the Santa Monica Mountains. In *Cultural Affiliation and Lineal Descent of Chumash Peoples in the Channel Islands and Santa Monica Mountains*, Vol. 1, prepared by Sally McLendon and John R. Johnson. Submitted to Archeology and Ethnography Program, National Park Service.

King, Linda B.

1969. The Medea Creek Cemetery (LAN-243): An Investigation of Social Organization from Mortuary Practices. *Archaeological Survey Annual Report* 11:23–68. University of California, Los Angeles.

1982. *Medea Creek Cemetery: Late, Inland Chumash Patterns of Social Organization, Exchange and Warfare.* Unpublished Ph.D. Dissertation, Department of Antrhopology, University of California, Los Angeles.

Kirch, Patrick V.

1984. *The Evolution of Polynesian Chiefdoms.* Cambridge University Press, Cambridge.

1991. Prehistoric Change in Western Melanesia. *Annual Review of Anthropology* 20:141–165.

2000. *On the Roads of the Winds: An Archaeological History of the Pacific Islands before European Contact.* University of California Press, Berkeley and Los Angeles.

Kirk, Donald

1970. *Wild Edible Plants of the Western United States.* Naturegraph Publishers, Healdsburg.

Kirkish, Alex N. and Brian F. Smith

1997. *Chumash Cemetery Location Information at the Village of Mishopshnow (CA-SBA-7) at Carpinteria State Beach.* Submitted to State of California, Department of Parks and Recreation.

Klar, Katherine A.

2000. The Island Chumash Language: Implications for Interdisciplinary Work. In *Proceedings of the Fifth California Islands Symposium*, edited by D. R. Browne, K. L. Mitchell, and H. W. Chaney, pp. 654–658. U. S. Department of the Interior, Mineral Management Service, Washington, D.C.

Koenig, W. D., R.L. Mumme, W.J Carmen and M.T Stanback

1994. Acorn Production by Oaks in Central Coastal California: Variation within and Among Years. *Ecology* 75:99–109.

Kowta, M.

1961. Excavations at Goleta, Artifact Description: Chipped Lithic Material. *Annual Reports of the University of California Archaeological Survey* 3:3349–384. Los Angeles.

Kroeber, Alfred L.

1925. Handbook of the Indians of California. *Bulletin 78*, Bureau of American Ethnology, Smithsonian Institution, Washington, D.C.

1932. The Patwin and their Neighbors. *University of California Publications in American Archaeology and Ethnology* 29(4):253–423. Berkeley.

Kunkel, Peter H.

1962. *Yokuts and Pomo Political Institutions: A Comparative Study.* Unpublished Ph.D. Dissertation, Department of Anthropology, University of California, Los Angeles.

Lambert, Patricia M.

1994. *War and Peace on the Western Front: A Study of Violent Conflict and its Correlates in Prehistoric Hunter-Gatherer Societies of Coastal Southern California.* Unpublished Ph.D. Dissertation, Department of Anthropology, University of California, Santa Barbara.

1997. Patterns of Violence in Prehistoric Hunter-Gatherer Societies of Coastal Southern California. In *Troubled Times: Violence and Warfare in the Past*, edited by Debra L. Martin and David W. Frayer, pp. 77–109. Gordon and Breach Publishers, Amsterdam.

2002. The Archaeology of War: A North American Perspective. *Journal of Archaeological Research* 10:207–241.

Lambert, Patricia M. and Phillip L. Walker

1991. The Physical Anthropological Evidence for the Evolution of Social Complexity in Coastal Southern California. *Antiquity* 65:963–973.

Landberg, Leif C.W.

1965. *The Chumash Indians of Southern California*. Southwest Museum, Los Angeles.

Langenwalter, Paul E.

1985. Appendix E: The Mescalitan Island Site III (CA-SBA-46) Archaeofauna Exclusive of Fish and Birds. In *SBA-46 Test Program, Vol. III*, edited by Scientific Resource Surveys, Inc. Prepared for Goleta Sanitary District and Brown and Caldwell.

Larson, Daniel O. and Joel C. Michaelsen

1989. *Climatic Variability: A Compounding Factor Causing Culture Change among Prehistoric Coastal Populations*. Manuscript on file, Department of Anthropology, California State University, Long Beach.

Larson, Daniel O., John R. Johnson and Joel C. Michaelsen

1994. Missionization among the Coastal Chumash of Central California: A Study of Risk Minimization Strategies. *American Anthropologist* 96: 263–299.

Lathrap, Donald W. and Robert L. Hoover

1975. Excavations at Shilimaqshtush: SBA-205. *San Luis Obispo County Archaeological Society Occasional Papers No. 10*, San Luis Obispo.

LeBlanc, Steven A.

1999. *Prehistoric Warfare in the American Southwest*. University of Utah Press, Salt Lake City.

2003. *Constant Battles: The Myth of the Peaceful Savage*. St. Martins Press, New York.

LeBlanc, Steven A. and Glen E. Rice

2001. Southwestern Warfare: The Value of Case Studies. In *Deadly Landscapes: Case Studies in Prehistoric Southwestern Warfare*, edited by Glen E. Rice and Steven A. LeBlanc, pp. 1–18. University of Utah Press, Salt Lake City.

Lee, Georgia

1993. Fake Effigies from the Southern California Coast? Robert Heizer and the Effigy Controversy. *Journal of California and Great Basin Anthropology* 15(2)195–215.

Lekson, Stephen H.

2002. War in the Southwest, War in the World. *American Antiquity* 67: 607–624.

Lightfoot, Kent G.

1995. Culture Contact Studies: Redefining the Relationship between Prehistoric and Historical Archaeology. *American Antiquity* 60:199–217.

2005. *Indians, Missionaries, and Merchants: The Legacy of Colonial Encounters on the California Frontiers*. University of California Press, Berkeley.

Lightfoot, Kent G. and Gary M. Feinman

1982. Social Differentiation and Leadership Development in Early Pithouse Villages in the Mogollon Region of the Southwest. *American Antiquity* 47:64–86.

Lightfoot, Kent G. and William S. Simmons

1998. Culture Contact in Protohistoric California: Social Contexts of Native and European Encounters. *Journal of California and Great Basin Anthropology* 20:138–170.

Love, Holly

1980. *Marine Subsistence at Muwu: VEN-11*. Masters' Thesis. On file at the Department of Anthropology at the University of California, Los Angeles.

Love, Holly, and Rheta Resnick

1979. Muwu: After Forty-five Years in Storage. *Masterkey*, Vol. 53: 1, pp. 10–19.

Macko, Michael E.

1983. *Beads, Bones, Baptisms, and Sweatlodges: Analysis of Collections from "Elijman" (CA-SBA-485), A Late Period Inezeno Chumash Village in the Central Santa Inez Valley, California*. Unpublished Master's Thesis, Department of Anthropology, University of California, Santa Barbara.

Markgraf, Vera, and Henry F. Diaz

2000. The Past ENSO Record: A Synthesis. In *El Niño and the Southern Oscillation*, edited by Henry F. Diaz and Vera Markgraf, pp. 465–488. Cambridge University Press, Cambridge.

Marquardt, William H.

2001. The Emergence and Demise of the Calusa. In *Societies in Eclipse: Eastern North America at the Dawn of European Colonization*, edited by David S. Brose, C. Wesley Cown, and Robert C. Mainfort, Jr., pp. 151–171. Smithsonian Institution Press, Washington, D.C.

Martz, Patricia Carol

1984. *Social Dimensions of Chumash Mortuary Populations in the Santa Monica Mountains Region*. Unpublished Ph.D. Dissertation, Department of Anthropology, University of California, Los Angeles.

Martz, Patricia Carol, Caprice Harper and David Miller

1995. *Cultural Ecology for Mugu Lagoon*. Prepared for the Department of the Navy, Western Division, Naval Facilities Engineering Command. California State University, Los Angeles.

Maschner, Herbert D.G.

1991. The Emergence of Cultural Complexity on the Northern Northwest Coast. *Antiquity* 65:924–934.

Mathes, W. Michael

1986. *Vizcaíno and Spanish Expansion in the Pacific Ocean, 1580–1630*. California Historical Society, San Francisco.

Mauss, Marcel

1967. *The Gift: Forms and Functions of Exchange in Archaic Societies.* Translated by Ian Cunnison. W. W. Norton, New York.

McCarthy, Helen

1993. Managing Oaks and the Acorn Crop. In *Before the Wilderness: Environmental Management by Native Californians*, compiled and edited by Thomas C. Blackburn and Kat Anderson, pp. 213–228. Ballena Press, Menlo Park.

McClure, Sarah B.

2004. Small Mammal Procurement in Coastal Contexts: A California Perspective. *Journal of California and Great Basin Anthropology* 24:207–232.

McKern, W. C.

1922. Functional Families of the Patwin. *University of California Publications in American Archaeology and Ethnology* 13(7):236–258.

McKusick, M. B.

1961. Excavations at Goleta, Methodology. *Annual Reports of the University of California Archaeological Survey* 3:339–348.

McLendon, Sally

1993. Collecting Pomoan Baskets, 1889–1939. *Museum Anthropology* 17(2): 49–60.

McLendon, Sally and John R. Johnson

1999. *Cultural Affiliation and Lineal Descent of Chumash Peoples in the Channel Islands and the Santa Monica Mountains, Vol. 1.* Submitted to Archeology and Ethnography Program, National Park Service.

McLendon, Sally and Brenda Shears Holland

1978. The Basket-Maker: the Pomoans of California. Ancestors:103–129.

McLendon, Sally and Michael J. Lowy

1978. Eastern Pomo and Southeastern Pomo. In *Handbook of North American Indians, Vol. 8, California*, edited by Robert F. Heizer, pp. 306–323. Smithsonian Institution, Washington, D.C.

Mead, George R.

1972. The Ethnobotany of the California Indians [A–M only]. In *Occasional Publications in Anthropology*, Ethnology Series, No. 30 Museum of Anthropology, University of Northern Colorado, Greeley.

Meighan, Clement W.

1969. A Ritual Cave in Topanga, California. *Masterkey* 43(3):112–117.

Milliken, Randall

1995. *A Time of Little Choice: The Disintegration of Tribal Culture in the San Francisco Bay Area, 1769–1810* . Ballena Press, Palo Alto.

Milliken, Randall T. and James A. Bennyhoff

1993. Temporal Changes in Beads as Prehistoric California Grave Goods. In *There Grows a Green Tree: Papers in Honor of David A. Fredrickson*, edited by G. White, P. Mikkelsen, W. R. Hildebrandt, and M. E. Basgall, pp. 381–395. Center for Archaeological Research at Davis No. 11. University of California, Davis.

Milliken, Randall, Richard T. Fitzgerald, Mark G. Hylkema, Randy G. Groza, Tom Origer, David G. Bieling, Alan Leventhal, Randy S. Wiberg, Andrew Gottsfield, Donna Gillette, Viviana Bellifemine, Eric Strother, Robert Cartier and David A. Fredrickson

2007. Punctuated Culture Change in the San Francisco Bay Area. In *California Prehistory: Colonization, Culture, and Complexity*, edited by Terry L. Jones and Kathryn A. Klar, pp. 99–123. AltaMira Press, Lanham, Maryland.

Mithun, Marianne

1999. *The Languages of Native North America*. Cambridge University Press, Cambridge.

Moratto, Michael J.

1984. *California Archaeology*. Academic Press, Orlando.

Munz, Phillip A. in collaboration with David D. Keck

1970. *A California Flora*. University of California Press, Berkeley.

Neff, Hector and Teresa Rudolph

1986. Treatment Program for Prehistoric and Historic Sites found along the Celeron/All Celeron American Pipeline Right-of-Way in California from Celeron Pipeline MPM00.02 Pipeline MPM 69.3. Center for Archaeological Studies, Department of Anthropology, University of California, Santa Barbara. Report on file at the Information Center, University of California, Santa Barbara.

Noah, Anna

2005. *Household Economies: The Role of Animals in Historic Period Chiefdom on the California Coast*. Ph.D. Dissertation, Department of Anthropology, University of California, Los Angeles.

Olson, Ronald L.

1930. Chumash Prehistory. *University of California Publications in American Archaeology and Ethnology* 28(1):1–21.

Orr, Phil C.

1943. Archaeology of Mescalitan Island and the Customs of the Canaliño. *Santa Barbara Museum of Natural History Occasional Papers* 5.

n.d. Field notes on file at the Santa Barbara Museum of Natural History.

Osborn, A.J.

1977. *Aboriginal Exploitation of Marine Food Resources*. Ph.D. Dissertation. Department of Anthropology, University of New Mexico.

O'Shea, John

1981. Coping with Scarcity: Exchange and Social Storage. In *Economic Archaeology*. Edited by A. Sheridan and G. N. Bailey, pp. 167–183. British Archaeological Reports (International Series 96), Oxford.

O'Shea, John and Paul Halstead

1989. Conclusions: Bad Year Economics. In *Bad Year Economics: Cultural Responses to Risk and Uncertainty.* Edited by Paul Halstead and John O'Shea, pp. 123–126. Cambridge University Press, Cambridge.

Pauketat, Timothy R.

2004. *Ancient Cahokia and the Mississippians.* Cambridge University Press, Cambridge and New York.

Peregrine, Peter N.

2001. Matrilocality, Corporate Strategy, and the Organization of Production in the Chacoan World. *American Antiquity* 66:36–46.

Pierce, Christopher D., Eric Clingen and Lynn H. Gamble

1982. Petrology of Chipped Stone Artifacts. In *Archaeological Investigations at Talepop, (LAN-229)*, by Chester King, William W. Bloomer, Eric Clingen, Bob E. Edberg, Lynn H. Gamble, Julia E. Hammett, John R. Johnson, Truus H. Kemperman, Christopher D. Pierce, and Eric Wohlgemuth, pp. 7-1–7-8. Office of Public Archaeology, University of California, Santa Barbara.

Pisias, Niklas G.

1978. Paleoceanography of the Santa Barbara Basin during the last 8000 years. *Quaternary Research* 10:366–384.

1979. Model for Paleoceanographic Reconstructions of the California Current for the Last 8000 Years. *Quaternary Research* 11:373–386.

Pletka, Scott

2001. The Economics of Island Chumash Fishing Practices. In *The Origins of a Pacific Coast Chiefdom: The Chumash of the Channel Islands*, edited by J. E. Arnold, pp. 221–244. University of Utah Press, Salt Lake City.

Polanyi, Karl

1957. The Economy as Instituted Process. In *Trade and Market in the Early Empires: Economies in History and Theory.* Edited by Karl Polanyi, Conrad M. Arensberg, and Harry W. Pearson, pp. 243–270. The Free Press and the Falcon's Wing Press, Glencoe, Illinois.

Porcasi, Judith F. and Harumi Fujita

2000. The Dolphin Hunters: A Specialized Prehistoric Maritime Adaptation in the Southern California Channel Islands and Baja California. *American Antiquity* 65(3):543–566.

Porcasi, Judith F. and Sherri L. Andrews

2001. Evidence for a Prehistoric Mola Mola Fishery on the Southern California Coast. *Journal of California and Great Basin Anthropology* 23(1):51–65.

Pourade, Richard F.

1960. *The Explorers*. San Diego Union-Tribune Publishing Company, San Diego.

Preston, William

1996. Serpent in Eden: Dispersal of Foreign Diseases into Pre-Mission California. *Journal of California and Great Basin Anthropology* 18:2–37.

Price, T. Douglas

2006. *Principles of Archaeology*. McGraw-Hill, New York.

Price, T. Douglas and James A. Brown

1985. *Prehistoric Hunter-Gatherers: The Emergence of Cultural Complexity*. Academic Press, Orlando.

Priestley, Herbert Ingram, Translator

1937. *A Historical, Political, and Natural Description of California by Pedro Fages, Soldier of Spain, Dutifully Made for the Viceroy in the Year 1775*. University of California Press, Berkeley.

1972. *A Historical, Political, and Natural Description of California by Pedro Fages, Written for the Viceroy in 1775*. Ballena Press, Ramona.

Putnam, Frederic W., C. C. Abbott, S. S. Haldeman, H. C. Yarrow and H. W. Henshaw

1879. Archaeological and Ethnographic Collections from Vicinity of Santa Barbara, California and from Ruined Pueblos of Arizona and New Mexico, and Certain Interior Tribes. In *Report Upon United States Geographical Surveys West of the One Hundredth Meridian, Vol. VII, Archaeology*, edited by George M. Wheeler. U.S. Government Printing Office, Washington, D.C.

Raab, L. Mark, Katherine Bradford, Judith F. Porcasi and William J. Howard

1995. Return to Little Harbor, Santa Catalina Island, California: A Critique of the Marine Paleotemperature Model. *American Antiquity* 60:287–308.

Raab, L. Mark, and Daniel O. Larson

1997. Medieval Climatic Anomaly and Punctuated Cultural Evolution in Coastal Southern California. *American Antiquity* 62:319–336.

Raab, L. Mark, and Terry L. Jones

2004. The Future of California Prehistory. In *Prehistoric California: Archaeology and the Myth of Paradise*, edited by L. Mark Raab and Terry L. Jones, pp. 204–211. University of Utah Press, Salt Lake City.

Redmond, Elsa M.

1994. External Warfare and the Internal Politics of Northern South American Tribes and Chiefdoms. In *Factional Competition and Political Development in the New World*, edited by Elizabeth M. Brumfiel and John W. Fox, pp. 44–54. Cambridge University Press, Cambridge.

Reichlen, Henry and Robert F. Heizer

1964. The Scientific Expedition of Leon de Cessac to California, 1877–1879. *University of California Archaeological Survey Reports* 61. Berkeley.

Renfrew, Colin

1974. Beyond a Subsistence Economy: The Evolution of Social Organization in Prehistoric Europe. In *Reconstructing Complex Societies*, edited by C.B. Moore, pp. 69–85. Supplement to the American School of Oriental Research No. 20. Cambridge.

Renfrew, Colin and Paul Bahn

2004. *Archaeology: Theory, Methods, and Practice.* Thames and Hudson, New York.

Resnick, Rheta

1980. *Marine Subsistence Patterns at VEN-11, a Coastal Chumash Village.* Master's Thesis. Manuscript on file at the Department of Anthropology, California State University, Northridge.

Richie, C.F. and R.A. Hager

1973. The Chumash Canoe: The Structure and Hydrodynamics of a Model. *Ethnic Technology Notes*, No. 8. San Diego Museum of Man, San Diego.

Rick, Torben C.

2004. *Daily Activities, Community Dynamics, and Historical Ecology on California's Northern Channel Islands.* Unpublished Ph.D. Dissertation, Department of Anthropology, University of Oregon.

2007. *The Archaeology and Historical Ecology of Late Holocene San Miguel Island.* Costen Institute of Archaeology, University of California, Los Angeles.

Rick, Torben C., René L. Vellanoweth, Jon M. Erlandson and Douglas J. Kennett

2002. On the Antiquity of the Single-Piece Shell Fishhook: AMS Radiocarbon Evidence from the Southern California Coast. *Journal of Archaeological Science* 29(9):933–942. London.

Robinson, Eugene

1942. Plank Canoes of the Chumash. *Masterkey* 16:202–209.

1943. Plank Canoes of the Chumash: Concluded. *Masterkey* 17:13–19.

Rock, John

1930. Field notes entitled "Burial Ground Just East of (old) Asphalt Mine, Carpinteria, January 1, 1930." Manuscript on file at the Santa Barbara Museum of Natural History.

Rockwell, Thomas and Lynn Gamble

1990. Applications of Soil Geomorphology for Reconstruction of Original Site Topography and Interpretation of C-14 Dates at SBA-46. In *Archaeological Investigations at Helo' on Mescalitan Island*, edited by Lynn H. Gamble. Department of Anthropology, University of California, Santa Barbara.

Rogers, David B.

1929. *Prehistoric Man of the Santa Barbara Coast, California*. Santa Barbara Museum of Natural History Special Publications 1, Santa Barbara.

Romani, Gwendolyn

1982. *In Search of Soapstone*. Unpublished Master's Thesis, Department of Anthropology, California State University, Northridge.

Rowley-Conwy, P. and M. Zvebil

1989. Saving It for Later: Storage by Prehistoric Hunter-Gatherers in Europe. In *Bad Year Economics: Cultural Responses to Risk and Uncertainty*. Edited by Paul Halstead and John O'Shea, pp. 40–56. Cambridge University Press, Cambridge.

Ruth, Clarence.

1967. A Survey of Fifty Pre-Historic Chumash Indian Village Sites, 1930–1967. Unpublished Manuscript.

Sahlins, Marshall

1972. *Stone-Age Economics*. Aldine, Chicago.

Schumacher, Paul

1875. Ancient Graves and Shell Heaps of California. *Smithsonian Institution Annual Report, 1874*, 335–350. Smithsonian Institution, Washington, D.C.

1877. Researches in the Kjökkenmöddings and Graves of a Former Population of the Santa Barbara Islands and the Adjacent Mainland. *Bulletin of the United States Geological and Geographic Survey of Territories* III:37–56. Washington, D.C.

1879. The Method and Manufacture of Soapstone Pots. *Report Upon United States Geographical Surveys West of the 100th Meridian*, VII:117–121. Washington, D.C.

Scientific Resource Surveys, Inc.

1985. *SBA-46 Test Program, Volumes I–III*. Prepared for Goleta Sanitary District and Brown and Caldwell.

Scott, Linda J.

1986. Anasazi Subsistence Activity Areas Reflected in the Pollen Record. Paper presented at the 51st Annual Meeting of the Society for American Archaeology, New Orleans.

Service, Elman R.

1971. *Primitive Social Organization: An Evolutionary Perspective*. Random House, New York.

Shalom, Diane Lynn

2005. *Climate Change and Cultural Response: A Study of Fish Remains from the Pitas Point Site (CA-VEN-27)*. Unpublished Master's Thesis, Department of Anthropology, San Diego State University.

Silliman, Stephen W.

2004. *Lost Laborers in Colonial California: Native Americans and the Archaeology of Rancho Petaluma.* The University of Arizona Press, Tuscon.

Simpson, Lesley B., Translator and Editor

1939. *California in 1792: The Expedition of Longinos Martínez.* The Huntington Library, San Marino, California.

1961. *Journal of Longinos Martínez: Notes and Observations of the Naturalist of the Botanical Expedition in Old and New California and the South Coast 1791–1792.* John Howell Books, San Francisco.

Smith, Clifton E.

1976. *A Flora of the Santa Barbara Region, California.* Santa Barbara Museum of Natural History, Santa Barbara.

Smith, Michael E.

2004. The Archaeology of Ancient State Economies. *Annual Review of Anthropology* 33:73–102.

Spanne, Lawrence

1970. *Archaeological Site Survey Record.* Manuscript on file at Central Coastal Information Center, Department of Anthropology, University of California, Santa Barbara.

Spencer, Charles S. and Kent V. Flannery

1986. Spatial Variation of Debris at Guilá Naquitz: A Descriptive Approach. In *Guilá Naquitz: Archaic Foraging and Early Agriculture in Oaxaca, Mexico*, edited by Kent V. Flannery, pp. 331–367. Academic Press, Orlando.

Stewart, Omar C.

1943. Notes on Pomo Ethnogeography. *University of California Publications in American Archaeology and Ethnology* 40(2):29–62.

1980. Memorial to Ronald L. Olson (1895–1979). *Journal of California and Great Basin Anthropology* 2:162–164.

Stine, S.

1994. Extreme and Persistent Drought in California and Patagonia During Medieval Time. *Nature* 369:546–9.

Stone, David F.

1982. Sedimentation and Infilling of the Goleta Slough: A 1770 Reconstruction. Paper presented at the Symposium of Holocene Climate and Archaeology of California Coast and Desert, San Diego.

Strudwick, Ivan

1985. The Single-Piece Circular Fishhook: Classification and Chronology. *Pacific Coast Archaeological Society* 21(2):32–69.

Suchey J. M., W. J. Wood and S. Shermis

1972. Analysis of Human Skeletal Material from Malibu, California (LAN-264). *Annual Reports of the University of California Archaeological Survey* 14:39–78.

Tainter, Joe

1971. Climatic Fluctuations and Resource Procurement in the Santa Ynez Valley. *Pacific Coast Archaeological Society* 7(3):25–63.

Thomas, David Hurst

1976. *Figuring Anthropology: First Principles of Probability and Statistics.* Holt, Rinehart, and Winston, New York.

Thomas, David Hurst and Robert L. Kelly

2006. *Archaeology: The Past, Present, and Future of the Field.* Thomson Wadsworth, Belmont, California.

Timbrook, Jan

1984. Chumash Ethnobotany: A Preliminary Report. *Journal of Ethnobotany.* 4(2):141–169.

1990. Ethnobotany of the Chumash Indians, California, Based on Collections by John P. Harrington. *Economic Botany* 44(2):236–253.

2007. *Chumash Ethnobotany: Plant Knowledge among the Chumash People of Southern California.* Santa Barbara Museum of Natural History, Santa Barbara.

Timbrook, Jan, John R. Johnson and David D. Earle

1982. Vegetation Burning by the Chumash. *Journal of California and Great Basin Anthropology* 4(2):163–186.

Vayda, Andrew

1967. Pomo Trade Feasts. In *Tribal and Peasant Economies,* edited by G. Dalton, pp. 494–500. Natural History Press, Garden City, New York.

Voorhies, Barbara

1992. Albert C. Spaulding 1914–1990. *American Antiquity* 57:197–201.

Wagner, Henry R., Editor

1929. *Spanish Voyages to the Northwest Coast of America in the Sixteenth Century.* California Historical Society, San Francisco.

Walker, Phillip L.

1989. Cranial Injuries as Evidence of Violence in Prehistoric Southern California. *American Journal of Physical Anthropology* 80:313–323.

1990. Analysis of Tool Marks on Bones from SBA-46. In *Archaeological Investigations at Helo' on Mescalitan Island,* edited by Lynn H. Gamble. Department of Anthropology, University of California, Santa Barbara.

1996. Integrative Approaches to the Study of Ancient Health: An Example from the Santa Barbara Channel Area of Southern California. In *Populational Significance of Paleopathological Conditions: Health, Illness and*

Death in the Past, edited by A. Pérez-Pérez, pp. 98–105. Fundación Uriach, Barcelona.

1997. Evidence for Late Middle Period Island-Mainland Trade in Fur Seal Meat at Pitas Point (CA-VEN-27). Paper presented at the 31st Annual Meeting of the Society for California Archaeology, Rohnert Park.

2001. Bioarchaeological Perspective in the History of Violence. *Annual Review of Anthropology* 30:573–596.

Walker, Phillip L. and D. Travis Hudson

1993. *Chumash Healing: Changing Health and Medical Practices in an American Indian Society.* Malki Museum Press, Banning.

Walker, Phillip L. and John R. Johnson

1992. The Effects of European Contact on the Chumash Indians. In *Disease and Demography in the Americas: Changing Patterns Before and After 1492*, edited by J. Verano and D. Ubelaker, pp. 127–139. Smithsonian Institution, Washington, D.C.

1994. The Decline of the Chumash Indian Population. In *The Wake of Contact: Biological Responses to Conquest*, edited by C. S. Larsen and G. Milner, pp. 109–120. Wiley-Liss, New York.

2003. For Everything There is a Season: Chumash Indian Births, Marriages, and Deaths at the Alta California Missions. In *Human Biologists in the Archives: Demography, Health, Nutrition and Genetics in Human Populations*, edited by D. Ann Herring and Alan C. Swedlund, pp. 53–77. Cambridge University Press, Cambridge.

Walker, Phillip L., Patricia Lambert and Michael J. DeNiro

1989. The Effects of European Contact on the Health of Alta California Indians. In *Columbian Consequences, Volume I: Archaeological and Historical Perspective on the Spanish Borderlands West*, edited by David Hurst Thomas, pp. 349–364. Smithsonian Institution Press, Washington, D.C.

Walker, P. L., F. J. Drayer and S. K. Siefkin

1996. *Malibu Human Skeletal Remains: A Bioarchaeological Analysis.* Submitted to California Department of Parks and Recreation, Sacramento, California.

Walker, Phillip L., Patricia M. Lambert, Michael Schultz and Jon M. Erlandson

2005. The Evolution of Treponemal Disease in the Santa Barbara Channel Area of Southern California. In *The Myth of Syphilis: The Natural History of Treponematosis in North America*, edited by M. Lucas Powell and Della C. Cook, pp. 281–305. University of Florida Press, Gainesville.

Wallace, William J.

1987. A Remarkable Group of Carved Stone Objects from the Pacific Palisades. *Pacific Coast Archaeological Society Quarterly* 23(1):47–58.

Watt, B.K. and A.L. Merrill

1963. Composition of Foods. *Agricultural Handbook* 8. U.S. Department of Agriculture, Washington, D.C.

West, James

1969. *A Descriptive Report of Salvage Excavations at 4-SBA-87, Refugio Bay, Santa Barbara County, California*. Report Submitted to the California Department of Parks and Recreation.

White, Gregory G.

2003. *Population Ecology of the Prehistoric Colusa Reach*. Unpublished Ph.D. Dissertation, Department of Anthropology, University of California, Davis.

Wlodarski, Robert J.

1979. Catalina Island Soapstone Manufacture. *Journal of California and Great Basin Anthroplogy* 1(2):331–355.

Wood, Don

1972. *Carpinteria State Beach, SBA-6*. Manuscript on file at the California Department of Parks and Recreation, Cultural Resource Division, Sacramento, CA.

Woodward, Arthur

1932. Field notes on file at the Smithsonian Institute (No. 6042–Archaeology of California).

1933. Los Angeles Museum Work at Muwu and Simomo, Ventura County, in 1932. *American Anthropologist* 35:490–491.

1934. An Early Account of the Chumash. *Masterkey* 8(4):118–123.

1938. The First Ethnologists in California. *Masterkey* 12:141–151.

Yates, Lorenzo G.

1877 [1975]. Notes on the Aboriginal Money of California. In *Seven Early Accounts of the Pomo Indians and their Culture*, assembled and edited by Robert F. Heizer, pp. 5–7. Archaeological Research Facility, Berkeley.

Yesner, D. R.

1980. Maritime Hunter-Gatherers: Ecology and Prehistory. *Current Anthropology* 21:727–750.

Young, Robert W.

1958. Richard Fowler Van Valkenburgh 1904–1957. *American Antiquity* 23(4):421.

Index

Page numbers followed by (fig) refer to figures and (t) refer to tables.

Lynn H. Gamble

Lynn H. Gamble is professor of anthropology at San Diego State University. Her recent publications have focused on a wide-range of topics, including the origin of the plank canoe in the New World, exchange in southern California, adaptations to paleoclimatic change, representation and forgeries in museum collections, and the challenges surrounding site preservation. She currently is the editor of the *Journal of California and Great Basin Anthropology.*

Compositor: Michael Bass Associates
Text: 10/13 Galliard OS
Display: Galliard
Indexer: Indexing Solutions